Blackstone's Police Manual

Evidence and Procedure

Blackstone's Police Manual

Volume 2

Evidence and Procedure

2016

David Johnston

LLB, LLM, Barrister

and

Glenn Hutton

BA, MPhil, FCIPD

Consultant Editor: Paul Connor

OXFORD
UNIVERSITY PRESS

OXFORD
UNIVERSITY PRESS

Great Clarendon Street, Oxford, OX2 6DP,
United Kingdom

Oxford University Press is a department of the University of Oxford.
It furthers the University's objective of excellence in research, scholarship,
and education by publishing worldwide. Oxford is a registered trade mark of
Oxford University Press in the UK and in certain other countries

First Edition published in 1998
Eighteenth Edition published in 2015

Impression: 1

Published in the United States of America by Oxford University Press
198 Madison Avenue, New York, NY 10016, United States of America

British Library Cataloguing in Publication Data

Data available

ISBN 978–0–19–874343–9

Printed in Italy by
L.E.G.O. S.p.A.

Foreword for 2016 Blackstone's Police Manuals

The police service currently faces a series of challenges; from the changes that police forces must make to deliver savings and reduce crime to the increasing complexity of the threats to national security, public safety and public order. Underpinning the ability of officers to deal effectively with these challenges is the knowledge and understanding of relevant law and procedure and the ability to apply this on a daily basis. This understanding is the cornerstone in providing a professional policing service.

The College of Policing plays a vital role in the development of police officers and staff, helping them to obtain and retain the skills and knowledge they need to fight crime and protect the public. The College has a remit to develop, maintain and test standards to ensure suitability for promotion. Part of this responsibility requires the College to ensure a comprehensive and relevant syllabus is produced. As such, the College works alongside Oxford University Press to ensure these Manuals are an accurate and up-to-date source of information and that they reflect what is required by people working across policing.

The *Blackstone's Police Manuals 2016* are the definitive reference source and official study guide for the national legal examination which all candidates must successfully pass in order to be promoted to sergeant or inspector. Their content is derived from evidence gathered from operational sergeants and inspectors alongside input from the wider police service. Whilst they are primarily designed to support officers seeking to progress their careers in preparing for their promotion examinations, they also provide a reference point for officers and staff seeking to continue their professional development and maintain their knowledge as a professional in policing. If you are using these Manuals to prepare for your promotion examinations I would like to take this opportunity to wish you the very best of luck in your studies, and I hope these books will assist you in progressing your career within the police service.

Alex Marshall
Chief Executive Officer of
the College of Policing

Preface

The Blackstone's Police Manuals are the only official study guides for Police Promotion Examinations—if the law is not in the Manuals, it will not be in the exams.

All the Manuals include explanatory keynotes and case law examples, providing clear and incisive analysis of important areas. As well as covering basic law and procedure they take full account of the PACE Codes of Practice and human rights implications. They can also be used as a training resource for police probationers, special constables and police community support officers, or as an invaluable reference tool for police staff of all ranks and positions. In relation to being used as a reference tool, this is particularly relevant to officers and others involved in the procedures connected with the custody, identification and interviews of offenders, all of which are detailed in Part III of the Manual.

The *Evidence and Procedure* Manual contains a wide range of activities to cover the complex and demanding legislative framework governing the increasing depth and breadth of policing delivery. In an attempt to present this shifting and growing body of national and European law the Manual has been structured in three distinct parts: Part I—The Criminal Justice System; Part II—The Law of Evidence; and Part III—Police Station Procedure.

The 2016 edition of the Manual includes the Anti-social Behaviour, Crime and Policing Act 2014, the Offender Rehabilitation Act 2014 and the Criminal Procedure Rules 2014. Further provisions have been brought into force in relation to the Youth Justice and Criminal Evidence Act 1999, and the Crime and Security Act 2010. This edition also includes a number of recent criminal cases decided by the appellate courts.

As with previous editions, the findings of the College of Policing review of the most recent police promotion examinations, together with editorial and customer feedback, have been taken into account in the revisions to the Manual.

Although every care is taken to ensure the accuracy of the contents of the Manual, neither the authors nor the publisher can accept any responsibility for any actions taken, or not taken, on the basis of the information contained within it.

Oxford University Press are always happy to receive any useful written feedback from any reader on the content and style of the Manual, especially from those involved in or with the criminal justice system. Please email this address with any comments or queries: police.uk@ oup.com.

The law is stated as at 1 June 2015.

Acknowledgements

The *Evidence and Procedure* Manual, as with each edition, has been greatly influenced by the support it receives from across the police service and other parts of the criminal justice system. In particular we would like to express our thanks to the staff of the Legal Services Department of the College of Policing and Examinations and Assessment. The monthly Digest produced by the Legal Services Department is an invaluable reference and the informative review conducted by Examinations and Assessment helps to shape the content and style of the Manual.

Thanks to George Cooper (Northamptonshire Police), Stuart K. Fairclough (Metropolitan Police), Paul Murphy (Greater Manchester Police) and Kevin Whitehouse (West Midlands Police).

Our thanks, as always, to all the staff involved in the production of the Manual in the Academic and Professional Law Department at Oxford University Press, especially Peter Daniell, Lucy Alexander, Matthew Humphrys, Janice Sayer, Pam Birkby and Lorna Richerby. Special thanks also to Rosalie for her continued support and forbearance and thanks to Bertie and Hilda.

David Johnston and Glenn Hutton

Contents

PART III Police Station Procedure   109

Table of Cases

Table of Statutes

Table of Statutory Instruments

Table of Codes of Practice

Table of European Legislation

Table of Guidelines

Table of Home Office Circulars

Table of International Treaties and Conventions

Table of Practice Directions

How to use this Manual

Volume numbers for the Manuals

The 2016 Blackstone's Police Manuals each have a volume number as follows:

Volume 1: *Crime*
Volume 2: *Evidence and Procedure*
Volume 3: *Road Policing*
Volume 4: *General Police Duties*

The first digit of each paragraph number in the text of the Manuals denotes the Manual number. For example, paragraph 2.3 is chapter 3 of the *Evidence and Procedure* Manual and 4.3 is chapter 3 of the *General Police Duties* Manual.

All index entries and references in the Tables of Legislation and the Table of Cases, etc. refer to paragraph numbers instead of page numbers, making information easier to find.

Material outside the scope of the police promotion examinations syllabus—blacklining

These Manuals contain some information which is outside the scope of the police promotion examinations. A full black line down the margin indicates that the text beside it is excluded from Inspectors' examinations.

PACE Code Chapters

The PACE Codes of Practice have been taken out of the appendices and are now incorporated within chapters in the main body of the *Blackstone's Police Manuals*. A thick grey line down the margin is used to denote text that is an extract of the PACE Code itself (i.e. the actual wording of the legislation) and does not form part of the general commentary of the chapter.

The PACE Codes of Practice form an important part of the police promotion examinations syllabus and are examinable for both Sergeants and Inspectors. They are not to be confused with 'blacklined' content that is excluded from the syllabus for Inspectors' examinations (see 'Material outside the scope of the police promotion examinations syllabus—blacklining' section.).

Length of sentence for an offence

Where a length of sentence for an offence is stated in this Manual, please note that the number of months or years stated is the maximum number and will not be exceeded.

Any feedback regarding content or other editorial matters in the Manuals can be emailed to police.uk@oup.com.

Police Promotion Examinations Rules and Syllabus Information

The rules and syllabus for the police promotion examinations system are defined within the Rules & Syllabus document published by College of Policing Selection and Assessment on behalf of the Police Promotion Examinations Board (PPEB). The Rules & Syllabus document is published annually each September, and applies to all police promotion assessments scheduled for the calendar year following its publication. For example, the September 2015 Rules & Syllabus document would apply to all police promotion assessments held during 2016.

The document provides details of the law and procedure to be tested within the National Police Promotion Framework Step 2 Legal Examination, and also outlines the rules underpinning the police promotion examination system.

All candidates who are taking a police promotion examination are strongly encouraged to familiarise themselves with the Rules & Syllabus document during their preparation. The police promotion examination rules apply to candidates undertaking the National Police Promotion Framework.

The document can be downloaded from the Development Section of the College of Policing website, which can be found at <http://www.college.police.uk>. Electronic versions are also supplied to all force examination officers.

If you have any problems obtaining the Rules & Syllabus document from the above source, please contact the Candidate Administration Team via the 'Contact us' section of the College of Policing website (see above).

Usually, no further updates to the Rules & Syllabus document will be issued during its year-long lifespan. However, in exceptional circumstances, the College of Policing (on behalf of the PPEB) reserves the right to issue an amended syllabus prior to the next scheduled annual publication date.

For example, a major change to a key area of legislation or procedure (e.g. the Codes of Practice) during the lifespan of the current Rules & Syllabus document would render a significant part of the current syllabus content obsolete. In such circumstances, it may be necessary for an update to the syllabus to be issued, which would provide guidance to candidates on any additional material which would be examinable within their police promotion examinations.

In such circumstances, an update to the Rules & Syllabus document would be made available through the College of Policing website, and would be distributed to all force examination contacts. The College of Policing will ensure that any syllabus update is distributed well in advance of the examination date, to ensure that candidates have sufficient time to familiarise themselves with any additional examinable material. Where possible, any additional study materials would be provided to candidates free of charge.

Please note that syllabus updates will only be made in *exceptional* circumstances; an update will not be made for every change to legislation included within the syllabus. For further guidance on this issue, candidates are advised to check regularly the College of Policing website, or consult their force examination officer, during their preparation period.

PART I

The Criminal Justice System

2.1 | Sources of Law and the Courts

2.1.1 Introduction

Sources of criminal law are found partly in common law and partly in statute law. These sources are impacted on by decisions made by the courts and the rights protected by the European Convention for the Protection of Human Rights and Fundamental Freedoms. These are all the subject of this chapter, together with an overview of the categories of offences and the criminal courts where these are dealt with and the law in relation to juries.

2.1.2 Common Law

There is no authoritative text of the common law; its sources lie in the principles of the law declared by the judges in the course of deciding cases. The common law can only be declared authoritatively by judge(s) of the superior courts (i.e. from the High Court) and then only to the extent that it is necessary for the purpose of deciding a particular case. The development of the common law has always been dependent upon the incidence of cases arising for decision, and the particular facts of those cases.

Those decisions are the *authoritative sources* of certain offences and powers, in the same way as an Act (such as the Theft Act 1968), and will be relevant irrespective of how ancient the case is—if anything, the older a case authority is, the more persuasive it is.

2.1.3 Legislation

Statutes, in the form of Acts of Parliament, have always been regarded as supplementary to the common law. The major part of criminal law and procedure is now in statutory form, but the principles of common law, notably in relation to criminal liability generally, homicide and the rules of evidence and procedure at a criminal trial, have not lessened in importance.

Statutes are enacted by Parliament and it is the duty of the court, as and when the occasion arises, to interpret and give effect to the intention of Parliament as expressed in the words of the statute. The courts have the same task in relation to delegated legislation, e.g. statutory instruments and bye-laws made by ministers under powers delegated to them by Parliament. In looking at the intentions of Parliament, the courts may consider the content of any debates within either House as reported in *Hansard*.

2.1.4 Judicial Precedents

Juries decide questions of *fact* (such as whether a person is innocent or guilty); judges decide questions of *law* and magistrates decide both *fact and law* (in relation to the latter, magistrates are advised by the court clerk (**see para. 2.1.8.2**)).

Matters of law are solely for the judge, who frequently has to rule on these during the course of a trial. Ultimately, the judge directs the jury on the law in summing up. In a trial by jury these rulings and directions alone are important in the development and illustration of the law.

2.1.4.1 The Courts and Decided Cases

The system of courts in England and Wales is a hierarchy; an inferior court is generally bound by the decision and directions of a superior court. For example, judges of the Crown Courts are bound by the decisions of the Court of Appeal. It should be noted that, although the Crown Court is superior to a magistrates' court and enjoys wider powers, it is still a 'lower' court and its decisions are not generally binding on other courts.

When it is said that a decision is a binding and authoritative precedent, what is meant is that the *principle of law* on which the decision was based, or the reason for the decision, is binding. This principle of the law is known as the *ratio decidendi* of the case, i.e. the rule of law on which a judicial decision is based.

The *ratio decidendi* consists only of the principle(s) of law essential to a decision. A judge, or court as a whole, may sometimes go beyond the facts of a particular case and give an *opinion* on some connected matter, intended to be of guidance in future cases. This opinion is known as an *obiter dictum*, and may be persuasive, but not binding, on other courts in a future case. Such *obiter dicta* are often made where an important point has arisen from the arguments in an appeal case but that point has not been directly raised by either party to the case.

Where a case decision becomes authoritative or binding, it is a 'reported' or 'decided' case.

2.1.4.2 Law Reports

Since 1865, the Incorporated Council of Law Reporting in England and Wales has published the series known as 'The Law Reports'. These are cited according to the court (e.g. Appeal Court; Queen's Bench Divisional Court) in which the case was heard and the year in which the case is reported (e.g. *R v Brown* [1994] 1 AC 212; *R v Bryant* [1979] QB 108).

These reports are supplemented by various commercial series, of which the best known are:

- Criminal Appeal Reports (e.g. *R v Bray* (1989) 88 Cr App R 354);
- Justice of the Peace Reports (e.g. *R v Britzman* (1983) 147 JP 531);
- All England Law Reports (e.g. *R v Bryce* [1992] 4 All ER 567);
- Weekly Law Reports (e.g. *R v Khan* [1996] 3 WLR 162);
- Criminal Law Review (e.g. *R v Deakin* [1972] Crim LR 781).

All cases from the Court of Appeal, all divisions of the High Court, and the Supreme Court are assigned what are known as neutral citations. Each case is given a unique number to identify the case which is not tied to any law report series, and which may be cited in court. These include:

- England and Wales Court of Appeal, Criminal Division (e.g. *R v Clancy* [2012] EWCA Crim 8);
- England and Wales High Court, Administrative Division (e.g. *R (On the Application of AS)* v *Great Yarmouth Youth Court* [2011] EWHC 2059 (Admin));
- England and Wales High Court, Civil Division (e.g. *R (On the Application of Moos)* v *Commissioner of Police of the Metropolis* [2012] EWCA Civ 12);
- United Kingdom Supreme Court (e.g. *R v Gnango* [2011] UKSC 59).

All cases assigned with neutral citations can be accessed on the website of the British and Irish Legal Information Institute (<http://www.bailii.org>). The England and Wales database on the website contains the Court of Appeal and High Court cases, and the United Kingdom database contains the cases from the Supreme Court and Tribunals.

Regarding the European Court of Human Rights, cases are cited in relation to the appellant and country concerned, e.g. *Kennedy* v *United Kingdom* (2011) 52 EHRR 4.

2.1.5 Determination of Court Venue

Criminal trials in England and Wales are either trials on indictment or summary trials. Trials on indictment take place in the Crown Court presided over by a judge and jury. Summary trials take place in the magistrates' court before at least two lay magistrates or a single district judge. Trials for a child or young person generally take place in the youth court that is part of the magistrates' court.

2.1.6 Classification of Offences and Mode of Trial

In relation to mode of trial there are three classes of offences as contained within the Interpretation Act 1978, sch. 1, that states:

In relation to England and Wales—
(a) 'indictable offence' means an offence which, if committed by an adult, is triable on indictment, whether it is exclusively so triable or triable either way;
(b) 'summary offence' means an offence which, if committed by an adult, is triable only summarily;
(c) 'offence triable either way' means an offence, other than an offence triable on indictment only by virtue of [s. 40] of the Criminal Justice Act 1988 which, if committed by an adult, is triable either on indictment or summarily;
and the terms 'indictable', 'summary' and 'triable either way', in their application to offences, are to be construed accordingly.

KEYNOTE

Schedule 1 qualifies the above definition by providing that an offence to which s. 22 of the Magistrates' Courts Act 1980 applies, broadly offences of criminal damage (s. 1 of the Criminal Damage Act 1971) involving damage worth less than £5,000, must be dealt with only summarily.

In relation to (c) above, s. 40 of the Criminal Justice Act 1988 provides that certain specified summary offences which are linked to indictable offences may be sent to the Crown Court for trial, e.g. driving while disqualified, taking a motor vehicle without the owner's consent, etc.

2.1.6.1 Summary Offences

Where statutes create offences and provide for a maximum penalty imposable on summary conviction, but do not provide for a penalty on conviction on indictment, the offences are summary offences.

Summary offences can only be tried in the magistrates' court (s. 2 of the Magistrates' Courts Act 1980). The Powers of Criminal Courts (Sentencing) Act 2000, s. 78 provides that the maximum sentence of imprisonment or detention in a young offender institution a magistrates' court can impose for a summary offence is six months, unless this limit is expressly excluded.

KEYNOTE

The maximum aggregate term of imprisonment which magistrates can impose is six months unless two of the terms are imposed for offences triable either way, in which case the maximum aggregate term is 12 months (Magistrates' Courts Act 1980, s. 133).

2.1.6.2　Indictable Offences

Where statutes create offences and provide only for a penalty on conviction on indictment, the offences are indictable offences. All common law offences are indictable offences.

Indictable only offences are sent, through an administrative exercise, directly to the Crown Court to be dealt with (Crime and Disorder Act 1998, s. 51).

2.1.6.3　Either Way Offences

Where statutes create offences and provide for both a maximum penalty imposable on summary conviction and for a penalty on conviction on indictment, the offences are known as triable either way offences.

If an either way offence is dealt with in the magistrates' court the maximum sentencing powers of the court are the same as those for summary offences.

2.1.6.4　Determining Mode of Trial: Adults

Where a person aged over 18 is charged with an offence that is triable either way, the magistrates' court convenes a mode of trial hearing.

If a defendant pleads not guilty or has not indicated an intention to plead guilty to an offence triable either way, a magistrates' court must decide whether the offence is more suitable for summary trial or trial on indictment (Magistrates' Courts Act 1980, s. 19).

The court is required to give the prosecutor and the accused the opportunity to make representations as to which court is more suitable for the conduct of the trial (s. 19(2)).

The court must also have regard to: the nature of the case; whether the circumstances make the offence one of a serious character; details of the accused's previous convictions (these include previous convictions in another European Union Member State); whether the punishment which a magistrates' court would have the power to inflict for the offence would be adequate; and any other circumstances which appear to the court to make the offence more suitable for it to be tried in one way rather than the other (s. 19(1) and (3)).

Generally, either way offences should be tried summarily unless it is likely that the court's sentencing powers will be insufficient. Its powers will generally be insufficient if the outcome is likely to result in a sentence in excess of six months' imprisonment for a single offence.

The magistrates' court may send a defendant to the Crown Court for sentence where the court is of the opinion that the offence (and any associated offences) is so serious that the Crown Court should, in the court's opinion, have the power to deal with the offender in any way it could deal with him if he had been convicted on indictment (Powers of Criminal Courts (Sentencing) Act 2000, s. 3). Certain offences triable either way can only be tried summarily if the value involved is small, i.e. does not exceed the sum of £5,000 (Magistrates' Courts Act 1980, s. 22). These offences are those under s. 1 of the Criminal Damage Act 1971 (destroying or damaging property), excluding any offence committed by destroying or damaging property by fire, and under s. 12A of the Theft Act 1968 (aggravated vehicle-taking) where no allegation is made under s.12A(1)(b) other than of damage, whether to the vehicle or other property or both (sch. 2 to the 1980 Act). In addition, s. 22A of the Magistrates' Courts Act 1980 relates to low value shoplifting and provides that, where the value of the stolen goods does not exceed £200, the offence is triable only summarily. However, under s. 22A(2) a person must nonetheless be allowed to elect trial in the Crown Court.

2.1.6.5　Determining Mode of Trial: Juveniles

Where a person under the age of 18 years is charged with an indictable offence, subject to ss. 51 and 51A of the Crime and Disorder Act 1998 and to ss. 24A and 24B of the Magistrates' Courts Act 1980, they shall be tried summarily (s. 24(1) of the 1980 Act). The general principle is that persons under the age of 18 years should be tried and sentenced in the youth court for both summary and indictable offences.

The Crime and Disorder Act 1998, ss. 51 and 51A deal with those cases where a juvenile must be tried on indictment or the magistrates have a discretion to send a juvenile to the Crown Court for trial. Section 51A(2) and (3) require the magistrates' court to send juveniles directly to the Crown Court for trial where they are charged with:

(a) homicide; or
(b) a firearms offence where there is a mandatory minimum sentence (Firearms Act 1968, s. 51A), or an offence under the Violent Crime Reduction Act 2006, s. 29(3) (minimum sentences in certain cases of using someone to mind a weapon);
(c) an offence to which the provisions of the Powers of Criminal Courts (Sentencing) Act 2000, s. 91, apply and the court considers that it ought to be possible to sentence the juvenile to detention under that section in the event of his being convicted of the offence; or
(d) the offence is a 'specified offence' (under the Criminal Justice Act 2003, s. 224) and it appears to the court that, if he is found guilty of the offence, the criteria for the imposition of a sentence under the Criminal Justice Act 2003, s. 226B (extended sentence for certain violent or sexual offences) would be met.

KEYNOTE

Juveniles may also be sent to the Crown Court to be tried jointly with an adult where they are jointly charged (including cases where one is alleged to have aided and abetted the other), the adult is to be tried in that court, and the magistrates decide it is in the interests of justice to do so (Crime and Disorder Act 1998, s. 51).

A juvenile has no right to elect Crown Court trial as it is up to the magistrates where the juvenile will be tried.

Trials of juveniles in the Crown Court should be reserved for the most serious and exceptional cases, which truly merit the description 'grave crimes' (*R (On the Application of B)* v *Norfolk Youth Court* [2013] EWHC 1459 (Admin)). In *BH (A Child)* v *Llandudno Youth Court* [2014] EWHC 1833 (Admin) it was held that if there was no real prospect that the Crown Court would impose a custodial sentence then the proper venue for trial was the youth court.

The magistrates' court may also commit a person under the age of 18 to the Crown Court for sentence, where they have been convicted on the summary trial of certain serious offences mentioned in s. 91(1) of the Powers of Criminal Courts (Sentencing) Act 2000, s. 3B.

There are two instances where a juvenile can be tried in the adult magistrates' court. Generally, these are where a child or young person is jointly charged with a person who has attained the age of 18 (Children and Young Persons Act 1933, s. 46(1)), or where a child or young person is charged with aiding, abetting, causing, procuring, allowing or permitting an offence with which a person who has attained the age of 18 is charged at the same time, or with an offence arising out of circumstances which are the same as or connected with those giving rise to an offence with which a person who has attained the age of 18 is charged at the same time (Children and Young Persons Act 1963, s. 18).

2.1.7 Limitation on Proceedings

In the law of England and Wales the general rule is that there is no restriction on the time which may elapse between the commission of an offence and the commencement of a prosecution for it. However, there are a number of statutory provisions prohibiting proceedings once a certain time has elapsed. The relevant provisions are outlined below.

2.1.7.1 Summary Offences

Section 127 of the Magistrates' Courts Act 1980 states:

> (1) Except as otherwise expressly provided by any enactment and subject to subsection (2) below, a magistrates' court shall not try an information...unless the information was laid...within 6 months from the time when the offence was committed...

KEYNOTE

Where there is uncertainty as to whether an information has been laid in time, the magistrates should use the ordinary criminal standard of proof (*Atkinson* v *DPP* [2004] EWHC 1457 (Admin)). In *R* v *Clerk to the Medway Justices, ex parte DHSS* (1986) 150 JP 401, the clerk refused to issue a summons because four months had been allowed to elapse between the interview of the suspect and the laying of an information.

Where a prosecutor issues a written charge, references in any enactment to an 'information' are to be construed as references to a 'written charge' and therefore the six-month limitation period applies (s. 30(5) of the Criminal Justice Act 2003).

2.1.7.2 Indictable Offences (Either Way and Indictable Only)

Section 127 of the Magistrates' Courts Act 1980 states:

> (2) Nothing in—
>   (a) subsection (1) above; or
>   (b) subject to subsection (4) below, any other enactment (however framed or worded) which, as regards any offence to which it applies, would but for this section impose a time-limit on the power of a magistrates' court to try an information summarily or impose a limitation on the time for taking summary proceedings,
> shall apply in relation to any indictable offence.
> (3) ...
> (4) Where, as regards any indictable offence, there is imposed by any enactment (however framed or worded, and whether falling within subsection (2)(b) above or not) a limitation on the time for taking proceedings on indictment for that offence no summary proceedings for that offence shall be taken after the latest time for taking proceedings on indictment.

KEYNOTE

Section 127(2) makes it clear that s. 127(1) does not apply to indictable offences and either way offences. This means that an offence triable either way such as theft (s. 1 of the Theft Act 1968), can be tried summarily after the six months limitation has expired. However, as provided by s. 127(4), some indictable offences may have a time limit prescribed within the legislation and in this event that time limit also applies to summary proceedings.

Although there is no time limit on instituting proceedings for indictable (and either way) offences it has been held that there is a reasonable time requirement that must be interpreted and applied in a way that will tend to achieve its purpose, i.e. avoid undue uncertainty on the part of the accused (*Burns* v *HM Advocate* [2008] UKPC 63). In *Bullen and Soneji* v *UK* [2009] ECHR 28 the European Court of Human Rights provided criteria by which the reasonableness of the length of the proceedings could be assessed: the complexity of the case, the conduct of the applicants and the relevant authorities and what was at stake for the applicants.

2.1.8 Magistrates' Courts

The Magistrates' Courts Act 1980 provides that a magistrates' court has the jurisdiction:

- to try any summary offence;
- to try summarily certain either way offences;
- to try summarily an indictable offence;

- over offences conferred on the court by any other enactment;
- sending adults and juveniles to the Crown Court for trial under ss. 51 and 51A of the Crime and Disorder Act 1998.

Section 1(1) of the 1980 Act provides that a justice of the peace may issue a summons or warrant where a person has or is suspected of having committed an offence.

2.1.8.1 Justices of the Peace

Magistrates' courts consist of justices of the peace (otherwise known as 'lay justices'), the majority of whom are unpaid lay men and women. A minority of justices are paid and are known as District Judges (Magistrates' Courts) and Deputy District Judges (Magistrates' Courts).

2.1.8.2 Justices' Clerks and Assistant Clerks

Section 27 of the Courts Act 2003 provides that a justices' clerk may be appointed by the Lord Chancellor only if he/she has a five-year magistrates' court qualification, is a barrister or solicitor who has served for not less than five years as an assistant to a justices' clerk or has previously been a justices' clerk. A justices' clerk is assigned to one or more local justice areas.

An assistant clerk may be employed as a clerk in court only if he/she is a barrister or solicitor of the Supreme Court or has passed the necessary examinations for either of those professions, or has been granted an exemption in relation to any examination by the appropriate examining body (Assistants to Justices' Clerks Regulations 2006 (SI 2006/3405 as amended by SI 2007/1448), reg. 3).

The functions of a justices' clerk include giving advice to any or all of the justices of the peace to whom he/she is clerk about matters of law (including procedure and practice) on questions arising in connection with the discharge of their functions (s. 28(4)).

The Justices' Clerks Rules 2005 (SI 2005/545), rr. 2, 3, and 3A, make provisions enabling things to be done by a single justice of the peace also to be done by a justices' clerk or an assistant clerk.

2.1.9 Youth Courts

A youth court is a special type of magistrates' court and hears any charge against a child or young person (s. 45 of the Children and Young Persons Act 1933). A 'child' is aged 10 and under 14 and a 'young person' is aged 14 and under 18.

A youth court is presided over by either a district judge or a bench of two or three lay magistrates who receive specialist training on dealing with young people. Unless there are unforeseen circumstances, the bench must include both a man and a woman (Youth Courts (Constitution of Committees and Right to Preside) Rules 2007, r. 10(1) (SI 2007/1611)). Where either no man or woman is available a decision to proceed with the case must be made in open court after hearing submissions from all the parties (*R v Birmingham Youth Court, ex parte F (a minor)* [2000] Crim LR 588).

2.1.9.1 Restrictions on Persons Present and Reporting

Restrictions are placed on those persons who may be present during proceedings in the youth court and this is contained in s. 47 of the Children and Young Persons Act 1933 which states:

(2) No person shall be present at any sitting of a youth court except—
  (a) members and officers of the court;
  (b) parties to the case before the court, their legal representatives, and witnesses and other persons directly concerned in that case;
  (c) bona fide representatives of newspapers or news agencies;
  (d) such other persons as the court may specially authorise to be present.

The reporting restrictions that apply automatically to proceedings in which children and young persons are concerned in youth courts are: no report shall be published which reveals the name, address or school of any child or young person concerned in the proceedings or includes any particulars likely to lead to the identification of any child or young person concerned in the proceedings; and no picture shall be published in any newspaper as being or including a picture of any child or young person so concerned in the proceedings as aforesaid (s. 49(1)).

However, the restrictions may be lifted by the court:

- for the purpose of avoiding injustice to the child or young person (s. 49(5)(a));
- in respect of a child or young person who is unlawfully at large, and where it is necessary to do so for the purpose of apprehending him/her. This only applies to a child or young person who is charged with, or convicted of, a violent or sexual offence or an offence punishable in the case of an adult with imprisonment for 14 years or more (s. 49(5)(b));
- in respect of a child who has been convicted of an offence, in the public interest (s. 49(4A));
- as respects a child or young person who is charged with or has been convicted of a violent offence or sexual offence (s. 49(6)).

For the purposes of this section a child or young person is 'concerned' in any proceedings whether as being the person against or in respect of whom the proceedings are taken or as being a witness in the proceedings (s. 49(4)). If during the course of proceedings a defendant attains the age of 18 the provisions of s. 49 no longer apply (*T* v *DPP; North East Press Ltd* (2004) 168 JP 194). Where a young person is tried in any other court, s. 39 of the 1933 Act allows the court discretion in imposing reporting restrictions to any proceedings other than criminal proceedings. However, in *R (On the Application of JC) v Central Criminal Court* [2014] EWHC 1041 (Admin) it was held that no order made by any court could restrict reporting of the proceedings after the subject of the order had reached the age of 18.

2.1.9.2 Attendance of Parent or Guardian

The youth court has the power to order the juvenile's parent or guardian to attend the proceedings. If the juvenile is aged under 16 the court *must* (and if the juvenile is aged 16 or 17, the court *may*) require such attendance, unless and to the extent that the court is satisfied that it would be unreasonable to require such attendance, having regard to the circumstances of the case (s. 34A(1) of the 1933 Act). This power equally applies to the attendance of the parent or guardian in the adult magistrates' court and Crown Court.

2.1.10 Crown Court

The Crown Court is a single court though it sits in many locations across England and Wales. The court has exclusive jurisdiction over trials on indictment and will normally hear cases which involve offences committed within its geographical area, but there are no territorial restrictions on the cases it can hear. The Senior Courts Act 1981, s. 46 states:

(2) The jurisdiction of the Crown Court with respect to proceedings on indictment shall include jurisdiction in proceedings on indictment for offences wherever committed, and in particular on indictment for offences within the jurisdiction of the Admiralty of England.

2.1.10.1 Judges

The Senior Courts Act 1981, s. 8 states:

(1) The jurisdiction of the Crown Court shall be exercisable by—
    (a) any judge of the High Court; or

(b) any Circuit judge, Recorder, qualifying judge advocate, or District Judge (Magistrates' Courts); or

(c) subject to and in accordance with the provisions of sections 74 and 75(2), a judge of the High Court, Circuit judge, recorder or qualifying judge advocate sitting with not more than four justices of the peace,

and any such persons when exercising the jurisdiction of the Crown Court shall be judges of the Crown Court.

KEYNOTE

All proceedings in the Crown Court must be heard and disposed of by a single judge except where a justice is permitted to sit with such a judge (s. 73(1) of the 1981 Act).

A qualifying judge advocate may not exercise the jurisdiction of the Crown Court on an appeal from a youth court (s. 8(1A)).

2.1.10.2 Modes of Address

The following is reproduced from the *Criminal Practice Directions, Division XII, General Application B: Modes of Address and Titles of Judges and Magistrates*, that states:

Modes of Address

B.1 The following judges, when sitting in court, should be addressed as 'My Lord' or 'My Lady', as the case may be, whatever their personal status:

(a) Judges of the Court of Appeal and of the High Court:

(b) any Circuit Judge sitting as a judge of the Court of Appeal (Criminal Division) or the High Court under s. 9(1) of the Senior Courts Act 1981;

(c) any judge sitting at the Central Criminal Court;

(d) any Senior Circuit Judge who is an Honorary Recorder.

B.2 Subject to the paragraph above, Circuit Judges, qualifying judge advocates, Recorders and Deputy Circuit Judges should be addressed as 'Your Honour' when sitting in court.

District Judges (Magistrates Courts) should be addressed as 'Sir (or Madam)' or 'Judge' when sitting in court.

Magistrates in court should be addressed through the chairperson as 'Sir (or Madam)' or collectively as 'Your Worships'.

2.1.10.3 Juries

Qualification for jury service is provided by s. 1 of the Juries Act 1974, which states:

Subject to the provisions of this Act, every person shall be qualified to serve as a juror in the Crown Court, the High Court and county courts and be liable accordingly to attend for jury service when summoned under this Act if—

(a) he is for the time being registered as a parliamentary or local government elector and is not less that eighteen nor more than seventy years of age;

(b) he has been ordinarily resident in the United Kingdom, the Channel Islands or the Isle of Man for any period of at least five years since attaining the age of thirteen;

but not if he is for the time being ineligible or disqualified for jury service; and the persons who are ineligible, and those who are disqualified, are those respectively listed in Parts I and II of Schedule 1 to this Act.

KEYNOTE

A jury generally consists of 12 jurors whose role is to determine the guilt or innocence of an accused where he/she has pleaded not guilty in relation to the offence(s) charged. The 12 jurors are selected by ballot in open court from the panel of jurors summoned to attend on a particular date (Juries Act 1974, s. 11).

Serving police officers, and staff of the CPS, can serve on juries as this does not offend against principles of fairness where there are no circumstances which would give rise to concerns of bias (*R* v *Abdroikov, Green and*

Williamson [2007] UKHL 37). Where two police officers and a member of the CPS were on the same jury it was held that neither of the officers had any connection with the police force, or the individual officers involved in the trial, and there was no reason why their position should cause any concern. However, in relation to the member of the CPS, the court considered that 'justice is not seen to be done if one discharging the very important neutral role of juror is a full-time, salaried, long-serving employee of the prosecutor' (*R v L* [2011] EWCA Crim 65). In relation to police officers the position would, however, be different where they had special knowledge of the individuals involved, or the facts of the case, or where the credibility or reliability of police evidence was a central issue (*Hanif and Khan* v *United Kingdom* [2011] ECHR 2247). In *R v Yemoh* [2009] EWCA Crim 930, the court held that even where a case contained contentious police evidence there was no reason why a police officer should not be a juror. However, in *R* v *Khan* [2008] EWCA Crim 531, the Court of Appeal advised that the trial judge should be made aware if any juror in waiting is or has been a police officer, a member of the prosecuting authority or is a serving prison officer.

2.2 Instituting Criminal Proceedings

2.2.1 Introduction

There is a number of ways that the appearance of a defendant before a magistrates' court can be secured:

- by the accused being arrested and, following CPS advice, charged by the police and brought before a court; or
- by the accused being arrested and then granted police bail to give the CPS time to decide whether to prosecute; the CPS may then start a prosecution by using the 'written charge and requisition procedure'; or
- by the accused being arrested and then granted bail subject to a requirement to return to the police station on a specified date; where the CPS decide there is sufficient evidence to charge the police will charge the accused when they answer their bail; or
- by the accused being served with a 'written charge and requisition' without first having been arrested; or
- in the case of a private prosecution, by the laying of an information by the prosecutor before a magistrate resulting in the issue of a summons requiring the accused to attend at court on a specified day to answer the allegation in the information; or
- by the laying of an information by a prosecutor before a magistrate resulting in the issue of a warrant for the defendant to be arrested and brought before the court. Alternatively, the warrant may be backed for bail where the defendant is arrested and then released on bail to attend court on a specified day.

2.2.2 Written Charge and Requisition

The procedure in relation to instituting criminal proceedings is provided by the Criminal Justice Act 2003, s. 29, which states:

(1) A relevant prosecutor may institute criminal proceedings against a person by issuing a document (a 'written charge') which charges the person with an offence.

(2) Where a relevant prosecutor issues a written charge, it must at the same time issue—
    (a) a requisition, or
    (b) a single justice procedure notice.

(2A) A requisition is a document which requires the person on whom it is served to appear before a magistrates' court to answer the written charge.

(2B) A single justice procedure notice is a document which requires the person on whom it is served to serve on the designated officer for a magistrates' court specified in the notice a written notification stating—
    (a) whether the person desires to plead guilty or not guilty, and
    (b) if the person desires to plead guilty, whether or not the person desires to be tried in accordance with section 16A of the Magistrates' Courts Act 1980.

(3) Where a relevant prosecutor issues a written charge and a requisition, the written charge and requisition must be served on the person concerned, and a copy of both must be served on the court named in the requisition.

(3A) Where a relevant prosecutor issues a written charge and a single justice procedure notice, the written charge and notice must be served on the person concerned, and a copy of both must be served on the designated officer specified in the notice.

(3B) If a single justice procedure notice is served on a person, the relevant prosecutor must—

(a) at the same time serve on the person such documents as may be prescribed by Criminal Procedure Rules, and

(b) serve copies of those documents on the designated officer specified in the notice.

(3C) The written notification required by a single justice procedure notice may be served by the legal representative of the person charged on the person's behalf.

KEYNOTE

In relation to subsection (2B)(b) above, s. 16A of the 1980 Act makes provision for a single justice to exercise the jurisdiction of a magistrates' court in certain cases.

A relevant prosecutor authorised to issue a requisition does not have the power to lay an information for the purpose of obtaining the issue of a summons under s. 1 of the Magistrates' Courts Act 1980 (s. 29(4)).

Section 29(5) defines a 'relevant prosecutor' and includes a police force, the Director of Public Prosecutions (i.e. all Crown Prosecution Service prosecutions), the Director of the Serious Fraud Office, the Director General of the National Crime Agency, the Attorney General, a Secretary of State, or a person so authorised by any of the above.

This section was amended by the Criminal Justice and Courts Act 2015, s. 46, which substituted 'relevant prosecutor' for the previous 'public prosecutor' and inserted the 'single justice procedure notice'.

2.2.3 Service of the Summons or Requisition

The Criminal Procedure Rules 2014 provide that a summons, requisition or witness summons may be served on a person by the following means:

Service by handing over a document (Rule 4.3)

(1) A document may be served on—

(a) an individual by handing it to him or her;

(b) a corporation by handing it to a person holding a senior position in that corporation;

(c) an individual or corporation who is legally represented in the case by handing it to that representative;

(2) If an individual is under 18, a copy of a document served under paragraph (1)(a) may be handed to his or her parent, or another appropriate adult, unless no such person is readily available.

Service by leaving or posting a document (Rule 4.4)

(1) A document may be served by addressing it to the person to be served and leaving it at the appropriate address for service under this rule, or by sending it to that address by first class post or by the equivalent of first class post.

(2) The address for service under this rule on—

(a) an individual is an address where it is reasonably believed that he or she will receive it;

(b) a corporation is its principal office, and if there is no readily identifiable principal office then any place where it carries on its activities or business;

(c) an individual or corporation who is legally represented in the case is that representative's office;

KEYNOTE

A document served under r. 4.3 is served on the day it is handed over (r. 4.10).

The person who serves a document may prove that by signing a certificate explaining how and when it was served (r. 4.11).

2.2.4 Service Outside England and Wales

The following legislation deals with the service of documents outside England and Wales:

• Section 39 of the Criminal Law Act 1977 (service in Scotland and Northern Ireland) provides that a summons, written charge, requisition and a single justice procedure notice, requiring a person charged with an offence to appear before a court in England or Wales, and any other document which, by virtue of any enactment, may or must be served on a person with, or at the same time as, a document mentioned in paragraph (a), (b), (c) or (ca) above, may, in such manner as may be prescribed by rules of court, be served on him in Scotland or Northern Ireland (s. 1). This also applies to a summons directed to a person that is issued after the person's trial has begun (s. 1A).

- Section 1139(4) of the Companies Act 2006 (service of copy summons, etc. on company's registered office in Scotland and Northern Ireland).
- Sections 3 and 4 of the Crime (International Co-operation) Act 2003, and rr. 32.1 and 32.2 of the Criminal Procedure Rules 2014 (service of summons, etc. outside the United Kingdom).
- Section 1139(2) of the Companies Act 2006 (service on overseas companies).

2.2.5 Issue of Warrants

There are several different types of warrants which may be issued by justices, some of which are detailed below.

2.2.5.1 Warrant to Arrest an Offender

The terms of a warrant for arrest require each person to whom it is directed to arrest the defendant and either bring him/her to a court specified in the warrant or required or allowed by law, or release the defendant on bail (with or without conditions) to attend court at a date, time and place specified or to be notified by the court (Criminal Procedure Rules 2014, r. 18.2).

Section 1(1)(b) of the Magistrates' Courts Act 1980 provides that, whenever a justice before whom an information is laid has power to issue a summons, he/she may alternatively issue a warrant for the arrest of the person named in the information, save that:

- the information must be in writing (s. 1(3)); and
- where the person in respect of whom the warrant is to be issued has attained the age of 18, the offence is an indictable offence or is punishable with imprisonment or else the person's address is not sufficiently established for a summons, or a written charge and requisition, to be served on him/her (s. 1(4)).

KEYNOTE

An arrest warrant may not be issued in the case of private prosecutions without the consent of the DPP (s. 1(4A)).

Warrants for arrest under s. 1(1)(b) of the 1980 Act are not commonly issued as police officers may arrest (without warrant) for any offence to allow its prompt and effective investigation, or to prevent the prosecution for an offence being hindered by the disappearance of the defendant (s. 24 of the Police and Criminal Evidence Act 1984). However, any warrant to arrest a person in connection with an offence, and certain other warrants, may be executed by a constable even though it is not in his/her possession at the time (s. 125D).

2.2.5.2 Warrant to Arrest a Witness

The Magistrates' Courts Act 1980 provides that a justice of the peace may issue a warrant where he/she is satisfied that it is in the interests of justice to secure the attendance of a person who could give material evidence. However, a warrant may only be issued where the justice of the peace is satisfied, by evidence on oath, that a summons would not procure the attendance of the person (s. 97(2)). In addition, a warrant may also be issued where a person fails to attend the court in answer to a summons where there is proof of its service, if it appears to the court that there is no just excuse for the failure (s. 97(3)).

Similar powers exist for witness warrants (and summonses) for the High Court and the Crown Court.

2.2.5.3 Warrant to Arrest in Default

This warrant is issued where a person defaults in payment of a fine or other sum and is a type of commitment warrant.

2.2.5.4 Warrant to Commit to Detention or Imprisonment

The person who executes a warrant of detention or imprisonment must take the defendant to any place specified in the warrant, or if that is not immediately practicable, to any other place at which the defendant may be lawfully detained; obtain a receipt from the custodian; and notify the court officer that the defendant has been taken to that place (Criminal Procedure Rules 2014, r. 18.5(4)).

2.2.5.5 Warrant to Distrain Property

This warrant is issued in an effort to collect money. It allows certain goods to be seized and sold as prescribed by the Criminal Procedure Rules 2014, Part 52: Enforcement of Fines and Other Orders for Payment.

2.2.6 Execution of Warrants

The Criminal Procedure Rules 2014, r. 18.5 states:

(1) A warrant may be executed—
    (a) by any person to whom it is directed; or
    (b) if the warrant was issued by a magistrates' court, by anyone authorised to do so by section 125 (warrants), 125A (civilian enforcement officers) or 125B (execution by approved enforcement agency) of the Magistrates' Courts Act 1980.

(2) The person who executes a warrant must—
    (a) explain, in terms the defendant can understand, what the warrant requires, and why;
    (b) show the defendant the warrant, if that person has it; and
    (c) if the defendant asks—
        (i) arrange for the defendant to see the warrant, if that person does not have it, and
        (ii) show the defendant any written statement of that person's authority required by section 125A or 125B of the 1980 Act.

KEYNOTE

The Magistrates' Courts Act 1980, s. 125 provides that a warrant issued by a magistrates' court may be executed by any person to whom it is directed or by any constable acting within that constable's police area.

Certain warrants issued by a magistrates' court (arrest, commitment, detention, distress, or in connection with the enforcement of a fine or other order) may be executed anywhere in England and Wales by a civilian enforcement officer (s. 125A) or by an approved enforcement agency (s. 125B). In either case, the person executing the warrant must, if the defendant asks, show a written statement indicating: that person's name; the authority or agency by which that person is employed, or in which that person is a director or partner; that that person is authorised to execute warrants; and, where s. 125B applies, that the agency is registered as one approved by the Lord Chancellor. A warrant to which s. 125A applies may be executed by any person entitled to execute it even though it is not in that person's possession at the time (s. 125D).

In order to execute a warrant of arrest issued in connection with, or arising out of criminal proceedings, or a warrant of commitment issued under s. 76 of the 1980 Act, a constable may enter and search any premises where he/she has reasonable grounds for believing the person sought is on the premises. The search may only be to the extent required and is restricted to the parts of the premises where the constable reasonably believes the person may be. Reasonable force may be used when necessary. These powers are derived from ss. 17(1) (a) and 117 of the Police and Criminal Evidence Act 1984. Civilian enforcement officers and approved enforcement agencies may be authorised to enter and search premises for the purposes of executing a warrant (for

---

or in connection with any criminal offence), only to the extent reasonably required, and where they have reasonable grounds for believing the person is on the premises (sch. 4A to the 1980 Act).

The Criminal Procedure Rules 2014, r. 18.5(3) states that a person who executes a warrant of arrest requiring the defendant to be released on bail must make a record of:

- the defendant's name;
- the reason for the arrest;
- the defendant's release on bail; and
- when and where the warrant requires the defendant to attend court; and serve the record on the defendant, and the court officer.

Other types of warrants that may be executed by a constable are listed in s. 125D(3) of the 1980 Act as a warrant under the: Armed Forces Act 2006; General Rate Act 1967 (insufficiency of distress); Family Law Act 1996 (failure to comply with occupation order or non-molestation order); Crime and Disorder Act 1998 (unwilling witnesses); Powers of Criminal Courts (Sentencing) Act 2000 (offenders referred to court by youth offender panel); and Magistrates' Courts Act 1980 (warrants relating to the non-appearance of a defendant, warrants of commitment, warrants of distress and warrants to arrest a witness).

2.2.6.1   Disclosure of Information for Enforcing Warrants

The Magistrates' Courts Act 1980, s. 125CA states:

(1) A magistrates' court may make a disclosure order if satisfied that it is necessary to do so for the purpose of executing a warrant to which this section applies.

(2) This section applies to a warrant of arrest, commitment, detention or distress issued by a justice of the peace in connection with the enforcement of a fine or other order imposed or made on conviction.

(3) A disclosure order is an order requiring the person to whom it is directed to supply the designated officer for the court with any of the following information about the person to whom the warrant relates—

(a) his name, date of birth or national insurance number;

(b) his address (or any of his addresses).

(4) A disclosure order may be made only on the application of a person entitled to execute the warrant.

KEYNOTE

The disclosure order may require that basic personal information (name, date of birth, national insurance number and address or addresses) held by a relevant public authority be supplied by that authority to the court for the purpose of facilitating the enforcement of a s. 125A(1) warrant which is so specified (s. 125C(1)).

A 'relevant public authority' means a Minister of the Crown, government department, local authority or chief officer of police specified in an order made by the Lord Chancellor (s. 125C(2)).

The information supplied for the purpose of facilitating the enforcement of a s. 125A(1) warrant may be supplied to any person entitled to execute the warrant; any employee of a body or person who, for the purposes of s. 125B, is an approved enforcement agency in relation to the warrant; or any justices' clerk or other person appointed under s. 2(1) of the Courts Act 2003 (s. 125C(3)).

Under s. 125C(4) it is an offence for a person to intentionally or recklessly disclose information supplied to him/her under this section otherwise than as permitted by subs. (3), or use information so supplied otherwise than for the purpose of facilitating the enforcement of the s. 125A(1) warrant concerned. However, it is not an offence to disclose any information in accordance with any enactment or order of a court or for the purposes of any proceedings before a court, or to disclose any information which has previously been lawfully disclosed to the public (s. 125C(5)).

2.2.6.2 Execution of Warrants throughout the United Kingdom

Section 136 of the Criminal Justice and Public Order Act 1994 states:

(1) A warrant issued in England, Wales or Northern Ireland for the arrest of a person charged with an offence may (without any endorsement) be executed in Scotland by any constable of any police force of the country of issue or of the country of execution, or by a constable appointed under section 53 of the British Transport Commission Act 1949, as well as by any other persons within the directions of the warrant.

(2) A warrant issued in—

    (a) Scotland; or

    (b) Northern Ireland,

for the arrest of a person charged with an offence may (without any endorsement) be executed in England and Wales by any constable of any police force of the country of issue or of the country of execution, or by a constable appointed under section 53 of the British Transport Commission Act 1949, as well as by any other persons within the directions of the warrant.

KEYNOTE

In addition to a warrant for the arrest of a person charged with an offence, this section also relates to: (a) a warrant of commitment and a warrant to arrest a witness issued in England, Wales or Northern Ireland; and (b) a warrant for committal, a warrant to imprison (or apprehend and imprison) and a warrant to arrest a witness issued in Scotland. In addition, the section also applies to a warrant for the arrest of an offender referred back to court by a youth offender panel (sch. 1, para. 3(2) to the Powers of Criminal Courts (Sentencing) Act 2000), issued in England and Wales.

Section 38A of the Criminal Law Act 1977 provides for the cross-border execution of Scottish commitment warrants for non-payment of fines, and s. 38B contains similar provisions for such warrants being executed between England, Wales and Northern Ireland.

The Indictable Offences Act 1848, s. 13 provides that warrants from the Isle of Man and the Channel Islands may be executed in England and Wales where they have been endorsed by a justice of the peace.

The execution of warrants from other countries is dealt with by the Extradition Act 2003. This provides a fast-track extradition arrangement with Member States of the European Union and Gibraltar. Such warrants must state that the person in question is accused in the territory issuing the warrant of the commission of a specified offence and that the warrant has been issued for the purposes of arrest and prosecution.

Bail

2.3.1 Introduction

The Bail Act 1976 is the primary source of legislation in relation to bail in criminal proceedings granted by the police and courts. Other legislation also impacts upon bail, in particular the Police and Criminal Evidence Act 1984 and the Criminal Justice and Public Order Act 1994.

The meaning of 'bail in criminal proceedings' is contained in s. 1 of the Bail Act 1976 which states:

(1) In this Act 'bail in criminal proceedings' means—
    (a) bail grantable in or in connection with proceedings for an offence to a person who is accused or convicted of the offence, or
    (b) bail grantable in connection with an offence to a person who is under arrest for the offence or for whose arrest for the offence a warrant (endorsed for bail) is being issued, or
    (c) bail grantable in connection with extradition proceedings in respect of an offence.

KEYNOTE

This section provides that bail can be granted immaterial of whether the offence was committed in 'England or Wales or elsewhere', and immaterial as to which country's law the offence relates (s. 1(5)).

2.3.2 Police Bail

Bail can either be granted by a custody officer at a police station or by a constable elsewhere than at a police station (known as 'street bail').

2.3.2.1 Street Bail

The Police and Criminal Evidence Act 1984, s. 30A provides for persons arrested elsewhere than at a police station to be released on bail without being required to attend a police station.

2.3.2.2 Release on Bail

Section 30A(1)   A constable may release on bail a person who is arrested or taken into custody in the circumstances mentioned in s. 30(1).

Section 30A(2)   A person may be released on bail under subs. (1) at any time before he arrives at a police station.

Section 30A(3)   A person released on bail under subs. (1) must be required to attend a police station.

Section 30A(3A)   Where a constable releases a person on bail under subs. (1)—
    (a) no recognizance for the person's surrender to custody shall be taken from the person,
    (b) no security for the person's surrender to custody shall be taken from the person or from anyone else on the person's behalf,
    (c) the person shall not be required to provide a surety or sureties for his surrender to custody, and
    (d) no requirement to reside in a bail hostel may be imposed as a condition of bail.

Section 30A(3B)	Subject to subs. (3A), where a constable releases a person on bail under subs. (1) the constable may impose, as conditions of the bail, such requirements as appear to the constable to be necessary— (a) to secure that the person surrenders to custody, (b) to secure that the person does not commit an offence while on bail, (c) to secure that the person does not interfere with witnesses or otherwise obstruct the course of justice, whether in relation to him or any other person, or (d) for the person's own protection or, if the person is under the age of 18, for the person's own welfare or in the person's own interests.
Section 30A(4)	Where a person is released on bail under subs. (1), a requirement may be imposed on the person as a condition of bail only under the preceding provisions of this section.
Section 30A(5)	The police station which the person is required to attend may be any police station.

KEYNOTE

Section 30A(3B) enables the officer granting bail to consider attaching conditions relevant and proportionate to the suspect and the offence. The conditions that may be considered are the same as those available to a custody officer as contained in s. 3A(5) of the 1976 Act, except for those specified in s. 30A(3A).

Guidance on street bail is contained in Home Office Circular 61/2003, *Bail Elsewhere than at a Police Station*. Although there is no limit on the time for which 'street' bail may be granted, the Circular suggests a normal maximum time of six weeks.

2.3.2.3 Notice in Writing

Section 30B(1)	Where a constable grants bail to a person under s. 30A, he must give that person a notice in writing before he is released.
Section 30B(2)	The notice must state: (a) the offence for which he was arrested, and (b) the grounds on which he was arrested.
Section 30B(3)	The notice must inform him that he is required to attend a police station.
Section 30B(4)	It may also specify the police station which he is required to attend and the time when he is required to attend.
Section 30B(4A)	If the person is granted bail subject to conditions under s. 30A(3B), the notice also— (a) must specify the requirements imposed by those conditions, (b) must explain the opportunities under ss. 30CA(1) and 30CB(1) for variation of those conditions, and (c) if it does not specify the police station at which the person is required to attend, must specify a police station at which the person may make a request under s. 30CA(1)(b),
Section 30B(5)	If the notice does not include the information mentioned in subs. (4), the person must subsequently be given a further notice in writing which contains that information.
Section 30B(6)	The person may be required to attend a different police station from that specified in the notice under subs. (1) or (5) or to attend at a different time.
Section 30B(7)	He must be given notice in writing of any such change as is mentioned in subs. (6) but more than one such notice may be given to him.

KEYNOTE

This section requires that the person bailed be given a written notice identifying the offence and grounds for arrest and informing the person that he/she is required to attend a police station. The notice may specify a police station and a time to attend, but if not, or where the person is required to attend a different police station, a further notice must be issued detailing the rearranged place and time. The notice must also include details of how the person bailed may apply for variation to any conditions (s. 30CA(1)(b)).

2.3.2.4 Release, Attendance and Re-arrest

Section 30C(1)   A person who has been required to attend a police station is not required to do so if he is given notice in writing that his attendance is no longer required.

Section 30C(2)   If a person is required to attend a police station which is not a designated police station he must be:
(a) released, or
(b) taken to a designated police station, not more than six hours after his arrival.

Section 30C(3)   Nothing in the Bail Act 1976 applies in relation to bail under s. 30A.

Section 30C(4)   Nothing in s. 30A or 30B or in this section prevents the re-arrest without warrant of a person released on bail under s. 30A if new evidence justifying a further arrest has come to light since his release.

2.3.2.5 Variation of Bail Conditions: Police

Section 30CA(1)   Where a person released on bail under s. 30A(1) is on bail subject to conditions—
(a) a relevant officer at the police station at which the person is required to attend, or
(b) where no notice under s. 30B specifying that police station has been given to the person, a relevant officer at the police station specified under s. 30B(4A)(c),
may, at the request of the person but subject to subs. (2), vary the conditions.

Section 30CA(2)   On any subsequent request made in respect of the same grant of bail, subs. (1) confers power to vary the conditions of the bail only if the request is based on information that, in the case of the previous request or each previous request, was not available to the relevant officer considering that previous request when he/she was considering it.

Section 30CA(3)   Where conditions of bail granted to a person under s. 30A(1) are varied under subs. (1)—
(a) paragraphs (a) to (d) of s. 30A(3A) apply,
(b) requirements imposed by the conditions as so varied must be requirements that appear to the relevant officer varying the conditions to be necessary for any of the purposes mentioned in paragraphs (a) to (d) of s. 30A(3B), and
(c) the relevant officer who varies the conditions must give the person notice in writing of the variation.

Section 30CA(4)   Power under subs. (1) to vary conditions is, subject to subs. (3)(a) and (b), power—
(a) to vary or rescind any of the conditions, and
(b) to impose further conditions.

KEYNOTE

The 'relevant officer' (s. 30CA(3)(c)) means a custody officer in relation to a designated police station. In relation to any other police station the 'relevant officer' means a constable who is not involved in the investigation of the offence for which the person making the request under subsection (1) was under arrest when granted bail under section 30A(1), if such a constable is readily available. If no such constable is readily available, the 'relevant officer' means a constable other than the one who granted bail to the person, if such a constable is readily available, and if no such constable is readily available, it means the constable who granted bail (s. 30CA(5)).

2.3.2.6 Variation of Bail Conditions: Court

Section 30CB(1)   Where a person released on bail under s. 30A(1) is on bail subject to conditions, a magistrates' court may, on an application by or on behalf of the person, vary the conditions if—
(a) the conditions have been varied under s. 30CA(1) since being imposed under s. 30A(3B),

(b) a request for variation under s. 30CA(1) of the conditions has been made and refused, or

(c) a request for variation under s. 30CA(1) of the conditions has been made and the period of 48 hours beginning with the day when the request was made has expired without the request having been withdrawn or the conditions having been varied in response to the request.

KEYNOTE

Where the court varies the conditions they must be seen as necessary for any of the purposes mentioned in s. 30A(3B)(a)–(d), and bail continues subject to the varied conditions (s. 30CB(3)(b) and (c)). It was held in *R (On the Application of Ajaib)* v *Birmingham Magistrates' Court* [2009] EWHC 2127 (Admin) that in deciding to vary bail conditions, the court was entitled to rely on a police officer's evidence whilst allowing him to withhold specific information. In this case the police asserted that they held material disclosure of which would prejudice their inquiries, suggesting that the suspect was liquidating his assets to travel abroad.

2.3.2.7 Power of Arrest for Non-attendance and Breach of Bail Conditions

Section 30D(1) A constable may arrest without warrant a person who:
(a) has been released on bail under s. 30A subject to a requirement to attend a specified police station, but
(b) fails to attend the police station at the specified time.

Section 30D(2) A person arrested under subs. (1) must be taken to a police station (which may be the specified police station or any other police station) as soon as practicable after the arrest.

Section 30D(2A) A person who has been released on bail under s. 30A may be arrested without a warrant by a constable if the constable has reasonable grounds for suspecting that the person has broken any of the conditions of bail.

Section 30D(2B) A person arrested under subs. (2A) must be taken to a police station (which may be the specified police station mentioned in subs. (1) or any other police station) as soon as practicable after the arrest.

Section 30D(3) In subs. (1), 'specified' means specified in a notice under subs. (1) or (5) of s. 30B or, if notice of change has been given under subs. (7) of that section, in that notice.

KEYNOTE

Section 30D(1) and (2) relates to a person's failure to answer his/her bail at the specified time and place. Section 30D(2A) and (2B) provides a power of arrest where a constable has reasonable grounds to suspect that a person has broken any of the conditions of bail.

2.3.3 Pre-charge Police Bail

Broadly, the Police and Criminal Evidence Act 1984 provides the following pre-charge scenario. The custody officer may decide to grant bail, with or without conditions, or withhold bail altogether where:

* there is as insufficient evidence to charge with an offence suspects whom it is necessary to continue to investigate without their having to be held in custody (s. 37(2));
* the police consider there is sufficient evidence to charge but the case has been referred to the CPS for a charging decision (s. 37(7)(a));
* there is sufficient evidence to charge but not for the purposes outlined in s. 37(7)(a) (this would usually be where further inquiries are to be made) (s. 37(7)(b));
* there is sufficient evidence and the person is charged with an offence (s. 37(7)(d));

- the officer conducting the review concludes that the detention without charge can no longer be justified (s. 40(8));
- at the end of 24 hours' detention without charge, unless the detained person is suspected of committing an indictable offence and continued detention up to 36 hours is authorised by a superintendent (s. 41(7)).

KEYNOTE

It is the decision of the custody officer as to whether a person is detained or released on bail while awaiting the outcome of the CPS charging decision. Where a person is released on bail, conditions may be applied to the bail and these may be varied by the custody officer by notice in writing (s. 37D(1) and (2)).

Conditions imposed by the custody officer may be varied by the magistrates' court on application by the suspect (s. 47(1E)). The magistrates can confirm the same conditions, impose different conditions or direct that bail shall be unconditional (Criminal Procedure Rules 2014, part 19). Irrespective of the outcome, it continues to be police bail.

Conditional bail before charge is not permitted when a person is bailed pending further (possibly lengthy) investigation (s. 34(5)).

Nothing in the Bail Act 1976 prevents the re-arrest without warrant of a person released on bail to attend at a police station, if new evidence justifying a further arrest has come to light since his/her release (s. 47(2)). Where a person has been re-arrested, s. 37C(2)(b) gives the police the power to release (again) 'without charge, either on bail or without bail'. Section 37C(4) states explicitly that if a person is released on bail under s. 37C(2)(b), that person shall be subject to whatever conditions applied before the 're-arrest'. It appears that there is no power to change conditions of bail at this point.

A custody officer, having granted bail to a person subject to a duty to appear at a police station, may give notice in writing that the person's appearance is not required (s. 47(4)).

Any period where a person is on bail is not calculated as part of his/her time in police detention (s. 47(6)).

There is NO time limit for which bail may be granted under the 1984 Act and the courts will only intervene where there are exceptional circumstances (*R (On the Application of C)* v *Chief Constable of A* [2006] EWHC 2352 (Admin)). In *Fitzpatrick and Others* v *Commissioner of Police of the Metropolis* [2012] EWHC 12 (QB) police bail was granted on 12 September 2007 and the suspects remained on bail and subject to investigation until it was confirmed that no action would be taken against them in June 2009. The court held that there had been no breach of Article 8 of the European Convention on Human Rights (the right to respect for private and family life) due to the complex nature of the case.

2.3.4 Police Bail After Charge

Where a person is charged at the police station (otherwise than a warrant backed for bail) the custody officer must make a decision to keep the person in custody until they can be brought before a magistrates' court, or to release the person either on bail or without bail, unless one or more conditions in the Police and Criminal Evidence Act 1984, s. 38, are satisfied (s. 38(1)).

Where the custody officer decides to bail a person who has been charged, s. 47(3) of the 1984 Act provides they may do so:

(a) to appear before a magistrates' court at such time and such place as the custody officer may appoint;

(b) to attend at such police station as the custody officer may appoint at such time as he may appoint for the purposes of—

    (i) proceedings in relation to a live link direction under section 57C of the Crime and Disorder Act 1998 (use of live link direction at preliminary hearings where accused is at police station); and

    (ii) any preliminary hearing in relation to which such a direction is given; or

(c) to attend at such police station as the custody officer may appoint at such time as he may appoint for purposes other than those mentioned in paragraph (b).

2.3.5   Police Bail Restrictions

The Criminal Justice and Public Order Act 1994 provides for those occasions when bail may only be granted in *exceptional circumstances* where a person is charged with certain specified offences. Section 25 of the 1994 Act states:

(1) A person who in any proceedings has been charged with or convicted of an offence to which this section applies in circumstances to which it applies shall be granted bail in those proceedings only if the court or, as the case may be, the constable considering the grant of bail is of the opinion that there are exceptional circumstances which justify it.

(2) This section applies, subject to subsection (3) below, to the following offences, that is to say—
   (a) murder;
   (b) attempted murder;
   (c) manslaughter;
   (d) rape under the law of Scotland;
   (e) an offence under section 1 of the Sexual Offences Act 1956 (rape);
   (f) an offence under section 1 of the Sexual Offences Act 2003 (rape);
   (g) an offence under section 2 of that Act (assault by penetration);
   (h) an offence under section 4 of that Act (causing a person to engage in sexual activity without consent) where the activity caused involved penetration within subsection (4)(a) to (d) of that section;
   (i) an offence under section 5 of that Act (rape of a child under 13);
   (j) an offence under section 6 of that Act (assault of a child under 13 by penetration);
   (k) an offence under section 8 of that Act (causing or inciting a child under 13 to engage in sexual activity), where an activity involving penetration within subsection (3)(a) to (d) of that section was caused;
   (l) an offence under section 30 of that Act (sexual activity with a person with a mental disorder impeding choice), where the touching involved penetration within subsection (3)(a) to (d) of that section;
   (m) an offence under section 31 of that Act (causing or inciting a person, with a mental disorder impeding choice, to engage in sexual activity), where an activity involving penetration within subsection (3)(a) to (d) of that section was caused;
   (n) an attempt to commit an offence within any of paragraphs (d) to (m).

(3) This section applies in the circumstances described in subsection (3A) or (3B) only.

(3A) This section applies where—
   (a) the person has been previously convicted by or before a court in any part of the United Kingdom of any offence within subsection (2) or of culpable homicide, and
   (b) if that previous conviction is one of manslaughter or culpable homicide—
      (i) the person was then a child or young person, and was sentenced to long-term detention under any of the relevant enactments, or
      (ii) the person was not then a child or young person, and was sentenced to imprisonment or detention.

(3B) This section applies where—
   (a) the person has been previously convicted by or before a court in another member State of any relevant foreign offence corresponding to an offence within subsection (2) or to culpable homicide, and
   (b) if the previous conviction is of a relevant foreign offence corresponding to the offence of manslaughter or culpable homicide—

(i) the person was then a child or young person, and was sentenced to detention for a period in excess of 2 years, or

(ii) the person was not then a child or young person, and was sentenced to detention.

(4) This section applies whether or not an appeal is pending against conviction or sentence.

(5) In this section—

'conviction' includes—

(a) a finding that a person is not guilty by reason of insanity;

(b) a finding under section 4A(3) of the Criminal Procedure (Insanity) Act 1964 (cases of unfitness to plead) that a person did the act or made the omission charged against him; and

(c) a conviction of an offence for which an order is made discharging the offender absolutely or conditionally;

and 'convicted' shall be construed accordingly;

'relevant foreign offence', in relation to a member State other than the United Kingdom, means an offence under the law in force in that member State; and

'the relevant enactments' means—

(a) as respects England and Wales, section 91 of the Powers of Criminal Courts (Sentencing) Act 2000;

(b) as respects Scotland, sections 205(1) to (3) and 208 of the Criminal Procedure (Scotland) Act 1995;

(c) …

(5A) For the purposes of subsection (3B), a relevant foreign offence corresponds to another offence if the relevant foreign offence would have constituted that other offence if it had been done in any part of the United Kingdom at the time when the relevant foreign offence was committed.

KEYNOTE

Section 25 provides that bail may not be granted where a person is charged with murder, attempted murder, manslaughter, rape or attempted rape if he/she has been previously convicted of any of these offences unless there are exceptional circumstances. A person charged with murder may not be granted bail except by order of a Crown Court judge (s. 115 of the Coroners and Justice Act 2009). This does not apply to attempted murder or conspiracy to murder.

Even where a person's custody time limit had expired, s. 25 could still be applied and the evidential burden was on the defence to demonstrate that exceptional circumstances existed. Also, in the case of *Hurnam* v *State of Mauritius* [2005] UKPC 49, the Privy Council stated that the seriousness of the offence is not a conclusive reason for refusing bail and the court must consider whether or not the accused is likely to abscond if released on bail.

In all other cases the custody officer must consider the issue of bail and s. 38(1) of the 1984 Act sets out the occasions where bail can be refused.

2.3.5.1 Condition of Detained Person and Communication of Refused Bail

A detained person should be informed of the bail decision as soon as it is made. This can be delayed if the conditions set out in PACE Code C, para. 1.8 apply, in which case the detainee should be informed as soon as practicable.

In reaching a decision as to whether a person should be refused bail the custody officer should consider whether the same objective can be achieved by imposing conditions to the bail, that is, for the person to appear at an appointed place at an appointed time. If conditions attached to a person's bail are likely to achieve the same objective as keeping the person in detention, bail must be given.

In *Gizzonio* v *Chief Constable of Derbyshire* (1998) *The Times*, 29 April, Gizzonio had been remanded in custody in respect of certain charges which had not ultimately been pursued. Damages (for the wrongful exercise of lawful authority) were sought on the basis that the police had wrongly opposed the grant of bail. It was held that the decision regarding bail is part of the process of investigation of crime with a view to prosecution and so the police enjoyed immunity in that respect.

2.3.6   Grounds for Refusing Police Bail

The Police and Criminal Evidence Act 1984, s. 38(1) provides that where an arrested person is charged with an offence, the custody officer, subject to s. 25 of the Criminal Justice and Public Order Act 1994, need not grant bail if the person arrested *is not an arrested juvenile* and one or more of the following grounds apply:

(a) the person's name or address cannot be ascertained or the custody officer has reasonable grounds for doubting whether a name or address furnished is his/her real name or address;

(b) the custody officer has reasonable grounds for believing that the person arrested will fail to appear in court to answer to bail;

(c) in the case of a person arrested for an imprisonable offence, the custody officer has reasonable grounds for believing that the detention of the person arrested is necessary to prevent him/her from committing an offence;

(d) in a case of a person aged 18 or over, where a sample may be taken from the person under s. 63B (where there is a provision for drug testing in force for that police area and station), the custody officer has reasonable grounds for believing that the detention of the person is necessary to enable the sample to be taken;

(e) in the case of a person arrested for an offence which is not an imprisonable offence, the custody officer has reasonable grounds for believing that the detention of the person arrested is necessary to prevent him/her from causing physical injury to any other person or from causing loss of or damage to property;

(f) the custody officer has reasonable grounds for believing that the detention of the person arrested is necessary to prevent him/her from interfering with the administration of justice or with the investigation of offences or of a particular offence; or

(g) the custody officer has reasonable grounds for believing that the detention of the person arrested is necessary for his/her own protection.

If the person arrested is *an arrested juvenile* and one or more of the following grounds apply:

(a) any of the requirements of paras (a) to (g) above, but in the case of para. (d) only if the arrested juvenile has attained the minimum age;

(b) the custody officer has reasonable grounds for believing that the arrested juvenile ought to be detained in his/her own interests;

(c) the offence with which the juvenile is charged is murder.

KEYNOTE

Juveniles being detained 'in their own interests' means for their own welfare. The expression 'welfare' has a wider meaning than just 'protection' and might apply to juveniles who, if released, might be homeless or become involved in prostitution or vagrancy (Bail Act 1976, sch. 1, part I, para. (3)).

In taking the decisions required by s. 38(1), except where a defendant's name and address cannot be ascertained, detention is necessary for the person's own protection, or a juvenile is detained in his/her own interests, the custody officer is required to have regard to the same considerations as those which a court is required to have regard to in taking corresponding decisions under the Bail Act 1976, sch. 1, part I, para. 2(1) (s. 38(2A)).

Schedule 1, part I, para. 2(1) provides that the defendant need not be granted bail if the court (custody officer) is satisfied that there are substantial grounds for believing that the defendant, if released on bail (whether subject to conditions or not) would:

- fail to surrender to custody, or
- commit an offence while on bail, or
- interfere with witnesses or otherwise obstruct the course of justice, whether in relation to him/herself or any other person.

In *R (On the Application of Ajaib)* v *Birmingham Magistrates' Court* [2009] EWHC 2127 (Admin), it was held that a police officer's opinion that the accused is a 'flight risk' was sufficient even though the source of information giving rise to the officer's opinion was not disclosed.

Schedule 1, part I, para. 9 provides that in taking the decisions required by para. 2(1), the court (custody officer) will have regard to such of the following considerations as appear to be relevant:

(a) the nature and seriousness of the offence or default (and the probable method of dealing with the defendant for it);
(b) the character, antecedents, associations and community ties of the defendant;
(c) the defendant's record as respects the fulfilment of his/her obligations under previous grants of bail in criminal proceedings;
(d) except in the case of a defendant whose case is adjourned for inquiries or a report, the strength of the evidence of his/her having committed the offence or having defaulted;
(e) if the court is satisfied that there are substantial grounds for believing that the defendant, if released on bail (whether subject to conditions or not), would commit an offence while on bail, the risk that the defendant may do so by engaging in conduct that would, or would be likely to, cause physical or mental injury to any person other than the defendant, as well as to any others which appear to be relevant.

Where bail is refused, the custody officer must inform the detained person of the reasons why and make an entry as to these reasons in the custody record (s. 38(3) and (4)).

In relation to juveniles, Article 37(b) of the United Nations Convention on the Rights of the Child 1989 requires that the arrest, detention or imprisonment of a child shall be in conformity with the law and shall be used as a measure of last resort and for the shortest appropriate period of time.

2.3.7 Custody Officer: Granting Bail

The granting of bail in criminal proceedings is provided by s. 3 of the Bail Act 1976 and this section examines the general provisions in relation to bail granted by a custody officer, the conditions that may be attached and applications to vary or remove those conditions.

2.3.7.1 General Provisions

Section 3 states:

(1) A person granted bail in criminal proceedings shall be under a duty to surrender to custody, and that duty is enforceable in accordance with section 6 of this Act.
(2) No recognizance for his surrender to custody shall be taken from him.
(3) Except as provided by this section—
    (a) no security for his surrender to custody shall be taken from him,
    (b) he shall not be required to provide a surety or sureties for his surrender to custody, and
    (c) no other requirement shall be imposed on him as a condition of bail.
(4) He may be required, before release on bail, to provide a surety or sureties to secure his surrender to custody.
(5) He may be required, before release on bail, to give security for his surrender to custody. The security may be given by him or on his behalf.
(6) He may be required to comply, before release on bail or later, with such requirements as appear to the court to be necessary to secure that—
    (a) he surrenders to custody,
    (b) he does not commit an offence while on bail,
    (c) he does not interfere with witnesses or otherwise obstruct the course of justice whether in relation to himself or any other person,
    (ca) for his own protection or, if he is a child or young person, for his own welfare or in his own interests.
(7) If a parent or guardian of a person under the age of seventeen consents to be surety for the person for the purposes of this subsection, the parent or guardian may be required to secure that

the person complies with any requirement imposed on him by virtue of subsection (6) . . . above but—

(a) no requirement shall be imposed on the parent or the guardian by virtue of this subsection where it appears that the person will attain the age of 17 before the time to be appointed for him to surrender to custody, and

(b) the parent or guardian shall not be required to secure compliance with any requirement to which his consent does not extend and shall not, in respect of those requirements to which his consent does extend, be bound in a sum greater than £50.

KEYNOTE

Guidance to courts, applicable also to a custody officer, when approaching the decision to grant bail was given in *R* v *Mansfield Justices, ex parte Sharkey* [1985] QB 613, where it was held that any relevant risk, for example, absconding, must be a 'real' risk, not just a fanciful one.

Where a custody officer grants bail there is a requirement for a record to be made of the decision in the prescribed manner and containing the prescribed particulars. If requested, a copy of the record of the decision must, as soon as practicable, be given to the person in relation to whom the decision was taken (s. 5(1)).

2.3.7.2 Custody Officer: Conditions of Bail

The power of a custody officer to impose bail conditions is provided by s. 3A of the 1976 Act, which states:

(5) Where a constable grants bail to a person no conditions shall be imposed under subsections (4), (5), (6) or (7) of section 3 of this Act unless it appears to the constable that it is necessary to do so—

(a) for the purpose of preventing that person from failing to surrender to custody, or

(b) for the purpose of preventing that person from committing an offence while on bail, or

(c) for the purpose of preventing that person from interfering with witnesses or otherwise obstructing the course of justice, whether in relation to himself or any other person, or

(d) for that person's own protection, or if he is a child or young person, for his own welfare or in his own interests.

KEYNOTE

Where a custody officer decides to grant bail and considers one or more of the requirements in s. 3A(5)(a)–(d) apply, one or more of the following conditions can be imposed:

- the accused is to live and sleep at a specified address;
- the accused is to notify any changes of address;
- the accused is to report periodically (daily, weekly or at other intervals) to his/her local police station;
- the accused is restricted from entering a certain area or building or to go within a specified distance of a specified address;
- the accused is not to contact (whether directly or indirectly) the victim of the alleged offence and/or any other probable prosecution witness;
- the accused is to surrender his/her passport;
- the accused's movements are restricted by an imposed curfew between set times (i.e. when it is thought the accused might commit offences or come into contact with witnesses);
- the accused is required to provide a surety or security.

In *McDonald* v *Dickson* [2003] SLT 476, it was held that a condition for an accused to remain in his dwelling at all times except between 10 am and 12 noon did not amount to detention or deprivation of his liberty and did not constitute an infringement of his right to liberty under the European Convention on Human Rights, Article 5.

In *R (On the Application of Carson)* v *Ealing Magistrates' Court* [2012] EWHC 1456 (Admin) the defendant was subject to pre-charge bail conditions, one of which was not to reside at her home address. The police investigation was in relation to racially aggravated harassment, the complainants being her neighbours. The

---

condition that the claimant cease to reside at her home address was held to be disproportionate as it is a serious matter to exclude a person from her own home.

In relation to non-imprisonable offences it has been held that a hunt protester who was arrested for an offence under s. 5 of the Public Order Act 1986 was rightly required as a condition of his bail not to attend another hunt meeting before his next court appearance (*R* v *Bournemouth Magistrates' Court, ex parte Cross* [1989] Crim LR 207).

The conditions outlined in this section can also be imposed by a constable granting bail elsewhere than at a police station under s. 30A(3B) of the Police and Criminal Evidence Act 1984.

2.3.7.3 Applications to Vary or Remove Bail Conditions

The power to vary or remove conditions is provided by s. 3A of the Bail Act 1976. Section 3A(4) substitutes s. 3(8) and states:

> Where a custody officer has granted bail in criminal proceedings he or another custody officer serving at the same police station may, at the request of the person to whom it was granted, vary the conditions of bail and in doing so he may impose conditions or more onerous conditions.

KEYNOTE

Section 3A(5) (see para. 2.3.7.2) also applies on any request to a custody officer to vary or remove conditions of bail.

There is a requirement that a custody officer either imposing or varying the conditions of bail must include a note of the reasons in the custody record and give a copy of that note to the person in relation to whom the decision was taken (s. 5A(3)).

An accused may also apply to the magistrates' court under s. 43B(1) of the Magistrates' Courts Act 1980, to vary conditions of police bail. The prosecution may apply to the magistrates' court to reconsider bail and vary the conditions of bail, impose conditions in respect of bail that has been granted unconditionally, or withhold bail (s. 5B(1)). This only applies to bail granted by the magistrates' court or a constable and only in relation to offences triable on indictment or either way (s. 5B(2)). The application can only be on the basis of information that was not available to the court or constable when the original decision was taken (s. 5B(3)).

2.3.7.4 Police Bail: Surety

The Bail Act 1976, s. 8 states:

(1) This section applies where a person is granted bail in criminal proceedings on condition that he provides one or more surety or sureties for the purpose of securing that he surrenders to custody.
(2) In considering the suitability for that purpose of a proposed surety, regard may be had (amongst other things) to—
    (a) the surety's financial resources;
    (b) his character and any previous convictions of his; and
    (c) his proximity (whether in point of kinship, place of residence or otherwise) to the person for whom he is to be surety.

KEYNOTE

The question as to whether or not sureties are necessary is at the discretion of the custody officer (or court). A person cannot stand as his/her own surety (s. 3(2)).

There is no power to grant conditional bail with a surety to ensure no further offending; a surety can be sought only for the purpose of securing surrender to custody and not for any other purpose (*R (On the Application of Shea)* v *Winchester Crown Court* [2013] EWHC 1050 (Admin)).

The decision as to the suitability of individual sureties is a matter for the custody officer. Where no surety, or suitable surety, is available, the custody officer can fix the amount of cash or security in which the surety is to be bound for the purpose of enabling the recognizance of the surety to be entered into subsequently (s. 8(3)).

Where a court grants bail but is unable to release the person where no surety or no suitable surety is available, the court may fix the amount in which the surety is to be bound, and the recognizance of the surety may later be entered into before a police officer who is either of the rank of inspector or above or who is in charge of a police station, or other person as specified in s. 8(4) in conjunction with the Criminal Procedure Rules 2014, r. 19(14)(3)(b)).

The normal consequence for a surety, where an accused fails to answer bail, is that he/she is required to forfeit the entire cash or security in which he/she stood surety. The power to forfeit recognizances is a matter for a court (Magistrates' Courts Act 1980, s. 120).

It is not necessary to prove that the surety had any involvement in the accused's non-appearance (*R* v *Warwick Crown Court, ex parte Smalley* [1987] 1 WLR 237). However, in *R* v *York Crown Court, ex parte Coleman* (1988) 86 Cr App R 151, it was held that where a surety had taken all reasonable steps to ensure the accused's appearance the recognizance ought not to be forfeited.

The Bail Act 1976 provides that a surety may notify a constable *in writing* that the accused is unlikely to surrender to custody and for that reason he/she wishes to be relieved of his/her obligations as surety. This written notification provides a constable with the power to arrest the accused without warrant (s. 7(3)).

2.3.7.5 Security

A person granted bail may be required to give security for his/her surrender to custody (Bail Act 1976, s. 3(5)). The security can be money or some other valuable item which will be liable to forfeiture in the event of non-attendance in answer to bail.

A security may be required as a condition of bail but only if it is considered necessary to prevent the person absconding.

A third party may make an asset available to an accused to enable him/her to provide it as security for his/her release on bail (*R (On the Application of Stevens)* v *Truro Magistrates' Court* [2001] EWHC Admin 558).

2.3.7.6 Acknowledging Bail

OFFENCE: **Acknowledging Bail in the Name of Another—***Forgery Act 1861, s. 34*
- Triable on indictment • Seven years' imprisonment

The Forgery Act 1861, s. 34 states:

> Whosoever, without lawful authority or excuse (the proof whereof shall lie on the party accused), shall in the name of any other person acknowledge any recognizance or bail, . . . or judgment or any deed or other instrument, before any court, judge, or other person lawfully authorised in that behalf, shall be guilty of felony . . .

KEYNOTE

This offence occurs where a person impersonates another person for the purpose of acting as a surety.

Provided the bail or recognizance is valid, this offence would appear to apply equally to bail granted by a court or the police.

2.3.8 Detention of Juveniles After Charge

The Children (Secure Accommodation) Regulations 1991 (SI 1991/1505 as amended by SI 2012/3134) provide that a child who is detained by the police under s. 38(6) of the Police and Criminal Evidence Act 1984, and who is aged 12 or over but under the age of 17, must be moved to local authority accommodation unless this is impracticable or there is no secure accommodation available and local authority accommodation would be inadequate to protect the child or public from serious harm. Where no secure accommodation is available and the serious harm criterion is met, the child can be kept in police detention. In *R (On the Application of BG)* v *West Midlands Constabulary* [2014] EWHC 4374 (Admin) it was held that the police were fulfilling their responsibilities by investigating whether secure local authority accommodation was available even where there was no such accommodation available.

Where the detained child is aged 10 or 11, the police must move the child to local authority accommodation unless this is impracticable, e.g. in extreme weather conditions. The type of accommodation in which the local authority proposes to place the youth is not a factor which the custody officer may take into account in considering whether the transfer is acceptable.

The obligation to transfer a child to local authority accommodation applies equally to a child charged during the daytime as it does to a child to be held overnight, subject to a requirement to bring the child before a court in accordance with s. 46 of the 1984 Act.

KEYNOTE

A police officer may arrest a juvenile without warrant if the juvenile has been remanded by a court to local authority accommodation and conditions were imposed, and the officer has reasonable grounds for suspecting that the juvenile has broken any of these conditions (Legal Aid, Sentencing and Punishment of Offenders Act 2012, s. 97(1)). Where a juvenile is arrested under this power he/she must be brought before a magistrate within 24 hours.

2.3.9   Live Link Bail

The use of a live link at preliminary hearings where the accused is at police station is provided by the Crime and Disorder Act 1998. Section 57C of the Act states:

(1)   This section applies in relation to a preliminary hearing in a magistrates' court.
(2)   Where subsection (3) or (4) applies to the accused, the court may give a live link direction in relation to his attendance at the preliminary hearing.
(3)   This subsection applies to the accused if—
    (a) he is in police detention at a police station in connection with the offence; and
    (b) it appears to the court that he is likely to remain at that station in police detention until the beginning of the preliminary hearing.
(4)   This subsection applies to the accused if he is at a police station in answer to live link bail in connection with the offence.
(5)   A live link direction under this section is a direction requiring the accused to attend the preliminary hearing through a live link from the police station.
(6)   But a direction given in relation to an accused to whom subsection (3) applies has no effect if he does not remain in police detention at the police station until the beginning of the preliminary hearing.
(6A) A live link direction under this section may not be given unless the court is satisfied that it is not contrary to the interests of justice to give the direction.

KEYNOTE

A magistrates' court may rescind a live link direction under this section at any time during a hearing to which it relates (s. 57C(8)).

Where a live link direction is given to an accused who is answering to live link bail he/she is to be treated as having surrendered to the custody of the court (as from the time when the direction is given) (s. 57C(10)).

The accused is to be treated as present in court when he/she attends via a live link and he/she must be able to see and hear, and to be seen and heard by, the court during the hearing (s. 57A(2)).

In this section, 'live link bail' means bail granted under part 4 of the Police and Criminal Evidence Act 1984 subject to the duty mentioned in s. 47(3)(b) of that Act (s. 57C(11)).

A person who fails to answer to live link bail or leaves the police station at any time before the beginning of proceedings in relation to a live link direction may be arrested (see s. 46A of the Police and Criminal Evidence Act 1984 at para. 2.3.10).

2.3.9.1 Searches of Persons Answering to Live Link Bail

The Police and Criminal Evidence Act 1984, s. 54B states:

(1) A constable may search at any time—
  (a) any person who is at a police station to answer to live link bail; and
  (b) any article in the possession of such a person.
(2) If the constable reasonably believes a thing in the possession of the person ought to be seized on any of the grounds mentioned in subsection (3), the constable may seize and retain it or cause it to be seized and retained.
(3) The grounds are that the thing—
  (a) may jeopardise the maintenance of order in the police station;
  (b) may put the safety of any person in the police station at risk; or
  (c) may be evidence of, or in relation to, an offence.
(4) The constable may record or cause to be recorded all or any of the things seized and retained pursuant to subsection (2).
(5) An intimate search may not be carried out under this section.
(6) The constable carrying out a search under subsection (1) must be of the same sex as the person being searched.

KEYNOTE

A constable may retain a thing seized under s. 54B in order to establish its lawful owner where there are reasonable grounds for believing that it has been obtained in consequence of the commission of an offence (s. 54C(2)).

If a thing seized under s. 54B may be evidence of, or in relation to, an offence, a constable may retain it for use as evidence at a trial for an offence, or for forensic examination or for investigation in connection with an offence (s. 54C(3)).

Nothing may be retained for either of the purposes mentioned in subs. (3) if a photograph or copy would be sufficient for that purpose (s. 54C(4)).

Designated detention officers, as well as constables, can use the powers in ss. 54B and 54C to search and seize. Where a detention officer exercises the power to seize things found pursuant to a search the officer must deliver the things seized to a constable as soon as practicable and in any case before the person from whom it was seized leaves the police station (Police Reform Act 2002, sch. 4, part 3, para. 27A).

Section 46A(1ZB) (see para. 2.3.10) provides a constable with a power of arrest for defendants who attend the police station to answer live link bail but refuse to be searched under s. 54B.

2.3.10 Power of Arrest for Failure to Answer to Police Bail

The Police and Criminal Evidence Act 1984, s. 46A states:

(1) A constable may arrest without a warrant any person who, having been released on bail under this Part of this Act subject to a duty to attend at a police station, fails to attend at that police station at the time appointed for him to do so.
(1ZA) The reference in subsection (1) to a person who fails to attend at a police station at the time appointed for him to do so includes a reference to a person who—
  (a) attends at a police station to answer to bail granted subject to the duty mentioned in section 47(3)(b), but (b) leaves the police station at any time before the beginning of

proceedings in relation to a live link direction under section 57C of the Crime and Disorder Act 1998 in relation to him.

(1ZB) The reference in subsection (1) to a person who fails to attend at a police station at the time appointed for the person to do so includes a reference to a person who—

(a) attends at a police station to answer to bail granted subject to the duty mentioned in section 47(3)(b), but

(b) refuses to be searched under section 54B.

(1A) A person who has been released on bail under section 37, 37C(2)(b) or 37CA(2)(b) above may be arrested without warrant by a constable if the constable has reasonable grounds for suspecting that the person has broken any of the conditions of bail.

(2) A person who is arrested under this section shall be taken to the police station appointed as the place at which he is to surrender to custody as soon as practicable after the arrest.

(3) For the purposes of—

(a) section 30 above (subject to the obligation in subsection (2) above), and

(b) section 31 above,

an arrest under this section shall be treated as an arrest for an offence.

KEYNOTE

Breach of conditions of bail is not a Bail Act offence, nor is it a contempt of court unless there is some additional feature (*R* v *Ashley* [2003] EWCA Crim 2571).

The offence for which a person is arrested under subs. (1) is the offence for which he/she was granted bail (s. 34(7)).

Section 46A(1) provides a power of arrest only where a person *fails to attend at that police station at the time appointed.* This should be contrasted with s. 46A(1A) where a person released on bail under s. 37 (release on bail without charge), s. 37C(2)(b) (breach of bail following release under s. 37(7)(a)) or s. 37CA(2)(b) (breach of bail following release under s. 37(7)(b)), may be arrested if there are *reasonable grounds for suspecting that the person has broken any of the conditions of bail.*

2.3.11 Liability to Arrest for Absconding or Breaking Bail Conditions

The Bail Act 1976, s. 7 states:

(1) If a person who has been released on bail in criminal proceedings and is under a duty to surrender into the custody of a court fails to surrender to custody at the time appointed for him to do so the court may issue a warrant for his arrest.

(1A) Subsection (1B) applies if—

(a) a person has been released on bail in connection with extradition proceedings;

(b) the person is under a duty to surrender into the custody of a constable; and

(c) the person fails to surrender to custody at the time appointed for him to do so.

(1B) A magistrates' court may issue a warrant for the person's arrest.

(2) If a person who has been released on bail in criminal proceedings absents himself from the court at any time after he has surrendered into the custody of the court and before the court is ready to begin or to resume the hearing of the proceedings, the court may issue a warrant for his arrest but no warrant shall be issued under this subsection where that person is absent in accordance with leave given to him by or on behalf of the court.

(3) A person who has been released on bail in criminal proceedings and is under a duty to surrender into the custody of a court may be arrested without warrant by a constable—

(a) if the constable has reasonable grounds for believing that person is not likely to surrender to custody;

(b) if the constable has reasonable grounds for believing that that person is likely to break any of the conditions of his bail or has reasonable grounds for suspecting that that person has broken any of those conditions; or

(c) in a case where that person was released on bail with one or more surety or sureties, if a surety notifies a constable in writing that that person is unlikely to surrender to custody and that for that reason the surety wishes to be relieved of his obligations as a surety.

Where a person is arrested under s. 7 he/she shall be brought before a magistrate as soon as practicable and in any event within 24 hours (s. 7(4)(a)). However, in the case of a person charged with murder, or with murder and one or more other offences, he/she must be brought before a judge of the Crown Court (s. 7(8)).

This section requires that a detainee not merely be brought to the court precincts or cells but actually be dealt with by a justice within 24 hours of being arrested (*R (On the Application of Culley)* v *Dorchester Crown Court* [2007] EWHC 109 (Admin)).

In *R* v *Evans* [2011] EWCA Crim 2842, the Court of Appeal stated:

> The general practice of accepting surrender by way of entry into the dock accords not only with common experience and general practice but also with principle . . . Crown Court surrender may also be accomplished by the commencement of any hearing before the judge where the defendant is formally identified and whether he enters the dock or not.

The word 'court' includes a judge of the court or a justice of the peace. Also a bail notice stating a particular time of attendance is a notice that may happen at any time from 9.30 am onwards. Mere arrival at the Crown Court building does not constitute surrender, neither does reporting to an advocate. Surrender has to be accomplished personally by the defendant.

Section 7 does not create an offence, it merely confers a power of arrest (*R* v *Gangar* [2008] EWCA Crim 2987).

2.3.12 Offence of Absconding by Person Released on Bail

The Bail Act 1976 s. 6 creates two offences in relation to absconding and states:

(1) If a person who has been released on bail in criminal proceedings fails without reasonable cause to surrender to custody he shall be guilty of an offence.
(2) If a person who—
  (a) has been released on bail in criminal proceedings, and
  (b) having reasonable cause therefor, has failed to surrender to custody, fails to surrender to custody at the appointed place as soon after the appointed time as is reasonably practicable he shall be guilty of an offence.

Section 6 applies where:

- the police grant bail to a suspect to appear at the police station;
- the police grant bail to a defendant to appear at court on the first appearance;
- the court grants bail to the defendant to return to court at a later date.

The burden of proof in relation to showing 'reasonable cause' (s. 6(1)) is a matter for the accused (s. 6(3)).

A person who has 'reasonable cause' still commits the offence if he/she fails to surrender 'as soon after the appointed time as is reasonably practicable'. Where an accused was half an hour late in appearing at court it was held that he/she had absconded (*R* v *Scott* [2007] EWCA Crim 2757). In *Laidlaw* v *Atkinson* (1986) The *Times*, 2 August, it was held that being mistaken about the day on which one should have appeared was not a reasonable excuse. Also, there is no requirement on the court to inquire as to whether a person arrested for failing to comply with bail conditions had any reasonable excuse for breaching bail (*R (On the Application of Vickers)* v *West London Magistrates' Court* (2003) EWHC 1809 (Admin)).

Failure to give to a person granted bail in criminal proceedings a copy of the record of the decision does not constitute reasonable cause for that person's failure to surrender to custody (s. 6(4)).

Failing to answer bail granted by a police officer is a summary offence and the decision to initiate proceedings is for the police/prosecutor using the written charge and requisition procedure. Such an offence may not be tried unless proceedings are commenced either within six months of the commission of the offence, or within three months: (a) after the person surrenders to custody at the appointed place; (b) is arrested, or attends at a police station, in connection with the bail offence or the offence for which he/she was granted bail; or (c) the person appears or is brought before a court in connection with the bail offence or the offence for which he/she was granted bail (s. 6(12)–(14)).

2.3.13 Remands in Police Custody

Where a person is remanded in custody it normally means detention in prison. However, s. 128 of the Magistrates' Courts Act 1980 provides that a magistrates' court may remand a person to police custody:

- for a period not exceeding three clear days (24 hours for persons under 18 (s. 91(5) of the Legal Aid, Sentencing and Punishment of Offenders Act 2012) (s. 128(7));
- for the purpose of inquiries into offences (other than the offence for which he/she appears before the court) (s. 128(8)(a));
- as soon as the need ceases he/she must be brought back before the magistrates (s. 128(8)(b));
- the conditions of detention and periodic review apply as if the person was arrested without warrant on suspicion of having committed an offence (s. 128(8)(c) and (d)).

2.3.14 Release of Short-term Prisoners on Licence and Subject to Home Curfew

The following paragraphs examine the law, practice and police powers in relation to the release of short-term prisoners who are on licence and subject to home curfew.

2.3.14.1 Release of Short-term Prisoners on Licence

Section 246 of the Criminal Justice Act 2003 provides the Secretary of State with the power to release a prisoner on licence where the prisoner has served the 'requisite period' for the term of his/her sentence. Eligible prisoners can choose to take their period of home detention curfew any time after a defined period of imprisonment.

Release may be subject to conditions that may include conditions for either securing the electronic monitoring of his/her compliance with any other conditions of his/her release (s. 62(1) and (2) of the Criminal Justice and Court Services Act 2000). Electronic monitoring does not include monitoring a curfew condition imposed under s. 253 of the Criminal Justice Act 2003 (s. 62(3) of the 2000 Act).

2.3.14.2 Release of Short-term Prisoners Subject to Home Curfew

The release of short-term prisoners subject to home curfews is provided by s. 253 of the Criminal Justice Act 2003.

The Home Detention Curfew scheme allows prisoners aged 18 years and over, serving sentences of three months or more but less than four years, to spend up to the last 60 days of their custodial sentence on a home curfew, enforced by electronic monitoring.

The prisoner is required to agree to the curfew conditions. The governor at the relevant prison determines the details of the curfew. This will normally be from 7 pm to 7 am and may be varied. The minimum period of curfew is nine hours, but there is no maximum. HM Prison Service Parole Unit is responsible for the management and monitoring of home detention curfews. The curfew equipment is operated and monitored by an approved private contractor. The contractor installs a home monitoring unit at the approved address and fits the prisoner with the personal identification device at this address on the day of release.

Although there is no involvement in the release process, the police are notified of all prisoners subject to home detention curfew 14 days prior to release. The police may request information from the monitoring contractor as to the offender's compliance, or otherwise, with the curfew, including any short-term 'unexplained' absences. Such requests for information are authorised by an officer of the rank of superintendent or above. Electronic monitoring contractors are obliged to provide such information within 24 hours of the request being made.

2.3.14.3 Recall of Prisoners Released Early

Where a person released on licence under s. 246 fails to comply with the curfew condition included in the licence, or his/her whereabouts can no longer be electronically monitored at the place specified in the curfew condition, the Secretary of State may revoke the licence and recall the person to prison (s. 255(1)). On the revocation of a person's licence that person is liable to be detained in pursuance of his sentence and, if at large, is to be treated as being unlawfully at large, and is liable for immediate return to custody by the police (s. 255(5)).

2.3.14.4 Police Arrests

The guidance provided to police forces in relation to persons who are the subject of a home detention curfew is as follows:
  Where arrested:

- custody officer to notify the monitoring contractor immediately of:
  - details of the prisoner;
  - details of the offence;
  - whether the prisoner is to be bailed or retained in custody;
  - whether the prisoner continues to wear the electronic tag;
- custody officer to notify the monitoring contractor when the prisoner is released.

Where charged:

- custody officer to immediately inform HM Prison Service Parole Unit;
- custody officer to inform contractor *if* the prisoner is to be returned to prison to remove and collect the monitoring unit.

Where a person is charged with an offence while subject to a home detention curfew, the PACE Code C in relation to detention following charge continues to apply.

Where a prisoner has been charged with an offence, the decision to revoke the prisoner's licence is a matter for HM Prison Service Parole Unit and not the police.

2.3.14.5 Police Requests for Revocation

Where the police consider that a prisoner subject to a home detention curfew represents a serious risk to the public, they may make a request for it to be revoked. Any such request should be authorised by an officer of the rank of superintendent or above and made to HM Prison Service Parole Unit at the Home Office.
  'Serious risk' means:

- offenders convicted of a sexual or violent offence: death or serious injury (physical or psychological) occasioned by further offences committed by the offender. Sexual and violent offences are considered the same in that a prisoner convicted of an offence of violence may be recalled following concerns about offences of a sexual nature.

- offenders convicted of a non-sexual or violent offence: death or serious injury, etc. The offence which may cause that risk need not be the same as the original offence.

It is only necessary to demonstrate that the prisoner has acted in such a way as to give *reasonable cause for belief* that recall is necessary to protect the public.

The chief of police and local parole board for an area also have a statutory duty to make suitable arrangements for managing dangerous offenders.

2.4 | Court Procedure and Witnesses

2.4.1 Introduction

This chapter deals with the conditions where an accused can plead guilty by post for certain summary offences, the procedure in dealing with offenders for summary either way and indictable offences, and the law in relation to witnesses.

2.4.2 Plea of Guilty by Post

The procedure for a defendant to plead guilty by post is provided by the Magistrates' Courts Act 1980 and applies to proceedings for summary offences started by way of summons (or requisition) in the magistrates' court (s. 12(1)), or in the youth court for persons aged 16 or 17 (s. 12(2)). The summons (or requisition) is served on the defendant together with a 'statement of facts' and a prescribed form of explanation. This allows the defendant an opportunity to plead guilty and put forward any mitigation in his/her absence. The magistrates' designated officer informs the prosecution of any written guilty plea.

Where a guilty plea has been received from the defendant, the 'statement of facts' and any mitigation are read out by the magistrates' clerk in open court. Failure to read out any mitigation submitted by the defendant will nullify the proceedings (*R v Epping and Ongar Justices, ex parte Breach* [1987] RTR 233). No further facts or evidence can be given by the prosecution. In fact neither the prosecution nor the defendant need attend when the court deals with the case, but if the defendant is present they must be given an opportunity of giving any mitigation in person (s. 12A).

The magistrates have the discretion to decide that a case is not appropriate to be dealt with under the 'statement of facts' procedure and may adjourn the case for the defendant to appear in court. In these circumstances the guilty plea entered by the defendant is disregarded (s. 12(9)).

At any time before the hearing, a defendant may withdraw his/her guilty plea by notifying the magistrates' clerk in writing. Also the court may allow a defendant to change his/her plea at the hearing and contest the case (*R v Bristol Justices, ex parte Sawyers* [1988] Crim LR 754). In *Rymer v DPP* [2010] EWHC 1848 (Admin) there was a postal plea of guilty and after conviction the hearing was adjourned to consider disqualifying the defendant from driving. At the adjourned hearing the defendant appeared and wished to change his plea to not guilty. It was held that there was no automatic right allowing the defendant to change his plea and that he would need to show good reason why this should be allowed.

KEYNOTE

This section is most commonly used for driving offences, and provision is made for a printout from the DVLA to be admissible as evidence of previous convictions for traffic offences without the need to give an accused notice of intention to refer to these previous convictions (Road Traffic Offenders Act 1988, s. 13).

2.4.3 Mode of Trial

Trials on indictment take place in the Crown Court; summary trials take place in the magistrates' court. The classification of the offence determines in which court the trial takes place; generally, summary offences in the magistrates' court and indictable offences in the Crown Court.

In the case of an either-way offence the magistrates must determine whether a person who has attained the age of 18 should be tried summarily in the magistrates' court or be sent to the Crown Court to be tried (ss. 17A to 21 of the Magistrates' Courts Act 1980). (Mode of trial is dealt with in more detail in **para. 2.1.6.4** (Determining Mode of Trial (Adults)) and **para. 2.1.6.5** (Determining Mode of Trial (Juveniles)).

2.4.3.1 Pre-trial Hearings

In the magistrates' court there is a system of pre-trial hearings. These are known as an 'Early First Hearing' where a guilty plea is anticipated or an 'Early Administrative Hearing' where a not guilty plea is expected. Section 8A of the Magistrates' Courts Act 1980 provides that at a pre-trial hearing, once a not guilty plea has been entered, the court may make rulings on any question as to the admissibility of evidence and any other question of law relating to criminal cases to be tried in the magistrates' court. However, such rulings can only be made if the accused is legally represented or he/she has been offered and granted or otherwise the right to representation by the Legal Services Commission as part of the Criminal Defence Service.

These rulings are binding and will continue to be so until the case is disposed of by the accused being acquitted, the prosecutor deciding not to proceed with the case, or the information is dismissed (s. 8B).

2.4.4 Summary Trial

Summary trials take place in the magistrates' court before at least two lay justices or a single District or Deputy District Judge (Magistrates' Courts).

The prosecution and defence may conduct their own case in person or be represented by counsel or solicitor (s. 122(1) of the Magistrates' Courts Act 1980). In the Crown Court the prosecution must appear by legal representative, but the accused may still conduct his/her own case. An accused conducting his/her own case may be allowed a friend to accompany him/her as an adviser, though such an adviser may not question witnesses or address the court (*McKenzie* v *McKenzie* [1971] P 33).

Where there is a 'guilty' plea in the magistrates' court, the hearing starts with the prosecution stating the facts of the case and introducing the offender's previous convictions, if there are any that are relevant. The defence then put any mitigation to the court before sentence is passed.

A 'not guilty' plea in the magistrates' court allows the prosecution to call their evidence. The prosecution will begin proceedings by addressing the court in an opening speech. If the prosecution have established that there is a case to answer, the defendant can then call evidence. Very occasionally this may be followed by rebuttal evidence being called by the prosecution which is confined to unexpected matters raised by the defence. At the end of the evidence for the defence (and the rebuttal evidence, if any), the defence will usually address the court, if they have not already done so, in a closing speech. If the defence consider that the prosecution have not established a case to answer, they may make a submission of 'no case to answer'. There is no clear direction as to what would constitute 'no case to answer' in the magistrates' court, and if the prosecution have provided the necessary minimum amount of evidence on which a reasonable court could convict, the trial should continue.

In *Moran v DPP* (2002) EWHC 89 (Admin) it was held that the justices are not required to give reasons in rejecting a submission of 'no case to answer'.

2.4.5 Trial on Indictment

Trials on indictment take place in the Crown Court before a judge of the High Court, circuit judge, a recorder, a qualifying judge advocate, or a District Judge (magistrates' courts).

Where there is a 'guilty plea', which must be entered personally by the accused (*R v Ellis* (1973) 57 Cr App R 571), the only evidence which the prosecution need to call is details of the accused's antecedents and criminal record. Occasionally, where there is disagreement about the precise facts of the offence, the prosecution may be required to call evidence to support their version of the facts; known as *Newton* hearings (*R v Newton* (1983) 77 Cr App R 13).

Where there is a 'not guilty' plea, the prosecution are required to satisfy the jury beyond reasonable doubt that the accused committed the offence. Where the prosecution fail to provide sufficient evidence as to *any* element of the offence, the accused is entitled to be acquitted. This acquittal would take place on the direction of the judge, at the end of the prosecution case, following a defence submission of 'no case to answer'.

There are occasions where an accused may plead not guilty to the offence charged but guilty to a lesser offence (s. 6(1)(b) of the Criminal Law Act 1967). If the prosecution accept the plea of guilty to the lesser offence, the court proceeds to sentence the accused for that lesser offence and treats him/her as being acquitted of the original offence charged (s. 6(5) of the 1967 Act). However, if the prosecution refuse to accept the plea of guilty to the lesser offence, the case proceeds as if the accused had pleaded not guilty (*R v Hazeltine* [1967] 2 QB 857).

An accused may be allowed to change his/her plea from not guilty to guilty as long as this occurs before the jury returns its verdict. The judge then directs the jury to return a formal verdict of guilty (*R v Heyes* [1951] 1 KB 29). Similarly, an accused may be allowed to change his/her plea from guilty to not guilty and the judge has the discretion to allow this at any stage before sentence is passed (*R v Plummer* [1902] 2 KB 339).

The Criminal Justice Act 2003, s. 44 provides that a trial on indictment in the Crown Court may be conducted without a jury where there is a danger of jury tampering, or continued without a jury where the jury has been discharged because of jury tampering (*R v Twomey* [2009] EWCA Crim 1035).

2.4.6 Defendant's Non-appearance

Where an accused fails to appear in the magistrates' court in answer to bail the court may:

- issue a warrant for the accused's arrest under s. 7 of the Bail Act 1976 (**see para. 2.3.11**);
- appoint a later time when the accused has to appear in accordance with s. 129(3) of the Magistrates' Courts Act 1980;
- proceed in the accused's absence under s. 11(1) of the Magistrates' Courts Act 1980.

Where the accused's appearance was by way of summons, the court must be satisfied that the summons was served in the prescribed manner before commencing in the accused's absence (s. 11(2)).

Where an accused is under 18 years of age the court *may* proceed in his/her absence (s. 11(1)(a)), and if the accused has attained the age of 18 the court *must* proceed in his/her absence unless it appears to the court to be contrary to the interests of justice do so (s. 11(1)(b)). The court is not required to inquire into the reasons for the accused's failure to appear (s. 11(6)).

In *James* v *Tower Bridge Magistrates' Court* [2009] EWHC 1500 (Admin), where the accused was two hours late for trial, the decision to proceed in the absence of the accused was held to be unlawful as the court failed to inquire as to why the accused was late or consider an adjournment. On occasions where a person is deliberately absent, and indifferent to the consequences of their absence, the court may proceed without the accused being present (*R* v *Umerji* [2014] EWCA Crim 421).

If the court imposes a custodial sentence the accused must be brought before the court before commencing the custodial sentence (s. 11(3A)).

Where the court proceeds in the defendant's absence, a not guilty plea is entered and the prosecution are required to prove the case to the normal criminal standard. If the prosecution evidence is insufficient to reach the standard, the defendant should be acquitted. Where the case is proved, the court may pass sentence or adjourn for the defendant to be present, either giving the defendant notice that he/she should attend or issuing a warrant for his/her arrest (ss. 10(3) and (4), and 11(3) and (4)).

The Crown Court does have the discretion to conduct a trial in the absence of the defendant and the seriousness of the offence is not a matter which is relevant to the exercise of this discretion. It is generally desirable that the defendant is represented by counsel during the trial, even where he/she had voluntarily absconded (*R* v *Jones* [2002] UKHL 5). Where the accused is absent involuntarily, for example through illness, the court may adjourn the trial, but it is in the public interest not to allow the trial to be put off for an indefinite period (*R* v *Taylor* [2008] EWCA Crim 680). In *R (On the Application of Davies)* v *Solihull Justices* [2008] EWHC 1157 (Admin) it was held that even where the accused had been excluded from the court premises due to his disorderly behaviour, this misbehaviour did not justify excluding him from his own trial. The European Court of Human Rights has held that it is for the authorities to satisfy the court that the accused was aware of the proceedings and adequate steps had been taken to trace the accused (*Colozza* v *Italy* (1985) 7 EHRR 516). In *Re X* [2001] Dalloz Jur 1899, the European Court held that where a judgment was made in the absence of the accused the court must hear the defence counsel and any written plea from the accused.

2.4.7 Adjournments and Remands

A magistrates' court may need to adjourn proceedings for a variety of reasons: where an accused wishes to obtain legal advice; the preparation of advance information for the defence; where an accused pleads not guilty and more time is required for the hearing; for reports, etc. In *R (On the Application of DPP)* v *North and East Hertfordshire Justices* [2008] EWHC 103 (Admin) it was held that an adjournment should not be refused to punish the inefficiency of the CPS or the failure of a witness to attend court. Where an adjournment is necessary, the court may have the power to remand an accused in custody.

2.4.7.1 Adjournments

Section 10 of the Magistrates' Courts Act 1980 provides that a magistrates' court may adjourn a summary trial at any time before or after beginning to try an information or 'written charge'. It need not remand the defendant unless one of the following conditions apply:

- the defendant has attained the age of 18 years; and
- the offence is triable 'either way'; and
- the accused has been in custody when first appearing or having been released on bail was surrendering to the custody of the court; or
- the accused has been remanded at any time during the proceedings.

Where a person aged 18 years or over is charged with an offence which may only be tried on indictment, the magistrates' court may adjourn the proceedings but must remand the defendant (s. 52(5) of the Crime and Disorder Act 1998).

'Remands' can be either by committing the defendant to custody or to remand on bail in accordance with the provisions of the Bail Act 1976.

2.4.7.2 Remands

Section 128(6) of the Magistrates' Courts Act 1980 provides that a magistrates' court shall not remand a person for a period exceeding eight clear days except where the person is:

- remanded on bail and the prosecution and defendant consent;
- remanded for inquiries to be made or of determining the most suitable method of dealing with the case; but, if the person is remanded, the remand can be no longer than four weeks on bail or three weeks in custody (s. 10(3) of the 1980 Act);
- remanded for a medical report (s. 11 of the Powers of Criminal Courts (Sentencing) Act 2000); or
- remanded where the court is to try an either way offence summarily and needs to be constituted for that purpose even where the remand is for a period exceeding eight clear days.

KEYNOTE

A magistrates' court may also remand an adult defendant in custody by committing him/her to detention at a police station for a period not exceeding three clear days (s. 128(7) of the Magistrates' Courts Act 1980), or 24 hours for persons under 18 (Legal Aid, Sentencing and Punishment of Offenders Act 2012, s. 91(5)).

'Eight clear days' in s. 128(6) means, for example, from Monday (when the court remanded a person) to Wednesday of the following week.

2.4.7.3 Custody Time Limits

Under regs 4 and 5 of the Prosecution of Offences (Custody Time Limits) Regulations 1987 (SI 1987/299), unless the court extends the time limit, the maximum period during which the defendant may be in pre-trial custody is:

(a) in a case which can be tried only in a magistrates' court, 56 days pending the beginning of the trial;

(b) in a magistrates' court, in a case which can be tried either in that court or in the Crown Court:
  (i) 70 days, pending committal for trial proceedings or the beginning of a trial in the magistrates' court, or
  (ii) 56 days, pending the beginning of a trial in the magistrates' court, if the court decides on such a trial during that period;

(c) in the Crown Court, pending the beginning of the trial:
  (i) 112 days from the defendant's committal for trial, or
  (ii) 182 days from the sending of the defendant for trial, less any period or periods during which the defendant was in custody in the magistrates' court.

KEYNOTE

Under s. 22(3)(a) of the Prosecution of Offences Act 1985, the court cannot extend a custody time limit that has expired, and must not extend such a time limit unless satisfied:

2.4.8   Witnesses

A witness is a person called by a party in court proceedings with a view to proving a particular matter material to the case. This section examines the key issues in relation to witnesses.

2.4.8.1   Attendance of Witnesses at Court

The prosecution or defence can apply for a summons, warrant or order requiring a witness to attend a magistrates' court (s. 97 or 97A of the Magistrates' Courts Act 1980, or para. 4 of sch. 3 to the Crime and Disorder Act 1998) or the Crown Court (s. 2 of the Criminal Procedure (Attendance of Witnesses) Act 1965). Where appropriate, such an application can be used as a pre-emptive measure to secure the attendance of witnesses.

The conditions that must be satisfied before a court issues a summons, warrant or order are:

- what evidence the proposed witness can give or produce;
- why it is likely to be material evidence;
- why it would be in the interests of justice to issue a summons.

There are two conditions that must be satisfied before a court issues a summons:

- that the person is likely to be able to give evidence which is likely to be material evidence, or produce any document or thing likely to be material evidence for the purpose of any criminal proceedings; and
- that it is in the interests of justice.

The Criminal Procedure Rules 2014, r. 4.7(1) provides that a witness summons may be served:

(a) on an individual, only under rule 4.3(1)(a) (handing over) or rule 4.4(1) and (2)(a) (leaving or posting), and

(b) on a corporation, only under rule 4.3(1)(b) (handing over) or rule 4.4(1) and (2)(b) (leaving or posting).

In *R* v *Popat* [2008] EWCA Crim 1921 it was held that a witness summons did not have to be served in accordance with the Criminal Procedure Rules if the date of the court hearing was actually brought to the attention of the witness.

Where witnesses are summoned but refuse to give evidence or to answer questions asked of them, they may be in contempt of court. The court has a range of powers to deal with contempt and these include imprisonment (*R* v *Haselden* [2000] All ER (D) 56).

The European Court has taken the view that where repeated and unsuccessful attempts have been made to bring a witness before the court—and in this case where he was forcibly brought before the court but absconded before giving evidence—it is open to domestic courts to have regard to any statement the witness made to the police, particularly where it is corroborated by other evidence (*Doorson v Netherlands* (1996) 22 EHRR 330).

2.4.8.2 Competence and Compellability

In looking at witnesses, it is crucial to consider two related questions:

- whether there are any restrictions to a witness being called to provide testimony. This question is frequently one of whether a witness is *competent;*
- whether a witness may be compelled or made to provide testimony. This is a question of whether a witness is *compellable.*

Competence in its simplest interpretation is whether in law a witness is allowed to be a witness. For a witness to be compellable two aspects must be considered:

- the witness must be competent; *and*
- the law requires the witness to give evidence even if the witness would rather not do so.

2.4.8.3 General Rule of Competence and Compellability

There is a general rule in English law that 'All people are competent and all competent witnesses are compellable'. The rule was sanctioned by the provisions of s. 53 of the Youth Justice and Criminal Evidence Act 1999. Section 53 states:

> (1) At every stage in criminal proceedings all persons are (whatever their age) competent to give evidence.

2.4.8.4 Exceptions to the Rule of Competence and Compellability

The exceptions to the general rule of competence and compellability are set out in various statutes.

The European Court of Human Rights has accepted that some categories of witness may not be compellable under a country's domestic law to give evidence, for example, spouses, cohabitees and family members. In *Unterpertinger v Austria* (1991) 13 EHRR 1, the Court held that the Convention:

> ...makes allowance for the special problems that may be entailed in a confrontation between someone 'charged with a criminal offence' and a witness from his own family and is calculated to protect such a witness by avoiding his being put in a moral dilemma . . .

2.4.8.5 The Accused

Evidence on Behalf of the Prosecution

The competence of the accused to give evidence on behalf of the prosecution is dealt with under s. 53 of the Youth Justice and Criminal Evidence Act 1999, which states:

> (4) A person charged in criminal proceedings is not competent to give evidence in the proceedings for the prosecution (whether he is the only person, or is one of two or more persons, charged in the proceedings).

However, a person charged in criminal proceedings will be competent to give evidence for the prosecution at such time as:

- he/she pleads guilty;
- he/she is convicted;
- the charges against him/her are dropped (referred to as entering a *nolle prosequi*—a promise not to prosecute) (s. 53(5)).

It follows from the application of s. 53(4) and (5) of the 1999 Act that should the prosecution wish to use the testimony of an accused against a co-accused, they must first make that person competent to be able to give that evidence. The person can only give evidence if that person pleads guilty, or he/she is convicted of the offence or the charges are dropped against him/her. In *R* v *McEwan* [2011] EWCA Crim 1026 it was held that where the accused pleads guilty, they are competent for the prosecution even if they suggest in their evidence that they were not a participant in the offence, unless the plea is set aside.

However, the Commission has directed domestic courts to adopt a 'critical approach' in their assessment of 'accomplice' evidence where the accomplice stood to lose the benefit of sentence reductions if he/she retracted previous statements or confessions. In such cases it was considered crucial that the accomplice evidence could be challenged and that such evidence was not the sole basis for a conviction (*Baragiola* v *Switzerland* (1993) 75 DR 76).

Evidence on Behalf of the Defence

The Criminal Evidence Act 1898 sets out the position of whether an accused person is competent and compellable for the defence. Section 1 of the 1898 Act states:

(1) A person charged in criminal proceedings shall not be called as a witness in the proceedings except upon his own application.

...

(4) Every person charged in criminal proceedings who is called as a witness in the proceedings shall, unless otherwise ordered by the court, give his evidence from the witness-box or other place from which the other witnesses give their evidence.

KEYNOTE

When an accused elects to give evidence, s. 72 of the Criminal Justice Act 1982 requires that such evidence be given on oath and that the accused is liable to cross-examination.

In being cross-examined, an accused may also be questioned by the prosecution about a co-accused (*R* v *Paul* [1920] 2 KB 183).

2.4.8.6 Competence and Compellability of Accused's Spouse or Civil Partner

The Police and Criminal Evidence Act 1984, s. 80 states:

(2) In any proceedings the spouse or civil partner of a person charged in the proceedings shall, subject to subsection (4) below, be compellable to give evidence on behalf of that person.

(2A) In any proceedings the spouse or civil partner of a person charged in the proceedings shall, subject to subsection (4) below, be compellable—

    (a) to give evidence on behalf of any other person charged in the proceedings but only in respect of any specified offence with which that other person is charged; or

    (b) to give evidence for the prosecution but only in respect of any specified offence with which any person is charged in the proceedings.

(3) In relation to the spouse or civil partner of a person charged in any proceedings, an offence is a specified offence for the purposes of subsection (2A) above if—

    (a) it involves an assault on, or injury or a threat of injury to, the spouse or civil partner or a person who was at the material time under the age of 16;

    (b) it is a sexual offence alleged to have been committed in respect of a person who was at the material time under that age; or

    (c) it consists of attempting or conspiring to commit, or of aiding, abetting, counselling, procuring or inciting the commission of, an offence falling within paragraph (a) or (b) above.

(4) No person who is charged in any proceedings shall be compellable by virtue of subsection (2) or (2A) above to give evidence in the proceedings.

(4A) References in this section to a person charged in any proceedings do not include a person who is not, or is no longer, liable to be convicted of any offence in the proceedings (whether as a result of pleading guilty or for any other reason).

(5)　In any proceedings a person who has been but is no longer married to the accused shall be compellable to give evidence as if that person and the accused had never been married.

(5A)　In any proceedings a person who has been but is no longer the civil partner of the accused shall be compellable to give evidence as if that person and the accused had never been civil partners.

KEYNOTE

In relation to s. 30(3)(c), 'inciting' is to be construed as 'encouraging or assisting crime' (s. 63 of the Serious Crime Act 2007).

The Marriage (Same Sex Couples) Act 2013 extended marriage to same sex couples, where marriage has the same effect in law in relation to such a couple as it does in relation to an opposite sex couple (s. 11(1)).

Whether an offence is one where a spouse can be compelled to give evidence under s. 80 must be decided by reference to the legal nature of the offence and not the surrounding factual circumstances. In *R* v *BA* [2012] EWCA Crim 1529 a husband was charged with 'threatening to destroy or damage property' belonging to his wife, contrary to s. 2(a) of the Criminal Damage Act 1971. The offence under s. 2(a) is directed at property where it cannot be said to give rise to the real possibility of an assault or injury or threat of injury. The Court of Appeal held that it was not a specified offence for the purposes of s. 80(2A) and (3)(a) and the wife was not a compellable witness.

There is no requirement to tell a wife that she was not a compellable witness against her husband before interviewing her about a crime of which her husband was suspected. A statement obtained from the wife in such circumstances could be admitted in evidence even though the wife refused to give evidence against her husband, provided it did not lead to an injustice (*R* v *L* [2008] EWCA Crim 973). However, the prosecution's hand is likely to be strengthened if it were shown that she was told that there was no obligation for her to make a statement (*R* v *Horsnell* [2012] EWCA Crim 227).

A person who is no longer married or in a civil partnership with the accused is compellable to give evidence as if they had never been married or been in a civil partnership (Police and Criminal Evidence Act 1984, s. 80(5) and (5A)). The person must have been divorced, or where it was a voidable marriage this must have been annulled.

The failure of the wife or husband of the accused to give evidence shall not be made the subject of any comment by the prosecution (s. 80(8)). Also s. 80A provides that where a spouse or civil partner of an accused is not compellable to give evidence, his/her failure to do so shall not be made the subject of any comment by the prosecution.

Cohabitees are not afforded the same concessions as a wife, husband or civil partner in giving evidence against each other (that of being competent but not compellable).

2.4.8.7　Children

The Youth Justice and Criminal Evidence Act 1999 deals with the position of children to act as witnesses in criminal proceedings.

Section 55 of the 1999 Act states:

(1)　Any question whether a witness in criminal proceedings may be sworn for the purpose of giving evidence on oath, whether raised—
　(a)　by a party to the proceedings, or
　(b)　by the court of its own motion, shall be determined by the court in accordance with this section.

(2)　The witness may not be sworn for that purpose unless—
　(a)　he has attained the age of 14, and
　(b)　he has a sufficient appreciation of the solemnity of the occasion and of the particular responsibility to tell the truth which is involved in taking an oath.

(3)　The witness shall, if he is able to give intelligible testimony, be presumed to have sufficient appreciation of those matters if no evidence tending to show the contrary is adduced (by any party).

(4)　If any such evidence is adduced, it is for the party seeking to have the witness sworn to satisfy the court that, on a balance of probabilities, the witness has attained the age of 14 and has a sufficient appreciation of the matters mentioned in subsection (2)(b).

2.4.8.8   Issues of Age

The time at which a person attains a particular age expressed in years shall be the commencement of the relevant anniversary of the date of his/her birth (s. 9(1) of the Family Law Act 1969).

Section 150 of the Magistrates' Courts Act 1980 states:

(4) Where the age of any person at any time is material for the purposes of any provision of this Act regulating the powers of a magistrates' court, his age at the material time shall be deemed to be or to have been that which appears to the court after considering any available evidence to be or to have been his age at that time.

2.4.8.9   People with a Disorder or Disability of the Mind

Under the Youth Justice and Criminal Evidence Act 1999, in determining whether a witness is competent to give evidence, proceedings take place in the absence of any jury (s. 55(5)). Expert evidence can be received as to the witness's competence (s. 55(6)), and the questioning of the witness is conducted by the court in the presence of the prosecution and defence (s. 55(7)).

In considering whether a witness is able to give 'intelligible testimony', s. 55(8) defines this as testimony where the witness is able to:

(a) understand questions put to him as a witness, and
(b) give answers to them which can be understood.

The decision in *R* v *Hayes* [1977] 1 WLR 234 may still apply to a witness's competence, where the courts are likely to take the view that the ability to understand and tell the truth is more important than an understanding of the religious meaning attached to the oath. Where such a person gives evidence, it is for the jury to determine how much weight to attach to the testimony.

Clearly, there is no inherent reason why a person suffering from a disorder or disability of the mind would not make a reliable witness. In *R v Barratt* [1996] Crim LR 495, a witness was suffering from a psychiatric condition and the court considered that her evidence was as reliable as that of any other witness save for certain aspects affected by her condition. The videotaped interview of a witness suffering from Alzheimer's disease was admitted in evidence where she was deemed unfit to attend trial (*R v Ali Sed* [2004] EWCA Crim 1294).

In *R v Watts* [2010] EWCA Crim 1824, where the complainants in a sexual abuse case were all seriously handicapped, the court illustrated a number of ways in which special measures directions (**see para. 2.4.10**), including electronic communication devices and the assistance of intermediaries, can be used to enable seriously handicapped witnesses to give intelligible evidence, although it also illustrated the fact that such evidence may be difficult to present and difficult to assess in terms of both content and credibility.

2.4.8.10   Other Groups

In addition to the main exceptions outlined above, other people and groups may be incompetent or not compellable as witnesses. These situations are likely to be less frequent than the earlier exceptions:

- The Sovereign and Heads of State are competent but not compellable.
- Diplomats and consular officers may have total or partial immunity from being compelled.
- Restrictions also apply in respect of bankers and judges.

2.4.8.11   Hostile Witnesses

A party calling a witness, whether it be the defence or prosecution, would ordinarily do so in the expectation that the witness will be providing testimony that supports a point being advanced by that party. A witness may, however, provide unfavourable testimony to the side calling him/her. In such circumstances, it is said that the witness has failed to come up to proof. In other words, his/her oral testimony has not been consistent with his/her original witness statement, e.g. by not proving the matter intended or by proving the opposite. It is a general rule that a party calling a witness does not impeach the credit of his/her witness by asking leading questions and cross-examining the witness on his/her earlier previous inconsistent statement.

However, should a witness not give his/her evidence fairly and show no regard for the truth as against the party calling him/her, the judge may deem that witness to be a hostile witness. In this instance, the party calling the witness may contradict him/her with other evidence or, with the leave of the judge, prove that on an earlier occasion he/she made a statement inconsistent with the present testimony.

Where such cross-examination occurs as a result of a witness being treated as hostile, the jury should be reminded in clear terms what weight should be attached to it, namely that the previous inconsistent statement is not evidence as such, but simply goes to undermine the credibility of the witness's oral testimony. This is the case even where the 'hostile witness' gives evidence that is consistent with his/her previous statement. The rationale for this is that the witness would not otherwise have given evidence if he/she had not been treated as hostile (*R v Ugorji* (1999) *The Independent*, 5 July).

It is important to distinguish between an unfavourable witness and one who is hostile. Simply because a witness does not provide testimony to prove a matter does not make him/her hostile. A hostile witness deliberately goes beyond this.

EXAMPLE

Consider the situation where the defence call witness A to provide evidence of a particular issue, e.g. that A saw a particular car at a particular place. However, in giving testimony, A, in good faith or as a result of an earlier misunderstanding, believes he was mistaken. In this instance A is an unfavourable witness. If, however, A in fact decides to lie and say that he did not in fact see the car when he really did then A may be deemed by the judge to be a hostile witness.

2.4.8.12 Witness Anonymity

The Coroners and Justice Act 2009, provides for witness anonymity orders and s. 86 of the Act states:

(1) In this Chapter a 'witness anonymity order' is an order made by a court that requires such specified measures to be taken in relation to a witness in criminal proceedings as the court considers appropriate to ensure that the identity of the witness is not disclosed in or in connection with the proceedings.

(2) The kinds of measures that may be required to be taken in relation to a witness include measures for securing one or more of the following—

    (a) that the witness's name and other identifying details may be—

        (i) withheld;

        (ii) removed from materials disclosed to any party to the proceedings;

    (b) that the witness may use a pseudonym;

    (c) that the witness is not asked questions of any specified description that might lead to the identification of the witness;

    (d) that the witness is screened to any specified extent;

    (e) that the witness's voice is subjected to modulation to any specified extent.

KEYNOTE

A 'witness anonymity order' may only be granted on the application of the prosecutor or defendant if the following three conditions, contained in s. 88, are satisfied:

- Condition A: the order is necessary to protect the safety of the witness, or another person, or the prevention of serious damage to property or to prevent real harm to the public interest;
- Condition B: having regard to all the circumstances, the taking of these measures would be consistent with the defendant receiving a fair trial; and
- Condition C: it is in the interests of justice that the witness ought to testify and the witness would not testify without the order being made, and there would be real harm to the public interest if the witness were to testify without the proposed order being made.

In making an order, the court must have regard to any reasonable fear on the part of the witness that he/she or another person would suffer death or injury, or that there would be serious damage to property, if the witness were to be identified (s. 88(6)). In *R* v *Powar* [2009] EWCA Crim 594, it was emphasised that regard must be had to the fear of the witnesses and the circumstances of the case. A different form of necessity, which the court recognised was equally valid, was the protection of witnesses such as undercover officers and agents of the security services.

An analysis of the conditions and court considerations was provided in *R* v *Mayers* [2008] EWCA Crim 2989, and in relation to 'Condition B' in *R* v *Khan* [2010] EWCA Crim 1962. In *R* v *Nazir* [2009] EWCA Crim 213, such orders were considered a 'special measure of last practicable resort'. Where the anonymous evidence is the 'sole and decisive' evidence against the accused, that evidence may still be afforded the protection of anonymity where it is in the interests of justice to do so as the only reasonable means of securing that evidence (*R* v *Horncastle* [2010] EWCA Crim 964; see also *Donovan* v *R* [2012] EWCA Crim 2749). However, the *Director's Guidance on Witness Anonymity* (December 2009, updated 28 February 2013), published by the CPS, suggests that if the evidence provided by a proposed anonymous witness is truly the sole or decisive evidence against an accused, the application for an anonymity order is likely to fail.

2.4.9 Live Links for Witnesses

Witnesses will ordinarily give their evidence from the witness box. However, some witnesses may give their testimony by other means, e.g., through a live television link. The statutory developments in this area are summarised below.

2.4.9.1 Criminal Justice Act 1988

Section 32(1) of the Criminal Justice Act 1988 provides that a witness outside the United Kingdom (other than the accused) may give evidence through a live television link. This provision applies to trials on indictment, proceedings in the youth court, appeals from the youth court and Crown Court, and in extradition proceedings.

Requests for assistance to hear witnesses outside their jurisdiction can be made by judicial authorities and designated prosecuting authorities under s. 7 of the Crime (International Co-operation) Act 2003.

> **KEYNOTE**
>
> There is no presumption in favour of using a television link, under any of the legislative provisions, and its use has to be justified for displacing the general rule that a witness should give evidence in the presence of the defendant (*R (On the Application of DPP)* v *Redbridge Youth Court* [2001] EWHC 209 (Admin)).
>
> A court has no inherent power to permit evidence to be given by telephone, even with the consent of the parties (*R* v *Hampson* [2012] EWCA Crim 1807).

2.4.9.2 Criminal Justice Act 2003

Section 51 of the Criminal Justice Act 2003 provides that witnesses, other than the accused, may give evidence through a 'live link' from another location in the United Kingdom, rather than from just overseas. 'Live link' means a closed circuit television link, but could apply to any technology with the same effect such as video conferencing facilities or the internet (s. 56(2)).

A court may only authorise the use of a live link if it is satisfied that it is in the interests of the efficient or effective administration of justice for the person to give his/her evidence in this manner (s. 51(4)).

> **KEYNOTE**
>
> This section requires the court, before authorising the use of a live link, to consider several factors in relation to the witness, including his/her availability, the importance of the evidence, and any impact there might be on the effective testing of the witness's evidence (s. 51(7)).

2.4.10 Special Measures

The Youth Justice and Criminal Evidence Act 1999 contains a range of measures designed to help young, disabled, vulnerable or intimidated witnesses to give evidence in criminal proceedings.

2.4.10.1 Eligible Witnesses

The Youth Justice and Criminal Evidence Act 1999 provides that both prosecution and defence witnesses are eligible for special measures, and the categories of eligibility include:

- all witnesses under the age of 18 at the time of the hearing or video recording (s. 16(1)(a));
- vulnerable witnesses who are affected by a mental disorder, impairment of intelligence and social functioning (s. 16(2)(a));
- vulnerable witnesses who are affected by physical disability or disorder (s. 16(2)(b));
- witnesses in fear or distress about testifying (s.17(2));
- any witness to a 'relevant offence', currently defined to include homicide offences and other offences involving a firearm or knife (s. 17(5)–(7), sch. 1A);
- adult complainants of sexual offences (as defined by s. 62 of the 1999 Act), human trafficking offences (s. 59A of the Sexual Offences Act 2003 or s. 4 of the Asylum and Immigration (Treatment of Claimants, etc) Act 2004), indecent photographs of children offences (s. 1 of the Protection of Children Act 1978 (take, permit to be taken or publish etc. such a photograph) and s. 160 of the Criminal Justice Act 1988 (possession of such a photograph).

KEYNOTE

While the primary rule is that all witnesses under the age of 18, regardless of the nature of the offence charged, are eligible for their evidence to be given by video interview and the use of live link, this does not prohibit a child witness who wishes to testify in court (ss. 21 and 22).

Regulation 2 of the Special Measures for Child Witnesses (Sexual Offences) Regulations 2013 (SI 2013/2971) amended the 1999 Act so that a complainant of a relevant offence whose age is uncertain will be presumed to be under the age of 18 if there are reasons to believe that person is under the age of 18. The effect is that a complainant to whom the presumption applies will be eligible for 'special measures' under s. 16.

In relation to the category 'any witness to a "relevant offence" involving a firearm, offensive weapon or knife', the 'relevant offence' is an offence specified in sch. 1A to the 1999 Act that includes murder, manslaughter, wounding, assault, etc. All witnesses involved in such cases, including police officers, are automatically eligible for a special measures direction unless they decline (s. 17(5)).

Generally, special measures directions in the case of vulnerable and intimidated witnesses apply to proceedings in relation to anti-social behaviour injunctions (s. 16 of the Anti-social Behaviour, Crime and Policing Act 2014) and criminal behaviour orders (s. 31 of the 2014 Act).

2.4.10.2 Special Measures Directions

There is a range of special measures available to the court for eligible witnesses which is provided by the 1999 Act and includes:

- screening the witness from seeing the defendant (s. 23);
- allowing a witness to give evidence by live link, accompanied by a supporter (s. 24);
- hearing a witness's evidence in private in a sex offence case, a trafficking for exploitation case, or where there is a fear the witness may be intimidated (s. 25);
- dispensing with the wearing of wigs and gowns (s. 26);
- admitting video recording of evidence-in-chief (s. 27);
- admitting video recording of cross-examination and re-examination (s. 28) (currently only in force in proceedings before the Crown Court sitting at Kingston-upon-Thames, Leeds or Liverpool (Youth Justice and Criminal Evidence Act 1999 (Commencement No. 13) Order 2013 (SI 2013/3236));
- questioning a witness through an intermediary in the case of a young or incapacitated witness (s. 29);
- provision of aids to communication for a young or incapacitated witness (s. 30);
- an investigation anonymity order or a witness anonymity order (s. 86 of the Coroners and Justice Act 2009).

2.4.11 Refreshing Memory

The Criminal Justice Act 2003 provides for the use of documents and transcripts by witnesses to refresh their memory.

Section 139 of the 2003 Act states:

(1) A person giving oral evidence in criminal proceedings about any matter may, at any stage in the course of doing so, refresh his memory of it from a document made or verified by him at an earlier time if—

    (a) he states in his oral evidence that the document records his recollection of the matter at that earlier time, and

    (b) his recollection of the matter is likely to have been significantly better at that time than it is at the time of his oral evidence.

(2) Where—

    (a) a person giving oral evidence in criminal proceedings about any matter has previously given an oral account, of which a sound recording was made, and he states in that evidence that the account represented his recollection of the matter at that time,

    (b) his recollection of the matter is likely to have been significantly better at the time of the previous account than it is at the time of his oral evidence, and

    (c) a transcript has been made of the sound recording,

he may, at any stage in the course of giving his evidence, refresh his memory of the matter from that transcript.

2.4.12 Evidence of Oral Statement made through an Interpreter

It is inadmissible for a police officer to give evidence of a conversation held through the use of an interpreter. The only valid witness would be the interpreter (*R* v *Attard* (1959) 43 Cr App R 90).

2.4.13 Victims' Personal Statements and Code of Practice

Victim Personal Statements are statements by the victims of a crime or crimes, or Family Impact Statements by families bereaved by homicide and other criminal conduct. The police may also prepare a Community Impact Statement making the court aware of particular local crime trends and their impact on the local community. *Criminal Practice Directions (Amendment No. 1)* [2013] EWCA Crim 2328, introduced an amendment to create a presumption that Victim Personal Statements will be read to the court if the victim so requests, subject to judicial discretion, and a new Practice Direction to be included on Impact Statements for Businesses.

Their purpose is to allow people a more structured opportunity to explain how they have been affected by the crime or crimes of which they were victims. They provide a practical way of ensuring that the sentencing court will consider 'any harm which the offence caused', reflecting on the evidence of the victim about the specific and personal impact of the offence or offences or, in the cases of homicide, on the family of the deceased. The statements may, albeit incidentally to the purposes of the sentencing court, identify a need for additional or specific support or protection for the victims of crime, to be considered at the end of the sentencing process. In *Attorney-General's Reference (No. 64 of 2014); H* [2014] EWCA Crim 2050 the principle that victims cannot determine the appropriate level of sentence, even when calling for mercy, was reaffirmed.

When a police officer takes a statement from a victim, the victim will be told about the scheme and given the chance to make a victim personal statement. A victim personal statement may be made or updated at any time prior to the disposal of the case. The decision about whether or not to make a victim personal statement is entirely for the victim (para. III.28.2).

The Domestic Violence, Crime and Victims Act 2004 introduced a Victims' Code setting out the services to be provided to victims of criminal conduct (s. 32(1)). The Domestic Violence, Crime and Victims Act 2004 (Victims' Code of Practice) Order 2013 (SI 2013/2907) introduced a revised code of practice entitled *The Code of Practice for Victims of Crime*, online copies of which can be found on the gov.uk website. The Code may include provision requiring or permitting the services which are to be provided to a victim to be provided to one or more others. This might include the relative of a deceased victim or the parent/guardian of a juvenile making a victim personal statement. A person can be a 'victim' even where no person has been charged with or convicted of an offence in respect of criminal conduct (s. 32(6)). 'Close relative' refers to the spouse, the partner, the relatives in direct line, the siblings and the dependants of the victim. Other family members, including guardians and carers, may be considered close relatives at the discretion of the service provider.

Where a person is convicted of a sexual or violent offence, and a relevant sentence has been imposed, victims may make representations through the local probation board as to any licence conditions or supervision requirements in the event of an offender's release from custody. The local probation board is also required to keep victims informed of any such conditions or requirements (s. 35).

The 2004 Act created the role of Commissioner for Victims and Witnesses ('Victims' Commissioner') who has a statutory duty to keep the Code of Practice under regular review and to help improve the services and support available.

2.4.14 Oaths and Affirmations

It is the general rule that every witness who gives evidence must be sworn, that is, take the oath or make an affirmation.

The manner in which the oath is administered is provided by s. 1 of the Oaths Act 1978. This requires the witness to hold the New Testament (Old Testament in the case of a Jew) in his uplifted hand and repeat, after the person administering the oath, the words 'I swear by Almighty God that...', followed by the oath prescribed by law.

Where the witness is neither a Christian nor a Jew he/she can object to taking the oath in the prescribed manner. Alternatively, the witness may affirm or take an oath upon a holy book appropriate to his/her religion or belief. For example, Hindus are sworn on the Vedas and Muslims are sworn on the Koran (*R* v *Morgan* (1764) 1 Leach 54).

An affirmation may be made by a witness who objects to being sworn or where his/her request for an alternative form of oath is not reasonably practicable and would delay or inconvenience the proceedings (s. 5 of the 1978 Act). The witness repeats after the person administering the affirmation, the words 'I [name] do solemnly, sincerely and truly declare and affirm', followed by the words of the oath prescribed by law (s. 6 of the 1978 Act).

There are two exceptions to the general rule:

- children may give unsworn evidence (s. 55 of the Youth Justice and Criminal Evidence Act 1999);
- witnesses merely producing a document need not be sworn (*Perry* v *Gibson* (1834) 1 A & E 48).

Where a compellable witness refuses to take an oath or make an affirmation in the Crown Court, he/she can be held in contempt of court and where appropriate face a penalty of imprisonment (s. 45(4) of the Senior Courts Act 1981).

Where a witness refuses, without just excuse, to be sworn or give evidence in the magistrates' court, he/she can be committed to custody for a period not exceeding one month and/or be fined (Magistrates' Courts Act 1980, s. 97(4)).

2.4.15 Examination-in-Chief

The party who calls a witness (prosecution or defence) is entitled to examine the witness by asking questions with a view to providing evidence which is favourable to that party's case. This is known as 'examination-in-chief'.

All witnesses are examined in chief with one exception: where the prosecution determine not to examine their witness in chief but allow the witness to be cross-examined by the defence. This is common in the case of police officers whose evidence-in-chief will be identical. Consequently, one police officer can give the evidence-in-chief but other officers involved may be required for cross-examination by the defence.

2.4.15.1 Leading Questions

The general rule is that leading questions, i.e. those which suggest the desired answer, may not be asked of a party's own witness. However, it is quite common practice for a party to lead a witness through certain parts of his/her evidence which are not in dispute.

There are two forms of leading questions: those which indicate to a witness the answer required and those which assume something to be true when it has not been established.

The first form is where a question puts words into the witness's mouth. For example, if evidence is given that A assaulted B and the question for the court is whether the defendant did in fact assault B, a prosecution witness should not be asked 'Did you see the defendant assault B?', but should be asked 'What did you see A do?'

Leading questions are admissible in the following circumstances:

- to refresh a witness's memory;
- where the witness is deemed 'hostile';
- for identification purposes;
- usually in matters accepted as being uncontroversial;
- in cross-examination.

2.4.16 Cross-examination

Under Article 6(3)(d) of the European Convention on Human Rights, everyone charged with a criminal offence shall be entitled:

> to examine or have examined witnesses against him and to obtain the attendance and examination of witnesses on his behalf under the same conditions as witnesses against him . . .

Cross-examination is the process by which one party may ask questions of the other party's witnesses. This examination is usually focused on either undermining their evidence or supporting that of the party's own witnesses. In *R v Shah* [2010] EWCA Crim 2326, a trial was held to be unfair if the defence were not afforded the opportunity to cross-examine key witnesses, where either through gross incompetence or as a deliberate act by the prosecution, the witnesses were not present in court.

Cross-examination, like any other form of questioning, is subject to the rules of evidence. The answers elicited from witnesses must be directly relevant to an issue in the case, or indirectly so, concerning evidence of collateral issues, which means that although all witnesses (except generally the defendant) may be asked credit questions, as a general rule, their answers to such questions will be final. A collateral issue is one which is only relevant to the credibility of the witness. In *Attorney-General v Hitchcock* (1847) 1 Exch 91, the court determined the general rule preventing a party from calling evidence on collateral issues. However, there are five exceptions to this general rule. These relate to where a witness:

- is biased;
- has previous convictions;
- has a reputation for untruthfulness;
- is unreliable because of some physical or mental disability or illness;
- has made a statement inconsistent with what he/she has said in the witness box.

If any of these exceptions apply, then further questions can be asked of the witness to disprove his/her answer to the credit question. In some cases, evidence that did not appear relevant to the prosecution case may acquire such relevance as a result of evidence given in chief by the defendant or their witnesses, and it may then be right to allow the prosecution to raise it in cross-examination (*R v Grocott* [2011] EWCA Crim 1962).

The rules in relation to cross-examination do not prevent a party from asking the other party's witnesses about any matter which, if accepted by the witness, will undermine the witness's evidence.

Where a party decides not to cross-examine an opponent's witness, this is held to be an *acceptance* of the witness's evidence-in-chief. Consequently, it is not open to the party that failed to cross-examine to criticise, in a closing speech, the unchallenged evidence of the witness (*R v Bircham* [1972] Crim LR 430).

In *R v Bingham* [1999] 1 WLR 598, it was held that a defendant who goes into the witness box and is sworn thereby exposes him/herself to cross-examination by the prosecution and any co-accused, even if he/she does not give any evidence-in-chief. The prosecution are entitled to cross-examine the defendant even where no questions have been put to him/her by the defence counsel and adverse inferences can be drawn if the defendant does not answer those questions. It was held that in a summary trial, where the prosecution fail to cross-examine an accused, the trial is not to be considered unfair as the magistrates are entitled to reject the accused's evidence (*R (On the Application of Wilkinson) v DPP* [2003] EWHC 865 (Admin)).

2.4.16.1 Protection of Complainants from Cross-examination

The Youth Justice and Criminal Evidence Act 1999, ss. 34–39, protect three categories of witness from cross-examination by an accused person.

Section 34 Complainants in proceedings for sexual offences

No person charged with a sexual offence may in any criminal proceedings cross-examine in person a witness who is the complainant, either—
  (a) in connection with that offence, or
  (b) in connection with any other offence (of whatever nature) with which that person is charged in the proceedings.

Section 35 Child complainants and other child witnesses.

(1) No person charged with an offence to which this section applies may in any criminal proceedings cross-examine in person a protected witness, either—
  (a) in connection with that offence, or
  (b) in connection with any other offence (of whatever nature) with which that person is charged in the proceedings.
(2) For the purposes of subsection (1) a 'protected witness' is a witness who—
  (a) either is the complainant or is alleged to have been a witness to the commission of the offence to which this section applies, and
  (b) either is a child or falls to be cross-examined after giving evidence in chief (whether wholly or in part)—
    (i) by means of a video recording made (for the purposes of section 27) at a time when the witness was a child, or
    (ii) in any other way at any such time.

Section 36 Direction prohibiting accused from cross-examining particular witness

(1) This section applies where, in a case where neither of sections 34 and 35 operates to prevent an accused in any criminal proceedings from cross-examining a witness in person—
  (a) the prosecutor makes an application for the court to give a direction under this section in relation to the witness, or
  (b) the court of its own motion raises the issue whether such a direction should be given.
(2) If it appears to the court—
  (a) that the quality of evidence given by the witness on cross-examination—
    (i) is likely to be diminished if the cross-examination (or further cross-examination) is conducted by the accused in person, and
    (ii) would be likely to be improved if a direction were given under this section, and
  (b) that it would not be contrary to the interests of justice to give such a direction,
  the court may give a direction prohibiting the accused from cross-examining (or further cross-examining) the witness in person.

KEYNOTE

The offences to which s. 35 apply are part 1 offences under the Sexual Offences Act 2003 and include: kidnapping, false imprisonment or an offence under ss. 1 or 2 of the Child Abduction Act 1984; any offence under s. 1 of the Children and Young Persons Act 1933; any offence which involves an assault on, or injury or threat of injury to, any person.

The restrictions on cross-examination of a vulnerable young witness are appropriate provided the defence case is understood and the jury are advised of any disadvantage caused to the defence (*R* v *Wills* [2011] EWCA Crim 1938 and *R* v *E* [2011] EWCA Crim 3028).

2.4.16.2 Cross-examination of Witnesses about Previous Sexual Behaviour

The Youth Justice and Criminal Evidence Act 1999, s. 41 states:

(1) If at a trial a person is charged with a sexual offence, then, except with the leave of the court—

(a) no evidence may be adduced, and

(b) no question may be asked in cross-examination,

by or on behalf of the accused at the trial, about any sexual behaviour of the complainant.

KEYNOTE

'Sexual behaviour' means any sexual behaviour or other sexual experience, whether or not involving any accused or other person, but excluding anything alleged to have taken place which is the subject matter of the charge against the accused (s. 42(1)(c)).

'Sexual behaviour' and 'other sexual experience' may refer to acts or events of a sexual character, as opposed to the existence of a relationship, acquaintanceship or familiarity. The phrases are wide enough to embrace the viewing of pornography, or sexually charged messaging over a live internet connection or answering questions in a sexually implicit quiz (*R* v *Ben-Rejab* [2011] EWCA Crim 1136).

A defendant's right to cross-examine must support the inference that the complainant's statement is false and not be to undermine the complainant's general credibility (*R* v *Evans* [2009] EWCA Crim 2668).

The House of Lords considered that it is common sense that a prior sexual relationship between a complainant and a defendant could be relevant to the defence of consent (*R* v *A* [2001] UKHL 25). Formal admissions by the prosecution as to the existence of a previous sexual relationship between the appellant and the complainant made it unnecessary to permit cross-examination of the complainant as to certain details of that previous relationship (*R* v *MM* [2011] EWCA Crim 1291).

Where a complainant claimed to have been sexually assaulted on four previous occasions but there was no evidence to suggest that any of the allegations were false, it was held that the number of allegations alone does not entitle the defence to explore the possibility that they were false (*A* [2012] EWCA Crim 1273).

2.4.17 Re-examination

Following cross-examination, the party calling the witness is entitled to re-examine. The questions put to the witness at this time may only relate to those matters upon which there was a cross-examination. No leading questions are allowed within the re-examination of a witness.

After the defendant has been re-examined, it is open to the judge to ask questions to clear up uncertainties, to fill gaps or to answer queries which might be lurking in the jury's mind. It is not appropriate for the judge to cross-examine the witness (*R* v *Wiggan* (1999) *The Times*, 22 March).

2.4.18 Further Evidence

It is the general rule that the prosecution must call the whole of their evidence before closing their case (*R* v *Francis* [1990] 1 WLR 1264).

However, there are three well-established exceptions to the general rule:

- evidence in rebuttal of defence evidence, that is, matters arising *ex improviso* (i.e. evidence which becomes relevant in circumstances which the prosecution could not have foreseen at the time when they presented their case) (*R* v *Owen* [1952] 2 QB 362 and *Malcolm* v *DPP* [2007] EWHC 363 (Admin));
- evidence not called by reason of oversight or inadvertence (*Royal* v *Prescott-Clarke* [1966] 1 WLR 788 and *Hammond* v *Wilkinson* [2001] Crim LR 323);
- evidence not previously available (*R* v *Pilcher* (1974) 60 Cr App R 1).

New evidence may be admitted in appeals for criminal cases as provided by s. 23(1) of the Criminal Appeal Act 1968. Section 23 allows the Court of Appeal, 'if they think it necessary or expedient in the interests of justice' to receive the evidence, if tendered, of any competent but not compellable witness or to order any compellable witness to attend for examination, whether or not that witness was called at the trial. In *R* v *Ahluwalia* [1992] 4 All ER 889, s. 23 was used to admit fresh evidence of the accused's alleged endogenous depression which, if put forward at the trial, may have provided an arguable defence to the charge of murder. Similarly, in *R* v *O'Brien* [2000] Crim LR 676, expert psychiatric evidence was admitted as fresh evidence to show that a defendant's abnormal disorder might render a confession or evidence unreliable. However, in *R* v *Horsman* [2001] EWCA Crim 3040, the Court of Appeal held that generally, at a retrial, a defendant could not adduce as fresh evidence a statement which he/she had withheld for tactical reasons during his/her first trial.

2.4.19 Contempt of Court

Section 12 of the Contempt of Court Act 1981 deals with criminal contempt in the magistrates' court and states:

(1) A magistrates' court has jurisdiction under this section to deal with any person who—
  (a) wilfully insults the justice or justices, any witness before an officer of the court or any solicitor or counsel having business in the court, during his or their sitting or attendance in court or in going to or returning from the court; or
  (b) wilfully interrupts the proceedings of the court or otherwise misbehaves in court.
(2) In any such case the court may order any officer of the court, or any constable, to take the offender into custody and detain him until the rising of the court; and the court may, if it thinks fit, commit the offender to custody for a specified period not exceeding one month or impose on him a fine not exceeding £2,500, or both.

KEYNOTE

The magistrates' court may also deal with any person for contempt where they are attending or brought before the court and refuse without just excuse to be sworn or give evidence, or to produce any document or thing (s. 97(4) of the Magistrates' Courts Act 1980). In addition, a magistrates' court can also punish as contempt the use of disclosed prosecution material in contravention of s. 17 of the Criminal Procedure and Investigations Act 1996 (confidentiality of disclosed information) (s. 18(1) of the 1996 Act).

2.5 Youth Justice, Crime and Disorder

2.5.1 Introduction

This chapter examines the framework of partnership created by the Crime and Disorder Act 1998 to deal with offending by children and young persons. It also includes the provisions of the Act in relation to youth cautions, orders against parents and police powers on dealing with truants.

2.5.2 Youth Justice System

The Crime and Disorder Act 1998 provides the aim of the youth justice system, and s. 37 states:

> (1) It shall be the principal aim of the youth justice system to prevent offending by children and young persons.
>
> (2) In addition to any other duty to which they are subject, it shall be the duty of all persons and bodies carrying out functions in relation to the youth justice system to have regard to that aim.

KEYNOTE

The 1998 Act requires that local authorities and the police work in partnership to develop and implement a strategy to reduce youth crime and disorder in their local areas. A number of other agencies including the probation services, local probation boards, clinical commissioning groups and local health boards or primary care trusts, are required to cooperate with the two responsible authorities (s. 38(2)).

Section 40(1) places a duty on each local authority, after consultation with the relevant persons and bodies, to formulate and implement for each year a 'youth justice plan', setting out:

(a) how youth justice services in their area are to be provided and funded; and

(b) how the youth offending team or teams established by them are to be composed and funded, how they are to operate and what functions they are to carry out.

2.5.3 Youth Offending Teams

Youth offending teams are multi-agency teams that are coordinated by a local authority with the intention of reducing the risk of young people offending and re-offending, and to provide counsel and rehabilitation to those who do offend.

The Crime and Disorder Act 1998, s. 39 states:

> (1) Subject to subsection (2) below, it shall be the duty of each local authority, acting in co-operation with the persons and bodies mentioned..., to establish for their area one or more youth offending teams.
>
> (2) Two (or more) local authorities acting together may establish one or more youth offending teams for both (or all) their areas;...
>
> (3) ...
>
> (4) ...

(5) A youth offending team shall include at least one of each of the following, namely—

    (a)   an officer of a local probation board or an officer of a provider of probation services;

    (aa) where the local authority is in England, a person with experience of social work in relation to children nominated by the director of children's services appointed by the local authority under section 18 of the Children Act 2004;

    (b)   where the local authority is in Wales, a social worker of the local authority social services department;

    (c)   a police officer;

    (d)   a person nominated by a Clinical Commissioning Group or a Local Health Board any part of whose area lies within the local authority's area;

    (da) where the local authority is in England, a person with experience in education nominated by the director of children's services appointed by the local authority under section 18 of the Children Act 2004;

    (e)   where the local authority is in Wales, a person nominated by the chief education officer appointed by the local authority under section 532 of the Education Act 1996.

KEYNOTE

In addition to those included as members of a youth offending team it may also include such other persons as the local authority thinks appropriate after consulting the other bodies involved (s. 39(6)).

Youth offending teams carry out those functions which are required of the team with the local authority's youth justice plan.

In addition, youth offending teams are required to establish youth offender panels to deal with referral orders (s. 21 of the Powers of Criminal Courts (Sentencing) Act 2000). Generally, a referral order is a way of dealing with an offender under the age of 18 on first conviction. The order may be made by the youth court (or exceptionally an adult magistrates' court) (s. 16). The young offender is referred to the youth offender panel, where a 'contract' is agreed with the offender and their family, aimed at tackling the offending behaviour and its causes. The 'contract' may include: financial or other reparation to the victim; attendance at mediation sessions; unpaid work or service; curfew requirements; educational attendance; rehabilitation for drugs or alcohol misuse (ss. 23 to 27 of the 2000 Act).

2.5.4   Young Offenders: Youth Cautions

A youth caution is a formal out-of-court disposal intended to provide a proportionate and effective response to offending behaviour and can be used for any offence provided that the statutory criteria are satisfied.

The Crime and Disorder Act 1998, s. 66ZA states:

(1) A constable may give a child or young person ('Y') a caution under this section (a 'youth caution') if—

    (a) the constable decides that there is sufficient evidence to charge Y with an offence,

    (b) Y admits to the constable that Y committed the offence, and

    (c) the constable does not consider that Y should be prosecuted or given a youth conditional caution in respect of the offence.

(2) A youth caution must be given in the presence of an appropriate adult.

(3) If a constable gives a youth caution to a person, the constable must explain the matters referred to in subsection (4) in ordinary language to—

    (a) that person, and

    (b) the appropriate adult.

(4) Those matters are—

    (a) the effect of subsections (1) to (3) and (5) to (7) of section 66ZB, and

    (b) any guidance issued under subsection (4) of that section.

2.5.5 Orders Against Parents

These orders are about influencing parental responsibility and control. The orders are designed to give parents more help and support to change the criminal and/or anti-social behaviour of their children in providing a framework where parents participate in their child's supervision. The strategy here is one of prevention in attempting to dissuade a recurrence of criminality or truancy.

2.5.5.1 Parenting Orders

Parenting orders are provided by the Crime and Disorder Act 1998, s. 8 of which states:

(1) This section applies where, in any court proceedings—
  (a) a child safety order is made in respect of a child, or the court determines on an application under section 12(6) below that a child has failed to comply with any requirement included in such an order;
  (aa) a parental compensation order is made in relation to a child's behaviour;
  (b) an injunction is granted under section 1 of the Anti-social Behaviour, Crime and Policing Act 2014, an order is made under section 22 of that Act or a sexual harm prevention order is made in respect of a child or young person;
  (c) a child or young person is convicted of an offence; or
  (d) a person is convicted of an offence under section 443 (failure to comply with a school attendance order) or section 444 (failure to secure regular attendance at a school of registered pupil) of the Education Act 1996.
(2) Subject to subsection (3) and section 9(1) below, if in the proceedings the court is satisfied that the relevant condition is fulfilled, it may make a parenting order in respect of a person who is a parent or guardian of the child or young person or, as the case may be, the person convicted of the offence under section 443 or 444 ('the parent').
(3) ...

(4) A parenting order is an order which requires the parent—

    (a) to comply, for a period not exceeding twelve months, with such requirements as are specified in the order; and

    (b) subject to subsection (5) below, to attend, for a concurrent period not exceeding three months, such counselling or guidance programme as may be specified in directions given by the responsible officer.

(5) A parenting order may, but need not, include such a requirement as is mentioned in subsection 4(b) above in any case where a parenting order under this section or any other enactment has been made in respect of the parent on a previous occasion.

KEYNOTE

In relation to s. 8(1)(b), the order under s. 22 of the 2014 Act is a criminal behaviour order, and a sexual harm prevention order means an order under s. 103A of the Sexual Offences Act 2003.

A parenting order may be made against one or both biological parents (this would include an order against a father who may not be married to the mother), and a person who is a guardian. Guardians are defined as any person who, in the opinion of the court, has for the time being the care of a child or young person (s. 117(1)).

The courts generally have the discretion as to whether or not a parenting order is made. Where a person under the age of 16 is convicted of an offence, the court shall, if satisfied that the relevant condition is fulfilled, make a parenting order (s. 9(1)). The requirements and directions of a parenting order should, as far as practicable, avoid any conflict with the parent's religious beliefs, and any interference with when they normally work or attend an educational establishment (s. 9(4)).

2.5.5.2 Breach of a Parenting Order

The Crime and Disorder Act 1998, s. 9 states:

(7) If while a parenting order is in force the parent without reasonable excuse fails to comply with any requirement included in the order, or specified in directions given by the responsible officer, he shall be liable on summary conviction to a fine not exceeding level 3 on the standard scale.

KEYNOTE

The section does not specify who would be responsible for instituting proceedings but it is assumed that this will be the 'responsible officer' (usually a member of the youth offending team) and that the normal processes will be followed whereby the CPS will make decisions as to a prosecution applying the usual test of public interest.

2.5.5.3 Binding Over of Parent or Guardian

The Powers of Criminal Courts (Sentencing) Act 2000, s. 150 provides for the binding over of a parent or guardian and states:

(1) Where a child or young person (that is to say, any person aged under 18) is convicted of an offence, the powers conferred by this section shall be exercisable by the court by which he is sentenced for that offence, and where the offender is aged under 16 when sentenced it shall be the duty of the court—

    (a) to exercise those powers if it is satisfied, having regard to the circumstances of the case, that their exercise would be desirable in the interests of preventing the commission by him of further offences; and

    (b) if it does not exercise them, to state in open court that it is not satisfied as mentioned in paragraph (a) above and why it is not so satisfied;

but this subsection has effect subject to section 19(5) above and paragraph 13(5) of Schedule 1 to this Act (cases where referral orders made or extended).

(2) The powers conferred by this section are as follows—

    (a) with the consent of the offender's parent or guardian, to order the parent or guardian to enter into a recognizance to take proper care of him and exercise proper control over him; and

    (b) if the parent or guardian refuses consent and the court considers the refusal unreasonable, to order the parent or guardian to pay a fine not exceeding £1,000;

and where the court has passed on the offender a sentence which consists of or includes a youth rehabilitation order, it may include in the recognizance provision that the offender's parent or guardian ensure that the offender complies with the requirements of that sentence.

KEYNOTE

The recognizance can be imposed on the parent or guardian for up to three years or until the offender is aged 18, whichever is the shorter (s. 150(4)).

For the purposes of s. 150, taking 'care' of a person includes giving him/her protection and guidance, and 'control' includes discipline (s. 150(11)).

2.5.5.4   Parental Compensation Orders

The Crime and Disorder Act 1998 provides for parental compensation orders. Section 13A states:

(1) A magistrates' court may make an order under this section (a 'parental compensation order') if on the application of a local authority it is satisfied, on the civil standard of proof—

    (a) that the condition mentioned in subsection (2) below is fulfilled with respect to a child under the age of 10; and

    (b) that it would be desirable to make the order in the interests of preventing a repetition of the behaviour in question.

(2) The condition is that the child has taken, or caused loss of or damage to, property in the course of—

    (a) committing an act which, if he had been aged 10 or over, would have constituted an offence; or

    (b) acting in a manner that caused or was likely to cause harassment, alarm or distress to one or more persons not of the same household as himself.

KEYNOTE

The 'civil standard of proof' is 'on the balance of probability'.

The amount of compensation specified cannot exceed £5,000 in all (s. 13A(4)). Collection and enforcement conditions are the same as if the parent had been convicted of an offence (s. 13A(6)).

2.5.6   Child Safety Orders

These orders are designed to help prevent children under 10 from turning to crime. Such orders are concerned with the child's potential offending behaviour and in practice are likely to be used in conjunction with parenting orders under s. 8 of the Crime and Disorder Act 1998.

The Crime and Disorder Act 1998, s. 11 states:

(1) Subject to subsection (2) below, if the family court, on the application of a local authority, is satisfied that one or more of the conditions specified in subsection (3) below are fulfilled with respect to a child under the age of 10, it may make an order (a 'child safety order') which—

    (a) places the child, for a period (not exceeding the permitted maximum) specified in the order, under the supervision of the responsible officer; and

    (b) requires the child to comply with such requirements as are so specified.

2.5.7   Removal of Truants to Designated Premises, etc.

The Crime and Disorder Act 1998, s. 16 states:

(1) This section applies where a local authority—
   (a) designates premises in a police area ('designated premises') as premises to which children and young persons of compulsory school age may be removed under this section; and
   (b) notifies the chief officer of police for that area of the designation.
(2) A police officer of or above the rank of superintendent may direct that the powers conferred on a constable by subsection (3) and (3ZA) below—
   (a) shall be exercisable as respects any area falling within the police area and specified in the direction; and
   (b) shall be so exercisable during a period specified;
   and references in each of those subsections to a specified area and a specified period shall be construed accordingly.

2.5.7.1   Police Powers

The Crime and Disorder Act 1998, s. 16 provides that:

(3)   if a constable has reasonable cause to believe that a child or young person found by him in a public place in a specified area during a specified period—
   (a) is of compulsory school age; and
   (b) is absent from school without lawful authority,
   the constable may remove the child or young person to designated premises, or to the school from which he is so absent.
(3ZA)   If a constable has reasonable cause to believe that a child or young person found by him in a public place in a specified area during a specified period and during school hours—
   (a) is of compulsory school age;
   (b) has been excluded on disciplinary grounds from a relevant school for a fixed period or permanently;
   (c) remains excluded from that school;
   (d) has not subsequently been admitted as a pupil to any other school; and
   (e) has no reasonable justification for being in the public place;
   the constable may remove the child or young person to designated premises.

The power of a constable to remove a child or young person to 'designated premises' is not an arrest in the traditional sense of detention, and statutory powers relating to arrests will not apply. However, the duty to explain the reason for a person's 'seizure' may well apply in such cases.

As with the powers conferred in relation to curfew notices, it appears probable that the common law rule entitling a constable to use reasonable force would apply. However, legal commentators are not convinced that this is the case, as the use of force could be seen as having a damaging effect on relations between the police and young persons and the possibility of criminal or civil action against individual officers. The requirement for the officer to have 'reasonable cause to believe' that the person meets the criteria at (a) and (b) is more stringent than mere suspicion.

The Education Act 1996 provides that penalty notices can be issued to parents or guardians who fail to ensure the regular attendance of their child of compulsory school age (5–16) who is registered at a state school, or fail to ensure that their excluded child is not found in a public place during school hours without a justifiable reason. If a child is found in such circumstances, designated local authority officers, headteachers (and authorised deputy headteachers and assistant headteachers), police officers and community support officers can issue a fixed penalty notice (ss. 444A and 444B).

The penalty to be paid will be £60 for those who pay within 21 days and £120 for those who pay within 28 days (Education (Penalty Notices) (England) (Amendment) Regulations 2007 (SI 2007/1867) and Education (Penalty Notices) (Wales) Regulations 2013 (SI 2013/1983)).

PART II

The Law of Evidence

2.6 Exclusion of Admissible Evidence

2.6.1 Introduction

In ensuring that a person has a fair trial, the court may exclude evidence, *even though the evidence itself is admissible*. The court may exclude any evidence in certain circumstances and has additional powers in relation to evidence obtained by confession. The courts' powers to exclude evidence come generally from s. 78 of the Police and Criminal Evidence Act 1984 (and specifically in relation to confession evidence from s. 76(2) of that Act), although the courts also have common law powers to exclude evidence.

2.6.2 Confessions

Where the suspect initially confesses to the offence, he/she may still plead not guilty, alleging that the confession was obtained by oppression and/or in circumstances that would render it unreliable or that it should be excluded as having been unfairly obtained. The courts are concerned with the reliability of evidence and often regard confessions as the least reliable way to prove a person's involvement in an offence.

A confession, which is defined by s. 82 of the Police and Criminal Evidence Act 1984 (see below), is an out-of-court statement made by a person and therefore falls into the category of evidence known as 'hearsay' evidence. Hearsay evidence is inadmissible unless it falls within one of the statutory or common law exceptions.

Confessions are such an exceptional category and are admissible in evidence as outlined in s. 76(1) of the 1984 Act. However, evidence of confession may be excluded by a court under either s. 76(2) or 78 of the 1984 Act.

Section 76 of the Police and Criminal Evidence Act 1984 states:

(1) In any proceedings a confession made by an accused person may be given in evidence against him insofar as it is relevant to any matter in issue in the proceedings and is not excluded by the court in pursuance of this section.

A 'confession' is defined by s. 82 of the 1984 Act, which states:

(1) In this Part of this Act—'confession' includes any statement wholly or partly adverse to the person who made it, whether made to a person in authority or not and whether made in words or otherwise;

KEYNOTE

A confession, therefore, is a positive action by the person making it. The person must use words or some other method of communication (e.g. nodding his/her head to a question, or a video tape of the suspect taking police to a murder weapon). Therefore confessions do not include silence by a person (although this may be relevant to special warnings, **see chapter 2.10**). It could include a filmed re-enactment of the crime (*Li Shu-Ling* v *The Queen* [1989] AC 270).

The confession does not have to be a pure statement of guilt and can include the answers to questions asked in interview which are *adverse to the defendant*. In *R* v *Z* [2003] EWCA Crim 191 the Court of Appeal considered the meaning of 'confession' for the purposes of the Police and Criminal Evidence Act 1984 in light

---

of the Human Rights Act 1998. The court held that the decision as to whether or not a statement was a confession was to be made at the time it was sought to give the statement in evidence as opposed to at the time the statement was made by the person.

A confession by one defendant can be indirectly used in evidence against another defendant. In *R v Hayter* [2005] UKHL 6 the House of Lords held that there was no reason why one defendant's guilt established by that defendant's own out-of-court confession could not be taken into account by a jury when considering the guilt of another defendant.

2.6.2.1 The Exclusion of Confession Evidence

Section 76(2) of the Police and Criminal Evidence Act 1984 gives the courts a responsibility to exclude confessions where they have been obtained by oppression (s. 76(2)(a)), or where the court considers that they are unreliable (s. 76(2)(b)). There is also a general power (under s. 78 of the 1984 Act and at common law) to exclude any evidence that the court considers would be detrimental to the fairness of the trial if allowed, which can also be applicable to the exclusion of confessions. Once the defence raises the issue of oppression and/or unreliability, it is for the prosecution to prove that the confession was not obtained in such circumstances (*R v Allen* [2001] EWCA Crim 1607).

Section 76A (which makes similar provisions for exclusion as those under s. 76), states that so long as it has not been excluded by the court, that in any proceedings where a confession was made by one accused person it may be given in evidence for another person charged in the same proceedings (a co-accused). The key part of this subsection is that the co-accused must be 'charged in the same proceedings'; for instance, in *R v Finch* [2007] EWCA Crim 36, where one suspect pleaded guilty the House of Lords held that he was no longer a person charged or accused in the trial; accordingly, s. 76A of the 1984 Act did not apply and what he said to the police was not admissible.

2.6.2.2 Section 76 PACE

Section 76 of the Police and Criminal Evidence Act 1984 states:

(2) If, in any proceedings where the prosecution proposes to give in evidence a confession made by an accused person, it is represented to the court that the confession was or may have been obtained—
(a) by oppression of the person who made it; or
(b) in consequence of anything said or done which was likely, in the circumstances existing at the time, to render unreliable any confession which might be made by him in consequence thereof,
the court shall not allow the confession to be given in evidence against him except in so far as the prosecution proves to the court beyond reasonable doubt that the confession (notwithstanding that it may be true) was not obtained as aforesaid.

2.6.2.3 Oppression

A court is under a duty to exclude a confession where it has been, or may have been, obtained by the oppression of the person making the confession. This means that there must be some link between the oppressive behaviour and the confession. So for instance, if the confession was made before the oppressive behaviour, this would not justify exclusion under this subsection (it may, however, justify exclusion under the general power of the courts). Where a confession has been obtained by oppression, any later confession obtained properly may also be excluded from evidence (*R v Ismail* [1990] Crim LR 109). It does not matter whether or not the confession is true; the issue under s. 76(2)(a) is how the person has been treated and whether any mistreatment led, or might have led, the person to make the confession. This issue is of particular importance in the interviewing of suspects. In looking at this the courts seem to take into account the nature of the person being interviewed. It was said in *R* v *Gowan* [1982] Crim LR 821, that hardened criminals must expect vigorous police interrogation.

2.6.2.4 What is Oppression?

In s. 76(8) of the Police and Criminal Evidence Act 1984, 'oppression' includes torture, inhuman or degrading treatment and the use or threat of violence (whether or not amounting to torture).

KEYNOTE

In *R* v *Fulling* [1987] QB 426, the Court of Appeal held that oppression is:

> [The] exercise of authority or power in a burdensome, harsh or wrongful manner; unjust or cruel treatment of subjects, inferiors etc., the imposition of unreasonable or unjust burdens.

It is suggested by some commentators that oppression involves some kind of impropriety on the part of the police, which might be suggested by a deliberate failure to follow the PACE Codes of Practice, although a failure to follow the Codes is not of itself an automatic reason for excluding evidence. Given that the courts have occasionally excluded evidence even where the relevant Code of Practice *has* been followed, the converse does not appear to be true and it is possible that a court might conclude that treatment had been 'oppressive' under all the circumstances even though the Codes of Practice had been followed.

The oppression must have been against the person who makes the confession.

When the defence raise the issue of oppression, it will be for the prosecution to show beyond reasonable doubt (*R* v *Miller* (1993) 97 Cr App R 99) that this was not the case. For these reasons (as well as those of professional ethics) it is of great importance to comply with the PACE Codes of Practice. It is also important to keep records of how a case is investigated, together with the reasons for taking decisions during the course of the investigation so that the prosecution can present a case which demonstrates that there was no oppressive or improper conduct in obtaining the confession.

It is a question of fact on each occasion whether a person's treatment was oppressive and whether there was any link between that person's treatment and his/her decision to make the confession. It might be possible for the defence to use evidence against officers involved in the case who have allegedly 'mistreated' suspects in other cases (*R* v *Twitchell* [2000] 1 Cr App R 373).

It will be for the prosecution to satisfy the judge that the confession was made voluntarily; even where the confession is admissible a jury would still need to be directed that they should disregard the confession if they considered that it was or may have been obtained by oppression or in consequence of anything said or done that was likely to render it unreliable (*R* v *Mushtaq* [2005] UKHL 25).

The legislation itself gives little guidance as to what will amount to oppression. For this reason it is necessary to look at the case law. Below are examples where the courts have held that the treatment of a person was 'oppressive':

- A person who was on the border of being mentally impaired, admitted the offence after denying it over 300 times because of the bullying manner of the questioning (*R* v *Paris* (1993) 97 Cr App R 99). This case does not mean that interviewers cannot go over the same point several times or even suggest to the interviewee that he/she is lying. However, *Paris* does suggest that this should be done in moderation and not to the point where it becomes oppressive.
- A person confessed but had been kept in custody longer than the court felt was justified and therefore unlawfully (*R* v *Davison* [1988] Crim LR 442).
- The suspect was wrongly informed that he/she had been recognised when this was not true (*R* v *Heron* (1993), unreported).
- There was a failure to have an appropriate adult present (*R* v *Silcott* (1991) *The Times*, 9 December).

- The defendant was a choir master and the police had told him that if he did not make a statement they would have to interview all the members of the choir and this could disclose other offences on his part (*R v Howden-Simpson* [1991] Crim LR 49).
- A confession was obtained where the person was being held without access to a solicitor (*Barbera v Spain* (1989) 11 EHRR 360).
- Interviews had extended over a three-hour period and were conducted in a manner that was persistent, aggressive and calculated to get a conviction as opposed to necessarily getting to the truth (*R v Ridley* (1999) 17 December, unreported). The court went on to comment that the manner in which the interviews were conducted was to be deplored and was an exploitation of a naïve man by methods which were unacceptable and had prejudiced the fair conduct of the trial.

2.6.2.5 Unreliability

A court is under a duty to exclude a confession where it is, has been or may have been obtained in consequence of anything which was likely, in the circumstances that existed at the time, to render it unreliable.

When looking at whether a confession is reliable, the court will consider the circumstances as they actually were at the time and not as they were believed to be. For instance, if it was believed that a suspect was in a fit state to be interviewed but it later transpires that he/she was medically unfit, there is likely to be some doubt as to whether a confession made at that time is reliable. (The belief of the officers at the time of acting, however, may be relevant to any disciplinary matters.)

For instance, in *R v Walker* [1998] Crim LR 211 the court held that the defendant's mental state may be taken into account when considering the surrounding circumstances, regardless of whether it was known to the police. The prosecution bore the burden of proof to show that the confession was admissible. The court went further and said that s. 76(2)(b) was not restricted in its application to use by the police of oppression. It was not necessary to show that the confession was unreliable by reference to the old common law test of 'threat or inducement'. A successful submission under s. 76(2)(b) does not require a breach of a Code of Practice.

Once again, it is for the prosecution to show (beyond reasonable doubt) that the confession is reliable once the question of unreliability has been raised by the defence.

In *R v Fulling* [1987] QB 426 it was suggested that questioning had been:

...by its nature, duration, or other attendant circumstances (including the fact of custody) excites hopes (such as the hope of release) or fears, or so affects the mind of the subject that his will crumbles and he speaks when otherwise he would have stayed silent.

Thus the circumstances of a case can affect the reliability of the accused's statement.

2.6.2.6 What is Unreliable?

It is a question of fact on each occasion whether the reliability of a person's confession is in question as a result of something said or done. Below are examples where the courts have held that a confession was unreliable:

- No caution was given to the suspect, the suspect was not asked if he wanted his solicitor present and was not shown the note of the interview (*R v Trussler* [1998] Crim LR 446).
- The PACE Codes of Practice were flagrantly breached (*R v Delaney* (1989) 88 Cr App R 338).
- A suspect who had just vomited was interviewed (any medical condition could affect the reliability of a confession; if in doubt the person should be examined by a doctor) (*R v McGovern* (1991) 92 Cr App R 228).
- The appropriate adult had a low IQ and was unable to assist the detained person (*R v Silcott* [1987] Crim LR 765).

- In a case where the suspect was a vulnerable person, the fact that he/she confessed to the offence without an appropriate adult being called made the confession unreliable. The court found that had the adult been present, a solicitor would in all probability have been instructed and there was a realistic likelihood that the suspect would not have made any admissions (*R v W* [2010] EWCA Crim 2799).
- It was suggested to a suspect of a sexual assault that it would be better for him/her to receive treatment than go to prison (*R v Delaney*).
- A person had been kept in custody for 14 hours, had been interviewed four times before confessing and had been refused any visits from family (*R v Silcott*).
- An offer of bail was made subject to the suspect admitting the offence or, conversely, the suspect was told that he/she would be kept in custody until he/she admitted the offence (*R v Barry* (1992) 95 Cr App R 384).
- Psychiatric evidence suggested that the suspect suffered from a severe personality disorder and that her admissions in her interview were unreliable (*R v Walker* [1998] Crim LR 211).
- A suspect had been forcibly overcome, and a confession was obtained in response to a question designed to elicit details of the offence from him without any prior caution having been administered (*R v Allen* [2001] EWCA Crim 1607).
- A defendant who was told by his employer that if he admitted to the theft no further action would be taken, but if he did not admit it, the police would be called. The suspect admitted it; nevertheless, the manager called the police. The manager's untrue inducement to the defendant made his confession unreliable, therefore the confession had been wrongfully admitted, which rendered the conviction unsafe (*R v Roberts* [2011] EWCA Crim 2974).

2.6.2.7 Effect of Excluding Confessions

Often further evidence is obtained after a person makes a confession. If a court excludes all or any part of a confession, then this may impact on the value of the additional evidence obtained by the prosecution.

While the additional evidence obtained after a confession may be admissible, much of the value of the evidence may be lost because s. 76(5) of the 1984 Act prevents the prosecution from linking the discovery of the additional evidence to any confession which has been excluded.

If the additional evidence cannot be linked to the confession, then it might not be possible to link the evidence to the suspect (and the evidence may also be excluded under s. 78 of the 1984 Act or at common law).

....

EXAMPLE

In the case of a murder, if a suspect confesses to the murder and tells the investigators where he/she has hidden the murder weapon, this would be good evidence that the person committed the offence. If the confession is excluded then, although evidence can be given that the weapon found is in fact the murder weapon, it will not be possible to show any connection between the suspect and the weapon. Therefore, unless there is some other evidence to link the weapon to the suspect (e.g. fingerprint evidence), the case may fail. The reason is that it would not be possible to say that the police went to the location where the weapon was hidden without at least implying that the suspect had indicated that it was there when interviewed. All that can be said is that the weapon was found at the particular location, which could be accessible to any number of people.

Section 76(4) of the Police and Criminal Evidence Act 1984 provides that the exclusion of such additional evidence is not affected by the exclusion of the confession. Even where a confession is excluded, it may still be admissible for other matters such as the fact that the accused speaks in a certain way or writes or expresses him/herself in a particular fashion. In such a case it would only be that part of the confession which is necessary to prove the point that will be admissible. Once again, this illustrates the point that evidence is often only admissible for a specific purpose.

....

2.6.3 Exclusion of Evidence Generally

The courts in England and Wales can exclude any evidence under certain circumstances. Those circumstances will usually be concerned with the way in which the evidence has been obtained or with the potential effect of allowing it to be adduced at trial.

2.6.3.1 Exclusion of Unfair Evidence

Section 78 of the Police and Criminal Evidence Act 1984 states:

(1) In any proceedings the court may refuse to allow evidence on which the prosecution proposes to rely to be given if it appears to the court that, having regard to all the circumstances, including the circumstances in which the evidence was obtained, the admission of the evidence would have such an adverse effect on the fairness of the proceedings that the court ought not to admit it.
(2) Nothing in this section shall prejudice any rule of law requiring a court to exclude evidence.

KEYNOTE

Section 78 is wider than s. 76 and applies to *all evidence that the prosecution intend to produce in court.*

When applying s. 78, the courts will look at the fairness of allowing the evidence to be admitted against the defendant.

Compliance with the Codes of Practice is vital. In *Batley* v *DPP* (1998) *The Times*, 5 March, the court said that where steps required by the Codes were not observed and where material was entered as evidence without those checks which formed an important aspect of the case, there was a real risk to the fairness of the proceedings against the defendant. This must be balanced against *R* v *Parris* (1989) 89 Cr App R 68, where the court held that a breach of the Codes is not an automatic exclusion of evidence. It is important to note that the court may take account of any changes to the Codes of Practice (even when changed after the person was in police detention) on the basis that the new Code reflects what is considered to be fair (*R* v *Word* (1994) 98 Cr App R 337).

In *R* v *Samuel* [1988] QB 615 the court stated that it is undesirable to attempt any general guidance as to the way in which a judge's discretion under s. 78 should be exercised. It is a question of fact in each case and, while s. 76 requires links with the treatment of the person spoken to, the only issue under s. 78 is whether it would be unfair to admit the evidence in court. *Stanesby* v *DPP* [2012] EWHC 1320 (Admin) is a case that supports this position; this was a drink drive procedure where the defendant told the custody sergeant that he was taking medication for depression, which should have triggered an appropriate adult being called (Code C1.4). The Court held that each case had to be determined on its facts; the breath test had been properly administered, by persons acting in good faith, to somebody who appeared to understand, and in fact did understand, what was required of him; even if an appropriate adult had attended it would not have made any difference to the administration of the breath test. Under s. 78, admission of the breath test results would not have such an adverse effect on the fairness of the proceedings that they should be excluded.

2.6.3.2 Evidence which will be Excluded

It is therefore difficult to give specific guidance, but the following are examples of evidence that has been excluded:

- Evidence of a driver being over the prescribed limit where the officer did not suspect that the driver had alcohol in his/her body.
- Some cases of 'entrapment' where the court is not satisfied that the person would have committed such an offence had it not been for the action of the police/customs officers. The court may look to see whether the person was pressurised into committing the offence/providing information or whether, by some ruse, the person was given an opportunity of so doing.
- Informing the suspect and his/her solicitor that the suspect's fingerprints had been found on items at the scene of the offence when this was not true.

- Undercover operations where the officers failed to record conversations in accordance with the PACE Codes of Practice.
- Failure by custody officers to inform a detained person of his/her rights.
- Interviewing a suspect without informing the person of his/her rights.
- Failing to provide the detained person with adequate meals.
- 'Off the record' interviews that were not recorded as required by the PACE Codes of Practice.
- Failing to make a contemporaneous note of a conversation.
- Failing to get an interpreter or appropriate adult.
- Interviewing a person suffering from schizophrenia without an appropriate adult being present (*R v Aspinall* [1999] 2 Cr App R 115).
- Identification of a suspect by police officers who had seen the person after he had been arrested and in handcuffs (*R v Bazil* (1996) 6 April, unreported).
- Failing to inform a suspect arrested in respect of one offence that it was proposed to question him/her in respect of another more serious offence or failing to ensure that he/she was aware of the true nature of the investigation (*R v Kirk* [2000] 1 WLR 567).

2.6.3.3 Exclusion at Common Law

Section 82(3) of the Police and Criminal Evidence Act 1984 retained the courts' common law power to exclude evidence at its discretion (as to which, see *R v Sang* [1980] AC 402). For evidence to be excluded at common law the court will not so much concern itself with *how* evidence is obtained, but rather the *effect* that the evidence will have at trial. The court can exclude evidence at common law where the prejudicial effect of the evidence on the defendant greatly outweighs its probative value.

In these cases, the courts are looking at the trial process itself, as opposed to the investigation, and therefore this power has less impact on how investigations should be conducted.

2.6.3.4 Entrapment

The issue of entrapment falls into two categories: that is to say, trying to obtain evidence relating to offences that have already been committed; and those cases where evidence is obtained of offences yet to be committed.

In relation to investigations concerning offences already committed, the House of Lords in *R v Sang* [1980] AC 402 held that:

> Save with regard to admissions and confessions and generally with regard to evidence obtained from the accused after commission of the offence, [the judge] has no discretion to refuse to admit relevant admissible evidence on the ground that it was obtained by improper or unfair means. The court is not concerned with how it was obtained. It is no ground for the exercise of discretion to exclude that the evidence was obtained as the result of the activities of an *agent provocateur*.

(This is now subject to s. 78 of the 1984 Act but the principle still applies.)

The issues surrounding entrapment are considered by some to be an infringement of a person's human rights. In *Teixeira de Castro v Portugal* (1999) 28 EHRR 101, the European Court of Human Rights (subject to the following two qualifications) held that the use of undercover agents is not incompatible with Article 6 of the European Convention (right to a fair trial). Those qualifications were that:

- their use must be restricted and safeguards observed to prevent abuse;
- their actions must not exceed passive surveillance.

In the case of *Attorney-General's Reference (No. 3 of 2000); Looseley* [2002] 1 Cr App R 29 the court stated that it is simply not acceptable that the state through its agents should lure its citizens into committing acts forbidden by the law and then seek to prosecute them for doing so. The court held that that would be entrapment. That would be a misuse of state power, and an abuse of the process of the courts. The unattractive consequences, frightening and sinister in extreme cases, which state conduct of this nature could have are obvious. The role of the courts is to stand between the state and its citizens and make sure this does not happen. It was also stated in the judgment that entrapment is not a substantive defence in the sense of providing a ground upon which the accused is entitled to an acquittal. However, the court has jurisdiction in a case of entrapment to stay the prosecution on the ground that the integrity of the criminal justice system would be compromised by allowing the state to punish someone whom the state itself has caused to transgress. Where the court does find that there has been entrapment the question is not whether the proceedings would be a fair determination of guilt and therefore excluded under s. 78 of the 1984 Act but whether they should have been brought at all.

This is an area where the substantive criminal law overlaps with evidence and procedure. Evidential factors to consider in running an operation that involves forms of entrapment include:

- the nature of the offence, as some offences are difficult to detect otherwise. Therefore, the more difficult the offence is to detect without intrusive inducement from the police, the more such intrusion will be justifiable;
- what suspicion officers have that an offence of that kind would be committed in the locality, for example, the setting-up of a van containing cigarettes to see if someone took the opportunity to steal them (*Williams and O'Hare* v *DPP* [1993] 3 All ER 365). 'If the trick had been the individual enterprise of a policeman in an area where such crime was not suspected to be prevalent, it would have been an abuse of State power' (Lord Hoffmann in *Attorney-General's Reference (No. 3 of 2000)* [2001] UKHL 53).

The key question is whether the suspects voluntarily applied themselves to 'the trick' and that they were not enticed or provoked into committing a crime which they would otherwise not have committed.

Examples of cases where evidence was not excluded include *R* v *Breen* [2001] EWCA Crim 1213. In this case police officers had attended the suspect's address unannounced and asked for 'blow'. The suspect gave the police his mobile telephone number and they returned the following day and were supplied with £20 worth of cannabis resin. The officers were invited to return at any time and they were supplied with drugs on subsequent visits. The Court of Appeal held that the judge had been entitled to find that the undercover officers had done no more than give the appellants an opportunity to break the law, of which each of them freely took advantage.

In *R* v *Winter* [2007] EWCA Crim 3493 the defendant (W) had planned to kill his estranged wife. To carry out his plan, W solicited the help of a friend (M). M introduced W to a friend (T) with the intention that T drive W's car around areas with CCTV coverage to provide an alibi. T was in fact an undercover police officer. W was arrested in the living quarters of the public house where he had been hiding, and officers found a knife in his pocket. W argued that once the police became aware of his plan they should have arrested him immediately rather than embark upon further evidence-gathering by means of entrapment. The Court of Appeal held that police conduct that brought about state-created crime was not acceptable except where the individual concerned took the opportunity to break the law of his/her own free will. The court concluded that the jury were satisfied that W had formed the plan in advance of his encouraging M and T to join him but their presence had made the plan possible and did not amount to entrapment.

In *R* v *Jones* [2007] EWCA Crim 1118 the police had received reports of graffiti being written in black marker pen on the toilets of trains and stations seeking girls of 8–13 years old for sex, offering payment and leaving a contact number. Police began an undercover operation using an officer posing as a 12-year-old girl. The undercover officer exchanged several texts with the suspect which clarified her age and arrangements for a meeting; the defendant sent the officer further text messages of an explicit nature including various sexual acts that he expected he would be able to perform on her. The Court of Appeal held that the police did not incite or instigate a crime but merely provided the opportunity for the defendant to commit a similar offence and provide evidence for a conviction. The officer did no more than pretend to be a child of a particular age. The police did not behave improperly in choosing the age of 12. It was the defendant who had asked the officer for her age, and he therefore believed that he was inciting penetrative sexual activity with a child under 13.

2.7 Disclosure of Evidence

Criminal Procedure and Investigations Act 1996 and Code of Practice

> A thick grey line down the margin denotes text that is an extract of the Code itself (i.e. the actual wording of the legislation). This material is examinable for both Sergeants and Inspectors.

2.7.1 Introduction

Disclosure can be grouped under two main areas: the material the prosecution will use in court to prove the case against the defendant, and all other material not forming part of the prosecution case which might have a bearing on the decision the court makes.

The Criminal Procedure and Investigations Act 1996 (the 1996 Act) is made up of seven parts. It is the first two parts which are of interest to the police:

- part I sets out the procedures for disclosure and the effects of failing to comply with the Act; and
- part II sets out the duties of police officers in relation to the disclosure provisions.

The 1996 Act introduced a Code of Practice which sets out the manner in which police officers are to record, retain and reveal to the prosecutor material obtained in a criminal investigation and which may be relevant to the investigation, and related matters. The Code assumes that the defence have already been informed of the details of the prosecution case and is included within this chapter. In addition to the Code of Practice this chapter also makes reference to the Attorney-General's Guidelines on Disclosure for Investigators, Prosecutors and Defence Practitioners (referred to in this chapter as the A-G's Guidelines); as well as the CPS Disclosure Manual.

2.7.2 Failure to Comply

Compliance with the rules of disclosure, by both the defence and prosecution, is essential if the 1996 Act is to have any real value. First, in cases where the defence are obliged to make disclosure to the prosecution, failure to do so may lead to the court or jury drawing such inferences as appear proper in deciding the guilt or innocence of the accused (s. 11(5) of the 1996 Act). Should the prosecution fail to comply with their obligations then an accused does not have to make defence disclosure and no such inference can be made. Secondly, failure by the prosecution to comply with the rules could lead to the court staying the proceedings on the grounds that there has been an abuse of process (s. 10). It could also lead to an action for damages or such other relief as the court sees fit under the Human Rights Act 1998, particularly in relation to Article 6 of the European Convention on Human Rights and the right to a fair trial. Additionally, where the prosecution have not made disclosure on time or fully, a stay on the proceedings or a further adjournment is possible. Even if there has been a failure to comply with disclosure the case will not automatically be stayed and therefore any failings should be brought to the attention of the CPS so that the matter can be considered. In *R (On the Application of Ebrahim) v Feltham Magistrates' Court* [2001] EWHC Admin 130 the court stated that:

> It must be remembered that it is a commonplace in criminal trial for the defendant to rely on holes in the prosecution case. If in such a case, there is sufficient credible evidence, apart from the missing evidence, which, if believed, would justify safe conviction then the trial should proceed, leaving the defendant to seek to persuade the jury or magistrates not to convict because evidence that might otherwise have been available was not before the court through no fault of the defendant.

Further guidance was provided in *R v Brooks* [2004] EWCA Crim 3537, a case where the prosecution failed to comply with the disclosure requirements. The Court of Appeal held that if the court was satisfied that the prosecution had deliberately withheld evidence from the court or frustrated the defence, the court did have the power to stay the prosecution. If the court was not so satisfied it would consider whether, despite all that had gone wrong, a fair trial was possible.

Failure to disclose may result in convictions being overturned; for instance in *R v Poole* [2003] EWCA Crim 1753, the Court of Appeal overturned convictions for murder because the non-disclosure of prosecution evidence influenced the jury's assessment of the reliability of the evidence of a key eye-witness. In this case the witness gave an account that was false in a material particular. However, the police did not follow up those inconsistencies and they failed to inform the CPS that his evidence was unreliable.

The level of disclosure that is required will be a question of fact in each case. In *Filmer v DPP* [2006] EWHC 3450 (Admin) the court held that the extent of disclosure required from the prosecution depends on the evidence and issue in a particular case. The prosecution are required to provide sufficient disclosure to enable a defendant to present his/her case. The court went on to say that this has to be the approach otherwise the prosecution would have to second guess every question the defence may want to ask (this is where the defence disclosure becomes relevant, **see para. 2.7.11.1**).

2.7.3 Disclosing the Prosecution Case—Advanced Information

This refers to the material that the defence are entitled to have in order to consider whether to plead guilty or not guilty. In some cases, it is not a question of whether the defendant committed the crime but whether the prosecution are in a position to prove the offence and, in order to consider this, the defence are unlikely to agree to plead or decide on the mode of trial without knowing the strength of the prosecution case. It is clearly in the public interest that guilty pleas are entered or indicated as soon as possible (*R v Calderdale Magistrates' Court, ex parte Donahue* [2001] Crim LR 141) and often this cannot be achieved unless advanced information has been provided. The need to know as early as possible whether a defendant is going to plead not guilty can be particularly important as there are time limits by which the courts have to set trials and committals. Often these can be delayed because the prosecution have not complied with their disclosure duties.

Ensuring that all defendants receive copies of any advanced information (or any later disclosure) is also important. In *R v Tompkins* [2005] EWCA Crim 3035 the court held that where there has been non-disclosure at the time a plea had been entered, a defendant who had pleaded guilty should not in any way be in a worse position than a defendant who had pleaded not guilty.

2.7.3.1 Obligations on Prosecution Regarding Disclosing the Prosecution Case—Advanced Information

In the Magistrates' Court, part 10 of the Criminal Procedure Rules 2014 provides that where the offence is one that can be tried in a magistrates' court the prosecutor must provide initial details of the prosecution case to the court and the defendant at, or before, the beginning of the day of the first hearing. These initial details must include:

- a summary of the evidence on which that case will be based; or
- any statement, document or extract setting out facts or other matters on which that case will be based; or
- any combination of such a summary, statement, document or extract; and
- the defendant's previous convictions.

For trials at the Crown Court, the defence will receive the majority of the prosecution case through the disclosure of witness statements or depositions. If the prosecution wish to use any additional evidence after committal they must serve this on the defence.

It is suggested that Article 6 of the European Convention on Human Rights supports the need to provide advanced information to the defence and that this should be done as soon as possible. Article 6(3)(a) states that a person is:

...to be informed promptly...and in detail, of the nature and cause of the accusation against him;

Article 6(3)(b) states that an accused is entitled to:

...have adequate time...for the preparation of his defence.

The point concerning advanced information in summary cases was considered in *R v Stratford Justices, ex parte Imbert* [1999] 2 Cr App R 276, where the court gave its opinion that Article 6 does not give an absolute right to pre-trial disclosure; it will be a question of whether the defendant can have a fair trial. Clearly, it will be easier to satisfy this test where advanced information has been provided to the defence.

Advanced information might also include the following and so consideration should be had to providing this material to the prosecutor so that he/she can forward it to the defence where appropriate (ensuring that the addresses and other details of witnesses and victims are protected):

- a copy of the custody record;
- copies of any interview tape(s);
- a copy of any first descriptions where relevant;
- significant information that might affect a bail decision or enable the defence to contest the committal proceedings (A-G's Guidelines, para. 14);
- any material which is relevant to sentence (e.g. information which might mitigate the seriousness of the offence or assist the accused to lay blame in whole or in part upon a co-accused or another person);
- statements and/or a summary of the prosecution cases;
- a copy of any video evidence.

Where a person has made several statements but all the relevant evidence for the prosecution case is contained in one statement, it is only that one statement which needs to be disclosed. In order to comply with advanced information the defence need to be either given a copy of the document or allowed to inspect the document (or a copy of it). In *R v Lane and Lane* [2011] EWCA Crim 2745 one of the witnesses refused to put incriminating evidence into his statement due to fear of repercussions. The police had notified the prosecution of the witness's increased knowledge, but the prosecution failed to notify the defence that the statement had been a partial account. The Court of Appeal held that the statement was untruthful as it did not disclose all the information that it should have done. The witness should have been told to make a full statement or he should have been abandoned as a witness, but he should never have been allowed to make a partial statement.

2.7.4 Disclosure Code of Practice—1 Introduction

The following sections set out the Disclosure Code of Practice issued under the Criminal Procedure and Investigations Act 1996.

2.7.4.1 Disclosure Code of Practice —1 Introduction

1.1 This Code of Practice applies in respect of criminal investigations conducted by police officers which begin on or after the day on which this Code comes into effect. Persons other than police officers who are charged with the duty of conducting an investigation as defined in the Act are to have regard to the relevant provisions of the Code, and should take these into account in applying their own operating procedures.

1.2 This Code does not apply to persons who are not charged with the duty of conducting an investigation as defined in the Act.

1.3 Nothing in this Code applies to material intercepted in obedience to a warrant issued under section 2 of the Interception of Communications Act 1985 or section 5 of the Regulation of Investigatory Powers Act 2000, or to any copy of that material as defined in section 10 of the 1985 Act or section 15 of the 2000 Act.

1.4 This Code extends only to England and Wales.

2.7.4.2 KEYNOTE

Aims of the 1996 Act

The aim of the disclosure rules within the Criminal Procedure and Investigations Act 1996 is to make sure that a defendant gets a fair trial and speeds up the whole trial process. This was confirmed by *R* v *Stratford Justices, ex parte Imbert* [1999] 2 Cr App R 276, where the court said that the legislation was to try to ensure that nothing which might assist the defence was kept from the accused.

The Act creates an initial duty on the prosecution to disclose with a continuing duty to disclose until the accused is acquitted or convicted or the prosecutor decides not to proceed with the case.

The prosecution must, from the start, consider any material that might undermine the prosecution case or assist the defence (s. 3 of the 1996 Act). It is submitted that this requires the prosecution to consider in more detail the types of defence that might be used at trial. Once the prosecution have provided their initial disclosure the defence in some cases are obliged to provide a defence statement and in other cases this is optional (see para. 2.7.11.1). Once the defence have provided their defence statement it may provide greater focus to the prosecution as to what other unused material may need to be disclosed.

While the duty of disclosure is placed on the prosecutor, the police have a responsibility to assist in this process. It is therefore vital that police officers understand, not only the statutory requirements made of them, but also the extent of their role within the whole disclosure process.

2.7.5 Disclosure Code of Practice—2 Definitions

2.1 In this Code:
- *a criminal investigation* is an investigation conducted by police officers with a view to it being ascertained whether a person should be charged with an offence, or whether a person charged with an offence is guilty of it. This will include:
  - investigations into crimes that have been committed;
  - investigations whose purpose is to ascertain whether a crime has been committed, with a view to the possible institution of criminal proceedings; and
  - investigations which begin in the belief that a crime may be committed, for example when the police keep premises or individuals under observation for a period of time, with a view to the possible institution of criminal proceedings;

- charging a person with an offence includes prosecution by way of summons or postal requisition;
- *an investigator* is any police officer involved in the conduct of a criminal investigation. All investigators have a responsibility for carrying out the duties imposed on them under this Code, including in particular recording information, and retaining records of information and other material;
- the *officer in charge of an investigation* is the police officer responsible for directing a criminal investigation. He is also responsible for ensuring that proper procedures are in place for recording information, and retaining records of information and other material, in the investigation;
- the *disclosure officer* is the person responsible for examining material retained by the police during the investigation; revealing material to the prosecutor during the investigation and any criminal proceedings resulting from it, and certifying that he has done this; and disclosing material to the accused at the request of the prosecutor;
- the *prosecutor* is the authority responsible for the conduct, on behalf of the Crown, of criminal proceedings resulting from a specific criminal investigation;
- *material* is material of any kind, including information and objects, which is obtained in the course of a criminal investigation and which may be relevant to the investigation. This includes not only material coming into the possession of the investigator (such as documents seized in the course of searching premises) but also material generated by him (such as interview records);
- material may be *relevant to an investigation* if it appears to an investigator, or to the officer in charge of an investigation, or to the disclosure officer, that it has some bearing on any offence under investigation or any person being investigated, or on the surrounding circumstances of the case, unless it is incapable of having any impact on the case;
- *sensitive material* is material, the disclosure of which, the disclosure officer believes, would give rise to a real risk of serious prejudice to an important public interest;
- references to *prosecution disclosure* are to the duty of the prosecutor under sections 3 and 7A of the Act to disclose material which is in his possession or which he has inspected in pursuance of this Code, and which might reasonably be considered capable of undermining the case against the accused, or of assisting the case for the accused;
- references to the disclosure of material to a person accused of an offence include references to the disclosure of material to his legal representative;
- references to police officers and to the chief officer of police include those employed in a police force as defined in section 3(3) of the Prosecution of Offences Act 1985.

2.7.5.1   KEYNOTE

Criminal Investigation

Section 1 of the Criminal Procedure and Investigations Act 1996 defines in which type of cases the disclosure provisions apply. In reality, this applies to all cases other than those where the defendant pleads guilty at the magistrates' court. These rules only apply where no criminal investigation into the alleged offence took place before 1 April 1997. If an investigation began before 1 April 1997, then it will be necessary to refer to the common law rules; however, ACPO has stated that the 1996 Act should be followed in all cases when considering disclosure. For those investigations that started after 4 April 2005, the amendments introduced by the Criminal Justice Act 2003 will apply.

Some guidance is given by the case of *R* v *Uxbridge Magistrates' Court, ex parte Patel* (2000) 164 JP 209, as to the time an investigation begins. There it was said that the phrase 'criminal investigation' in s. 1(3) of the 1996 Act means that a criminal investigation could begin into an offence before it was committed. This could be so in a surveillance case or where a series of offences was committed, some before and some after the appointed day. Whether in any given case that was the correct view would be a question of fact for the court to determine.

Section 1 also defines a criminal investigation and states:

(4) For the purposes of this section a criminal investigation is an investigation which police officers or other persons have a duty to conduct with a view to it being ascertained—
   (a) whether a person should be charged with an offence, or
   (b) whether a person charged with an offence is guilty of it.

Consequently, this part of the Act also applies to other people, besides the police, who carry out investigations where they have a duty to ascertain whether criminal offences have been committed (e.g. National Crime Agency, HM Revenue and Customs, Department of Work and Pensions investigators). It does not apply to those whose primary responsibility does not relate to criminal offences (e.g. local authorities and schools).

2.7.5.2   KEYNOTE

Disclosure Officer

If not appointed at the start of an investigation, a disclosure officer must be appointed in sufficient time to be able to prepare the unused material schedules for inclusion in the full file submitted to the CPS (Disclosure Manual, para. 3.11).

2.7.5.3   KEYNOTE

Prosecutor

This role is defined by s. 2(3) of the 1996 Act as being 'any person acting as prosecutor whether an individual or a body'. In other words, the person who will be taking the case to court. On most occasions, this will be the CPS. It would also apply to the Serious Fraud Office or the Data Protection Registrar. In the case of private prosecutions, the prosecutor is obliged to comply with the disclosure provisions of the 1996 Act but does not have to comply with the Code of Practice. The prosecutor is responsible for ensuring that initial disclosure is made to the defence as well as any further disclosure as required under the continuing duty to disclose. The prosecutor should also be available to advise the OIC, disclosure officer and investigators on matters relating to the relevance of material recorded and retained by police, sensitive material and any other disclosure issues that might arise.

Should there need to be an application to the court to withhold material because of public interest (**see para. 2.7.9.3**), this will be done through the prosecutor.

A more detailed explanation of the roles and responsibilities of the prosecutor are set out in the CPS Disclosure Manual.

2.7.5.4   KEYNOTE

Relevant Material

The material will be *relevant* whether or not it is beneficial to the prosecution case, weakens the prosecution case or assists the defence case. It is not only material that will become 'evidence' in the case that should be considered; any information, record or thing which may have a bearing on the case can be material for the purposes of disclosure. The way in which evidence has been obtained may in itself be relevant.

What is relevant to the offence is once again a question of fact, and will not include everything. In *DPP* v *Metten* (1999) 22 January, unreported, it was claimed that the constables who had arrested the defendant had known the identities of potential witnesses to the arrest and these had not been disclosed. The court said that this was not relevant to the case as it did not fall within the definition of an investigation in s. 2(1) of the 1996 Act in that it concerned the time of arrest, and not what happened at the time the *offence* was committed. Paragraphs 5.4 and 5.5 of the Code give guidance on items that might be considered to be relevant material in a case.

Relevant material may relate to the credibility of witnesses, such as previous convictions, the fact that they have a grudge against the defendant or even the weather conditions for the day if relevant to the issue of identification. It may include information that house-to-house inquiries were made and that no one witnessed anything.

Particularly at the early stages of an investigation (sometimes not until the defence statement is provided outlining the defence case), it may not be possible to know whether material is relevant. If in doubt, it should be recorded and placed on the schedule of undisclosed material. Throughout the case, investigators and all others involved should continually review the material in the light of the investigation.

2.7.6 Disclosure Code of Practice—3 General Responsibilities

3.1 The functions of the investigator, the officer in charge of an investigation and the disclosure officer are separate. Whether they are undertaken by one, two or more persons will depend on the complexity of the case and the administrative arrangements within each police force. Where they are undertaken by more than one person, close consultation between them is essential to the effective performance of the duties imposed by this Code.

3.2 In any criminal investigation, one or more deputy disclosure officers may be appointed to assist the disclosure officer, and a deputy disclosure officer may perform any function of a disclosure officer as defined in paragraph 2.1.

3.3 The chief officer of police for each police force is responsible for putting in place arrangements to ensure that in every investigation the identity of the officer in charge of an investigation and the disclosure officer is recorded. The chief officer of police for each police force shall ensure that disclosure officers and deputy disclosure officers have sufficient skills and authority, commensurate with the complexity of the investigation, to discharge their functions effectively. An individual must not be appointed as disclosure officer, or continue in that role, if that is likely to result in a conflict of interest, for instance, if the disclosure officer is the victim of the alleged crime which is the subject of the investigation. The advice of a more senior officer must always be sought if there is doubt as to whether a conflict of interest precludes an individual acting as disclosure officer. If thereafter the doubt remains, the advice of a prosecutor should be sought.

3.4 The officer in charge of an investigation may delegate tasks to another investigator, to civilians employed by the police force, or to other persons participating in the investigation under arrangements for joint investigations, but he remains responsible for ensuring that these have been carried out and for accounting for any general policies followed in the investigation. In particular, it is an essential part of his duties to ensure that all material which may be relevant to an investigation is retained, and either made available to the disclosure officer or (in exceptional circumstances) revealed directly to the prosecutor.

3.5 In conducting an investigation, the investigator should pursue all reasonable lines of inquiry, whether these point towards or away from the suspect. What is reasonable in each case will depend on the particular circumstances. For example, where material is held on computer, it is a matter for the investigator to decide which material on the computer it is reasonable to inquire into, and in what manner.

3.6 If the officer in charge of an investigation believes that other persons may be in possession of material that may be relevant to the investigation, and if this has not been obtained under paragraph 3.5 above, he should ask the disclosure officer to inform them of the existence of the investigation and to invite them to retain the material in case they receive a request for its disclosure. The disclosure officer should inform the prosecutor that they may have such material. However, the officer in charge of an investigation is not required to make speculative enquiries of other persons; there must be some reason to believe that they may have relevant material. That reason may come from information provided to the police by the accused or from other inquiries made or from some other source.

3.7   If, during a criminal investigation, the officer in charge of an investigation or disclosure officer for any reason no longer has responsibility for the functions falling to him, either his supervisor or the police officer in charge of criminal investigations for the police force concerned must assign someone else to assume that responsibility. That person's identity must be recorded, as with those initially responsible for these functions in each investigation.

2.7.6.1   **KEYNOTE**

General Responsibility of the Disclosure Officer

The disclosure officer creates the link between the investigation team and the prosecutor (CPS) and is therefore very important to the disclosure process. For investigations carried out by the police, generally speaking there is no restriction on who performs this role; however, they must be suitably trained and experienced. The role and responsibility of the disclosure officer is set out in the Disclosure Manual at para. 3.9:

- examine, inspect, view or listen to all relevant material that has been retained by the investigator and that does not form part of the prosecution case
- examine, inspect, view or listen to all relevant material that has been retained by the investigator and that does not form part of the prosecution case
- create schedules that fully describe the material
- identify all material which satisfies the disclosure test using the MG6E
- submit the schedules and copies of disclosable material to the prosecutor
- at the same time, supply to the prosecutor a copy of material falling into any of the categories described in paragraph 7.3 of the Code and copies of all documents required to be routinely revealed and which have not previously been revealed to the prosecutor
- consult with and allow the prosecutor to inspect the retained material
- review the schedules and the retained material continually, particularly after the defence statement has been received, identify to the prosecutor material that satisfies the disclosure test using the MG6E and supply a copy of any such material not already provided
- schedule and reveal to the prosecutor any relevant additional unused material pursuant to the continuing duty of disclosure
- certify that all retained material has been revealed to the prosecutor in accordance with the Code
- where the prosecutor requests the disclosure officer to disclose any material to the accused, give the accused a copy of the material or allow the accused to inspect it.

2.7.6.2   **KEYNOTE**

Reasonable Lines of Inquiry

An officer who is classed as an investigator must pursue all reasonable lines of inquiry (Code, para. 3.5) and having done so retain all material which is relevant to the case (see para. 2.7.8.1), whether or not it is helpful to the prosecution (Code, para. 5.1). Failure to do so could lead to a miscarriage of justice. In *R* v *Poole* [2003] EWCA Crim 1753, Y provided a statement to police in a murder case. It transpired that N had been with Y at the relevant time and this cast doubt over Y's evidence. The police did not follow up the inconsistencies. The Court of Appeal held that the failure to disclose N's evidence was a material irregularity which in part led to a successful appeal by the defendant. The investigator also has a responsibility to identify material that could be sensitive and bring this to the attention of the CPS. This need to be proactive was reinforced in *R* v *Joof* [2012] EWCA Crim 1475 where the court held that the responsibilities imposed by the Criminal Procedure and Investigations Act 1996 and the A-G's Guidelines could not be circumvented by not making inquiries. An officer who believed that a person might have information which might undermine the prosecution case or assist the defence could not decline to make inquiries in order to avoid the need to disclose what might be said. Where material is identified steps must be taken to record and retain the material. For information recorded on computers, see chapter 30 of the Disclosure Manual and the Annex to the A-G's Guidelines.

2.7.6.3   **KEYNOTE**

Material that Undermines the Prosecution Case

There is only limited case law in this area but it is likely that such material will consist mainly of material which raises question marks over the strength of the prosecution case, the value of evidence given by witnesses and issues relating to identification. If officers feel that the material is not relevant to the prosecution case but may be useful to the defence in cross-examination, it may well come within the category of material which undermines the prosecution case. In *Tucker* v *CPS* [2008] EWCA Crim 3063, the prosecution did not reveal to the defence a record containing important information as to a possible motive for a witness lying about the defendant's involvement in the offence. This led to the conviction being overturned. It was clearly material that undermined the prosecution case as it raised questions over the value of the witness's evidence.

Disclosure of previous convictions and other matters that might affect the credibility of a witness may 'undermine the prosecution case' as it may limit the value of the witness's testimony. This factor may not be apparent at the time but may come to light after the initial disclosure, such as where it becomes known that the witness has a grudge against the defendant. This is one reason why the 1996 Act requires the decision as to whether material undermines the prosecution case to be continuously monitored throughout the case.

In *R (On the Application of Ebrahim)* v *Feltham Magistrates' Court* [2001] EWHC Admin 130 the court stated that the extent of the investigation should be proportionate to the seriousness of the matter being investigated. What is reasonable in a case may well depend on such factors as the staff and resources available, the seriousness of the case, the strength of evidence against the suspect and the nature of the line of inquiry to be pursued. If in doubt it is suggested that the CPS is contacted for guidance.

Paragraph 5.16 of the Disclosure Manual makes important observations concerning negative results: when making inquiries, 'negative results can sometimes be as significant to an investigation as positive ones'. It is impossible to define precisely when a negative result may be significant, as every case is different. However, it will include the result of any inquiry that differs from what might be expected, given the prevailing circumstances. Not only must material or information which points towards a fact or an individual be retained, but also that which casts doubt on the suspect's guilt, or implicates another person. Examples of negative information include:

- a CCTV camera that did not record the crime/location/suspect in a manner which is consistent with the prosecution case (the fact that a CCTV camera did not function or have videotape loaded will not usually be considered relevant negative information);
- where a number of people present at a particular location at the particular time that an offence is alleged to have taken place state that they saw nothing unusual;
- where a finger-mark from a crime scene cannot be identified as belonging to a known suspect;
- any other failure to match a crime scene sample with one taken from the accused.

2.7.6.4   **KEYNOTE**

Complaints against Police Officers Involved in a Case

Not only might the credibility of witnesses undermine the prosecution case, but so too might complaints against officers involved in the case, together with any occasions where officers have not been believed in court in the past. In these cases, it will be necessary to decide whether this information should be disclosed to the defence and, if disclosed, in how much detail. This question is probably best answered by the following extract from advice given to prosecutors by the DPP:

> It is, of course, necessary in the first instance for the police to bring such matters to the notice of the prosecutor, but it is submitted that the prosecutor should have a greater element of discretion than with the disclosure of previous convictions. With convictions against prosecution witnesses, disclosure normally follows, whereas in relation to disciplinary findings regard should be had to the nature of the finding and its likely relevance to the matters in issue. Findings which involve some element of dishonesty should invariably be disclosed, while matters such as disobedience to orders, neglect of duty and discreditable conduct will often have no relevance to the officer's veracity or the guilt or otherwise of a defendant. Certainly, there should be no duty on the prosecution to disclose details of unsubstantiated complaints even though this is a popular type of inquiry from some defence representatives. The imposition of such a duty would only encourage the making of false complaints in the hope that they might be used to discredit an officer in the future.

Whether a misconduct finding should be disclosed is a value judgement. The responsibility for that value judgement sits with Professional Standards Departments (PSDs), although the final responsibility to reveal relevant misconduct findings or criminal convictions/cautions rests with the police officer concerned, who will be aware of the issues in the case in which he/she is a witness. PSDs must seek to achieve consistency and balance in the exercise of their responsibility to provide advice and guidance to police officers in these matters. PSDs should always be ready to seek the advice of the CPS in appropriate cases (Disclosure Manual, paras 18.6 and 18.17).

Some guidance is given by the courts. In *R* v *Edwards* [1991] 1 WLR 207 the court held that a disciplinary finding and reprimand of a DCI for countersigning interview notes which had been wrongly re-written in another case should have been disclosed to the defence. *R* v *Guney* [1998] 2 Cr App R 242 followed *Edwards*. In *Guney* six police officers went to the defendant's home with a warrant to search for drugs. Three of the officers had formerly been members of a squad which had been subject to 'considerable internal police interest'. The court held that the defence were not entitled to be informed of every occasion when any officer had given evidence 'unsuccessfully' or whenever allegations were made against him/her. In this case, the information should have been disclosed. The court went on to say that the records available to the CPS should include transcripts of any decisions of the Court of Appeal Criminal Division where convictions were quashed because of the misconduct or lack of veracity of identified police officers as well as cases stopped by the trial judge or discontinued on the same basis. The systematic collection of such material was preferable to the existing haphazard arrangement.

If in doubt advice should be sought from the CPS.

2.7.6.5 **KEYNOTE**

Third Party Material

Third party material can be considered in two categories:

(a) that which is or has been in the possession of the police or which has been inspected by the police;
(b) all other material not falling under (a).

Material which falls into the first category is covered by the same rules of disclosure as any other material the police have. Where police do not have material that they believe may be relevant to the case, para. 3.6 of the Code provides direction.

In the vast majority of cases the third party will make the material available to the investigating officer. However, there may be occasions where the third party refuses to hand over the material and/or allow it to be examined.

If the OIC, the investigator or the disclosure officer believes that a third party holds material that may be relevant to the investigation, that person or body should be told of the investigation. They should be alerted to the need to preserve relevant material. Consideration should be given as to whether it is appropriate to seek access to the material and, if so, steps should be taken to obtain such material. It will be important to do so if the material or information is likely to undermine the prosecution case, or to assist a known defence. A letter should be sent to the third party together with the explanatory leaflet, specimens of which are provided in the Disclosure Manual at Annex B.

Where access to the material is declined or refused by the third party and it is believed that it is reasonable to seek production of the material before a suspect is charged, the investigator should consider making an application under sch. 1 to the Police and Criminal Evidence Act 1984 (special procedure material).

Where the suspect has been charged and the third party refuses to produce the material, application will have to be made to the court for a witness summons. In the magistrates' court this is covered by s. 97 of the Magistrates' Courts Act 1980 and in the Crown Court it is covered by ss. 2(2) and 2A to 2D of the Criminal Procedure (Attendance of Witnesses) Act 1965. The third party may still wish to resist the requirement to produce the material and the point was considered in *R* v *Brushett* [2001] Crim LR 471 (this was a case that concerned Social Services Department files relating to a children's home). The court considered a number of earlier cases and established some central principles as follows:

- To be material evidence documents must be not only relevant to the issues arising in the criminal proceedings, but also documents admissible as such in evidence.
- Documents which are desired merely for the purpose of possible cross-examination are not admissible in evidence and, thus, are not material for the purposes of s. 97.
- Whoever seeks production of documents must satisfy the justices with some evidence that the documents are 'likely to be material' in the sense indicated, likelihood for this purpose involving a real possibility, although not necessarily a probability.
- It is not sufficient that the applicant merely wants to find out whether or not the third party has such material documents. This procedure must not be used as a disguised attempt to obtain discovery.
- Where social services documents are supplied to the prosecution, the prosecution should retain control of such material as part of the disclosure regime. That is envisaged by the rules. It cannot be acceptable to return material to social services to avoid the obligations arising under the rules. In any event, the obligation would arise in relation to the notes taken and retained.
- The obligation laid on the prosecution by statute and rules cannot be avoided by a third party making an agreement with the prosecution that the prosecution will abrogate any duties laid upon it by either common law or statute.
- If circumstances arise where it would be unjust not to allow disclosure of certain other material, so a defendant would not receive a fair trial in the sense that he/she could not establish his innocence where he/she might otherwise do so, then that material must be disclosed.
- The fact that the prosecution have knowledge of the third party material may be a relevant factor to allow the defence access.
- Material concerning false allegations in the past may be relevant material (*R* v *Bourimech* [2002] FWCA Crim 2089).
- If the disputed material might prove the defendant's innocence or avoid a miscarriage of justice, the weight came down resoundingly in favour of disclosing it (*R* v *Reading Justices, ex parte Berkshire County Council* (1996) 1 Cr App R 239).

In *R* v *Alibhai* [2004] EWCA Crim 681 the Court of Appeal held that under the Criminal Procedure and Investigations Act 1996 the prosecutor was only under a duty to disclose material in the hands of third parties if that material had come into the prosecutor's hands and the prosecutor was of the opinion that such material undermined the case. However, the A-G's Guidelines went further by requiring a prosecutor to take steps pursuing third party disclosure if there was a suspicion that documents would be detrimental to the prosecution or of assistance to the defence. However, in such circumstances, the prosecutor enjoyed a margin of consideration as to what steps were appropriate. The provisions for disclosure are not intended to create duties for third parties to follow. The disclosure duties under the 1996 Act were created in respect of material that the prosecution or the police had and which the prosecution had inspected. Material was not prosecution material unless it was held by the investigator or by the disclosure officer (*DPP* v *Wood and McGillicuddy* [2006] EWHC 32 (Admin)).

The A-G's Guidelines also deal with materials held by third parties (including government agencies) in paras 53 to 58. Paragraphs 53 to 55 deal with material held by government departments or other Crown bodies and suggest that reasonable steps should be taken to identify and consider material that may be relevant to an issue in the case. Paragraph 56 examines the circumstances in which the prosecution should take steps to obtain access to material or information in the possession of other third parties. In such cases, consideration should be given to take steps to obtain such material or information. It will be important to do so if the material or information is likely to undermine the prosecution case, or assist a known defence. Paragraph 57 deals with the situation where the police or prosecutor meet with a refusal by the third party to supply such material or information. If, despite the reasons put forward for refusal by the third party, it still appears reasonable to seek its production, a witness summons requiring the third party to produce the material should be applied for (such an application can also be made by the defence). The third party can then argue at court that it is not material, or that it should not be disclosed on grounds of public interest immunity.

2.7.7 Disclosure Code of Practice—4 Recording of Information

4.1 If material which may be relevant to the investigation consists of information which is not recorded in any form, the officer in charge of an investigation must ensure that it is recorded in a durable or retrievable form (whether in writing, on video or audio tape, or on computer disk).

4.2 Where it is not practicable to retain the initial record of information because it forms part of a larger record which is to be destroyed, its contents should be transferred as a true record to a durable and more easily-stored form before that happens.

4.3 Negative information is often relevant to an investigation. If it may be relevant it must be recorded. An example might be a number of people present in a particular place at a particular time who state that they saw nothing unusual.

4.4 Where information which may be relevant is obtained, it must be recorded at the time it is obtained or as soon as practicable after that time. This includes, for example, information obtained in house-to-house enquiries, although the requirement to record information promptly does not require an investigator to take a statement from a potential witness where it would not otherwise be taken.

2.7.7.1 KEYNOTE

Contemporaneous Records

The need for contemporaneous records is also required under the Police and Criminal Evidence Act 1984 and if not complied with could affect the admissibility of important evidence (s. 78 of the 1984 Act).

2.7.8 Disclosure Code of Practice—5 Retention of Material

(a) Duty to retain material

5.1 The investigator must retain material obtained in a criminal investigation which may be relevant to the investigation. Material may be photographed, video-recorded, captured digitally or otherwise retained in the form of a copy rather than the original at any time, if the original is perishable; the original was supplied to the investigator rather than generated by him and is to be returned to its owner; or the retention of a copy rather than the original is reasonable in all the circumstances.

5.2 Where material has been seized in the exercise of the powers of seizure conferred by the Police and Criminal Evidence Act 1984, the duty to retain it under this Code is subject to the provisions on the retention of seized material in section 22 of that Act.

5.3 If the officer in charge of an investigation becomes aware as a result of developments in the case that material previously examined but not retained (because it was not thought to be relevant) may now be relevant to the investigation, he should, wherever practicable, take steps to obtain it or ensure that it is retained for further inspection or for production in court if required.

5.4 The duty to retain material includes in particular the duty to retain material falling into the following categories, where it may be relevant to the investigation:

- crime reports (including crime report forms, relevant parts of incident report books or police officer's notebooks);
- custody records;
- records which are derived from tapes of telephone messages (for example, 999 calls) containing descriptions of an alleged offence or offender;
- final versions of witness statements (and draft versions where their content differs from the final version), including any exhibits mentioned (unless these have been returned to their owner on the understanding that they will be produced in court if required);
- interview records (written records, or audio or video tapes, of interviews with actual or potential witnesses or suspects);
- communications between the police and experts such as forensic scientists, reports of work carried out by experts, and schedules of scientific material prepared by the expert for the investigator, for the purposes of criminal proceedings;
- records of the first description of a suspect by each potential witness who purports to identify or describe the suspect, whether or not the description differs from that of subsequent descriptions by that or other witnesses;
- any material casting doubt on the reliability of a witness.

5.5 The duty to retain material, where it may be relevant to the investigation, also includes in particular the duty to retain material which may satisfy the test for prosecution disclosure in the Act, such as:

- information provided by an accused person which indicates an explanation for the offence with which he has been charged;
- any material casting doubt on the reliability of a confession;
- any material casting doubt on the reliability of a prosecution witness.

5.6 The duty to retain material falling into these categories does not extend to items which are purely ancillary to such material and possess no independent significance (for example, duplicate copies of records or reports).

(b) Length of time for which material is to be retained

5.7 All material which may be relevant to the investigation must be retained until a decision is taken whether to institute proceedings against a person for an offence.

5.8 If a criminal investigation results in proceedings being instituted, all material which may be relevant must be retained at least until the accused is acquitted or convicted or the prosecutor decides not to proceed with the case.

5.9 Where the accused is convicted, all material which may be relevant must be retained at least until:

- the convicted person is released from custody, or discharged from hospital, in cases where the court imposes a custodial sentence or a hospital order;
- six months from the date of conviction, in all other cases.

If the court imposes a custodial sentence or hospital order and the convicted person is released from custody or discharged from hospital earlier than six months from the date of conviction, all material which may be relevant must be retained at least until six months from the date of conviction.

5.10 If an appeal against conviction is in progress when the release or discharge occurs, or at the end of the period of six months specified in paragraph 5.9, all material which may be relevant must be retained until the appeal is determined. Similarly, if the Criminal Cases Review Commission is considering an application at that point in time, all material which may be relevant must be retained at least until the Commission decides not to refer the case to the Court.

2.7.8.1   KEYNOTE

Retention of Material

In order to disclose material to the defence, there is a need first to find it and secondly retain it. Retention of material applies to documents and other evidence, including videos. Failure to retain material could lead to the prosecution losing the case, particularly where the court considers that its absence will lead to the defendant not being able to receive a fair trial (Article 6 of the European Convention on Human Rights). In *Mouat* v *DPP* [2001] EWHC Admin 130 the defendant had been charged with speeding. Police officers had recorded a video of the defendant driving at speed and had shown the video to the defendant prior to charge but had later recorded over it. The defendant contended that he had been intimidated by the unmarked police car being driven only inches from his rear bumper. The policy of the force was to keep videos for 28 days, unless they recorded an offence, in which case they were kept for 12 months. The court held that the police were under a duty to retain the video tapes at least until the end of the suspended enforcement period, during which time the defendant was entitled to consider whether he wished to contest his liability in court.

In deciding what material should be retained in an investigation, consideration should be given to any force orders, what powers there are to seize and retain the said material, as well as the Disclosure Code and the A-G's Guidelines. Where an investigator discovers material that is relevant to the case, he/she must record that information or retain the material (Code, para. 5.1).

When deciding if the material should be retained the A-G's Guidelines provide that: 'investigators should always err on the side of recording and retaining material where they have any doubt as to whether it may be relevant' (A-G's Guidelines, para. 25).

It is important to note that the material itself does not have to be admissible in court for it to undermine the prosecution case. This point was made in *R* v *Preston* [1994] 2 AC 130, where it was said that:

In the first place, the fact that an item of information cannot be put in evidence by a party does not mean that it is worthless. Often, the train of inquiry which leads to the discovery of evidence which is admissible at a trial may include an item which is not admissible, and this may apply, although less frequently, to the defence as well as the prosecution.

If, during the lifetime of a case, the OIC becomes aware that material which has been examined during the course of an investigation, but not retained, becomes relevant as a result of new developments, para. 5.3 of the Code will apply. That officer should take steps to recover the material wherever practicable, or ensure that it is preserved by the person in possession of it (Disclosure Manual, para. 5.25).

In some of these cases the investigation may well have started some time before the defendant became a suspect. In such cases all the material from the investigation/operation would have to be reviewed to see if it is relevant to the defence case. In cases where there is a surveillance operation or observation point, it may be that the details of the observation point and the surveillance techniques would not be revealed but it would be necessary to retain material generating from it (see para. 2.7.9.3).

KEYNOTE

CCTV

The likelihood of an incident being caught on CCTV can be quite strong, which raises the question as to the responsibility of the police to investigate the possibility of there being a recording and retaining the recording tape. This point was considered in *R (On the Application of Ebrahim)* v *Feltham Magistrates' Court* [2001] EWHC Admin 130. These cases related to the obliteration of video evidence. In coming to its judgment, the court considered a number of previous decisions where the police were not required to retain CCTV evidence. The general question for the court was whether the prosecution had been under a duty to obtain or retain video evidence. If there was no such duty, the prosecution could not have abused the process of the court simply because the material was no longer available, i.e. it was a reasonable line of inquiry (as to whether they were under a duty to obtain the evidence, **see para. 2.7.6.2**). *Ebrahim* shows that CCTV footage does not necessarily have to be retained in all cases. *R* v *Dobson* [2001] EWCA Crim 1606 followed *Ebrahim*. Dobson had been convicted of arson with intent to endanger life, his defence being that he was elsewhere at the time. There had been a strong possibility that the route that Dobson claimed to have taken would have been covered by CCTV but it would have depended on which side of the road he had been using and which way the cameras were pointing at the time. Dobson's solicitors had not asked for the tapes to be preserved at interview and the police confirmed that the possibility of investigating the tapes had been overlooked. The tapes had been overwritten after 31 days. In following the principles set down in *Ebrahim*, the police, by their own admissions, had failed in their duty to obtain and retain the relevant footage. While there was plainly a degree of prejudice in Dobson being deprived of the opportunity of checking the footage in the hope that it supported his case, that prejudice was held not to have seriously prejudiced his case given the uncertainty of the likelihood that it would assist and the fact that Dobson had equally been in a position to appreciate the possible existence and significance of the tapes. The fact that there was no suggestion of malice or intentional omission by the police was also an important consideration for the court.

2.7.9 Disclosure Code of Practice—6 Preparation of Material for Prosecutor

(a) Introduction

6.1 The officer in charge of the investigation, the disclosure officer or an investigator may seek advice from the prosecutor about whether any particular item of material may be relevant to the investigation.

6.2 Material which may be relevant to an investigation, which has been retained in accordance with this code, and which the disclosure officer believes will not form part of the prosecution case, must be listed on a schedule. This process will differ depending on whether the case is likely to be heard in the magistrates' court or the Crown Court.

(b) Magistrates Court

Anticipated Guilty pleas

6.3 If the accused is charged with a summary offence or an either-way offence that is likely to remain in the magistrates' court, and it is considered that he is likely to plead guilty (e.g. because he has admitted the offence), a schedule or streamlined disclosure certificate is not required. However, the Common Law duty to disclose material which may assist the defence at bail hearings or in the early preparation of their case remains, and where there is such material the certification on the Police Report (MG5/SDF) must be completed. Where there is no such material, a certificate to that effect must be completed in like form to that attached at the Annex [of the Codes].

6.4 If, contrary to the expectation of a guilty plea being entered, the accused pleads not guilty at the first hearing, the disclosure officer must ensure that the streamlined disclosure certificate is prepared and submitted as soon as is reasonably practicable after that happens.

Anticipated Not Guilty pleas

6.5 If the accused is charged with a summary offence or an either-way offence that is likely to remain in the magistrates' court, and it is considered that he is likely to plead not guilty, a streamlined disclosure certificate must be completed in like form to that attached at the Annex.

Material which may assist the defence

6.6 In every case, irrespective of the anticipated plea, if there is material known to the disclosure officer that might assist the defence with the early preparation of their case or at a bail hearing (e.g. a key prosecution witness has relevant previous convictions or a witness has withdrawn his or her statement), a note must be made on the MG5 (or other format agreed under the National File Standards). The material must be disclosed to the prosecutor who will disclose it to the defence if he thinks it meets this Common Law test.

No undermining or assisting material and sensitive material – magistrates' court cases

6.7 If there is no material which might fall to be disclosed as undermining the prosecution case or assisting the defence, the officer should complete the appropriate entry on the streamlined disclosure certificate. If there is any sensitive unused material the officer should complete a sensitive material schedule (MG6D or similar) and attach it to the prosecution file. In exceptional circumstances, when its existence is so sensitive that it cannot be listed, it should be revealed to the prosecutor separately.

(c) Crown Court

6.8 For cases to be held in the Crown Court, the unused material schedules (MG6 series) are used.

6.9 The disclosure officer must ensure that a schedule is prepared in the following circumstances:
- the accused is charged with an offence which is triable only on indictment;
- the accused is charged with an offence which is triable either way, and it is considered that the case is likely to be tried on indictment.

6.10 Material which the disclosure officer does not believe is sensitive must be listed on a schedule of non-sensitive material. The schedule must include a statement that the disclosure officer does not believe the material is sensitive.

Way in which material is to be listed on schedule

6.11 For indictable only cases or either-way cases sent to the Crown Court, schedules MG6C, D and E should be completed to facilitate service of the MG6C with the prosecution case, wherever possible. The disclosure officer should ensure that each item of material is listed separately on the schedule, and is numbered consecutively. The description of each item should make clear the nature of the item and should contain sufficient detail to enable the prosecutor to decide whether he needs to inspect the material before deciding whether or not it should be disclosed.

6.12 In some enquiries it may not be practicable to list each item of material separately. For example, there may be many items of a similar or repetitive nature. These may be listed in a block and described by quantity and generic title.

6.13 Even if some material is listed in a block, the disclosure officer must ensure that any items among that material which might satisfy the test for prosecution disclosure are listed and described individually.

(d) Sensitive material – Crown Court

6.14 Any material which is believed to be sensitive either must be listed on a schedule of sensitive material or, in exceptional circumstance

2.7.9.1

KEYNOTE

Initial Disclosure

Under s. 3 of the 1996 Act, all previously undisclosed material that might undermine the prosecution case must be disclosed to the defence. If there is no such material, then the accused must be given a written statement to that effect. This applies to all material in possession of the police or that has been inspected under the provisions of the Disclosure Code of Practice. This therefore requires the disclosure officer to know what material exists and what material has already been made available to the defence.

In magistrates' courts there is now a streamlined procedure in summary cases that are expected to end in a guilty plea, so that a schedule of unused material need not be served in such cases, but that the prosecution should perform its obligations at common law (as set out in *R* v *DPP ex parte Lee*, see **2.7.10.2**) and provide written confirmation that it has been done.

The prosecution only have to disclose material relevant to the prosecution in question. For instance, surveillance logs concerning another matter would not need to be disclosed (*R* v *Dennis* (2000) 13 April, unreported). It is up to the prosecutor to decide on the format in which material is disclosed to the accused. If material is to be copied, s. 3(3) of the 1996 Act leaves open the question of whether this should be done by the prosecutor or by the police. The prosecutor must also provide the defence with a schedule of all non-sensitive material (s. 4(2) of the 1996 Act). This includes all other information in police possession, or material that has been examined by the police other than 'sensitive material' (this is disclosed to the prosecutor separately). 'Sensitive material' is material which it is not in the public interest to disclose. At this stage, the defence are not entitled to inspect items on the schedule that have not been disclosed (s. 3(6) and (7)).

Material must not be disclosed to the extent that the court concludes that it is not in the public interest to disclose it and orders accordingly or it is material whose disclosure is prohibited by s. 17 of the Regulation of Investigatory Powers Act 2000 unless it falls within the exception provided by s. 18 of the Act.

KEYNOTE

Completing the Schedules

It is important that the schedules themselves are completed fully. Guidance is given by paras 6.9 to 6.11 of the Code and in detail in the Disclosure Manual, chapters 6 to 8. While items should be listed separately, there may be occasions where items are similar or the same, in which case these may be listed together (Disclosure Manual, para. 7.4). This also applies to sensitive schedules, in so far as is possible without compromising the confidentiality of the information (see also the Disclosure Manual, para. 7.4). Paragraph 21 and the Annex to the A-G's Guidelines also allows in some circumstances, because of the large volumes of material, not to examine all the material.

The following items should also be considered when deciding on initial disclosure in cases where the disclosure is in the public interest (that is where they are not *'sensitive material'*):

- records of previous convictions and cautions for prosecution witnesses;
- any other information which casts doubt on the reliability of a prosecution witness or on the accuracy of any prosecution evidence;
- any motives for the making of false allegations by a prosecution witness;
- any material which may have a bearing on the admissibility of any prosecution evidence;
- the fact that a witness has sought, been offered or received a reward;
- any material that might go to the credibility of a prosecution witness;
- any information which may cast doubt on the reliability of a confession. Any item which relates to the accused's mental or physical health, his intellectual capacity, or to any ill-treatment which the accused may have suffered when in the investigator's custody is likely to have the potential for casting doubt on the reliability of a purported confession;
- information that a person other than the accused was or might have been responsible or which points to another person whether charged or not (including a co-accused) having involvement in the commission of the offence (Disclosure Manual, para. 10.1).

The disclosure officer should be mindful of the need to demonstrate that he/she has taken all reasonable steps should it transpire that full disclosure had not been made.

It should be remembered that the prosecutor is required to advise the disclosure officer of any omissions or amendments or where there are insufficient or unclear descriptions, or where there has been a failure to provide schedules at all. The disclosure officer must then take all necessary remedial action and provide properly completed schedules to the prosecutor. Failure to do so may result in the matter being raised with a senior officer. There may also be occasions where schedules need to be edited; this is covered in the Disclosure Manual at paras 7.7 and 7.8. The responsibility to edit rests with the police but the prosecutor should be consulted where editing or separating is other than straightforward (para. 7.9).

KEYNOTE

Sensitive Material

This is material which the disclosure officer believes it is not in the public interest to disclose. While the general principle that governs the 1996 Act and Article 6 of the European Convention is that material should not be withheld from the defence, sensitive material is an exception to this. In *Van Mechelen* v *Netherlands* (1998) 25 EHRR 647, the court stated that in some cases it may be necessary to withhold certain evidence from the defence so as to preserve the fundamental rights of another individual or to safeguard an important public interest. However, only such measures restricting the rights of the defence which are strictly necessary are permissible under Article 6. It should be noted that the court did recognise that the entitlement of disclosure of relevant evidence was not an absolute right but could only be restricted as was strictly necessary. In *R* v *Keane* [1994] 1 WLR 746 Lord Taylor CJ stated that 'the judge should carry out a balancing exercise, having regard both to the weight of the public interest in non-disclosure and to the importance of the documents to the issues of interest, present and potential, to the defence, and if the disputed material might prove a defendant's innocence or avoid a miscarriage of justice, the balance came down resoundingly in favour of disclosure'.

Decisions as to what should be withheld from the defence are a matter for the court and, where necessary, an application to withhold the material must be made to the court (*R* v *Ward* [1993] 1 WLR 619). The application of public interest immunity was considered by the House of Lords in *R* v *H* [2004] UKHL 3. In this case, the defendants were charged with conspiracy to supply a Class A drug following a covert police investigation, and sought disclosure of material held by the prosecution relating to the investigation. The prosecution resisted the disclosure on grounds of public interest immunity. The court held that if the material did not weaken the prosecution case or strengthen the defence, there would be no requirement to disclose it. Once material is considered to be sensitive then it should be disclosed only if the public interest application fails (unless abandoning the case is considered more appropriate) or with the express written approval of the Treasury Solicitor (Disclosure Manual, chapters 33 to 34). Such material is not as wide as it seems; for instance it does not mean evidence which might harm the prosecution case. This category is limited and the Code of Practice, at para. 6.12, gives a number of examples of such material. It will be for the disclosure officer to decide what material, if any, falls into this category. Guidance is provided in chapters 13 and 18 of the Disclosure Manual.

Paragraph 6.12 of the Code provides examples of sensitive material. Many of these items are included within the common law principles of public interest immunity. The case law in this area will still apply to decisions regarding the disclosure of such material. These groups are not exclusive and the areas most likely to apply will be those concerning the protection of intelligence and intelligence methods. In any consideration as to what should be withheld, the provisions of part II of the Regulation of Investigatory Powers Act 2000 should be referred to. Part II of the Act will make provision, not only for the gathering and recording of intelligence, but also disclosure of any material gained and methods used. Claims to withhold material may be made by parties other than the prosecutor (who would do so on behalf of the police). In some cases, the relevant minister or the Attorney-General may intervene to claim immunity. Alternatively, the claim to immunity may be made by the party seeking to withhold the evidence, either on its own initiative or at the request of the relevant government department.

Guidance is also provided in para. 65 of the A-G's Guidelines: even where an application is made to the court to withhold material a prosecutor should aim to disclose as much of the material as he/she properly can (by giving the defence redacted or edited copies of summaries).

In deciding whether material attracts public interest immunity the court will have to be satisfied that the material in no way helps the defence or undermines the prosecution case. Where the material related to secret or confidential systems it should not be revealed as this would aid serious criminal enterprise in the future (*R* v *Templar* [2003] EWCA Crim 3186).

Where police consider that material should not be disclosed due to its sensitive nature, the Disclosure Manual should be followed. This is covered at paras 8.5 to 8.27. Some of the key points from these paragraphs include the following:

- Consultation should take place at a senior level, and a senior officer (who may be independent of the investigation) should be involved.
- The consultation should cover:
  - the reasons why the material is said to be sensitive;
  - the degree of sensitivity said to attach to the material, i.e. why it is considered that disclosure will create a real risk of serious prejudice to an important public interest;
  - the consequences of revealing to the defence:
    — the material itself,
    — the category of the material,
    — the fact that an application is being made;
  - the apparent significance of the material to the issues in the trial;
  - the involvement of any third parties in bringing the material to the attention of the police;

- where the material is likely to be the subject of an order for disclosure, what police views are regarding continuance of the prosecution.
- Any submission that is to be made to the court will be signed by the prosecutor, and by the senior officer, who will state that to the best of his/her knowledge and belief the assertions of fact on which the submission is based are correct. In applications for public interest immunity the CPS has an obligation to ensure that all such material is in its possession and the police have a duty to pass the material on (*R* v *Menga and Marshalleck* [1998] Crim LR 58).
- Whether it is possible to disclose the material without compromising its sensitivity.

Care must be taken to safeguard material that is sensitive and keep it separate from other material because if the material subject to a public interest immunity order for nondisclosure is inadvertently disclosed by the prosecution to lawyers for the defendants, those lawyers cannot be ordered not to further disseminate that material to any third party, including their own clients (*R* v *G* [2004] EWCA Crim 1368).

The investigator also has a responsibility to identify material that could be sensitive and bring this to the attention of the CPS. Where material is identified steps must be taken to record and retain the material. For information recorded on computers, see chapter 30 of the Disclosure Manual and the Annex to the A-G's Guidelines.

2.7.9.4   **KEYNOTE**

Informants

The courts recognise the need to protect the identity of informants to ensure that the supply of information about criminal activities does not dry up and to ensure the informants' own safety. However, there may be occasions where if the case is to continue the identity of an informant will have to be disclosed.

This is particularly so where there is a suggestion that an informant has participated in the events constituting, surrounding or following the crime; the judge must consider whether this role so impinges on an issue of interest to the defence, present or potential, as to make disclosure necessary (*R* v *Turner* [1995] 1 WLR 264).

The need to disclose details of informants has been considered by the Court of Appeal in two cases. The first case, *R* v *Denton* [2002] EWCA Crim 272, concerned a defendant who was a police informer. The defendant was charged with murder and alleged that he had been told by his police handlers not to tell his lawyers about his status. The court held that there was no duty for the Crown to disclose to the defence, or to seek a ruling from the judge, as to any information regarding an accused being a police informer. On any common sense view, the material had already been disclosed to the defendant, and the Crown had no duty to supply the defendant with information with which he was already familiar. This last point may also be relevant to other situations. The second case, *R* v *Dervish* [2001] EWCA Crim 2789, concerned an undercover operation that was commenced after an informant gave information. The court held in this case that the public interest in protecting the identification of an informant had to be balanced against the right of the defendant to a fair trial; if there was material that might assist the defence, the necessity for the defendant to have a fair trial would outweigh the other interests in the case and the material would have to be disclosed or the prosecution discontinued. There had been no such material in this case. In *R* v *Edwards (formerly Steadman)* [2012] EWCA Crim 5, a murder case, the prosecution failed to disclose the fact that they were seeking one of the witness's registration as an informant, and that this witness was willing to give information if he did not receive any additional custodial sentence in respect of the offences with which he had been charged. The court stated that these were factors which should have been made available to the jury in deciding the credibility of the witness. However, in the circumstances of the case, even with full and proper disclosure, the task of assessing this witness's reliability would have changed neither the landscape of the trial nor the jury's deliberations upon the evidence. The circumstantial case was compelling, and the verdict was safe.

Where an informant who has participated in the crime is called to give evidence at the trial there would have to be very strong reasons for this fact not to be disclosed (*R* v *Patel* [2001] EWCA Crim 2505).

There are strong links between the principles of informants and undercover police officers. In *R* v *Barkshire* [2011] EWCA Crim 1885 the Court of Appeal, upholding the appeal, held that recordings and the statement of an undercover police officer contained information which assisted the defence. They showed that the undercover officer had been involved in activities which went much further than the authorisation that he had been given. They appeared to show him as an enthusiastic supporter of criminal activity, arguably, as an *agent provocateur*. Further, the recordings supported the defendant's contentions that their intended activities were directed to the saving of life and avoidance of injury, and that they proposed to conduct the occupation in a careful and proportionate manner. This material was pertinent to a potential submission of abuse of process by way of entrapment and in any event had the capacity to support B's defence.

2.7.9.5 KEYNOTE

Observation Points and the *Johnson* Ruling

R v *Rankine* [1986] 2 WLR 1075, considering previous cases, stated that it was the rule that police officers should not be required to disclose sources of their information, whether those sources were paid informers or public spirited citizens, subject to a discretion to admit to avoid a miscarriage of justice and that observation posts were included in this rule.

In *R* v *Johnson* [1988] 1 WLR 1377, the appellant was convicted of supplying drugs. The only evidence against him was given by police officers, who testified that, while stationed in private premises in a known drug-dealing locality, they had observed him selling drugs. The defence applied to cross-examine the officers on the exact location of the observation posts, in order to test what they could see, having regard to the layout of the street and the objects in it. In the jury's absence, the prosecution called evidence as to the difficulty of obtaining assistance from the public, and the desire of the occupiers, who were also occupiers at the time of the offence, that their names and addresses should not be disclosed because they feared for their safety.

The judge ruled that the exact location of the premises need not be revealed. The appeal was dismissed; although the conduct of the defence was to some extent affected by the restraints placed on it, this led to no injustice. The jury were well aware of the restraints, and were most carefully directed about the very special care they had to give to any disadvantage they may have brought to the defence. *Johnson* was applied and approved in *R* v *Hewitt* (1992) 95 Cr App R 81 (see also *R* v *Grimes* [1994] Crim LR 213).

In *Johnson*, Watkins LJ at pp. 1385–6 gave the following guidance as to the minimum evidential requirements needed if disclosure is to be protected:

a) The police officer in charge of the observations to be conducted, no one of lower rank than a sergeant should usually be acceptable for this purpose, must be able to testify that beforehand he visited all observation places to be used and ascertained the attitude of occupiers of premises, not only to the use to be made of them, but to the possible disclosure thereafter of the use made and facts which could lead to the identification of the premises thereafter and of the occupiers. He may of course in addition inform the court of difficulties, if any, usually encountered in the particular locality of obtaining assistance from the public.

b) A police officer of no lower rank than a chief inspector must be able to testify that immediately prior to the trial he visited the places used for observations, the results of which it is proposed to give in evidence, and ascertained whether the occupiers are the same as when the observations took place and whether they are or are not, what the attitude of those occupiers is to the possible disclosure of the use previously made of the premises and of facts which could lead at the trial to identification of premises and occupiers.

Such evidence will of course be given in the absence of the jury when the application to exclude the material evidence is made. The judge should explain to the jury, as this judge did, when summing up or at some appropriate time before that, the effect of his ruling to exclude, if he so rules.

The guidelines in *Johnson* do not require a threat of violence before protection can be afforded to the occupier of an observation post; it suffices that the occupier is in fear of harassment (*Blake* v *DPP* (1993) 97 Cr App R 169).

This extended the rules established in *R* v *Rankine* [1986] QB 861 and is based on the protection of the owner or occupier of the premises, and not on the identity of the observation post. Thus, where officers have witnessed the commission of an offence as part of a surveillance operation conducted from an unmarked police vehicle, information relating to the surveillance and the colour, make and model of the vehicle should not be withheld (*R* v *Brown and Daley* (1988) 87 Cr App R 52).

2.7.10 Disclosure Code of Practice—7 Revelation of Material to Prosecutor

7.1 Certain unused material must be disclosed to the accused at Common Law if it would assist the defence with the early preparation of their case or at a bail hearing. This material may consist of items such as a previous relevant conviction of a key prosecution witness or the withdrawal of support for the prosecution by a witness. This material must be revealed to the prosecutor for service on the defence with the initial details of the prosecution case.

7.1A In anticipated not guilty plea cases for hearing in the magistrates' court the disclosure officer must give the streamlined disclosure certificate to the prosecutor at the same time as he gives the prosecutor the file containing the material for the prosecution case.

7.1B In cases sent to the Crown Court, wherever possible, the disclosure officer should give the schedules concerning unused material to the prosecutor at the same time as the prosecution file in preparation for the first hearing and any case management that the judge may wish to conduct at that stage.

7.2 The disclosure officer should draw the attention of the prosecutor to any material an investigator has retained (including material to which paragraph 6.13 applies) which may satisfy the test for prosecution disclosure in the Act, and should explain why he has come to that view.

7.3 At the same time as complying with the duties in paragraphs 7.1 and 7.2, the disclosure officer must give the prosecutor a copy of any material which falls into the following categories (unless such material has already been given to the prosecutor as part of the file containing the material for the prosecution case):
   • information provided by an accused person which indicates an explanation for the offence with which he has been charged;
   • any material casting doubt on the reliability of a confession;
   • any material casting doubt on the reliability of a prosecution witness;
   • any other material which the investigator believes may satisfy the test for prosecution disclosure in the Act.

7.4 If the prosecutor asks to inspect material which has not already been copied to him, the disclosure officer must allow him to inspect it. If the prosecutor asks for a copy of material which has not already been copied to him, the disclosure officer must give him a copy. However, this does not apply where the disclosure officer believes, having consulted the officer in charge of the investigation, that the material is too sensitive to be copied and can only be inspected.

7.5 If material consists of information which is recorded other than in writing, whether it should be given to the prosecutor in its original form as a whole, or by way of relevant extracts recorded in the same form, or in the form of a transcript, is a matter for agreement between the disclosure officer and the prosecutor.

2.7.10.1 KEYNOTE

What Satisfies the Test for Prosecution Disclosure

Paragraphs 7.2 to 7.3 of the Code create a catchall provision and presumably requires the disclosure officer to make inquiries of the other officers in the case to ensure that all material is included.

However, what needs to be disclosed should be balanced by A-G's Guidelines:

Properly applied, the CPIA should ensure that material is not disclosed which overburdens the participants in the trial process, diverts attention from the relevant issues, leads to unjustifiable delay, and is wasteful of resources. Consideration of disclosure issues should be an integral part of a good investigation and not something that exists separately.

Disclosure must not be an open-ended trawl of unused material. A critical element to fair and proper disclosure is that the defence play their role to ensure that the prosecution are directed to material which might reasonably be considered capable of undermining the prosecution case or assisting the case for the accused. This process is key to ensuring prosecutors make informed determinations about disclosure of unused material. The defence statement is important in identifying the issues in the case and why it is suggested that the material meets the test for disclosure (A-G's Guidelines, paras 3 and 9).

There will occasionally be cases where the police investigation has been intelligence-led; there may be a deputy disclosure officer appointed just to deal with intelligence material which, by its very nature, is likely to be sensitive (see para. 2.7.9.3). Where there are a number of disclosure officers assigned to a case, there should be a lead disclosure officer who is the focus for inquiries and whose responsibility it is to ensure that the investigator's disclosure obligations are complied with. Where appropriate, regular case conferences and other meetings should be held to ensure prosecutors are apprised of all relevant developments in investigations. Full records should be kept of such meetings (A-G's Guidelines, para. 18).

It should be noted that where material is available to police from a particular source, e.g. local authority records, a decision that some of the material is relevant does not mean that it all has to be disclosed. This point was reinforced by the case of *R* v *Abbott* [2003] EWCA Crim 350, where the Court of Appeal held that the defendant was not entitled to blanket disclosure of all the files.

2.7.10.2   **KEYNOTE**

Time Period for Initial Disclosure

While there are provisions to set specific time periods by which initial disclosure must be met, none currently exist. Until such time, disclosure at this stage must be made as soon as practicable after the duty arises.

In *R* v *Bourimech* [2002] EWCA Crim 2089, the defendant sought disclosure following the service of his defence statement of a previous crime report made by the victim. One day before the trial was scheduled to begin, the crime report relating to that incident was served among other papers on the defence. This report escaped the notice of the defence until the final day of the trial. The court held that the defect in disclosure amounted to unfairness in the proceedings and the court could not be confident that if the victim had been cross-examined in relation to the previous allegation the jury might have been influenced by the credit and credibility of the witness.

In most cases prosecution disclosure can wait until after this time without jeopardising the defendant's right to a fair trial. However, the prosecutor must always be alive to the need to make advance disclosure of material that should be disclosed at an earlier stage (*R* v *DPP, ex parte Lee* [1999] 1 WLR 1950). Examples include:

- previous convictions of a complainant or a deceased if that information could reasonably be expected to assist the defence when applying for bail;
- material that might enable a defendant to make a pre-committal application to stay the proceedings as an abuse of process;
- material that might enable a defendant to submit that he/she should only be committed for trial on a lesser charge, or perhaps that he/she should not be committed for trial at all;
- depending on what the defendant chooses to reveal about his/her case at this early stage, material that would enable the defendant and his/her legal advisers to make preparations for trial that would be significantly less effective if disclosure were delayed; for example, names of eye-witnesses whom the prosecution did not intend to use.

It should be noted that any disclosure by the prosecution prior to committal would not normally exceed the initial disclosure which, after committal, would be required by s. 3 of the 1996 Act.

Disclosure Code of Practice—8 Subsequent Action by Disclosure Officer

8.1 At the time when a streamlined disclosure certificate is prepared for magistrates' court cases, or a schedule of non-sensitive material is prepared for Crown Court cases, the disclosure officer may not know exactly what material will form the case against the accused. In addition, the prosecutor may not have given advice about the likely relevance of particular items of material. Once these matters have been determined, the disclosure officer must give the prosecutor, where necessary, an amended certificate or schedule listing any additional material:

- which may be relevant to the investigation,
- which does not form part of the case against the accused,
- which is not already listed on the schedule, and
- which he believes is not sensitive, unless he is informed in writing by the prosecutor that the prosecutor intends to disclose the material to the defence.

8.2 Section 7A of the Act imposes a continuing duty on the prosecutor, for the duration of criminal proceedings against the accused, to disclose material which satisfies the test for disclosure (subject to public interest considerations). To enable him to do this, any new material coming to light should be treated in the same way as the earlier material.

8.3 In particular, after a defence statement has been given, or details of the issues in dispute have been recorded on the effective trial preparation form, the disclosure officer must look again at the material which has been retained and must draw the attention of the prosecutor to any material which might reasonably be considered capable of undermining the case for the prosecution against the accused or of assisting the case for the accused; and he must reveal it to him in accordance with paragraphs 7.4 and 7.5 above.

2.7.11.1   **KEYNOTE**

Disclosure by the Defence

The duty on the defence to make disclosure only arises *after* the prosecution has made the initial disclosure (s. 5(1) of the 1996 Act). This duty falls into two categories: compulsory and voluntary. The disclosure required by the defence is limited to material that they intend to use at trial.

The defence statement should set out the nature of the defendant's defence, including any particular defences on which he/she intends to rely and particulars of the matters of fact on which the defendant intends to rely; this means the defence will need to disclose a factual narrative of their case. In addition, those issues, relevant to the case, which the accused disputes with the prosecution must be set out with reasons. From 4 April 2005 the defence statement must indicate any point of law (including any point as to the admissibility of evidence or an abuse of process) which the defendant wishes to raise, and any authority on which he/she intends to rely for that purpose (s. 6A of the 1996 Act). This requirement to give reasons is intended to stop the defence going on a 'fishing expedition' to speculatively look at material in order to find some kind of defence.

Where the defence case involves an alibi, the statement must give details of the alibi, including the name and address of any alibi witness. In cases where there are co-accused, there is no duty to disclose this information to the other defendants, although this could be done voluntarily.

An alibi for the purposes of the defence statement is defined as evidence tending to show that by reason of the presence of the accused at a particular place or in a particular area at a particular time, he/she was not, or was unlikely to have been, at the place where the offence is alleged to have been committed at the time of its alleged commission. Where this applies, the defence must provide details including the name, address and date of birth of any witness the accused believes is able to give evidence in support of the alibi, or as many of those details as are known to the accused when the statement is given. Where such details are not known, the statement must include any information in the accused's possession which might be of material assistance in identifying or finding any such witness (s. 6A(2) of the 1996 Act).

The defence must also give to the court and the prosecutor notice of any other witnesses other than the defendant will be called to give evidence. If any other witness is to be called then the name, address and date of birth of each such proposed witness, or as many of those details as are known to the accused must be provided. If any of this information is not available the defence must provide any information in their possession which might be of material assistance in identifying or finding any such proposed witness (s. 6C of the 1996 Act), see para. 2.7.11.7.

There may be occasions where the defence statement is allowed to be used in cross-examination when it is alleged that the defendant has changed his/her defence or in re-examination to rebut a suggestion of recent invention (*R* v *Lowe* [2003] EWCA Crim 3182).

2.7.11.2 KEYNOTE

Compulsory Disclosure by Defence (s. 5)

In proceedings before the Crown Court, where the prosecutor has provided initial disclosure, or purported to, the accused must serve a defence statement on the prosecutor and the court. The accused must also provide details of any witnesses he/ she intends to call at the trial. Where there are other accused in the proceedings and the court so orders, the accused must also give a defence statement to each of the other accused specified by the court, and a request for a copy of the defence statement may be made by any co-accused.

Once a defence statement has been provided (whether compulsorily or voluntarily), the prosecution must disclose any prosecution material that:

- might be reasonably expected to assist the accused's defence; and
- has not already been disclosed.

It will be a question of fact whether material in police possession might be reasonably expected to assist the defence case. If the court feels that material that was not disclosed would to any reasonable person have been expected to help the defence case, the case may fail.

If there is no additional material to be disclosed then the prosecutor must give a written statement to this effect. It is not the responsibility of the prosecutor or the police to examine material held by third parties which the defence have stated they wish to examine (the defence can request this from the third party or apply for a witness summons). However, there may be occasions where matters disclosed in the defence statement lead investigators to look at material held by third parties as it might impact on the prosecution case. This stage of the disclosure process may require further inquiries prompted by the defence statement. The result of those inquiries may then have to be disclosed because it either undermines the prosecution case or it assists the accused's defence.

Where the defence statement points the prosecution to other lines of inquiry, e.g. the investigation of an alibi, or where forensic expert evidence is involved, the disclosure officer should inform the officer in charge of the investigation and copy the defence statement to him/her, together with any CPS advice provided if appropriate (Disclosure Manual, para. 15.17).

2.7.11.3 KEYNOTE

Voluntary Disclosure by Accused (s. 6)

In the magistrates' court, the accused is not obliged to serve a defence statement but may choose to do so, in which case the statutory provisions apply. However, it is a mandatory requirement for the accused to provide details of his or her witnesses. The purpose of s. 6 of the 1996 Act is to allow the defence, in cases where the case is being tried summarily as a not guilty plea, to obtain further disclosure from the prosecution after the initial disclosure. This is only likely to happen where:

- the defence are not satisfied with the material disclosed at the initial disclosure stage or where they wish to examine items listed in the schedule of non-sensitive material;
- the defence wish to show the strength of their case in order to persuade the prosecution not to proceed.

If the defence decide to make a defence statement they must comply with the same conditions imposed on compulsory defence disclosure.

2.7.11.4   **KEYNOTE**

Time Period for the Defence Statement

Once the prosecution provides the initial disclosure, the defence have 14 days in respect of summary proceedings, or 28 days in respect of Crown Court proceedings within which the accused in criminal proceedings must give: a compulsory defence statement under s. 5 of the Act; a voluntary defence statement under s. 6 of the Act; or a notice of his/her intention to call any person, other than him/herself, as a witness at trial under s. 6C of the Act (Alibi witness). The court can only grant an extension if satisfied that the accused could not reasonably have given a defence statement or given notification within the relevant period. There is no limit on the number of days by which the relevant period may be extended or the number of applications for extensions that may be made (Criminal Procedure and Investigations Act 1996 (Defence Disclosure Time Limits) Regulations 2011 (SI 2011/209)).

2.7.11.5   **KEYNOTE**

Effect of Failure in Defence Disclosure

If the defence fail to give a defence statement under s. 5 or, where a defence statement is provided, they:

- are outside the time limits;
- set out inconsistent defences in a defence statement or at trial put forward a different defence; or
- at trial adduce evidence in support of an alibi without having given particulars of the alibi in a defence statement, or call a witness in support of an alibi without providing details of the witness or information that might help trace the witness;
  then the following sanctions may apply:
- the court or, with the leave of the court, any other party may make such comment as appears appropriate;
- the court or jury may draw such inferences as appear proper in deciding whether the accused is guilty of the offence concerned (but there must also be other evidence to convict the defendant);
- even if the defence serve the defence statement outside the time limits, the prosecution must still consider the impact of the statement in terms of the need for any further disclosure (*Murphy* v *DPP* [2006] EWHC 1753 (Admin)).

2.7.11.6   **KEYNOTE**

Continuing Duty of Prosecutor to Disclose (s. 7A)

Section 7A places a continuing duty on the prosecutor at any time between the initial disclosure and the accused being acquitted or convicted or the prosecutor deciding not to proceed with the case concerned, to keep under review the question of further disclosure. In considering the need for further disclosure the prosecutor must consider whether material might reasonably be considered capable of undermining the case for the prosecution against the accused or of assisting the case for the accused. If there is any such material, it must be disclosed to the accused as soon as is reasonably practicable. Consideration of what might need to be disclosed could change depending on the state of affairs at that time (including the case for the prosecution as it then stands) and so should be reviewed on a continuing basis (s. 7A(4)).

In *R* v *Tyrell* [2004] EWCA Crim 3279 this responsibility was clearly outlined. The court held that there was an obligation to consider whether there was any material in the hands of the prosecution which might undermine the case against the applicants or might reasonably be expected to assist the disclosed defences. In addition, the Crown had to consider whether there was any material which might be relevant to an issue which might feature in the trial; this clearly required a continuing duty. In this case, the court found that disclosure had been considered many times as the case progressed in relation to a variety of issues as they arose and ensured a fair trial.

Material must not be disclosed to the extent that the court concludes that it is not in the public interest to disclose it and orders accordingly or it is material whose disclosure is prohibited by s. 17 of the Regulation of Investigatory Powers Act 2000.

There is a duty on the prosecution to continue to review the disclosure of prosecution material right up until the case is completed (acquittal, conviction or discontinuance of the case). If the defence are not satisfied that the prosecution have disclosed all they should have, s. 8 of the 1996 Act allows for the defence to apply to the court for further disclosure.

2.7.11.7   KEYNOTE

Interviewing Defence Witnesses or Alibi Witnesses

Section 21A of the Criminal Procedure and Investigations Act 1996 introduced a Code of Practice for Arranging and Conducting Interviews of Witnesses Notified by the Accused. The Code sets out guidance that police officers and other persons charged with investigating offences must follow if they arrange or conduct interviews of proposed witnesses whose details are disclosed to the prosecution under the 1996 Act. These are set out below:

Arrangement of the interview

Information to be provided to the witness before any interview may take place

3.1   If an investigator wishes to interview a witness, the witness must be asked whether he consents to being interviewed and informed that:
- an interview is being requested following his identification by the accused as a proposed witness under section 6A(2) or section 6C of the Act,
- he is not obliged to attend the proposed interview,
- he is entitled to be accompanied by a solicitor at the interview (but nothing in this Code of Practice creates any duty on the part of the Legal Services Commission to provide funding for any such attendance), and
- a record will be made of the interview and he will subsequently be sent a copy of the record.

3.2   If the witness consents to being interviewed, the witness must be asked:
- whether he wishes to have a solicitor present at the interview,
- whether he consents to a solicitor attending the interview on behalf of the accused, as an observer, and
- whether he consents to a copy of the record being sent to the accused. If he does not consent, the witness must be informed that the effect of disclosure requirements in criminal proceedings may nevertheless require the prosecution to disclose the record to the accused (and any co-accused) in the course of the proceedings.

Information to be provided to the accused before any interview may take place

4.1   The investigator must notify the accused or, if the accused is legally represented in the proceedings, the accused's representatives:
- that the investigator requested an interview with the witness,
- whether the witness consented to the interview, and
- if the witness consented to the interview, whether the witness also consented to a solicitor attending the interview on behalf of the accused, as an observer.

4.2 If the accused is not legally represented in the proceedings, and if the witness consents to a solicitor attending the interview on behalf of the accused, the accused must be offered the opportunity, a reasonable time before the interview is held, to appoint a solicitor to attend it.

Identification of the date, time and venue for the interview

5 The investigator must nominate a reasonable date, time and venue for the interview and notify the witness of them and any subsequent changes to them.

Notification to the accused's solicitor of the date, time and venue of the interview

6 If the witness has consented to the presence of the accused's solicitor, the accused's solicitor must be notified that the interview is taking place, invited to observe, and provided with reasonable notice of the date, time and venue of the interview and any subsequent changes.

Conduct of the interview

The investigator conducting the interview

7 The identity of the investigator conducting the interview must be recorded. That person must have sufficient skills and authority, commensurate with the complexity of the investigation, to discharge his functions effectively. That person must not conduct the interview if that is likely to result in a conflict of interest, for instance, if that person is the victim of the alleged crime which is the subject of the proceedings. The advice of a more senior officer must always be sought if there is doubt as to whether a conflict of interest precludes an individual conducting the interview. If thereafter the doubt remains, the advice of a prosecutor must be sought.

Attendance of the accused's solicitor

8.1 The accused's solicitor may only attend the interview if the witness has consented to his presence as an observer. Provided that the accused's solicitor was given reasonable notice of the date, time and place of the interview, the fact that the accused's solicitor is not present will not prevent the interview from being conducted. If the witness at any time withdraws consent to the accused's solicitor being present at the interview, the interview may continue without the presence of the accused's solicitor.

8.2 The accused's solicitor may attend only as an observer.

Attendance of the witness's solicitor

9 Where a witness has indicated that he wishes to appoint a solicitor to be present, that solicitor must be permitted to attend the interview.

Attendance of any other appropriate person

10 A witness under the age of 18 or a witness who is mentally disordered or otherwise mentally vulnerable must be interviewed in the presence of an appropriate person.

Recording of the interview

11.1 An accurate record must be made of the interview, whether it takes place at a police station or elsewhere. The record must be made, where practicable, by audio recording or by visual recording with sound, or otherwise in writing. Any written record must be made and completed during the interview, unless this would not be practicable or would interfere with the conduct of the interview, and must constitute either a verbatim record of what has been said or, failing this, an account of the interview which adequately and accurately summarises it. If a written record is not made during the interview it must be made as soon as practicable after its completion. Written interview records must be timed and signed by the maker.

11.2 A copy of the record must be given, within a reasonable time of the interview, to:
   (a) the witness, and
   (b) if the witness consents, to the accused or the accused's solicitor.

2.7.12   Disclosure Code of Practice—9 Certification by Disclosure Officer

9.1 The disclosure officer must certify to the prosecutor that to the best of his knowledge and belief, all relevant material which has been retained and made available to him has been revealed to the prosecutor in accordance with this Code. He must sign and date the certificate. It will be necessary to certify not only at the time when the schedule and accompanying material is submitted to the prosecutor, and when relevant material which has been retained is reconsidered after the accused has given a defence statement, but also whenever a schedule is otherwise given or material is otherwise revealed to the prosecutor.

Disclosure Code of Practice—10 Disclosure of Material to Accused

10.1   Other than early disclosure under Common Law, in the magistrates' court the streamlined certificate at the Annex (and any relevant unused material to be disclosed under it) must be disclosed to the accused either:

- at the hearing where a not guilty plea is entered, or
- as soon as possible following a formal indication from the accused or representative that a not guilty plea will be entered at the hearing.

10.1A   If material has not already been copied to the prosecutor, and he requests its disclosure to the accused on the ground that:

- it satisfies the test for prosecution disclosure, or
- the court has ordered its disclosure after considering an application from the accused, the disclosure officer must disclose it to the accused.

10.2   If material has been copied to the prosecutor, and it is to be disclosed, whether it is disclosed by the prosecutor or the disclosure officer is a matter of agreement between the two of them.

10.3   The disclosure officer must disclose material to the accused either by giving him a copy or by allowing him to inspect it. If the accused person asks for a copy of any material which he has been allowed to inspect, the disclosure officer must give it to him, unless in the opinion of the disclosure officer that is either not practicable (for example because the material consists of an object which cannot be copied, or because the volume of material is so great), or not desirable (for example because the material is a statement by a child witness in relation to a sexual offence).

10.4   If material which the accused has been allowed to inspect consists of information which is recorded other than in writing, whether it should be given to the accused in its original form or in the form of a transcript is a matter for the discretion of the disclosure officer. If the material is transcribed, the disclosure officer must ensure that the transcript is certified to the accused as a true record of the material which has been transcribed.

10.5   If a court concludes that an item of sensitive material satisfies the prosecution disclosure test and that the interests of the defence outweigh the public interest in withholding disclosure, it will be necessary to disclose the material if the case is to proceed. This does not mean that sensitive documents must always be disclosed in their original form: for example, the court may agree that sensitive details still requiring protection should be blocked out, or that documents may be summarised, or that the prosecutor may make an admission about the substance of the material under section 10 of the Criminal Justice Act 1967.

2.7.13.1   KEYNOTE

Disclosing Material to the Defence

The court can order disclosure of material which the prosecution contend is sensitive. In such cases it may be appropriate to seek guidance on whether to disclose the material or offer no evidence, thereby protecting the sensitive material or the source of that material (e.g. where informants or surveillance techniques are involved).

Forces may have instructions as to providing further copies when requested by the defence in relation to procedures and costs. It is suggested that where copies are provided, some proof of delivery should be obtained.

2.7.13.2   KEYNOTE

Disclosure of Statements in Cases of Complaints against the Police

Statements made by witnesses during an investigation of a complaint against a police officer are disclosable; however, the timing of the disclosure may be controlled. In *R* v *Police Complaints Authority, ex parte Green*

[2002] EWCA Civ 389, the Court of Appeal stated that there is no requirement to disclose witness statements to eye-witness complainants during the course of an investigation. The evidence of such complainants could be contaminated and, therefore, disclosure would risk hindering or frustrating the very purpose of the investigation. A complainant's legitimate interests were appropriately and adequately safeguarded by his/her right to a thorough and independent investigation, to contribute to the evidence, to be kept informed of the progress of the investigation and to be given reasoned conclusions on completion of the investigation. However, a complainant had no right to participate in the investigation as though he/she were supervising it. The general rule was that complainants, whether victims or next of kin, were not entitled to the disclosure of witness statements used in the course of a police investigation until its conclusion at the earliest.

Police complaints and disciplinary files may also fall within sensitive material that does not have to be disclosed (*Halford* v *Sharples* [1992] 1 WLR 736). This would not apply to written complaints against the police prompting investigations or the actual statements obtained during the investigations, although immunity may be claimed in the case of a particular document by reason of its contents (*R* v *Chief Constable of the West Midlands Police, ex parte Wiley* [1995] 1 AC 274). However, the working papers and reports prepared by the investigating officers do form a class which is entitled to immunity and therefore production of such material should be ordered only where the public interest in disclosure of their contents outweighs the public interest in preserving confidentiality (*Taylor* v *Anderton* [1995] 1 WLR 447).

2.7.13.3   **KEYNOTE**

Confidentiality

The defence may only use material disclosed to them under the 1996 Act for purposes related to the defence case; any other use will be a contempt of court. Once evidence has been given in open court, however, the material is available for other purposes.

PART III

Police Station Procedure

2.8 Detention and Treatment of Persons by Police Officers

PACE Code of Practice for the Detention, Treatment and Questioning of Persons by Police Officers (Code C)

> A thick grey line down the margin denotes text that is an extract of the PACE Code itself (i.e. the actual wording of the legislation). This material is examinable for both Sergeants and Inspectors.

2.8.1 Introduction

The powers to detain people who have been arrested and the manner in which they must be dealt with are primarily contained in the Police and Criminal Evidence Act 1984 and the PACE Codes of Practice. These Codes are intended to protect the basic rights of detained people. If these Codes are followed, it is more likely that evidence obtained while people are in custody will be admissible; the provisions of the 1984 Act give guidance in numerous areas. The Human Rights Act 1998 makes it even more important to comply with the 1984 Act and its associated Codes of Practice. This can be seen from the case of *R* v *Chief Constable of Kent Constabulary, ex parte Kent Police Federation Joint Branch Board* [2000] 2 Cr App R 196, where the court stated that the 1984 Act and the Codes of Practice represented the balance between the important duty of the police to investigate crime and apprehend criminals and the rights of the private citizen. A breach of Code C is fundamental in affecting the fairness of the evidence (*R* v *Aspinall* [1999] 2 Cr App R 115).

This chapter examines the treatment of persons who have been detained by police. The majority of this is contained within PACE Code C, which was amended in October 2013. Some sections of Code C deal with the interviewing of suspects and as such are included in **chapter 2.10**. Code H is the corresponding Code which applies to persons detained for the purposes of a terrorist investigation; the two Codes are similar and provide further clarity on their application. They also reflect changes to legislation that apply to both these Codes. These include consequential changes to custody records as a result of the reduced stop and search recording requirements in s. 3 of the Police and Criminal Evidence Act 1984, introduced in March 2011. References to terrorism matters, where appropriate, are included in the keynotes to this chapter.

The main responsibility for a detained person lies with the custody officer; however, it is important that all staff, including supervisors involved in investigations or those dealing with detained persons, are aware of the provisions of the Act and the Codes.

As the key reference point for the treatment of detained persons lies in the PACE Codes, this chapter and the subsequent chapters that deal with those in police detention are based around the codes of practice with the keynotes combining the Notes for Guidance to the Codes of Practice, legislation, and case law that support the Codes.

As Code C uses terms such as 'custody officer' and 'designated person' (amongst others), it is useful to examine briefly what they mean before examining Code C in detail.

2.8.2 Custody Officers

Custody officers are responsible for the reception and treatment of prisoners detained at the police station.

The role of the custody officer is to act independently of those conducting the investigation, thereby ensuring the welfare and rights of the detained person (this requirement is contained in s. 36(5) of the 1984 Act). Section 36 requires that one or more custody officers must be appointed for each designated police station. However, in *Vince* v *Chief Constable of Dorset* [1993] 1 WLR 415, it was held that a chief constable was under a duty to appoint one custody officer for each designated police station and had a discretionary power to appoint more than one, but this duty did not go so far as to require a sufficient number to ensure that the functions of custody officer were always performed by them. The provision of the facility of a custody officer must be reasonable. Section 36(3) states that a custody officer must be an officer of at least the rank of sergeant. However, s. 36(4) allows officers of any rank to perform the functions of custody officer at a designated police station if a sergeant is not readily available to perform them. The effect of s. 36(3) and (4) is that the practice of allowing officers of any other rank to perform the role of custody officer where a sergeant *(who has no other role to perform)* is in the police station must therefore be unlawful. Should a decision be made to use acting sergeants or untrained custody officers, this may lead to a claim in negligence by the officer or the detained person where there is a breach of the Codes or someone is injured as a result of the failure to manage the custody suite effectively. It could also lead to a prosecution under health and safety legislation.

For cases where arrested people are taken to a non-designated police station, s. 36(7) states that an officer of any rank not involved in the investigation should perform the role of custody officer. If no such person is at the station, the arresting officer (or any other officer involved in the investigation) or the officer that granted him/her bail under s. 30A of the 1984 Act (bail prior to being taken to a police station) should perform the role. In these cases, an officer of at least the rank of inspector at a designated police station must be informed. It is suggested that once informed, that officer should consider the circumstances of the detained person.

Where a custody officer feels that he/she is unable to comply with the minimum standards of detention as required by the 1984 Act, it is suggested that he/she should draw this to the attention of the line manager and/or the superintendent responsible for the custody suite. Custody officers should be mindful of Article 5 of the European Convention on Human Rights in considering whether they are able to manage the number of detained persons in their custody to ensure that their detention is not longer than needed.

2.8.3 Designated Support Staff

Sections 38 and 39 of the Police Reform Act 2002 allow persons employed by the Local Policing Body or persons employed by a contractor of the Local Policing Body (in relation to detention and escort officers) to be designated as investigating officers, detention officers and escort officers.

Designated officers are given powers to carry out certain functions that would up to this time have been carried out by police officers only. Before a person can be given the powers of a designated officer, the chief officer of police must be satisfied that the person is a suitable person to carry out the functions for which he/she is designated, is capable of effectively carrying out those functions, and has received adequate training in the carrying out of those functions and in the exercise and performance of the powers and duties of a designated officer. It should be noted that not all designated officers will be designated with the same range of powers and it will be important to know what powers a particular designated officer has been given and therefore what his/her role will be. Schedule 4 to the Police Reform Act 2002 outlines these powers, some of which are set out below.

2.8.3.1 Investigating Officers

- To act as the supervisor of any access to seized material to which a person is entitled, to supervise the taking of a photograph of seized material or to photograph it him/herself.
- To arrest a detainee for a further offence if it appears to him/her that the detainee would be liable to arrest for that further offence if released from his/her initial arrest.
- Power for the custody officer to transfer to a designated civilian investigating officer responsibility for a detainee. This power includes a duty for the person investigating the offence, once the detainee is returned to the custody of the custody officer, to report back to the custody officer on how the Codes were complied with.
- To question an arrested person under ss. 36 and 37 of the Criminal Justice and Public Order Act 1994 about facts which may be attributable to the person's participation in an offence. The designated person may also give the suspect the necessary warning about the capacity of a court to draw inferences from a failure to give a satisfactory account in response to questioning.

2.8.3.2 Detention Officers

- Powers to search detained persons, to take fingerprints and certain samples without consent and to take photographs.
- To require certain defined categories of persons who have been convicted, cautioned, reprimanded or warned in relation to recordable offences to attend a police station to have their fingerprints taken.
- To carry out non-intimate searches of persons detained at police stations or elsewhere and to seize items found during such searches.
- To carry out searches and examinations in order to determine the identity of persons detained at police stations. Identifying marks found during such processes may be photographed.
- To carry out intimate searches in the same very limited circumstances that are applicable to constables.
- To take fingerprints without consent in the same circumstances that a constable can.
- To take non-intimate samples without consent and to inform the person from whom the sample is to be taken of any necessary authorisation by a senior officer and of the grounds for that authorisation.
- To require certain defined categories of persons who have been charged with or convicted of recordable offences to attend a police station to have a sample taken.
- To inform a person that intimate samples taken from him/her may be the subject of a speculative search (i.e. this will satisfy the requirement that the person must be informed that the sample will be the subject of a speculative search).
- To photograph detained persons in the same way that constables can.

2.8.3.3 Escort Officers

- To transport arrested persons to police stations and escort detained persons from one police station to another or between police stations and other locations specified by the custody officer.

- To carry out the duty of taking a person arrested by a constable to a police station as soon as practicable.
- With the authority of the custody officer, to escort detainees between police stations or between police stations and other specified locations.
- To conduct non-intimate searches of the detainee; and to seize or retain, or cause to be seized or retained, anything found on such a search (restrictions on power to seize personal effects are the same as for police officers, as is the requirement that the search be carried out by a member of the same sex).

Where any of the powers allow for the use of reasonable force when exercised by a police constable, a designated person has the same entitlement to use reasonable force as a constable.

It is important to note that not all support staff will be designated for the purposes of the Police Reform Act 2002 and non-designated staff will not have the additional powers as outlined above.

2.8.4 Designated Police Stations

Section 30 of the Police and Criminal Evidence Act 1984 requires that a person who has been arrested must be taken to a police station *as soon as practicable* after arrest, unless the arrested person has been bailed prior to arrival at the police station. Section 30A of the 1984 Act allows a constable to release on bail a person who is under arrest. However, not all police stations have charge rooms or facilities for dealing with prisoners, so the 1984 Act requires that prisoners who will be detained (or who are likely to be detained) for more than six hours must go to a 'designated' police station. A designated police station is one that has enough facilities for the purpose of detaining arrested people. Section 35 requires the Chief Officer of Police to designate sufficient police stations to deal with prisoners. It is for the Chief Officer to decide which stations are to be designated stations and these details are then published. Police stations can be designated permanently or for any specified periods provided that they are not designated for part of a day.

2.8.5 PACE Code of Practice for the Detention, Treatment and Questioning of Persons by Police Officers (Code C)

This Code applies to people in police detention after 00.00 on 2 June 2014, notwithstanding that their period of detention may have commenced before that time.

1 General

1.0 The powers and procedures in this Code must be used fairly, responsibly, with respect for the people to whom they apply and without unlawful discrimination. Under the Equality Act 2010, section 149, when police officers are carrying out their functions, they also have a duty to have due regard to the need to eliminate unlawful discrimination, harassment and victimisation, to advance equality of opportunity between people who share a relevant protected characteristic and people who do not share it, and to take steps to foster good relations between those persons.

1.1 All persons in custody must be dealt with expeditiously, and released as soon as the need for detention no longer applies.

1.1A A custody officer must perform the functions in this Code as soon as practicable. A custody officer will not be in breach of this Code if delay is justifiable and reasonable steps are taken to prevent unnecessary delay. The custody record shall show when a delay has occurred and the reason.

1.2 This Code of Practice must be readily available at all police stations for consultation by:
- police officers;
- police staff;
- detained persons;
- members of the public.

1.3 The provisions of this Code:
- include the Annexes
- do not include the *Notes for Guidance*.

1.4 If an officer has any suspicion, or is told in good faith, that a person of any age may be mentally disordered or otherwise mentally vulnerable, in the absence of clear evidence to dispel that suspicion, the person shall be treated as such for the purposes of this Code.

1.5 If anyone appears to be under 17, they shall in the absence of clear evidence that they are older, be treated as a juvenile for the purposes of this Code and any other Code.

1.5A If anyone appears to have attained the age of 17 and to be under the age of 18, they shall in the absence of clear evidence that they are older, be treated as a 17-year-old for the purposes of this and any other Code. The provisions and Notes for Guidance which in accordance with *paragraph 1.5* apply to a juvenile and the way they are to be treated shall also apply to them, except as described in sub-paragraphs (a) and (b) below:

(a) The statutory provisions in section 38 of PACE (Detention after charge) which apply only to an arrested juvenile as defined in section 37(15) of PACE and to which *paragraphs 16.7* and *16.10* and *Note 16D* of this Code relate, shall not apply to a person who appears to have attained the age of 17 for the purposes of:

   (i) the grounds to keep them in police detention after charge; and

   (ii) the requirement to transfer a person who has been kept in police detention after charge to local authority accommodation and the power of the local authority to detain them pending appearance at court.

(b) the statutory provisions in section 65(1) of PACE (appropriate consent) which require appropriate consent for a person who has not attained the age of 17 to be given by them and their parent or guardian shall not apply to a person who appears to have attained the age of 17 and whose consent alone shall be sufficient.

In this Code, section 65(1) applies *to Annex A, paragraphs 2(b)* and *2B* (Intimate searches) and *Annex K, paragraphs 1(b)* and *3* (X-Ray and ultrasound scan) and in Code D (Identification) to *paragraph 2.12* with regards to taking fingerprints, samples, footwear impressions, photographs and evidential searches and examinations.

1.6 If a person appears to be blind, seriously visually impaired, deaf, unable to read or speak or has difficulty orally because of a speech impediment, they shall be treated as such for the purposes of this Code in the absence of clear evidence to the contrary.

1.7 'The appropriate adult' means, in the case of a:

(a) juvenile:

   (i) the parent, guardian or, if the juvenile is in the care of a local authority or voluntary organisation, a person representing that authority or organisation;

   (ii) a social worker of a local authority

   (iii) failing these, some other responsible adult aged 18 or over who is not a police officer or employed by the police.

   Note: *Paragraph 1.5A* extends sub-paragraph (a) paragraph to the person called to fulfil the role of the appropriate adult for a 17-year-old detainee.

(b) person who is mentally disordered or mentally vulnerable.

   (i) a relative, guardian or other person responsible for their care or custody;

   (ii) someone experienced in dealing with mentally disordered or mentally vulnerable people but who is not a police officer or employed by the police;

   (iii) failing these, some other responsible adult aged 18 or over who is not a police officer or employed by the police.

1.8 If this Code requires a person be given certain information, they do not have to be given it if at the time they are incapable of understanding what is said, are violent or may become violent or in urgent need of medical attention, but they must be given it as soon as practicable.

1.9 References to a custody officer include any police officer who for the time being, is performing the functions of a custody officer.

1.9A When this Code requires the prior authority or agreement of an officer of at least inspector or superintendent rank, that authority may be given by a sergeant or chief inspector authorised to perform the functions of the higher rank under the Police and Criminal Evidence Act 1984 (PACE), section 107.

1.10 Subject to *paragraph 1.12*, this Code applies to people in custody at police stations in England and Wales, whether or not they have been arrested, and to those removed to a police station as a place of safety under the Mental Health Act 1983, sections 135 and 136, as a last resort (see *paragraph 3.16*). Section 15 applies solely to people in police detention, e.g. those brought to a police station under arrest or arrested at a police station for an offence after going there voluntarily.

1.11 No part of this Code applies to a detained person:

   (a) to whom PACE Code H applies because:

   • they are detained following arrest under section 41 of the Terrorism Act 2000 (TACT) and not charged; or

   • an authorisation has been given under section 22 of the Counter-Terrorism Act 2008 (CTACT) (post-charge questioning of terrorist suspects) to interview them.

   (b) to whom the Code of Practice issued under paragraph 6 of Schedule 14 to TACT applies because they are detained for examination under Schedule 7 to TACT.

1.12 This Code does not apply to people in custody:

   (i) arrested by officers under the Criminal Justice and Public Order Act 1994, section 136(2) on warrants issued in Scotland, or arrested or detained without warrant under section 137(2) by officers from a police force in Scotland. In these cases, police powers and duties and the person's rights and entitlements whilst at a police station in England or Wales are the same as those in Scotland;

   (ii) arrested under the Immigration and Asylum Act 1999, section 142(3) in order to have their fingerprints taken;

   (iii) whose detention is authorised by an immigration officer under the Immigration Act 1971;

   (iv) who are convicted or remanded prisoners held in police cells on behalf of the Prison Service under the Imprisonment (Temporary Provisions) Act 1980;

   (v) *Not used*

   (vi) detained for searches under stop and search powers except as required by Code A.

   The provisions on conditions of detention and treatment in *sections 8* and *9* must be considered as the minimum standards of treatment for such detainees.

1.13 In this Code:

   (a) 'designated person' means a person other than a police officer, designated under the Police Reform Act 2002, Part 4 who has specified powers and duties of police officers conferred or imposed on them;

   (b) reference to a police officer includes a designated person acting in the exercise or performance of the powers and duties conferred or imposed on them by their designation.

   (c) where a search or other procedure to which this Code applies may only be carried out or observed by a person of the same sex as the detainee, the gender of the detainee and other parties present should be established and recorded in line with *Annex L* of this Code.

1.14 Designated persons are entitled to use reasonable force as follows:

   (a) when exercising a power conferred on them which allows a police officer exercising that power to use reasonable force, a designated person has the same entitlement to use force; and

   (b) at other times when carrying out duties conferred or imposed on them that also entitle them to use reasonable force, for example:

- when at a police station carrying out the duty to keep detainees for whom they are responsible under control and to assist any police officer or designated person to keep any detainee under control and to prevent their escape.
- when securing, or assisting any police officer or designated person in securing, the detention of a person at a police station.
- when escorting, or assisting any police officer or designated person in escorting, a detainee within a police station.
- for the purpose of saving life or limb; or
- preventing serious damage to property.

1.15 Nothing in this Code prevents the custody officer, or other officer given custody of the detainee, from allowing police staff who are not designated persons to carry out individual procedures or tasks at the police station if the law allows. However, the officer remains responsible for making sure the procedures and tasks are carried out correctly in accordance with the Codes of Practice. Any such person must be:

(a) a person employed by a police force and under the direction and control of the Chief Officer of that force; or

(b) employed by a person with whom a police force has a contract for the provision of services relating to persons arrested or otherwise in custody.

1.16 Designated persons and other police staff must have regard to any relevant provisions of the Codes of Practice.

1.17 References to pocket books include any official report book issued to police officers or other police staff.

2.8.5.1 KEYNOTE

Code C recognises that detained persons are treated in accordance with the Equality Act 2010; for these Codes 'relevant protected characteristic' includes age, disability, gender reassignment, pregnancy and maternity, race, religion or belief, sex and sexual orientation. Code C does not affect the principle that all citizens have a duty to help police officers to prevent crime and discover offenders. This is a civic rather than a legal duty; but when a police officer is trying to discover whether, or by whom, an offence has been committed, he/she is entitled to question any person from whom he/she thinks useful information can be obtained, subject to the restrictions imposed by this Code. A person's declaration that he/she is unwilling to reply does not alter this entitlement.

Paragraph 1.1A is intended to cover delays which may occur in processing detainees, e.g. if a large number of suspects are brought into the station simultaneously to be placed in custody, or interview rooms are all being used, or perhaps there are difficulties contacting an appropriate adult, solicitor or interpreter. However, if that delay was not 'justified', it could lead to actions for unlawful detention and false imprisonment, and any evidence obtained as a result may be held to be inadmissible (*Roberts* v *Chief Constable of Cheshire Constabulary* [1999] 1 WLR 662).

Although certain sections of this Code apply specifically to people in custody at police stations, those there voluntarily to assist with an investigation should be treated with no less consideration, e.g. offered refreshments at appropriate times, and enjoy an absolute right to obtain legal advice or communicate with anyone outside the police station.

2.8.5.2 KEYNOTE

Meaning of Police Detention

Police detention is defined by s. 118 of the Police and Criminal Evidence Act 1984 which states:

(2) Subject to subsection (2A) a person is in police detention for the purposes of this Act if—

(a) he has been taken to a police station after being arrested for an offence or after being arrested under section 41 of the Terrorism Act 2000, or

(b) he is arrested at a police station after attending voluntarily at the station or accompanying a constable to it, and is detained there or is detained elsewhere in the charge of a constable, except that a person who is at a court after being charged is not in police detention for those purposes.

(2A) Where a person is in another's lawful custody by virtue of paragraph 22, 34(1) or 35(3) of Schedule 4 to the Police Reform Act 2002, he shall be treated as in police detention.

Paragraph 22 of sch. 4 to the Police Reform Act 2002 refers to the power to transfer persons into the custody of investigating officers, para. 34(1) relates to designated escort officers taking an arrested person to a police station and para. 35(3) deals with a designated escort officer transferring a detainee from one police station to another. Code C 2.1A states that a person is at a police station when they are in the boundary of any building or enclosed yard which forms part of that police station. Therefore they are in police detention when they are within that boundary/yard.

2.8.5.3   KEYNOTE

Mentally Vulnerable/Disordered

'Mentally vulnerable' applies to any detainee who, because of his/her mental state or capacity, may not understand the significance of what is said, of questions or of his/her replies. 'Mental disorder' is defined in the Mental Health Act 1983, s. 1(2) as 'any disorder or disability of mind'. When the custody officer has any doubt about the mental state or capacity of a detainee, that detainee should be treated as mentally vulnerable and an appropriate adult called.

2.8.5.4   KEYNOTE

Appropriate Adults

In *R* v *Aspinall* [1999] 2 Cr App R 115, the Court of Appeal emphasised the importance of appropriate adults. There it was held that an appropriate adult played a significant role in respect of a vulnerable person whose condition rendered him/her liable to provide information which was unreliable, misleading or self-incriminating.

A person, including a parent or guardian, should not be an appropriate adult if he/she is:

- suspected of involvement in the offence;
- the victim;
- a witness;
- involved in the investigation; or
- has received admissions prior to attending to act as the appropriate adult.

If a juvenile's parent is estranged from the juvenile, he/she should not be asked to act as the appropriate adult if the juvenile expressly and specifically objects to his/her presence.

If a juvenile admits an offence to, or in the presence of, a social worker or member of a youth offending team other than during the time that person is acting as the juvenile's appropriate adult, another appropriate adult should be appointed in the interest of fairness.

In the case of people who are mentally disordered or otherwise mentally vulnerable, it may be more satisfactory if the appropriate adult is someone experienced or trained in their care rather than a relative lacking such qualifications. But if the detainee prefers a relative to a better qualified stranger or objects to a particular person, his/her wishes should, if practicable, be respected.

A detainee should always be given an opportunity, when an appropriate adult is called to the police station, to consult privately with a solicitor in the appropriate adult's absence if he/she wants. An appropriate adult is not subject to legal privilege.

A solicitor or independent custody visitor (formerly a lay visitor) present at the police station in that capacity may not be the appropriate adult.

The custody officer must remind the appropriate adult and detainee about the right to legal advice and record any reasons for waiving it in accordance with section 6.

Evidence obtained while a person is in custody where the person called as an appropriate adult does not have that person's best interests in mind or is not capable of assisting that person could be excluded.

In the case of *R (on the application of HC)* v *Secretary of State for the Home Department and the Commissioner of Police for the Metropolis* [2013] EWHC 982 (Admin), the court held that treating 17-year-olds in detention as adults was contrary to Article 8 of the European Convention on Human Rights. The Codes were revised to comply with this judgment. Paragraph 1.5A is referred to throughout the codes; the purpose of para. 1.5A is to extend the safeguards for juveniles to 17-year-olds unless this is precluded by any statutory provisions. Sub-paragraphs 1.5A(a) and (b) identify the provisions of ss. 38 and 65 of PACE concerning detention after charge and appropriate consent which for this reason do not extend to 17-year-olds. All other safeguards in this and other Codes are extended and the requirements which are indicated in the relevant provisions and Notes for Guidance are as follows:

(a) under para. 3.13 of this Code, to identify and inform someone responsible for the welfare of a 17-year-old which is in addition to their right in section 5 of this Code not to be held incommunicado;

(b) under para. 3.14 to notify a person who has statutory responsibility under a court order to supervise or monitor a 17-year-old;

(c) under para. 8.8 with regard to cell accommodation and keeping 17-year-old detainees separate from adults;

(d) to call a person described by para. 1.7(a) in relation to testing for the presence of Class A drugs, to fulfil the role of the appropriate adult for the purposes of this or any other Code to support and assist a 17-year-old:

(i) by being present when:

- they are informed of their rights and entitlements and the grounds for their detention (see *paras 3.17* and *3.18*);
- they are cautioned or given a special warning (see *paras 10.12* and *10.11A*);
- they are being interviewed in accordance with this Code (see sections 11 and 12) or Codes E or F unless para. 11.15 of this Code allows the interview to go ahead without the adult being present;
- their detention is being reviewed or an extension is being considered (see *paras 15.3(c)* and *15.3C(a)*):
- they are charged and related action is taken (see *paras 16.1, 16.3, 16.4A* and *16.6*);
- samples to test for Class A drugs are requested from a person who has not attained the age of 18 (see *para. 17.7*);
- an intimate search is carried out (see *Annex A, paras 2A, 2B* and *5*);
- a strip search is carried out (see *Annex A, para. 11*(c));
- an x-ray or ultrasound scan is carried out (see *Annex K, paras 2 and 3*);
- procedures in Code D involving witness identification, taking fingerprints, samples, footwear impressions and photographs and when evidential searches and examinations are carried out (see *paras 2.14 and 2.15*).

(ii) by allowing:

- the adult to inspect their custody record and to have a copy of their record (see *paras 2.4, 2.4A* and *2.5*);
- a 17-year-old to consult the adult in private (see *para. 3.18*);
- the adult to request legal advice on their behalf to advise and assist them (see *paras 3.19, 6.5A* and *1.17*).

It is important to note that para. 1.5A does not amend s. 37(15) of PACE which defines the term 'arrested juvenile' for the purposes of ss. 34 to 51 of PACE, or provisions in any other enactment which expressly refer and apply to persons under the age of 17. Until amended by Parliament, these statutory provisions alone do not extend to persons who have attained the age of 17.

While an appropriate adult should be given access to a juvenile, this does not mean that he/she has free access to the custody area. In *Butcher* v *DPP* [2003] EWHC 580 (Admin), the custody officer physically escorted the detainee's appropriate adult from the custody suite as she had entered it without being invited and had been verbally abusive and aggressive. The court held that the custody sergeant had not detained the appropriate adult, but had merely used reasonable force to remove her in order to maintain the operational effectiveness of the custody suite. The court held that the custody sergeant was entitled to ask her to leave and to use reasonable force when she failed to comply with that request.

It is also important to consider the welfare of the appropriate adult. This is demonstrated by the case of *Leach* v *Chief Constable of Gloucestershire Constabulary* [1999] 1 WLR 1421. Here L was asked by a police officer to attend police interviews of a murder suspect who was also thought to be mentally disordered, as an 'appropriate adult' per the requirement of the Codes. She was told only that the suspect was a 52-year-old male, and was not informed of the nature of the case. The suspect was in fact Frederick West, who was being questioned in connection with murders committed in particularly harrowing and traumatic circumstances. For many weeks L acted as an appropriate adult, accompanying the officer and suspect to murder scenes, and on many occasions being left alone in a locked cell with the suspect. She claimed to be suffering from post-traumatic stress and psychological injury as well as a stroke as a result of her experiences. The Court of Appeal said that the Fred West case was notorious among modern crimes and it was foreseeable that psychiatric harm might arise. While there was no requirement to cases counselling or trained help should be offered.

2.8.6   2   Custody Records

2.1A   When a person:
- is brought to a police station under arrest
- is arrested at the police station having attended there voluntarily or
- attends a police station to answer bail

they must be brought before the custody officer as soon as practicable after their arrival at the station or if applicable, following their arrest after attending the police station voluntarily.

This applies to both designated and non-designated police stations. A person is deemed to be "at a police station" for these purposes if they are within the boundary of any building or enclosed yard which forms part of that police station.

2.1   A separate custody record must be opened as soon as practicable for each person brought to a police station under arrest or arrested at the station having gone there voluntarily or attending a police station in answer to street bail. All information recorded under this Code must be recorded as soon as practicable in the custody record unless otherwise specified. Any audio or video recording made in the custody area is not part of the custody record.

2.2   If any action requires the authority of an officer of a specified rank, subject to *paragraph 2.6A*, their name and rank must be noted in the custody record.

2.3   The custody officer is responsible for the custody record's accuracy and completeness and for making sure the record or copy of the record accompanies a detainee if they are transferred to another police station. The record shall show the:
- time and reason for transfer;
- time a person is released from detention.

2.3A   If a person is arrested and taken to a police station as a result of a search in the exercise of any stop and search power to which PACE Code A (Stop and search) or the 'search powers code' issued under TACT applies, the officer carrying out the search is responsible for ensuring that the record of that stop and search is made as part of the person's custody record. The custody officer must then ensure that the person is asked if they want a copy of the search record and if they do, that they are given a copy as soon as practicable. The person's entitlement to a copy of the search record which is made as part of their custody record is in addition to, and does not affect, their entitlement to a copy of their custody record or any other provisions of *section 2* (Custody records) of this Code. (See Code A, *paragraph 4.2B* and the TACT search powers code *paragraph 5.3.5*).

2.4 The detainee's solicitor and appropriate adult must be permitted to inspect the whole of the detainee's custody record as soon as practicable after their arrival at the station and at any other time on request, whilst the person is detained. This includes the following specific records relating to the reasons for the detainee's arrest and detention and the offence concerned, to which *paragraph 3.1(b)* refers:

(a) The information about the circumstances and reasons for the detainee's arrest as recorded in the custody record in accordance with *paragraph 4.3* of Code G. This applies to any further offences for which the detainee is arrested whilst in custody;

(b) The record of the grounds for each authorisation to keep the person in custody. The authorisations to which this applies are the same as those described at items (i)(a) to (d) in the table in *paragraph 2* of *Annex M* of this Code.

Access to the records in sub-paragraphs (a) and (b) is in addition to the requirements in *paragraphs 3.4(b), 11.1A, 15.0, 15.7A(c)* and *16.7A* to make certain documents and materials available and to provide information about the offence and the reasons for arrest and detention.

Access to the custody record for the purposes of this paragraph must be arranged and agreed with the custody officer and may not unreasonably interfere with the custody officer's duties. A record shall be made when access is allowed and whether it includes the records described in sub-paragraphs (a) and (b) above.

Note: *Paragraph 1.5A* extends this paragraph to the person called to fulfil the role of the appropriate adult for a 17-year-old detainee.

2.4A When a detainee leaves police detention or is taken before a court they, their legal representative or appropriate adult shall be given, on request, a copy of the custody record as soon as practicable. This entitlement lasts for 12 months after release.

Note: *Paragraph 1.5A* extends this paragraph to the person called to fulfil the role of the appropriate adult for a 17-year-old detainee.

2.5 The detainee, appropriate adult or legal representative shall be permitted to inspect the original custody record after the detainee has left police detention provided they give reasonable notice of their request. Any such inspection shall be noted in the custody record.

Note: *Paragraph 1.5A* extends this paragraph to the person called to fulfil the role of the appropriate adult for a 17-year-old detainee.

2.6 Subject to *paragraph 2.6A*, all entries in custody records must be timed and signed by the maker. Records entered on computer shall be timed and contain the operator's identification.

2.6A Nothing in this Code requires the identity of officers or other police staff to be recorded or disclosed:

(a) *Not used*

(b) if the officer or police staff reasonably believe recording or disclosing their name might put them in danger.

In these cases, they shall use their warrant or other identification numbers and the name of their police station.

2.7 The fact and time of any detainee's refusal to sign a custody record, when asked in accordance with this Code, must be recorded.

2.8.6.1 **KEYNOTE**

The purpose of using warrant or identification numbers instead of names referred to in Code C, para. 2.6A is to protect those involved in serious organised crime investigations or arrests of particularly violent suspects when there is reliable information that those arrested or their associates may threaten or cause harm to those involved. In cases of doubt, an officer of inspector rank or above should be consulted.

3 Initial Action

(a) Detained persons—normal procedure

3.1 When a person is brought to a police station under arrest or arrested at the station having gone there voluntarily, the custody officer must make sure the person is told clearly about:

(a) the following continuing rights, which may be exercised at any stage during the period in custody:

(i) their right to consult privately with a solicitor and that free independent legal advice is available as in *section 6*;

(ii) their right to have someone informed of their arrest as in *section 5*;

(iii) their right to consult the Codes of Practice; and

(iv) if applicable, their right to interpretation and translation (see *paragraph 3.12*) and their right to communicate with their High Commission, Embassy or Consulate (see *paragraph 3.12A*).

(b) their right to be informed about the offence and (as the case may be) any further offences for which they are arrested whilst in custody and why they have been arrested and detained in accordance with *paragraphs 2.4, 3.4(a)* and *11.1A* of this Code and *paragraph 3.3* of Code G.

3.2 The detainee must also be given a written notice, which contains information:

(a) setting out:

(i) their rights under *paragraph 3.1, paragraph 3.12* and *3.12A*;

(ii) the arrangements for obtaining legal advice, see *section 6*;

(iii) their right to a copy of the custody record as in *paragraph 2.4A*;

(iv) their right to remain silent as set out in the caution in the terms prescribed in *section 10*;

(v) their right to have access to materials and documents which are essential to effectively challenging the lawfulness of their arrest and detention for any offence and (as the case may be) any further offences for which they are arrested whilst in custody, in accordance with *paragraphs 3.4(b), 15.0, 15.7A(c)* and *16.7A* of this Code;

(vi) the maximum period for which they may be kept in police detention without being charged, when detention must be reviewed and when release is required.

(vii) their right to medical assistance in accordance with *section 9* of this Code

(viii) their right, if they are prosecuted, to have access to the evidence in the case before their trial in accordance with the Criminal Procedure and Investigations Act 1996, the Attorney General's Guidelines on Disclosure, the common law and the Criminal Procedure Rules.

(b) briefly setting out their other entitlements while in custody, by:

(i) mentioning:

• the provisions relating to the conduct of interviews;

• the circumstances in which an appropriate adult should be available to assist the detainee and their statutory rights to make representations whenever the need for their detention is reviewed.

(ii) listing the entitlements in this Code, concerning

• reasonable standards of physical comfort;

• adequate food and drink;

• access to toilets and washing facilities, clothing, medical attention, and exercise when practicable.

3.2A The detainee must be given an opportunity to read the notice and shall be asked to sign the custody record to acknowledge receipt of the notice. Any refusal to sign must be recorded on the custody record.

3.3 Not used.

3.3A An 'easy read' illustrated version should also be provided if available

3.4 (a) The custody officer shall:
- record the offence(s) that the detainee has been arrested for and the reason(s) for the arrest on the custody record. See *paragraph 10.3* and Code G *paragraphs 2.2* and *4.3*;
- note on the custody record any comment the detainee makes in relation to the arresting officer's account but shall not invite comment. If the arresting officer is not physically present when the detainee is brought to a police station, the arresting officer's account must be made available to the custody officer remotely or by a third party on the arresting officer's behalf. If the custody officer authorises a person's detention, subject to *paragraph 1.8*, that officer must record the grounds for detention in the detainee's presence and at the same time, inform them of the grounds. The detainee must be informed of the grounds for their detention before they are questioned about any offence;
- note any comment the detainee makes in respect of the decision to detain them but shall not invite comment;
- not put specific questions to the detainee regarding their involvement in any offence, nor in respect of any comments they may make in response to the arresting officer's account or the decision to place them in detention. Such an exchange is likely to constitute an interview as in *paragraph 11.1A* and require the associated safeguards in *section 11*.

Note: This sub-paragraph also applies to any further offences and grounds for detention which come to light whilst the person is detained.

See *paragraph 11.13* in respect of unsolicited comments.

(b) Documents and materials which are essential to effectively challenging the lawfulness of the detainee's arrest and detention must be made available to the detainee or their solicitor. Documents and materials will be 'essential' for this purpose if they are capable of undermining the reasons and grounds which make the detainee's arrest and detention necessary. The decision about whether particular documents or materials must be made available for the purpose of this requirement therefore rests with the custody officer who determines whether detention is necessary, in consultation with the investigating officer who has the knowledge of the documents and materials in a particular case necessary to inform that decision. A note should be made in the detainee's custody record of the fact that documents or materials have been made available under this sub-paragraph and when. The investigating officer should make a separate note of what is made available and how it is made available in a particular case. This sub-paragraph also applies (with modifications) for the purposes of sections 15 (Reviews and extensions of detention) and 16 (Charging detained persons). See *paragraphs 15.0* and *16.7A*.

3.5 The custody officer or other custody staff as directed by the custody officer shall:
(a) ask the detainee whether at this time, they:
(i) would like legal advice, see *paragraph 6.5*;
(ii) want someone informed of their detention, see *section 5*;
(b) ask the detainee to sign the custody record to confirm their decisions in respect of (a);
(c) determine whether the detainee:
(i) is, or might be, in need of medical treatment or attention, see *section 9*;
(ii) requires:
- an appropriate adult (see *paragraphs 1.4, 1.5, 1.5A* and *3.15*);
- help to check documentation (see *paragraph 3.20*);
- an interpreter (see *paragraph 3.12*).
(d) record the decision in respect of (c).

Where any duties under this paragraph have been carried out by custody staff at the direction of the custody officer, the outcomes shall, as soon as practicable, be reported to the custody officer who retains overall responsibility for the detainee's care and treatment and ensuring that it complies with this Code.

3.6 When these needs are determined, the custody officer is responsible for initiating an assessment to consider whether the detainee is likely to present specific risks to custody staff or themselves. Such assessments should always include a check on the Police National Computer, to be carried out as soon as practicable, to identify any risks highlighted in relation to the detainee. Although such assessments are primarily the custody officer's responsibility, it may be necessary for them to consult and involve others, e.g. the arresting officer or an appropriate healthcare professional, see *paragraph 9.13*. Reasons for delaying the initiation or completion of the assessment must be recorded.

3.7   Chief officers should ensure that arrangements for proper and effective risk assessments required by *paragraph 3.6* are implemented in respect of all detainees at police stations in their area.

3.8   Risk assessments must follow a structured process which clearly defines the categories of risk to be considered and the results must be incorporated in the detainee's custody record. The custody officer is responsible for making sure those responsible for the detainee's custody are appropriately briefed about the risks. If no specific risks are identified by the assessment, that should be noted in the custody record. See *paragraph 9.14*.

3.8A   The content of any risk assessment and any analysis of the level of risk relating to the person's detention is not required to be shown or provided to the detainee or any person acting on behalf of the detainee. But information should not be withheld from any person acting on the detainee's behalf, for example, an appropriate adult, solicitor or interpreter, if to do so might put that person at risk.

3.9   The custody officer is responsible for implementing the response to any specific risk assessment, e.g.:
- reducing opportunities for self harm;
- calling an appropriate healthcare professional;
- increasing levels of monitoring or observation;
- reducing the risk to those who come into contact with the detainee.

3.10   Risk assessment is an ongoing process and assessments must always be subject to review if circumstances change.

3.11   If video cameras are installed in the custody area, notices shall be prominently displayed showing cameras are in use. Any request to have video cameras switched off shall be refused.

(b) Detained persons—special groups

3.12   If the detainee appears to be someone who does not speak or understand English or who has a hearing or speech impediment, the custody officer must ensure:
- (a) that without delay, an interpreter is called for assistance in the action under *paragraphs 3.1 to 3.5*. If the person appears to have a hearing or speech impediment, the reference to 'interpreter' includes appropriate assistance necessary to comply with *paragraphs 3.1 to 3.5*. See *paragraph 13.1C* if the detainee is in Wales. See *section 13*;
- (b) that in addition to the continuing rights set out in *paragraph 3.1(a)(i) to (iv)*, the detainee is told clearly about their right to interpretation and translation;
- (c) that the written notice given to the detainee in accordance with *paragraph 3.2* is in a language the detainee understands and includes the right to interpretation and translation together with information about the provisions in *section 13* and *Annex M*, which explain how the right applies; and
- (d) that if the translation of the notice is not available, the information in the notice is given through an interpreter and a written translation provided without undue delay.

3.12A If the detainee is a citizen of an independent Commonwealth country or a national of a foreign country, including the Republic of Ireland, the custody officer must ensure that in addition to the continuing rights set out in *paragraph 3.1(a)(i) to (iv)*, they are informed as soon as practicable about their rights of communication with their High Commission, Embassy or Consulate set out in *section 7*. This right must be included in the written notice given to the detainee in accordance with *paragraph 3.2*.

3.13 If the detainee is a juvenile, the custody officer must, if it is practicable, ascertain the identity of a person responsible for their welfare. That person:

- may be:
  - ~ the parent or guardian;
  - ~ if the juvenile is in local authority or voluntary organisation care, or is otherwise being looked after under the Children Act 1989, a person appointed by that authority or organisation to have responsibility for the juvenile's welfare;
  - ~ any other person who has, for the time being, assumed responsibility for the juvenile's welfare.
- must be informed as soon as practicable that the juvenile has been arrested, why they have been arrested and where they are detained. This right is in addition to the juvenile's right in *section 5* not to be held incommunicado.

Note: *Paragraph 1.5A* extends the obligations in this paragraph to 17-year-old detainees.

3.14 If a juvenile is known to be subject to a court order under which a person or organisation is given any degree of statutory responsibility to supervise or otherwise monitor them, reasonable steps must also be taken to notify that person or organisation (the 'responsible officer'). The responsible officer will normally be a member of a Youth Offending Team, except for a curfew order which involves electronic monitoring when the contractor providing the monitoring will normally be the responsible officer.

Note: *Paragraph 1.5A* extends the obligations in this paragraph to 17-year-old detainees.

3.15 If the detainee is a juvenile, mentally disordered or otherwise mentally vulnerable, the custody officer must, as soon as practicable:

- inform the appropriate adult, who in the case of a juvenile may or may not be a person responsible for their welfare, as in *paragraph 3.13*, of:
  - ~ the grounds for their detention;
  - ~ their whereabouts.
- ask the adult to come to the police station to see the detainee.

Note: *Paragraph 1.5A* extends the obligation to call someone to fulfil the role of the appropriate adult to 17-year-old detainees.

3.16 It is imperative that a mentally disordered or otherwise mentally vulnerable person, detained under the Mental Health Act 1983, section 136, be assessed as soon as possible. A police station should only be used as a place of safety as a last resort but if that assessment is to take place at the police station, an approved mental health professional and a registered medical practitioner shall be called to the station as soon as possible to carry it out. The appropriate adult has no role in the assessment process and their presence is not required. Once the detainee has been assessed and suitable arrangements made for their treatment or care, they can no longer be detained under section 136. A detainee must be immediately discharged from detention under section 136 if a registered medical practitioner, having examined them, concludes they are not mentally disordered within the meaning of the Act.

3.17 If the appropriate adult is:

- already at the police station, the provisions of *paragraphs 3.1* to *3.5* must be complied with in the appropriate adult's presence;
- not at the station when these provisions are complied with, they must be complied with again in the presence of the appropriate adult when they arrive

and a copy of the notice given to the detainee in accordance with *paragraph 3.2*, shall also be given to the appropriate adult.

Note: *Paragraph 1.5A* extends the obligations in this paragraph to 17-year-old detainees.

3.18 The detainee shall be advised that:

- the duties of the appropriate adult include giving advice and assistance;
- they can consult privately with the appropriate adult at any time.

Note: *Paragraph 1.5A* extends the obligations in this paragraph to 17-year-old detainees.

3.19 If the detainee, or appropriate adult on the detainee's behalf, asks for a solicitor to be called to give legal advice, the provisions of *section 6* apply.

Note: *Paragraph 1.5A* extends the obligations in this paragraph to 17-year-old detainees.

3.20 If the detainee is blind, seriously visually impaired or unable to read, the custody officer shall make sure their solicitor, relative, appropriate adult or some other person likely to take an interest in them and not involved in the investigation is available to help check any documentation. When this Code requires written consent or signing the person assisting may be asked to sign instead, if the detainee prefers. This paragraph does not require an appropriate adult to be called solely to assist in checking and signing documentation for a person who is not a juvenile, or mentally disordered or otherwise mentally vulnerable (see *paragraph 3.15*).

(c) Persons attending a police station or elsewhere voluntarily

3.21 Anybody attending a police station or other location (see *paragraph 3.22*) voluntarily to assist police with the investigation of an offence may leave at will unless arrested. The person may only be prevented from leaving at will if their arrest on suspicion of committing the offence is necessary in accordance with Code G. See Code G *Note 2G*.

(a) If during an interview it is decided that their arrest is necessary, they must:
- be informed at once that they are under arrest and of the grounds and reasons as required by Code G, and
- be brought before the custody officer at the police station where they are arrested or, as the case may be, at the police station to which they are taken after being arrested elsewhere. The custody officer is then responsible for making sure that a custody record is opened and that they are notified of their rights in the same way as other detainees as required by this Code.

(b) If they are not arrested but are cautioned as in *section 10*, the person who gives the caution must, at the same time, inform them they are not under arrest, they are not obliged to remain at the station or other location but if they agree to remain, they may obtain free and independent legal advice if they want. They shall also be given a copy of the notice explaining the arrangements for obtaining legal advice and told that the right to legal advice includes the right to speak with a solicitor on the telephone and be asked if they want advice. If advice is requested, the interviewer is responsible for securing its provision without delay by contacting the Defence Solicitor Call Centre. The interviewer must ensure that other provisions of this Code and Codes E and F concerning the conduct and recording of interviews of suspects and the rights and entitlements and safeguards for suspects who have been arrested and detained are followed insofar as they can be applied to suspects who are not under arrest. This includes:
- informing them of the offence and, as the case may be, any further offences, they are suspected of and the grounds and reasons for that suspicion and their right to be so informed (see *paragraph 3.1(b)*);
- the caution as required in *section 10*;
- determining whether they require an appropriate adult and help to check documentation (see *paragraph 3.5(c)(ii)*); and
- determining whether they require an interpreter and the provision of interpretation and translation services and informing them of that right. See *paragraphs 3.1(a)(iv), 3.5(c)(ii)* and *3.12* and *section 13*.

but does not include any requirement to provide a written notice in addition to that above which concerns the arrangements for obtaining legal advice.

3.22 If the other location mentioned in *paragraph 3.21* is any place or premises for which the interviewer requires the person's informed consent to remain, for example, the person's home, then the references that the person is 'not obliged to remain' and that they 'may leave at will' mean that the person may also withdraw their consent and require the interviewer to leave.

(d) Documentation

3.23 The grounds for a person's detention shall be recorded, in the person's presence if practicable. See *paragraph 1.8*.

3.24 Action taken under *paragraphs 3.12* to *3.20* shall be recorded.

(e) Persons answering street bail

3.25 When a person is answering street bail, the custody officer should link any documentation held in relation to arrest with the custody record. Any further action shall be recorded on the custody record in accordance with *paragraphs 3.23* and *3.24* above.

3.26 The provisions of this section identify the information which must be given to suspects who have been cautioned in accordance with *section 10* of this Code according to whether or not they have been arrested and detained. It includes information required by EU Directive 2012/13 on the right to information in criminal proceedings. If a complaint is made by or on behalf of such a suspect that the information and (as the case may be) access to records and documents has not been provided as required, the matter shall be reported to an inspector to deal with as a complaint for the purposes of *paragraph 9.2*, or *paragraph 12.9* if the challenge is made during an interview. This would include, for example:

  (a) in the case of a detained suspect:
   • not informing them of their rights (see *paragraph 3.1*);
   • not giving them a copy of the Notice (see *paragraph 3.2(a)*);
   • not providing an opportunity to read the notice (see *paragraph 3.2A*);
   • not providing the required information (see *paragraphs 3.2(a)*, *3.12(b)* and, *3.12A*);
   • not allowing access to the custody record (see *paragraph 2.4*);
   • not providing a translation of the Notice (see *paragraph 3.12(c)* and *(d)*); and

  (b) in the case of a suspect who is not detained:
   • not informing them of their rights or providing the required information (see *paragraph 3.21(b)*).

2.8.7.1

KEYNOTE

Detention of People under Arrest

Section 37 of the 1984 Act states:

(1) Where—
   (a) a person is arrested for an offence—
      (i) without a warrant; or
      (ii) under a warrant not endorsed for bail,
   (b) repealed,
   the custody officer at each police station where he is detained after his arrest shall determine whether he has before him sufficient evidence to charge that person with the offence for which he was arrested and may detain him at the police station for such period as is necessary to enable him to do so.

(2) If the custody officer determines that he does not have such evidence before him, the person arrested shall be released either on bail or without bail, unless the custody officer has reasonable grounds for believing that his detention without being charged is necessary to secure or preserve evidence relating to an offence for which he is under arrest or to obtain such evidence by questioning him.

(3) If the custody officer has reasonable grounds for so believing, he may authorise the person arrested to be kept in police detention.

(4) Where a custody officer authorises a person who has not been charged to be kept in police detention, he shall, as soon as is practicable, make a written record of the grounds for the detention.

(5) Subject to subsection (6) below, the written record shall be made in the presence of the person arrested who shall at that time be informed by the custody officer of the grounds for his detention.

It is suggested that the custody officer record all the reasons for authorising the person's detention. It is suggested that detail of at least minimal level should be included, as it may be necessary in any criminal or civil proceedings. Indeed, it will be difficult for the custody officer to explain his/her decision without such information.

Section 37(6) states:

Subsection (5) above shall not apply where the person arrested is, at the time when the written record is made—
(a) incapable of understanding what is said to him;
(b) violent or likely to become violent; or
(c) in urgent need of medical attention.

People who have been arrested, returned on bail or have voluntarily given themselves up at a police station, which includes a person who has attended the police station after having been given street bail, will be brought before a custody officer who must decide whether the person should be detained at the police station or released. People who attend police stations voluntarily to assist the police with their investigations are not subject to this procedure; their treatment is dealt with by s. 29 of the 1984 Act (see *General Police Duties, chapter 4.5*). However, if an officer forms a view that the person should be arrested at the police station for the purpose of interview and informs the custody officer of this view, the custody officer can authorise detention for the interview and is entitled to assume that the arrest by the officer is lawful (*Fayed* v *Metropolitan Police Commissioner* [2004] EWCA Civ 1579).

If the grounds were not given at the time of arrest (on justifiable grounds) the custody officer should consider whether the arrested person is now in a position to be given the grounds for the arrest (as being the first practicable opportunity (s. 28(3) of the 1984 Act)). If the grounds for arrest were not given when they should have been, the arrest is unlawful regardless of what information is given later (*Wilson* v *Chief Constable of Lancashire* [2000] Po LR 367).

Having heard the details of and grounds for the arrest, the custody officer must decide whether or not there are reasons which justify authorising that person's detention (s. 37 of the 1984 Act deals with the procedures to be followed before a person is charged). Some commentators have suggested that it is also the role of the custody officer to establish that the arrest itself was lawful. While good practice, the custody officer's duty is confined to acting in accordance with the requirements set out in s. 37 of the 1984 Act. These duties do not appear to include considering whether the arrest was lawful unless this is relevant to the main question of whether there is sufficient evidence to charge the suspect. The view is supported by the decision of the Divisional Court in *DPP* v *L* [1999] Crim LR 752, where the court held that there was no express or implied requirement imposing a duty on a custody officer to inquire into the legality of an arrest and in that case the custody officer was therefore entitled to assume that it was lawful. A subsequent finding that the arrest was unlawful did not invalidate the decision of the custody officer to hold the person in custody. However, where the custody officer is aware that the arrest is unlawful, he/she will need to consider whether continued detention is justifiable, particularly in light of the Human Rights Act 1998. The Codes allow for the custody officer to delegate actions to other members of staff; a custody officer or other officer who, in accordance with this Code, allows or directs the carrying out of any task or action relating to a detainee's care, treatment, rights and entitlements to another officer or any police staff must be satisfied that the officer or police staff concerned is suitable, trained and competent to carry out the task or action in question.

Paragraphs 3.2, 3.4 and 3.12 set out the minimum of what should be included in the notice of entitlement, which should be available in Welsh, the main minority ethnic languages and the principal European languages, whenever they are likely to be helpful.

Access to 'easy read' illustrated versions should also be provided if they are available. For access to currently available notices see https://www.gov.uk/notice-of-rights-and-entitlements-a-persons-rights-in-police-detention.

The need for detained persons to understand their rights is fundamental to their fair treatment. A procedure for determining whether a person needs an interpreter might involve a telephone interpreter service or using cue cards or similar visual aids which enable detainees to indicate their ability to speak and understand English and their preferred language. This could be confirmed through an interpreter who could also assess the extent to which the person can speak and understand English.

Paragraph 3.21 sets out what information should be given to a person voluntarily attending a police station or other location; it should be noted that it does not include any requirement to provide a written notice other than the detail concerning the arrangements for obtaining legal advice.

In cases where a juvenile is in police detention it may be necessary to inform more than one person. For instance, if the juvenile is in local authority or voluntary organisation care but living with his/her parents or other adults responsible for his/her welfare, although there is no legal obligation to inform them, they should normally be contacted, as well as the authority or organisation, unless suspected of involvement in the offence concerned. Even if the juvenile is not living with his/her parents, consideration should be given to informing them.

If the person is arrested on a warrant, any directions given by the court in the warrant must be followed. Consideration can always be given to contacting the court to get a variation on the conditions of the warrant. (If the warrant was issued for the arrest of a person who has not yet been charged or summonsed for an offence, he/she should be dealt with as any other person arrested for an offence without warrant unless there are any additional directions on the warrant that must be followed.)

Where a person who has been bailed under s. 37(7)(a) in order that the DPP can make a case disposal decision answers his/her bail or is arrested for failing to return on bail, detention can only be authorised to allow him/her to be further bailed under s. 37D of the 1984 Act or in order that he/she can be charged or cautioned for offences connected with the original bail. If the person is not in a fit state to be dealt with he/she may be kept in police detention until he/she is (s. 37D of the 1984 Act).

2.8.7.2 KEYNOTE

Authorising a Person's Detention

A custody officer can authorise the detention of a person when there is sufficient evidence to charge and, more commonly, when there is *not* sufficient evidence to charge the suspect. If there is insufficient evidence to charge, the custody officer must decide if the detention is necessary to secure or preserve evidence relating to an offence for which the person is under arrest or to obtain such evidence by questioning him/her.

If a person representing the detained person does not consider that the detention is lawful he/she can apply to the court for the detainee's release (*habeas corpus*). A detainee may also be able to make an application for release or damages following the incorporation of the European Convention on Human Rights (Article 5(4)).

Where a detained person wishes to consult the Codes of Practice, this does not entitle the person concerned to delay unreasonably any necessary investigative or administrative action whilst he/she does so. Examples of action which need not be delayed unreasonably include: procedures requiring the provision of breath, blood or urine specimens under the Road Traffic Act 1988 or the Transport and Works Act 1992; searching detainees at the police station; taking fingerprints, footwear impressions or non-intimate samples without consent for evidential purposes.

2.8.7.3 KEYNOTE

Risk Assessments

The custody officer is responsible for initiating a risk assessment to consider whether detainees are likely to present specific risks to custody staff or themselves (Code C, para. 3.6). The risk assessment must follow a structured process which clearly defines the categories of risk to be considered (the Detention and Custody Authorised Professional Practice (APP) produced by the College of Policing (see http://www.app.college.po-lice.uk/app-content/) provides more detailed guidance on risk assessments). For this reason it is suggested that the risk assessment should be completed prior to the detainee being placed in a cell or detention room.

In addition to considering risk assessments for detained persons, the custody officer also needs to consider the safety of others who are in the custody area. Home Office Circular 34/2007 provides guidance on the arrangements for the safety and security of the custody suite, in particular in respect of solicitors and accredited and probationary representatives working in custody suites. The guidance has been issued following a number of incidents having been brought to the attention of the Home Office and the Health and Safety Executive (HSE), highlighting the actual and potential risks faced by solicitors, particularly when carrying out private consultations with their clients in the custody area, and the Authorised Professional Practice (APP) on Detention and Custody provides more detailed guidance on risk assessments and identifies key risk areas which should always be considered.

2.8.7.4

KEYNOTE

Documents or Material that Undermine the Need to keep a Suspect in Custody

For the purposes of paras 3.4(b) and 15.0: investigating officers are responsible for bringing to the attention of the officer who is responsible for authorising the suspect's detention, or (as the case may be) continued detention (before or after charge), any documents and materials in their possession or control which appear to undermine the need to keep the suspect in custody. In accordance with part IV of PACE, this officer will be either the custody officer, the officer reviewing the need for detention before or after charge (PACE, s. 40), or the officer considering the need to extend detention without charge from 24 to 36 hours (PACE, s. 42). The authorising officer is then responsible for determining, which, if any, of those documents and materials are capable of undermining the need to detain the suspect and must therefore be made available to the suspect or their solicitor. It is not the case that documents need to be copied and provided to the suspect or their solicitor; the way in which documents and materials are 'made available' is a matter for the investigating officer to determine on a case-by-case basis and having regard to the nature and volume of the documents and materials involved. For example, they may be made available by supplying a copy or allowing supervised access to view. However, for view-only access, it will be necessary to demonstrate that sufficient time is allowed for the suspect and solicitor to view and consider the documents and materials in question.

2.8.8

4 Detainee's Property

(a) Action

4.1 The custody officer is responsible for:
   (a) ascertaining what property a detainee:
      (i) has with them when they come to the police station, whether on:
         - arrest or re-detention on answering to bail;
         - commitment to prison custody on the order or sentence of a court;
         - lodgement at the police station with a view to their production in court from prison custody;
         - transfer from detention at another station or hospital;
         - detention under the Mental Health Act 1983, section 135 or 136;
         - remand into police custody on the authority of a court.
      (ii) might have acquired for an unlawful or harmful purpose while in custody;
   (b) the safekeeping of any property taken from a detainee which remains at the police station.

   The custody officer may search the detainee or authorise their being searched to the extent they consider necessary, provided a search of intimate parts of the body or involving the removal of more than outer clothing is only made as in *Annex A*. A search may only be carried out by an officer of the same sex as the detainee. See *Annex L*.

4.2 Detainees may retain clothing and personal effects at their own risk unless the custody officer considers they may use them to cause harm to themselves or others, interfere with evidence, damage property, effect an escape or they are needed as evidence. In this event the custody officer may withhold such articles as they consider necessary and must tell the detainee why.

4.3 Personal effects are those items a detainee may lawfully need, use or refer to while in detention but do not include cash and other items of value.

(b) Documentation

4.4 It is a matter for the custody officer to determine whether a record should be made of the property a detained person has with him or had taken from him on arrest. Any record made is not required to be kept as part of the custody record but the custody record should be noted as to where such a record exists. Whenever a record is made the detainee shall be allowed to check and sign the record of property as correct. Any refusal to sign shall be recorded.

4.5 If a detainee is not allowed to keep any article of clothing or personal effects, the reason must be recorded.

2.8.8.1 KEYNOTE

Section 54 of the 1984 Act states:

(1) The custody officer at a police station shall ascertain everything which a person has with him when he is—
   (a) brought to the station after being arrested elsewhere or after being committed to custody by an order or sentence of a court; or
   (b) arrested at the station or detained there, as a person falling within section 34(7), under section 37 above.

(2) The custody officer may record or cause to be recorded all or any of the things which he ascertains under subsection (1).

(2A) In the case of an arrested person, any such record may be made as part of his custody record.

(3) Subject to subsection (4) below, a custody officer may seize and retain any such thing or cause any such thing to be seized and retained.

(4) Clothes and personal effects may only be seized if the custody officer—
   (a) believes that the person from whom they are seized may use them—
      (i) to cause physical injury to himself or any other person;
      (ii) to damage property;
      (iii) to interfere with evidence; or
      (iv) to assist him to escape; or
   (b) has reasonable grounds for believing that they may be evidence relating to an offence.

(5) Where anything is seized, the person from whom it is seized shall be told the reason for the seizure unless he is—
   (a) violent or likely to become violent; or
   (b) incapable of understanding what is said to him.

(6) Subject to subsection (7) below, a person may be searched if the custody officer considers it necessary to enable him to carry out his duty under subsection (1) above and to the extent that the custody officer considers necessary for that purpose.

(6A) A person who is in custody at a police station or is in police detention otherwise than at a police station may at any time be searched in order to ascertain whether he has with him anything which he could use for any of the purposes specified in subsection (4) (a) above.

(6B) Subject to subsection (6C) below, a constable may seize and retain, or cause to be seized and retained, anything found on such a search.

(6C) A constable may only seize clothes and personal effects in the circumstances specified in subsection (4) above.

(7) An intimate search may not be conducted under this section.

(8) A search under this section shall be carried out by a constable.

(9) The constable carrying out a search shall be of the same sex as the person searched.

The custody officer must also consider what property the detained person might have in his/her possession for an unlawful or harmful purpose while in custody. The safekeeping of any property taken from the detained person and kept at the police station is the responsibility of the custody officer.

The custody officer does not need to record everything a detained person has with him/her. The custody officer will have a discretion as to the nature and detail of any recording and there is no requirement for this to be recorded in the custody record. However, custody officers should be mindful of any force instructions as to what will need to be recorded and where. It is suggested that it will still be necessary to make records, not least to ensure against claims that property has been mishandled or removed. The custody officer will have to make judgements about how to balance the need for recording against the amount of administrative work involved.

2.8.8.2

KEYNOTE

The Search

While the custody officer has a duty to ascertain what property a person has with him/her (often by means of searching the person), there is also a need to consider the rights of the detained person. The custody officer may authorise a constable to search a detained person, or may search the detained person him/herself in order to ascertain what property the detained person has with him/her (s. 54(6)). It should be noted that the custody officer must first authorise any search and the extent of the search; officers should not search a person until this authority has been given. Therefore the custody officer may only authorise a search to the extent that he/she considers necessary to comply with this duty. In order to safeguard the rights of the detained person, there are three levels to which searches can be conducted:

- searches that do not involve the removal of more than the detained person's outer clothing (this includes shoes and socks);
- strip searches;
- intimate searches.

Each of these is examined below.

The extent of the search is determined by the custody officer on the basis of what he/she honestly believes is necessary in order to comply with the above duties. Both the decision to search the detained person and the extent of the search must be decided on the facts of the case in question. It may be important to consider cultural issues that might affect the detained person; for instance, would it be necessary and justifiable to search a Sikh's turban? Force standing orders are not an automatic right to search all detained persons (*Brazil v Chief Constable of Surrey* [1983] 1 WLR 1155). A custody officer can authorise a strip search but an intimate search can only be authorised by an officer of the rank of inspector or above.

2.8.8.3

KEYNOTE

Searches that Do not Involve the Removal of More than the Detained Person's Outer Clothing

In effect, this is any search that does not become a strip search or an intimate search. This type of search applies to almost every person coming before the custody officer. Typically this will involve emptying out all items that are in the person's pockets, removing jewellery and the searching of other areas that can be conducted without the need to remove more than outer garments, such as coats and possibly items such as jumpers. This type of authorisation would also lend itself to a 'pat down' of the detained person. If there is any doubt as to whether the search goes beyond one that falls into this category, it is suggested that it should be treated as a strip search. Where metal detectors are used in custody suites, an indication from the device may give the grounds for authorising a strip search.

Not all detained persons need to be searched; s. 54(1) and para. 4.1 require a detainee to be searched when it is clear the custody officer will have continuing duties in relation to that detainee or when that detainee's behaviour or offence makes an inventory appropriate. They do not require every detainee to be searched, e.g. if it is clear that a person will only be detained for a short period and is not to be placed in a cell, the custody officer may decide not to search him/her. In such a case the custody record will be endorsed 'not searched', para. 4.4 will not apply, and the detainee will be invited to sign the entry. If the detainee refuses, the custody officer will be obliged to ascertain what property he/she has in accordance with para. 4.1.

2.8.8.4

KEYNOTE

Strip Searches

Strip searches are dealt with in Code C, Annex A, paras 9 to 12.

2.8.8.5

KEYNOTE

Intimate Searches

Intimate searches are dealt with in Code C, Annex A. An intimate search is a search which consists of the physical examination of a person's body orifices other than the mouth.

2.8.8.6

KEYNOTE

Drug Search—X-rays and Ultrasound Scans

Section 55A of the 1984 Act allows detained persons to have an X-ray taken of them or an ultrasound scan to be carried out on them (or both). This is dealt with in Code C, Annex K.

2.8.8.7

KEYNOTE

Conduct of a Search

- Reasonable force may be used (s. 117 of the 1984 Act).
- The custody officer should specify the level of the search to be conducted and this must be recorded in the person's record.
- Reference to Code A, para. 3.1 may be useful when considering how to conduct the search: 'Every reasonable effort must be made to minimise the embarrassment that a person being searched may experience.'
- Annex L should be referred to for guidance when establishing the gender of persons for the purpose of searching.

2.8.8.8

KEYNOTE

What Property can be Retained?

Once a person has been searched and the custody officer has ascertained what property the detained person has with him/her, a decision must be made as to what property will be returned to the detained person and what property will be retained by the police.

It is suggested that the custody officer may authorise the seizure of an article of clothing under s. 54(4)(b) of the 1984 Act, where he/she has reasonable grounds for believing that such clothing may be evidence relating to an offence. For instance, if the detained person is wearing a pair of trainers of the same type as those which are reasonably believed to have made impressions at the scene of a recent burglary and the detained person has a burglary record then, unless the custody officer knows of other facts clearly putting the suspect at some other place at the time of the offence, he/she is plainly justified in having those shoes forensically examined. However, it is submitted that this does not authorise the custody officer to seize footwear on the off-chance that some officer or some other police force may have obtained impressions at a burglary site which might match the trainers of the detained person.

Where property by virtue of its nature, quantity or size in the detainee's possession at the time of arrest has not been brought to the police station the custody officer is not required to record this on the custody record. Only items of clothing worn by the detained person which have been withheld need to be recorded on the custody record.

Unless the property has been seized and retained as evidence under s. 22 of the 1984 Act, it must be returned to the detained person on his/her release. If property has been seized from a third party in the course of the investigation the property can only be retained for so long as is necessary in accordance with s. 22(1) of the 1984 Act; even if it might be needed for another matter it should be returned to the third party unless there was an additional power to seize the item (*Settelen* v *Metropolitan Police Commissioner* [2004] EWHC 2171 (Ch)). If property is rightfully seized but retained unnecessarily this would be unlawful and could lead to a claim for damages (*Martin* v *Chief Constable of Nottinghamshire* (1998) 1 May, unreported). The seizure of a person's property is also protected by the European Convention on Human Rights, First Protocol, Article 1.

2.8.9   5 Right not to be Held Incommunicado

(a) Action

5.1   Subject to paragraph 5.7B, any person arrested and held in custody at a police station or other premises may, on request, have one person known to them or likely to take an interest in their welfare informed at public expense of their whereabouts as soon as practicable. If the person cannot be contacted the detainee may choose up to two alternatives. If they cannot be contacted, the person in charge of detention or the investigation has discretion to allow further attempts until the information has been conveyed.

5.2   The exercise of the above right in respect of each person nominated may be delayed only in accordance with *Annex B*.

5.3   The above right may be exercised each time a detainee is taken to another police station.

5.4   If the detainee agrees, they may at the custody officer's discretion, receive visits from friends, family or others likely to take an interest in their welfare, or in whose welfare the detainee has an interest.

5.5   If a friend, relative or person with an interest in the detainee's welfare enquires about their whereabouts, this information shall be given if the suspect agrees and *Annex B* does not apply.

5.6   The detainee shall be given writing materials, on request, and allowed to telephone one person for a reasonable time. Either or both of these privileges may be denied or delayed if an officer of inspector rank or above considers sending a letter or making a telephone call may result in any of the consequences in:

(a) *Annex B paragraphs 1* and *2* and the person is detained in connection with an indictable offence;

(b) *Not used*

Nothing in this paragraph permits the restriction or denial of the rights in *paragraphs 5.1* and *6.1*.

5.7   Before any letter or message is sent, or telephone call made, the detainee shall be informed that what they say in any letter, call or message (other than in a communication to a solicitor) may be read or listened to and may be given in evidence. A telephone call may be terminated if it is being abused. The costs can be at public expense at the custody officer's discretion.

5.7A   Any delay or denial of the rights in this section should be proportionate and should last no longer than necessary.

5.7B   In the case of a person in police custody for specific purposes and periods in accordance with a direction under the Crime (Sentences) Act 1997, Schedule 1 (productions from prison etc.), the exercise of the rights in this section shall be subject to any additional conditions specified in the direction for the purpose of regulating the detainee's contact and communication with others whilst in police custody.

(b) Documentation

5.8   A record must be kept of any:

(a) request made under this section and the action taken;

(b) letters, messages or telephone calls made or received or visit received;

(c) refusal by the detainee to have information about them given to an outside enquirer.

The detainee must be asked to countersign the record accordingly and any refusal recorded.

2.8.9.1

KEYNOTE

Right to Have Someone Informed

A person may request an interpreter to interpret a telephone call or translate a letter. In addition to Code C, this right can be denied or delayed where a person is detained under s. 41 of or sch. 7 to the Terrorism Act 2000 by an officer of the rank of inspector or above (Code H, section 5). The grounds are the same as those regulating the holding of people *incommunicado*. Should there be any delay in complying with a request by a detained person to have someone informed of his/her detention or to communicate with someone, the detained person should be informed of this and told the reason for it and a record kept (s. 56(6) of the 1984 Act). Subject to having sufficient personnel to supervise a visit and any possible hindrance to the investigation, the custody officer also has a discretion to allow visits to the detained person at the police station.

It is suggested that with the Codes of Practice outlining the limited rights for the detained person to make telephone calls and the right to restrict these calls, if the person has a mobile telephone it can be seized for the period of his/her detention. There is no case law on this point and any force policy should be followed. If the detainee does not know anyone to contact for advice or support or cannot contact a friend or relative, the custody officer should bear in mind any local voluntary bodies or other organisations which might be able to help. Paragraph 6.1 applies if legal advice is required.

In some circumstances, it may not be appropriate to use the telephone to disclose information under paras 5.1 and 5.5. So for example there may be occasions when officers wish to conduct a search under s. 18 of the 1984 Act and the detained person has requested to have someone informed. Clearly, if that person is informed before the search is conducted, vital evidence or property may be lost. Often, the custody officer has two methods by which he/she can inform the person requested about the detained person's detention: either in person or on the phone. Contacting the person by telephone is likely to be the quickest; however, there is no requirement to use the quickest method in order to pass on this information. While there is no case law on this point, Code C supports the view that, where the s. 18 search is to be conducted relatively quickly after the request is made by the detained person, it would be permissible to inform that person at the time the s. 18 search is conducted. Where the search is not to be conducted straight away, a lengthy delay may be seen as a breach of this right, which may lead to a stay of proceedings or a claim for damages as a breach of the detained person's human rights.

The additional conditions mentioned in para. 5.7B are contained in Prison Service Instruction 26/2012 (Production of Prisoners at the Request of Warranted Law Enforcement Agencies) which provides detailed guidance and instructions for police officers and Governors and Directors of Prisons regarding applications for prisoners to be transferred to police custody and their safe custody and treatment while in police custody.

2.8.10

6 Right to Legal Advice

(a) Action

6.1   Unless *Annex B* applies, all detainees must be informed that they may at any time consult and communicate privately with a solicitor, whether in person, in writing or by telephone, and that free independent legal advice is available. See *paragraph 3.1*.

6.2   *Not used.*

6.3   A poster advertising the right to legal advice must be prominently displayed in the charging area of every police station.

6.4   No police officer should, at any time, do or say anything with the intention of dissuading any person who is entitled to legal advice in accordance with this Code, whether or not they have been arrested and are detained, from obtaining legal advice.

6.5   The exercise of the right of access to legal advice may be delayed only as in *Annex B*. Whenever legal advice is requested, and unless *Annex B* applies, the custody officer must act without delay to secure the provision of such advice. If the detainee has the right to speak to a solicitor in person but declines to exercise the right the officer should point out that the right includes the right to speak with a solicitor on the telephone. If the detainee continues to waive this right, or a detainee whose right to free legal advice is limited to telephone advice from the Criminal Defence Service (CDS) Direct declines to exercise that right, the officer should ask them why and any reasons should be recorded on the custody record or the interview record as appropriate. Reminders of the right to legal advice must be given as in *paragraphs 3.5, 11.2, 15.4, 16.4, 16.5, 2B of Annex A, 3 of Annex K* and *5 of Annex M* of this Code and Code D, *paragraphs 3.17(ii)* and *6.3*. Once it is clear a detainee does not want to speak to a solicitor in person or by telephone they should cease to be asked their reasons.

6.5A   In the case of a person who is a juvenile or is mentally disordered or otherwise mentally vulnerable, an appropriate adult should consider whether legal advice from a solicitor is required. If the person indicates that they do not want legal advice, the appropriate adult has the right to ask for a solicitor to attend if this would be in the best interests of the person. However, the person cannot be forced to see the solicitor if they are adamant that they do not wish to do so.

Note: *Paragraph 1.5A* applies this paragraph to 17-year-old detainees.

6.6   A detainee who wants legal advice may not be interviewed or continue to be interviewed until they have received such advice unless:

(a) *Annex B* applies, when the restriction on drawing adverse inferences from silence in *Annex C* will apply because the detainee is not allowed an opportunity to consult a solicitor; or

(b) an officer of superintendent rank or above has reasonable grounds for believing that:

(i) the consequent delay might:
- lead to interference with, or harm to, evidence connected with an offence;
- lead to interference with, or physical harm to, other people;
- lead to serious loss of, or damage to, property;
- lead to alerting other people suspected of having committed an offence but not yet arrested for it;
- hinder the recovery of property obtained in consequence of the commission of an offence.

(ii) when a solicitor, including a duty solicitor, has been contacted and has agreed to attend, awaiting their arrival would cause unreasonable delay to the process of investigation.

Note: In these cases the restriction on drawing adverse inferences from silence in *Annex C* will apply because the detainee is not allowed an opportunity to consult a solicitor.

(c) the solicitor the detainee has nominated or selected from a list:

(i) cannot be contacted;

(ii) has previously indicated they do not wish to be contacted; or

(iii) having been contacted, has declined to attend; and
- the detainee has been advised of the Duty Solicitor Scheme but has declined to ask for the duty solicitor;
- in these circumstances the interview may be started or continued without further delay provided an officer of inspector rank or above has agreed to the interview proceeding.

Note: The restriction on drawing adverse inferences from silence in *Annex C* will not apply because the detainee is allowed an opportunity to consult the duty solicitor;

(d) the detainee changes their mind about wanting legal advice or (as the case may be) about wanting a solicitor present at the interview and states that they no longer wish to speak to a solicitor. In these circumstances, the interview may be started or continued without delay provided that:

    (i) an officer of inspector rank or above:

- speaks to the detainee to enquire about the reasons for their change of mind, and
- makes, or directs the making of, reasonable efforts to ascertain the solicitor's expected time of arrival and to inform the solicitor that the suspect has stated that they wish to change their mind and the reason (if given);

    (ii) the detainee's reason for their change of mind (if given) and the outcome of the action in (i) are recorded in the custody record;

    (iii) the detainee, after being informed of the outcome of the action in (i) above, confirms in writing that they want the interview to proceed without speaking or further speaking to a solicitor or (as the case may be) without a solicitor being present and do not wish to wait for a solicitor by signing an entry to this effect in the custody record;

    (iv) an officer of inspector rank or above is satisfied that it is proper for the interview to proceed in these circumstances and:

- gives authority in writing for the interview to proceed and, if the authority is not recorded in the custody record, the officer must ensure that the custody record shows the date and time of the authority and where it is recorded, and
- takes, or directs the taking of, reasonable steps to inform the solicitor that the authority has been given and the time when the interview is expected to commence and records or causes to be recorded, the outcome of this action in the custody record.

    (v) When the interview starts and the interviewer reminds the suspect of their right to legal advice (see *paragraph 11.2*, Code E *paragraph 4.5* and Code F *paragraph 4.5*), the interviewer shall then ensure that the following is recorded in the written interview record or the interview record made in accordance with Code E or F:

- confirmation that the detainee has changed their mind about wanting legal advice or (as the case may be) about wanting a solicitor present and the reasons for it if given;
- the fact that authority for the interview to proceed has been given and, subject to *paragraph 2.6A*, the name of the authorising officer;
- that if the solicitor arrives at the station before the interview is completed, the detainee will be so informed without delay and a break will be taken to allow them to speak to the solicitor if they wish, unless *paragraph 6.6(a)* applies, and
- that at any time during the interview, the detainee may again ask for legal advice and that if they do, a break will be taken to allow them to speak to the solicitor, unless *paragraph 6.6(a), (b)*, or *(c)* applies.

Note: In these circumstances, the restriction on drawing adverse inferences from silence in *Annex C* will not apply because the detainee is allowed an opportunity to consult a solicitor if they wish.

6.7   If *paragraph 6.6(a)* applies, where the reason for authorising the delay ceases to apply, there may be no further delay in permitting the exercise of the right in the absence of a further authorisation unless *paragraph 6.6(b), (c)* or *(d)* applies. If *paragraph 6.6(b)(i)* applies, once sufficient information has been obtained to avert the risk, questioning must cease until the detainee has received legal advice unless *paragraph 6.6(a), (b)(ii), (c)* or *(d)* applies.

6.8   A detainee who has been permitted to consult a solicitor shall be entitled on request to have the solicitor present when they are interviewed unless one of the exceptions in *paragraph 6.6* applies.

6.9   The solicitor may only be required to leave the interview if their conduct is such that the interviewer is unable properly to put questions to the suspect.

6.10   If the interviewer considers a solicitor is acting in such a way, they will stop the interview and consult an officer not below superintendent rank, if one is readily available, and otherwise an officer not below inspector rank not connected with the investigation. After speaking to the solicitor, the officer consulted will decide if the interview should continue in the presence of that solicitor. If they decide it should not, the suspect will be given the opportunity to consult another solicitor before the interview continues and that solicitor given an opportunity to be present at the interview.

6.11   The removal of a solicitor from an interview is a serious step and, if it occurs, the officer of superintendent rank or above who took the decision will consider if the incident should be reported to the Solicitors Regulatory Authority. If the decision to remove the solicitor has been taken by an officer below superintendent rank, the facts must be reported to an officer of superintendent rank or above, who will similarly consider whether a report to the Solicitors Regulatory Authority would be appropriate. When the solicitor concerned is a duty solicitor, the report should be both to the Solicitors Regulatory Authority and to the Legal Services Commission.

6.12   'Solicitor' in this Code means:
- a solicitor who holds a current practising certificate;
- an accredited or probationary representative included on the register of representatives maintained by the Legal Services Commission.

6.12A   An accredited or probationary representative sent to provide advice by, and on behalf of, a solicitor shall be admitted to the police station for this purpose unless an officer of inspector rank or above considers such a visit will hinder the investigation and directs otherwise. Hindering the investigation does not include giving proper legal advice to a detainee. Once admitted to the police station, *paragraphs 6.6* to *6.10* apply.

6.13   In exercising their discretion under *paragraph 6.12A*, the officer should take into account in particular:
- whether:
  ~ the identity and status of an accredited or probationary representative have been satisfactorily established;
  ~ they are of suitable character to provide legal advice, e.g. a person with a criminal record is unlikely to be suitable unless the conviction was for a minor offence and not recent.
- any other matters in any written letter of authorisation provided by the solicitor on whose behalf the person is attending the police station.

6.14   If the inspector refuses access to an accredited or probationary representative or a decision is taken that such a person should not be permitted to remain at an interview, the inspector must notify the solicitor on whose behalf the representative was acting and give them an opportunity to make alternative arrangements. The detainee must be informed and the custody record noted.

6.15   If a solicitor arrives at the station to see a particular person, that person must, unless *Annex B* applies, be so informed whether or not they are being interviewed and asked if they would like to see the solicitor. This applies even if the detainee has declined legal advice or, having requested it, subsequently agreed to be interviewed without receiving advice. The solicitor's attendance and the detainee's decision must be noted in the custody record.

(b) Documentation

6.16   Any request for legal advice and the action taken shall be recorded.

6.17   A record shall be made in the interview record if a detainee asks for legal advice and an interview is begun either in the absence of a solicitor or their representative, or they have been required to leave an interview.

2.8.10.1 KEYNOTE

Right to Legal Advice

A poster or posters of the right to legal advice containing translations into Welsh, the main minority ethnic languages and the principal European languages should be displayed wherever they are likely to be helpful and it is practicable to do so.

Section 58 of the Police and Criminal Evidence Act 1984 provides an almost inalienable right for a person arrested and held in custody at a police station or other premises to consult privately with a solicitor free of charge at any time if he/she requests it. In *R* v *Alladice* (1988) 87 Cr App R 380 the Court of Appeal made it clear that:

> ...no matter how strongly and however justifiably the police may feel that their investigation and detection of crime is being hindered by the presence of a solicitor...they are nevertheless confined to the narrow limits imposed by section 58.

A detainee has a right to free legal advice and to be represented by a solicitor. Note for Guidance 6B explains the arrangements which enable detainees to obtain legal advice. An outline of these arrangements is also included in the Notice of Rights and Entitlements given to detainees in accordance with para. 3.2. The arrangements also apply, with appropriate modifications, to persons attending a police station or other location voluntarily who are cautioned prior to being interviewed. See para. 3.21. When a detainee asks for free legal advice, the Defence Solicitor Call Centre (DSCC) must be informed of the request. Free legal advice will be limited to telephone advice provided by the Criminal Defence Service Direct (CDS) if a detainee is:

- detained for a non-imprisonable offence;
- arrested on a bench warrant for failing to appear and being held for production at court (except where the solicitor has clear documentary evidence available that would result in the client being released from custody);
- arrested for drink driving (driving/in charge with excess alcohol, failing to provide a specimen, driving/in charge whilst unfit through drink); or
- detained in relation to breach of police or court bail conditions

unless one or more exceptions apply, in which case the DSCC should arrange for advice to be given by a solicitor at the police station, for example:

- the police want to interview the detainee or carry out an eye-witness identification procedure;
- the detainee needs an appropriate adult;
- the detainee is unable to communicate over the telephone;
- the detainee alleges serious misconduct by the police;
- the investigation includes another offence not included in the list;
- the solicitor to be assigned is already at the police station.

When free advice is not limited to telephone advice, detainees can ask for free advice from a solicitor they know or if they do not know a solicitor or the solicitor they know cannot be contacted, from the duty solicitor.

To arrange free legal advice, the police should telephone the DSCC. The call centre will decide whether legal advice should be limited to telephone advice from CDS Direct, or whether a solicitor known to the detainee or the duty solicitor should speak to the detainee.

When detainees want to pay for legal advice themselves:

- the DSCC will contact a solicitor of their choice on their behalf;
- they may, when free advice is only available by telephone from CDS Direct, still speak to a solicitor of their choice on the telephone for advice, but the solicitor would not be paid by legal aid and may ask the person to pay for the advice;
- they should be given an opportunity to consult a specific solicitor or another solicitor from that solicitor's firm. If this solicitor is not available, they may choose up to two alternatives. If these alternatives are not available, the custody officer has discretion to allow further attempts until a solicitor has been contacted and agreed to provide advice;

- they are entitled to a private consultation with their chosen solicitor on the telephone or the solicitor may decide to come to the police station;
- If their chosen solicitor cannot be contacted, the DSCC may still be called to arrange free legal advice.

Apart from carrying out duties necessary to implement these arrangements, an officer must not advise the suspect about any particular firm of solicitors.

No police officer or police staff shall indicate to any suspect, except to answer a direct question, that the period for which he/she is liable to be detained, or if not detained, the time taken to complete the interview, might be reduced: if the suspect does not ask for legal advice or does not want a solicitor present when he/she is interviewed; or if he/she has asked for legal advice or (as the case may be) asked for a solicitor to be present when he/she is interviewed but changes his/her mind and agrees to be interviewed without waiting for a solicitor.

A detainee has a right to free legal advice and to be represented by a solicitor. A detainee is not obliged to give reasons for declining legal advice and should not be pressed to do so. The solicitor's only role in the police station is to protect and advance the legal rights of his/her client. On occasions, this may require the solicitor to give advice which has the effect of the client avoiding giving evidence which strengthens a prosecution case. The solicitor may intervene in order to seek clarification, challenge an improper question to the client or the manner in which it is put, advise the client not to reply to particular questions or if he/she wishes to give the client further legal advice.

An officer who takes the decision to exclude a solicitor must be in a position to satisfy the court that the decision was properly made. In order to do this he/she may need to witness what is happening. Paragraph 6.9 only applies if the solicitor's approach or conduct prevents or unreasonably obstructs proper questions being put to the suspect or the suspect's response being recorded. Examples of unacceptable conduct include answering questions on a suspect's behalf or providing written replies for the suspect to quote.

If an officer of at least inspector rank considers that a particular solicitor or firm of solicitors is persistently sending probationary representatives who are unsuited to provide legal advice, he/she should inform an officer of at least superintendent rank, who may wish to take the matter up with the Solicitors Regulation Authority.

Whenever a detainee exercises his/her right to legal advice by consulting or communicating with a solicitor, he/she must be allowed to do so in private. This right to consult or communicate in private is fundamental. If the requirement for privacy is compromised because what is said or written by the detainee or solicitor for the purpose of giving and receiving legal advice is overheard, listened to or read by others without the informed consent of the detainee, the right will effectively have been denied. When a detainee chooses to speak to a solicitor on the telephone, he/she should be allowed to do so in private unless this is impractical because of the design and layout of the custody area or the location of telephones. However, the normal expectation should be that facilities will be available, unless they are being used, at all police stations to enable detainees to speak in private to a solicitor either face to face or over the telephone.

This right to have a private consultation also applies to juveniles who, should they wish to have a private consultation without the appropriate adult being present, must be permitted to do so. This point was considered in *R (On the Application of M (A Child)) v Commissioner of the Police of the Metropolis* [2001] EWHC 533 (Admin), where the court said that ideally there ought be a consultation room at every police station and facilities for private telephone calls to be made for legal consultations. However, there was no breach of Article 6(3) of the European Convention on Human Rights where it could not be shown that a detainee had been denied adequate facilities for the preparation of his defence.

Once a person has indicated a wish to have a solicitor, and has not yet been advised by a solicitor, he/she can only be interviewed in limited circumstances as set out in Code C, para. 6.6. In considering whether a detainee can be interviewed or continue to be interviewed under para. 6.6 without having received legal advice which he/she has requested, the officer making this decision should, if practicable, ask the solicitor for an estimate of how long it will take to come to the station and relate this to the time that detention is permitted, the time of day (i.e. whether the rest period under para. 12.2 is imminent) and the requirements of other investigations. Subject to the constraints of Annex B, a solicitor may advise more than one client in an investigation if he/she wishes. Any question of a conflict of interest is for the solicitor under his/her professional code of conduct. If, however, waiting for a solicitor to give advice to one client may lead to unreasonable delay to the interview with another, the provisions of para. 6.6(b) may apply.

Where the solicitor is on the way or is to set off immediately, it will not normally be appropriate to begin an interview before he/she arrives. If it appears necessary to begin an interview before the solicitor's arrival, he/she should be given an indication of how long the police would be able to wait before starting the interview so that there is an opportunity to make arrangements for someone else to provide legal advice.

Code C, Annex B provides an exception to this right to legal advice. The same exception also applies where the person is held under prevention of terrorism legislation (Terrorism Act 2000, s. 41 or sch. 8) and the conditions in Code H, Annex B apply. In addition, a uniformed officer of at least the rank of inspector not connected with the case may be present if authorised by an Assistant Chief Constable or Commander (Terrorism Act 2000, sch. 8, para. 9 and Code H, paras 6.4, 6.5). The delay can only be for a maximum of 36 hours (48 hours from the time of arrest in terrorism cases) or until the time the person will first appear at court, whichever is the sooner (see below). The 36-hour period is calculated from the 'relevant time'.

Another exception is in relation to the drink-drive procedure for s. 7 of the Road Traffic Act 1988. In *DPP* v *Noe* [2000] RTR 351 a request to see a solicitor or alternatively to consult a law book to verify the legality of the police request for a specimen of breath was not a reasonable excuse under s. 7. This is confirmed by *Campbell* v *DPP* [2002] EWHC 1314 (Admin), in which it was held that it was entirely proportionate to allow a police officer to require a member of the community to provide a specimen, albeit that legal advice had not been obtained.

Where Code C, para. 6.6 is used it will have to be justified at court if the interview is to be admissible. This power might prove useful in circumstances where there are 'delaying tactics' by legal representatives, particularly where they are aware that the detained person's relevant time is due to expire within a short period.

When detainees who wanted legal advice change their mind, an officer of inspector rank or above must authorise the continuation of the interview. It is permissible for such authorisation to be given over the telephone, if the authorising officer is able to satisfy him/herself about the reason for the detainee's change of mind and is satisfied that it is proper to continue the interview in those circumstances.

In terrorism cases a direction may be given by an officer of at least the rank of Commander or Assistant Chief Constable which may provide that a detained person who wishes to exercise the right to consult a solicitor may do so only in the sight and hearing of a qualified officer, this person being a uniformed officer of at least the rank of inspector not connected with the investigation from the authorising officer's force (Code H, para. 6.5).

2.8.11

7 Citizens of Independent Commonwealth Countries or Foreign Nationals

(a) Action

7.1   A detainee who is a citizen of an independent Commonwealth country or a national of a foreign country, including the Republic of Ireland, has the right, upon request, to communicate at any time with the appropriate High Commission, Embassy or Consulate. That detainee must be informed as soon as practicable of this right and asked if they want to have their High Commission, Embassy or Consulate told of their whereabouts and the grounds for their detention. Such a request should be acted upon as soon as practicable.

7.2   A detainee who is a citizen of a country with which a bilateral consular convention or agreement is in force requiring notification of arrest must also be informed that subject to *paragraph 7.4*, notification of their arrest will be sent to the appropriate High Commission, Embassy or Consulate as soon as practicable, whether or not they request it. A list of the countries to which this requirement currently applies and contact details for the relevant High Commissions, Embassies and Consulates can be obtained from the Consular Directorate of the Foreign and Commonwealth Office (FCO) as follows:

- from the FCO web pages:
  - ~ https://gov.uk/government/publications/table-of-consular-conventions-and-mandatory-notification-obligations, and
  - ~ https://www.gov.uk/government/publications/foreign-embassies-in-the-uk
- by telephone to 020 7008 3100,
- by email to fcocorrespondence@fco.gov.uk.
- by letter to the Foreign and Commonwealth Office, King Charles Street, London, SW1A 2AH.

7.3 Consular officers may, if the detainee agrees, visit one of their nationals in police detention to talk to them and, if required, to arrange for legal advice. Such visits shall take place out of the hearing of a police officer.

7.4 Notwithstanding the provisions of consular conventions, if the detainee claims that they are a refugee or have applied or intend to apply for asylum, the custody officer must ensure that UK Visas and Immigration (UKVI) (formerly the UK Border Agency) is informed as soon as practicable of the claim. UKVI will then determine whether compliance with relevant international obligations requires notification of the arrest to be sent and will inform the custody officer as to what action police need to take.

(b) Documentation

7.5 A record shall be made:
- when a detainee is informed of their rights under this section and of any requirement in *paragraph 7.2*;
- of any communications with a High Commission, Embassy or Consulate, and
- of any communications with UKVI about a detainee's claim to be a refugee or to be seeking asylum and the resulting action taken by police.

2.8.11.1

KEYNOTE

The exercise of the rights in this section may not be interfered with even where Code C, Annex B applies.

2.8.12

8 Conditions of Detention

(a) Action

8.1 So far as it is practicable, not more than one detainee should be detained in each cell.

8.2 Cells in use must be adequately heated, cleaned and ventilated. They must be adequately lit, subject to such dimming as is compatible with safety and security to allow people detained overnight to sleep. No additional restraints shall be used within a locked cell unless absolutely necessary and then only restraint equipment, approved for use in that force by the chief officer, which is reasonable and necessary in the circumstances having regard to the detainee's demeanour and with a view to ensuring their safety and the safety of others. If a detainee is deaf, mentally disordered or otherwise mentally vulnerable, particular care must be taken when deciding whether to use any form of approved restraints.

8.3 Blankets, mattresses, pillows and other bedding supplied shall be of a reasonable standard and in a clean and sanitary condition.

8.4 Access to toilet and washing facilities must be provided.

8.5 If it is necessary to remove a detainee's clothes for the purposes of investigation, for hygiene, health reasons or cleaning, replacement clothing of a reasonable standard of comfort and cleanliness shall be provided. A detainee may not be interviewed unless adequate clothing has been offered.

8.6   At least two light meals and one main meal should be offered in any 24-hour period. Drinks should be provided at meal times and upon reasonable request between meals. Whenever necessary, advice shall be sought from the appropriate healthcare professional, on medical and dietary matters. As far as practicable, meals provided shall offer a varied diet and meet any specific dietary needs or religious beliefs the detainee may have. The detainee may, at the custody officer's discretion, have meals supplied by their family or friends at their expense.

8.7   Brief outdoor exercise shall be offered daily if practicable.

8.8   A juvenile shall not be placed in a police cell unless no other secure accommodation is available and the custody officer considers it is not practicable to supervise them if they are not placed in a cell or that a cell provides more comfortable accommodation than other secure accommodation in the station. A juvenile may not be placed in a cell with a detained adult.
Note: *Paragraph 1.5A* extends these requirements to 17-year-old detainees.

(b) Documentation

8.9   A record must be kept of replacement clothing and meals offered.

8.10 If a juvenile is placed in a cell, the reason must be recorded.
Note: *Paragraph 1.5A* extends this requirement to 17-year-old detainees.

8.11 The use of any restraints on a detainee whilst in a cell, the reasons for it and, if appropriate, the arrangements for enhanced supervision of the detainee whilst so restrained, shall be recorded. See *paragraph 3.9*.

2.8.12.1   **KEYNOTE**

The provision of bedding, medical and dietary matters are of particular importance in the case of a person likely to be detained for an extended period. In deciding whether to allow meals to be supplied by family or friends, the custody officer is entitled to take account of the risk of items being concealed in any food or package and the officer's duties and responsibilities under food handling legislation. Meals should, so far as practicable, be offered at recognised meal times, or at other times that take account of when the detainee last had a meal.

It is suggested that the custody officer should undertake a further risk assessment which should be recorded in the custody record before more than one person is placed in a cell. Any steps taken to minimise the risk should also be included in the custody record. (Paragraph 2.3 requires the time of release to be recorded; this is relevant in calculating any period of detention which may still be remaining if the person has been bailed, and periods in police detention also count towards the period a person serves in custody.)

Section 117 of the 1984 Act provides that where any provision of the Act confers a power on a constable and does not provide that the power may only be exercised with the consent of some person, other than a police officer, the officer may use reasonable force, if necessary, in the exercise of the power.

This is not a blanket power to use force. In *R* v *Jones* (1999) *The Times*, 21 April, the court said that s. 117 should not be interpreted as giving a right to police to exercise force whenever the consent of a suspect was not required.

2.8.13   ## 9 Care and Treatment of Detained Persons

(a) General

9.1   Nothing in this section prevents the police from calling an appropriate healthcare professional to examine a detainee for the purposes of obtaining evidence relating to any offence in which the detainee is suspected of being involved.

9.2   If a complaint is made by, or on behalf of, a detainee about their treatment since their arrest, or it comes to notice that a detainee may have been treated improperly, a report must be made as soon as practicable to an officer of inspector rank or above not connected with the investigation. If the matter concerns a possible assault or the possibility of the unnecessary or unreasonable use of force, an appropriate healthcare professional must also be called as soon as practicable.

9.3 Detainees should be visited at least every hour. If no reasonably foreseeable risk was identified in a risk assessment, see *paragraphs 3.6–3.10*, there is no need to wake a sleeping detainee. Those suspected of being under the influence of drink or drugs or both or of having swallowed drugs, or whose level of consciousness causes concern must, subject to any clinical directions given by the appropriate healthcare professional, see *paragraph 9.13*:

- be visited and roused at least every half hour;
- have their condition assessed as in *Annex H*;
- and clinical treatment arranged if appropriate.

9.4 When arrangements are made to secure clinical attention for a detainee, the custody officer must make sure all relevant information which might assist in the treatment of the detainee's condition is made available to the responsible healthcare professional. This applies whether or not the healthcare professional asks for such information. Any officer or police staff with relevant information must inform the custody officer as soon as practicable.

(b) Clinical treatment and attention

9.5 The custody officer must make sure a detainee receives appropriate clinical attention as soon as reasonably practicable if the person:
 (a) appears to be suffering from physical illness; or
 (b) is injured; or
 (c) appears to be suffering from a mental disorder; or
 (d) appears to need clinical attention.

9.5A This applies even if the detainee makes no request for clinical attention and whether or not they have already received clinical attention elsewhere. If the need for attention appears urgent, e.g. when indicated as in Annex H, the nearest available healthcare professional or an ambulance must be called immediately.

9.5B The custody officer must also consider the need for clinical attention in relation to those suffering the effects of alcohol or drugs.

9.6 *Paragraph 9.5* is not meant to prevent or delay the transfer to a hospital if necessary of a person detained under the Mental Health Act 1983, section 136. When an assessment under that Act is to take place at a police station, see *paragraph 3.16*, the custody officer must consider whether an appropriate healthcare professional should be called to conduct an initial clinical check on the detainee. This applies particularly when there is likely to be any significant delay in the arrival of a suitably qualified medical practitioner.

9.7 If it appears to the custody officer, or they are told, that a person brought to a station under arrest may be suffering from an infectious disease or condition, the custody officer must take reasonable steps to safeguard the health of the detainee and others at the station. In deciding what action to take, advice must be sought from an appropriate healthcare professional. The custody officer has discretion to isolate the person and their property until clinical directions have been obtained.

9.8 If a detainee requests a clinical examination, an appropriate healthcare professional must be called as soon as practicable to assess the detainee's clinical needs. If a safe and appropriate care plan cannot be provided, the appropriate healthcare professional's advice must be sought. The detainee may also be examined by a medical practitioner of their choice at their expense.

9.9 If a detainee is required to take or apply any medication in compliance with clinical directions prescribed before their detention, the custody officer must consult the appropriate healthcare professional before the use of the medication. Subject to the restrictions in *paragraph 9.10*, the custody officer is responsible for the safekeeping of any medication and for making sure the detainee is given the opportunity to take or apply prescribed or approved medication. Any such consultation and its outcome shall be noted in the custody record.

9.10 No police officer may administer or supervise the self-administration of medically prescribed controlled drugs of the types and forms listed in the Misuse of Drugs Regulations 2001, Schedule 2 or 3. A detainee may only self-administer such drugs under the personal supervision of the registered medical practitioner authorising their use or other appropriate healthcare professional. The custody officer may supervise the self-administration of, or authorise other custody staff to supervise the self-administration of, drugs listed in Schedule 4 or 5 if the officer has consulted the appropriate healthcare professional authorising their use and both are satisfied self-administration will not expose the detainee, police officers or anyone else to the risk of harm or injury.

9.11 When appropriate healthcare professionals administer drugs or authorise the use of other medications, supervise their self-administration or consult with the custody officer about allowing self-administration of drugs listed in Schedule 4 or 5, it must be within current medicines legislation and the scope of practice as determined by their relevant statutory regulatory body.

9.12 If a detainee has in their possession, or claims to need, medication relating to a heart condition, diabetes, epilepsy or a condition of comparable potential seriousness then, even though *paragraph 9.5* may not apply, the advice of the appropriate healthcare professional must be obtained.

9.13 Whenever the appropriate healthcare professional is called in accordance with this section to examine or treat a detainee, the custody officer shall ask for their opinion about:
- any risks or problems which police need to take into account when making decisions about the detainee's continued detention;
- when to carry out an interview if applicable; and
- the need for safeguards.

9.14 When clinical directions are given by the appropriate healthcare professional, whether orally or in writing, and the custody officer has any doubts or is in any way uncertain about any aspect of the directions, the custody officer shall ask for clarification. It is particularly important that directions concerning the frequency of visits are clear, precise and capable of being implemented.

(c) Documentation

9.15 A record must be made in the custody record of:
(a) the arrangements made for an examination by an appropriate healthcare professional under *paragraph 9.2* and of any complaint reported under that paragraph together with any relevant remarks by the custody officer;
(b) any arrangements made in accordance with *paragraph 9.5*;
(c) any request for a clinical examination under *paragraph 9.8* and any arrangements made in response;
(d) the injury, ailment, condition or other reason which made it necessary to make the arrangements in (a) to (c);
(e) any clinical directions and advice, including any further clarifications, given to police by a healthcare professional concerning the care and treatment of the detainee in connection with any of the arrangements made in (a) to (c);
(f) if applicable, the responses received when attempting to rouse a person using the procedure in *Annex H*.

9.16 If a healthcare professional does not record their clinical findings in the custody record, the record must show where they are recorded. However, information which is necessary to custody staff to ensure the effective ongoing care and well being of the detainee must be recorded openly in the custody record, see *paragraph 3.8* and *Annex G, paragraph 7*.

9.17   Subject to the requirements of *Section 4*, the custody record shall include:

- a record of all medication a detainee has in their possession on arrival at the police station;
- a note of any such medication they claim to need but do not have with them.

2.8.13.1   **KEYNOTE**

A 'health care professional' means a clinically qualified person working within the scope of practice as determined by his/her relevant professional body. Whether a health care professional is 'appropriate' depends on the circumstances of the duties he/she carries out at the time.

Paragraph 9.3 also applies to a person in police custody by order of a magistrates' court under the Criminal Justice Act 1988, s. 152 (as amended by the Drugs Act 2005, s. 8) to facilitate the recovery of evidence after being charged with drug possession or drug trafficking and suspected of having swallowed drugs. In the case of the healthcare needs of a person who has swallowed drugs, the custody officer, subject to any clinical directions, should consider the necessity for rousing every half hour. This does not negate the need for regular visiting of the suspect in the cell. Whenever possible, juveniles (which includes 17-year-olds) and mentally vulnerable detainees should be visited more frequently. The purpose of recording a person's responses when attempting to rouse them using the procedure in Annex H is to enable any change in the individual's consciousness level to be noted and clinical treatment arranged if appropriate.

Paragraph 9.5 does not apply to minor ailments or injuries which do not need attention. However, all such ailments or injuries must be recorded in the custody record and any doubt must be resolved in favour of calling the appropriate health care professional. The custody officer should always seek to clarify directions that the detainee requires constant observation or supervision and should ask the appropriate health care professional to explain precisely what action needs to be taken to implement such directions.

A detainee who appears drunk or behaves abnormally may be suffering from illness, the effects of drugs or may have sustained injury, particularly a head injury which is not apparent. A detainee needing or dependent on certain drugs, including alcohol, may experience harmful effects within a short time of being deprived of his/her supply. In these circumstances, when there is any doubt, police should always act urgently to call an appropriate health care professional or an ambulance.

Any information that is available about the detained person should be considered in deciding whether to request a medical examination. In *R v HM Coroner for Coventry, ex parte Chief Constable of Staffordshire Police* (2000) 164 JP 665 the detained person had been drunk on arrest and was detained to be interviewed. The detained person made no complaint of his condition but his sister called the police to advise them that he would get the shakes. It was clear at interview and the following morning that he did have the shakes but no complaint was made and no doctor was called. A verdict of accidental death aggravated by neglect was an option in the case as the deceased had died while in police custody. The court considered the facts, such as the deceased's withdrawal and the warning as to his condition, from which a properly directed jury could have concluded that had certain steps been taken it was at least possible that the deceased would not have died. In this case, a verdict of accidental death aggravated by neglect was left open to the jury, even though a doctor at the inquest gave evidence that he doubted whether calling a doctor would have made any difference to the eventual outcome.

Whenever practicable, arrangements should be made for persons detained for assessment under s. 136 of the Mental Health Act 1983 to be taken to a hospital. Chapter 10 of the Mental Health Act 1983 Code of Practice (as revised) provides more detailed guidance about arranging assessments under s. 136 of the 1983 Act and transferring detainees from police stations to other places of safety.

2.8.13.2   **KEYNOTE**

Medical Record Forming Part of the Custody Record

It is important to respect a person's right to privacy, and information about his/her health must be kept confidential and only disclosed with his/her consent or in accordance with clinical advice when it is necessary to protect the detainee's health or that of others who come into contact with him/her.

A solicitor or appropriate adult must be permitted to consult a detainee's custody record as soon as practicable after his/her arrival at the station and at any other time while the person is detained (Code C, para. 2.4). Therefore details required to be included in the custody record concerning the detainee's injuries and ailments will be accessible to both the solicitor and appropriate adult. However, paras 9.15 and 9.16 do not require any information about the cause of any injury, ailment or condition to be recorded on the custody record if it appears capable of providing evidence of an offence.

As the Codes specify matters which must be included within the custody record, it is suggested that all other matters recorded by the appropriate health care professional do not form part of the custody record and therefore do not need to be made available to the solicitor or appropriate adult under Code C, para. 2.4, i.e. the notes made by the health care professional.

2.8.13.3 KEYNOTE

Independent Custody Visiting (Lay Visitors)

Section 51 of the Police Reform Act 2002 introduced independent custody visitors on a statutory basis. The arrangements may confer on independent custody visitors such powers as the police authority considers necessary to enable them to carry out their functions under the arrangements and may, in particular, confer on them powers to:

- require access to be given to each police station;
- examine records relating to the detention of persons;
- meet detainees for the purposes of a discussion about their treatment and conditions while detained; and
- inspect the facilities including, in particular, cell accommodation, washing and toilet facilities and the facilities for the provision of food.

A Code of Practice on Independent Custody Visiting has been published outlining the role of the independent visitor (this can be found at <http://www.icva.org.uk>).

10 Cautions (see chapter 2.10)

11 Interviews—general (see chapter 2.10)

12 Interviews in police stations (see chapter 2.10)

2.8.14

13 Interpreters

(a) General

13.1 Chief officers are responsible for making arrangements to provide appropriately qualified independent persons to act as interpreters and to provide translations of essential documents for:
   (a) detained suspects who, in accordance with *paragraph 3.5(c)(ii)*, the custody officer has determined require an interpreter, and
   (b) suspects who are not under arrest but are cautioned as in *section 10* who, in accordance with *paragraph 3.21*, the interviewer has determined require an interpreter. In these cases, the responsibilities of the custody officer are, if appropriate, assigned to the interviewer. An interviewer who has any doubts about whether an interpreter is required or about how the provisions of this section should be applied to a suspect who is not under arrest should seek advice from an officer of the rank of sergeant or above.

   If the suspect has a hearing or speech impediment, references to 'interpreter' and 'interpretation' in this Code include appropriate assistance necessary to establish effective communication with that person. See *paragraph 13.1C* below if the person is in Wales.

13.1A The arrangements must comply with the minimum requirements set out in Directive 2010/64/EU of the European Parliament and of the Council of 20 October 2010 on the right to interpretation and translation in criminal proceedings. The provisions of this Code implement the requirements for those to whom this Code applies. These requirements include the following:

- That the arrangements made and the quality of interpretation and translation provided shall be sufficient to 'safeguard the fairness of the proceedings, in particular by ensuring that suspected or accused persons have knowledge of the cases against them and are able to exercise their right of defence'. This term which is used by the Directive means that the suspect must be able to understand their position and be able to communicate effectively with police officers, interviewers, solicitors and appropriate adults as provided for by this and any other Code in the same way as a suspect who can speak and understand English and who does not have a hearing or speech impediment and who would therefore not require an interpreter.

- The provision of a written translation of all documents considered essential for the person to exercise their right of defence and to 'safeguard the fairness of the proceedings' as described above. For the purposes of this Code, this includes any decision to authorise a person to be detained and details of any offence(s) with which the person has been charged or for which they have been told they may be prosecuted, see *Annex M*.

- Procedures to help determine:
  ~ whether a suspect can speak and understand English and needs the assistance of an interpreter, see *paragraph 13.1*; and
  ~ whether another interpreter should be called or another translation should be provided when a suspect complains about the quality of either or both, see *paragraphs 13.10A* and *13.10C*.

13.1B All reasonable attempts should be made to make the suspect understand that interpretation and translation will be provided at public expense.

13.1C With regard to persons in Wales, nothing in this or any other Code affects the application of the Welsh Language Schemes produced by police and crime commissioners in Wales in accordance with the Welsh Language Act 1993. See *paragraphs 3.12* and *13.1*.

(b) Interviewing suspects–foreign languages

13.2 Unless *paragraphs 11.1* or *11.18(c)* apply, a suspect who for the purposes of this Code requires an interpreter because they do not appear to speak or understand English (see *paragraphs 3.5(c)(ii)* and *3.12*) must not be interviewed in the absence of a person capable of interpreting.

13.2A An interpreter should also be called if a juvenile is interviewed and their parent or guardian, present as the appropriate adult, does not appear to speak or understand English, unless the interview is urgent and *paragraphs 11.1* or *11.18(c)* apply.
Note: *Paragraph 1.5A* extends the requirement in this paragraph to interviews of 17-year-old suspects.

13.3 When a written record of the interview is made (see *paragraph 11.7*), the interviewer shall make sure the interpreter makes a note of the interview at the time in the person's language for use in the event of the interpreter being called to give evidence, and certifies its accuracy. The interviewer should allow sufficient time for the interpreter to note each question and answer after each is put, given and interpreted. The person should be allowed to read the record or have it read to them and sign it as correct or indicate the respects in which they consider it inaccurate. If an audio or visual record of the interview is made, the arrangements in Code E or F shall apply.

13.4 In the case of a person making a statement under caution to a police officer or other police staff other than in English:

(a) the interpreter shall record the statement in the language it is made;

(b) the person shall be invited to sign it;

(c) an official English translation shall be made in due course.

(c) Interviewing suspects who have a hearing or speech impediment

13.5 Unless *paragraphs 11.1* or *11.18(c)* (urgent interviews) apply, a suspect who for the purposes of this Code requires an interpreter or other appropriate assistance to enable effective communication with them because they appear to have a hearing or speech impediment (see *paragraphs 3.5(c)(ii)* and *3.12*) must not be interviewed in the absence of an independent person capable of interpreting or without that assistance.

13.6 An interpreter should also be called if a juvenile is interviewed and their parent or guardian, present as the appropriate adult, appears to have a hearing or speech impediment, unless the interview is urgent and *paragraphs 11.1* or *11.18(c)* apply.

Note: *Paragraph 1.5A* extends the requirement in this paragraph to interviews of 17-year-old suspects.

13.7 The interviewer shall make sure the interpreter is allowed to read the interview record and certify its accuracy in the event of the interpreter being called to give evidence. If the interview is audibly recorded or visually recorded, the arrangements in Code E or F apply.

(d) Additional rules for detained persons

13.8 *Not used.*

13.9 If *paragraph 6.1* applies and the detainee cannot communicate with the solicitor because of language, hearing or speech difficulties, an interpreter must be called. A police officer or any other police staff may not be used for this purpose.

13.10 After the custody officer has determined that a detainee requires an interpreter (see *paragraph 3.5(c)(ii)*) and following the initial action in *paragraphs 3.1* to *3.5*, arrangements must also be made for an interpreter to:

- explain the grounds and reasons for any authorisation for their continued detention, before or after charge and any information about the authorisation given to them by the authorising officer and which is recorded in the custody record. See *paragraphs 15.3, 15.4* and *15.16(a)* and *(b)*;

- be present at the magistrates' court for the hearing of an application for a warrant of further detention or any extension or further extension of such warrant to explain any grounds and reasons for the application and any information about the authorisation of their further detention given to them by the court (see PACE, sections 43 and 44 and *paragraphs 15.2* and *15.16(c)*), and

- explain any offence with which the detainee is charged or for which they are informed they may be prosecuted and any other information about the offence given to them by or on behalf of the custody officer, see *paragraphs 16.1* and *16.3*.

13.10A If a detainee complains that they are not satisfied with the quality of interpretation, the custody officer or (as the case may be) the interviewer, is responsible for deciding whether a different interpreter should be called in accordance with the procedures set out in the arrangements made by the chief officer, see *paragraph 13.1A*.

(e) Translations of essential documents

13.10B Written translations, oral translations and oral summaries of essential documents in a language the detainee understands shall be provided in accordance with *Annex M* (Translations of documents and records).

13.10C If a detainee complains that they are not satisfied with the quality of the translation, the custody officer or (as the case may be) the interviewer, is responsible for deciding whether a further translation should be provided in accordance with the procedures set out in the arrangements made by the chief officer, see *paragraph 13.1A*.

(f) Decisions not to provide interpretation and translation

13.10D If a suspect challenges a decision:
- made by the custody officer or (as the case may be) by the interviewer, in accordance with this Code (see *paragraphs 3.5(c)(ii)* and *3.21*) that they do not require an interpreter; or
- made in accordance with *paragraphs 13.10A, 13.10B* or *13.10C* not to provide a different interpreter or another translation or not to translate a requested document, the matter shall be reported to an inspector to deal with as a complaint for the purposes of *paragraph 9.2* or *12.9* if the challenge is made during an interview.

(g) Documentation

13.11 The following must be recorded in the custody record or, as applicable, the interview record:
- (a) Action taken to call an interpreter;
- (b) Action taken when a detainee is not satisfied about the standard of interpretation or translation provided, see *paragraphs 13.10A* and *13.10C*;
- (c) When an urgent interview is carried out in accordance with *paragraph 13.2* or *13.5* in the absence of an interpreter;
- (d) When a detainee has been assisted by an interpreter for the purpose of providing or being given information or being interviewed;
- (e) Action taken in accordance with *Annex M* when:
  - a written translation of an essential document is provided;
  - an oral translation or oral summary of an essential document is provided instead of a written translation and the authorising officer's reason(s) why this would not prejudice the fairness of the proceedings (see *Annex M, paragraph 3*);
  - a suspect waives their right to a translation of an essential document (see *Annex M, paragraph 4*);
  - when representations that a document which is not included in the table is essential and that a translation should be provided are refused and the reason for the refusal (see *Annex M, paragraph 8*).

2.8.14.1 **KEYNOTE**

Where the detained person is unable to speak effectively in English, an interpreter must be called to safeguard the rights of the person and to allow him/her to communicate. A procedure for determining whether a person needs an interpreter might involve a telephone interpreter service or using cue cards or similar visual aids which enable detainees to indicate their ability to speak and understand English and their preferred language.

This could be confirmed through an interpreter who could also assess the extent to which the person can speak and understand English. There should also be a procedure for determining whether suspects who require an interpreter require assistance in accordance with para. 3.20 to help them check and if applicable sign any documentation. Chief Officers have discretion when determining the individuals or organisations they use to provide interpretation and translation services for their forces provided that these services are compatible with the requirements of the Directive.

The importance of the role of the interpreter in proceedings can be seen in *Bielecki* v *DPP* [2011] EWHC 2245 (Admin). This was a drink-drive case where the defendant, who was Polish, had been required to provide breath specimens for analysis under the Road Traffic Act; this had been communicated through a Polish-speaking interpreter, who was present to translate at the police station. The defendant failed to provide the breath specimens and his defence was that he did not understand the requirement. The court held that it was a legitimate inference for the magistrates to draw that the words had been translated accurately. There was no evidence that the interpreter suggested to the officers that the defendant had not understood what was being said. A court could draw the inference, if the evidence supported it, that someone being asked to do something in a police station by a police officer with the assistance of an accredited interpreter of the relevant language had been asked the correct question and understood it and also the consequences of not responding to it (*Bielecki* v *DPP* [2011] EWHC 2245 (Admin)).

The interpreter is there for the benefit of the detained person and should not be considered to be part of the prosecution team. The case of *R (On the Application of Bozkurt)* v *Thames Magistrates' Court* [2001] EWHC Admin 400, demonstrates the importance of the interpreter's independence in proceedings. In *Bozkurt*, the police arranged for an interpreter to attend the custody suite and interpret for the drink-drive procedure at the police station. The police then arranged for the interpreter to attend court. The interpreter translated for the defendant while he took advice from the duty solicitor at court. The interpreter failed to inform the solicitor that he had translated for the drink-drive procedure at the police station. The court held that an interpreter was under an equal duty to that of the solicitor to keep confidential what he might hear during a conference. In these circumstances, it would have been preferable for a different interpreter to be used, or at least for the interpreter to have obtained the permission of the solicitor to interpret for the conference.

The revised Codes provide consistency with paras 3.5(c)(ii) and 3.12 where the need for an interpreter is determined according to a person's ability to speak and understand English. The routine (non-urgent) exception if the interviewer speaks the suspect's own language is deleted to accord with the EU Directive which requires interpreters to be independent. In any event, this would be operationally impracticable in that an English translation of the interview is required. Amendments to para. 11.18(c) of Code C still allow for urgent interviews. It is important to note that reference to police officers acting as interpreters has been removed as this causes a conflict with the requirement for interpreters to be independent.

2.8.15   14 Questioning—Special Restrictions

14.1   If a person is arrested by one police force on behalf of another and the lawful period of detention in respect of that offence has not yet commenced in accordance with PACE, section 41 no questions may be put to them about the offence while they are in transit between the forces except to clarify any voluntary statement they make.

14.2   If a person is in police detention at a hospital they may not be questioned without the agreement of a responsible doctor.

2.8.15.1   KEYNOTE

If questioning takes place at a hospital under paragraph 14.2, or on the way to or from a hospital, the period of questioning concerned counts towards the total period of detention permitted.

15 Reviews and Extensions of Detention

(a) Persons detained under PACE

15.0 The requirement in *paragraph 3.4(b)* that documents and materials essential to challenging the lawfulness of the detainee's arrest and detention must be made available to the detainee or their solicitor, applies for the purposes of this section as follows:

(a) The officer reviewing the need for detention without charge (PACE, s. 40), or (as the case may be) the officer considering the need to extend detention without charge from 24 to 36 hours (PACE, s. 42), is responsible, in consultation with the investigating officer, for deciding which documents and materials are essential and must be made available.

(b) When *paragraph 15.7A* applies (application for a warrant of further detention or extension of such a warrant), the officer making the application is responsible for deciding which documents and materials are essential and must be made available before the hearing.

15.1 The review officer is responsible under PACE, section 40 for periodically determining if a person's detention, before or after charge, continues to be necessary. This requirement continues throughout the detention period and, except as in paragraph 15.10, the review officer must be present at the police station holding the detainee.

15.2 Under PACE, section 42, an officer of superintendent rank or above who is responsible for the station holding the detainee may give authority any time after the second review to extend the maximum period the person may be detained without charge by up to 12 hours. Further detention without charge may be authorised only by a magistrates' court in accordance with PACE, sections 43 and 44.

15.2A An authorisation under section 42(1) of PACE extends the maximum period of detention permitted before charge for indictable offences from 24 hours to 36 hours. Detaining a juvenile or mentally vulnerable person for longer than 24 hours will be dependent on the circumstances of the case and with regard to the person's:

(a) special vulnerability;

(b) the legal obligation to provide an opportunity for representations to be made prior to a decision about extending detention;

(c) the need to consult and consider the views of any appropriate adult; and

(d) any alternatives to police custody.

Note: *Paragraph 1.5A* extends sub-paragraph (c) to 17-year-old detainees.

15.3 Before deciding whether to authorise continued detention the officer responsible under *paragraph 15.1* or *15.2* shall give an opportunity to make representations about the detention to:

(a) the detainee, unless in the case of a review as in *paragraph 15.1*, the detainee is asleep;

(b) the detainee's solicitor if available at the time; and

(c) the appropriate adult if available at the time.

Note: *Paragraph 1.5A* extends the requirement in sub-paragraph (c) to 17-year-old detainees.

15.3A Other people having an interest in the detainee's welfare may also make representations at the authorising officer's discretion.

15.3B Subject to *paragraph 15.10*, the representations may be made orally in person or by telephone or in writing. The authorising officer may, however, refuse to hear oral representations from the detainee if the officer considers them unfit to make representations because of their condition or behaviour.

15.3C The decision on whether the review takes place in person or by telephone or by video conferencing is a matter for the review officer. In determining the form the review may take, the review officer must always take full account of the needs of the person in custody. The benefits of carrying out a review in person should always be considered, based on the individual circumstances of each case with specific additional consideration if the person is:

(a) a juvenile (and the age of the juvenile); or

Note: *Paragraph 1.5A extends this sub-paragraph to 17-year-old detainees.*

(b) suspected of being mentally vulnerable; or

(c) in need of medical attention for other than routine minor ailments; or

(d) subject to presentational or community issues around their detention.

15.4   Before conducting a review or determining whether to extend the maximum period of detention without charge, the officer responsible must make sure the detainee is reminded of their entitlement to free legal advice, see *paragraph 6.5*, unless in the case of a review the person is asleep.

15.5   If, after considering any representations, the review officer under *paragraph 15.1* decides to keep the detainee in detention or the superintendent under *paragraph 15.2* extends the maximum period for which they may be detained without charge, then any comment made by the detainee shall be recorded. If applicable, the officer shall be informed of the comment as soon as practicable. See also *paragraphs 11.4* and *11.13*.

15.6   No officer shall put specific questions to the detainee:

- regarding their involvement in any offence; or
- in respect of any comments they may make:
    - ~ when given the opportunity to make representations; or
    - ~ in response to a decision to keep them in detention or extend the maximum period of detention.

Such an exchange could constitute an interview as in *paragraph 11.1A* and would be subject to the associated safeguards in *section 11* and, in respect of a person who has been charged, *paragraph 16.5*. See also *paragraph 11.13*.

15.7   A detainee who is asleep at a review, see paragraph 15.1, and whose continued detention is authorised must be informed about the decision and reason as soon as practicable after waking.

15.7A   When an application is made to a magistrates' court under PACE, s. 43 for a warrant of further detention to extend detention without charge of a person arrested for an indictable offence, or under s. 44, to extend or further extend that warrant, the detainee:

(a) must be brought to court for the hearing of the application;

(b) is entitled to be legally represented if they wish, in which case, Annex B cannot apply; and

(c) must be given a copy of the information which supports the application and states:

(i) the nature of the offence for which the person to whom the application relates has been arrested;

(ii) the general nature of the evidence on which the person was arrested;

(iii) what inquiries about the offence have been made and what further inquiries are proposed;

(iv) the reasons for believing continued detention is necessary for the purposes of the further inquiries;

Note: A warrant of further detention can only be issued or extended if the court has reasonable grounds for believing that the person's further detention is necessary for the purpose of obtaining evidence of an indictable offence for which the person has been arrested and that the investigation is being conducted diligently and expeditiously. See *paragraph 15.0(b)*.

15.8   *Not used.*

(b) Review of detention by telephone and video conferencing facilities

15.9 PACE, section 40A provides that the officer responsible under section 40 for reviewing the detention of a person who has not been charged, need not attend the police station holding the detainee and may carry out the review by telephone.

15.9A PACE, section 45A(2) provides that the officer responsible under section 40 for reviewing the detention of a person who has not been charged, need not attend the police station holding the detainee and may carry out the review by video conferencing facilities.

15.9B A telephone review is not permitted where facilities for review by video conferencing exist and it is practicable to use them.

15.9C The review officer can decide at any stage that a telephone review or review by video conferencing should be terminated and that the review will be conducted in person. The reasons for doing so should be noted in the custody record.

15.10 When a review is carried out by telephone or by video conferencing facilities, an officer at the station holding the detainee shall be required by the review officer to fulfil that officer's obligations under PACE section 40 and this Code by:

(a) making any record connected with the review in the detainee's custody record;

(b) if applicable, making the record in (a) in the presence of the detainee; and

(c) for a review by telephone, giving the detainee information about the review.

15.11 When a review is carried out by telephone or by video conferencing facilities, the requirement in *paragraph 15.3* will be satisfied:

(a) if facilities exist for the immediate transmission of written representations to the review officer, e.g. fax or email message, by allowing those who are given the opportunity to make representations, to make their representations:

(i) orally by telephone or (as the case may be) by means of the video conferencing facilities; or

(ii) in writing using the facilities for the immediate transmission of written representations; and

(b) in all other cases, by allowing those who are given the opportunity to make representations, to make their representations orally by telephone or by means of the video conferencing facilities.

(c) Documentation

15.12 It is the officer's responsibility to make sure all reminders given under *paragraph 15.4* are noted in the custody record.

15.13 The grounds for, and extent of, any delay in conducting a review shall be recorded.

15.14 When a review is carried out by telephone or video conferencing facilities, a record shall be made of:

(a) the reason the review officer did not attend the station holding the detainee;

(b) the place the review officer was;

(c) the method representations, oral or written, were made to the review officer, see *paragraph 15.11*.

15.15 Any written representations shall be retained.

15.16 A record shall be made as soon as practicable of:

(a) the outcome of each review of detention before or after charge, and if *paragraph 15.7* applies, of when the person was informed and by whom;

(b) the outcome of any determination under PACE, section 42 by a superintendent whether to extend the maximum period of detention without charge beyond 24 hours from the relevant time. If an authorisation is given, the record shall state the number of hours and minutes by which the detention period is extended or further extended.

(c) the outcome of each application under PACE, section 43, for a warrant of further detention or under section 44, for an extension or further extension of that warrant. If a warrant for further detention is granted under section 43 or extended or further extended under 44, the record shall state the detention period authorised by the warrant and the date and time it was granted or (as the case may be) the period by which the warrant is extended or further extended.

Note: Any period during which a person is released on bail does not count towards the maximum period of detention without charge allowed under PACE, sections 41 to 44.

2.8.16.1

KEYNOTE

Relevant Time

There are limits on how long a person can be detained. The Police and Criminal Evidence Act 1984 and the Codes of Practice talk of the 'relevant time'. This is the time from which the limits of detention are calculated. The relevant time of a person's detention starts in accordance with s. 41(2)–(5) of the 1984 Act. Section 41 states:

(2) The time from which the period of detention of a person is to be calculated (in this Act referred to as 'the relevant time')—

    (a) in the case of a person to whom this paragraph applies, shall be—

        (i) the time at which that person arrives at the relevant police station; or

        (ii) the time 24 hours after the time of that person's arrest,

        whichever is the earlier;

    (b) in the case of a person arrested outside England and Wales, shall be—

        (i) the time at which that person arrives at the first police station to which he is taken in the police area in England or Wales in which the offence for which he was arrested is being investigated; or

        (ii) the time 24 hours after the time of that person's entry into England and Wales,

        whichever is the earlier;

    (c) in the case of a person who—

        (i) attends voluntarily at a police station; or

        (ii) accompanies a constable to a police station without having been arrested, and is arrested at the police station,

        the time of his arrest;

    (ca) in the case of a person who attends a police station to answer to bail granted under section 30A, the time he arrives at the police station;

    (d) in any other case, except where subsection (5) below applies, shall be the time at which the person arrested arrives at the first police station to which he is taken after his arrest.

(3) Subsection (2)(a) above applies to a person if—

    (a) his arrest is sought in one police area in England and Wales;

    (b) he is arrested in another police area; and

    (c) he is not questioned in the area in which he is arrested in order to obtain evidence in relation to an offence for which he is arrested;

  and in sub-paragraph (i) of that paragraph 'the relevant police station' means the first police station to which he is taken in the police area in which his arrest was sought.

(4) Subsection (2) above shall have effect in relation to a person arrested under section 31 above as if every reference in it to his arrest or his being arrested were a reference to his arrest or his being arrested for the offence for which he was originally arrested.

(5) If—

    (a) a person is in police detention in a police area in England and Wales ('the first area'); and

    (b) his arrest for an offence is sought in some other police area in England and Wales ('the second area'); and

    (c) he is taken to the second area for the purposes of investigating that offence, without being questioned in the first area in order to obtain evidence in relation to it,

  the relevant time shall be—

        (i) the time 24 hours after he leaves the place where he is detained in the first area; or

        (ii) the time at which he arrives at the first police station to which he is taken in the second area, whichever is the earlier.

Note that under s. 41(5) the relevant time may vary, depending on whether the detainee is interviewed in relation to the offence while still in the first police area.

For those detained under the Terrorism Act 2000 the detention clock starts from the time the person is arrested, not the time he/she arrives at the police station.

The Criminal Justice Act 2003 inserted s. 41(2)(ca) into the Police and Criminal Evidence Act 1984. This allows for a person who has been arrested to be bailed before being taken to a police station. When the person attends the police station to which he/she has been bailed the relevant time starts when he/she arrives at the police station.

For the provisions of s. 31 of the 1984 Act relating to people who have been arrested for one offence and if released from the police station would be liable to arrest for some other offence, see *General Police Duties*, chapter 4.5.

Some situations occur where a person is arrested at one police station and has been circulated as wanted by another police station in the same force area. In these cases, where the person is not wanted on warrant, the detention clock for the second offence starts at the same time as for the original offence for which he/she was arrested. Consideration will need to be given as to how to protect the detention period for the second offence while officers are dealing with the first matter. Options that might be considered would include bailing the person for one of the offences or conducting both investigations at the same station. Here there may be a risk of 'confusing' the suspect, which may allow him/her to retract or qualify any confession he/she might make.

In *Henderson* v *Chief Constable of Cleveland* [2001] EWCA Civ 335 the court considered the policy of not executing a court warrant until after other matters for which the person had been detained were completed. The court held that, once a warrant was executed, there was a requirement to follow the directions of the warrant. The police, however, had a discretion as to *when* to execute the warrant. This may be relevant where a person has been arrested for one offence and it is discovered that he/she is also wanted for another offence or where there are warrants in existence for that person at more than one court. In such cases, if the warrant is executed immediately, the direction on the warrant tells officers to take the person before the next available court, an action which could interfere with the investigation. If *Henderson* is followed there is no requirement to execute the warrant straight away and the other matters can be dealt with before the requirement to produce the person at court under the warrant applies.

2.8.16.2   **KEYNOTE**

Limits on Detention and Review

Once detention has been authorised this does not mean that a person can be detained indefinitely. Section 34 of the Police and Criminal Evidence Act 1984 requires the custody officer to release a person if he/she becomes aware that the grounds for detention no longer apply and that no other grounds exist for the continuing detention (unless the person appears to have been unlawfully at large when he/she was arrested). Failure to comply with this could also lead to a breach of Article 5 of the European Convention on Human Rights. If there are additional grounds, these should be recorded in the custody record and the person informed of these additional grounds in the same way as when a person is first detained. For example, this could be for new offences or it could be that it becomes necessary to preserve evidence by questioning the detained person.

It is only the *custody officer* who can authorise the release of a detained person (s. 34(3)). In addition to the requirement to release a person should the grounds for detention no longer exist, there are also maximum time limits for which a person can be detained without charge. Once this limit has been reached any prosecution will need to proceed by summons or by warrant.

KEYNOTE

Time Limits: Without Charge

While a person is in police detention there is a requirement that his/her continuing detention is reviewed. There are minimum time requirements for when these reviews must be conducted, with the timing of the first review being calculated from the time detention is authorised. This time can be considered as the 'review time'. The question of whether a person should be kept in custody is a continuous one and the review process is intended as an added protection to the detained person.

The maximum period that a person can be detained without charge is 96 hours (with the exception of suspected acts of terrorism, in which case it is 14 days). The necessity for the continued detention of the person must be reviewed throughout this time. The period of detention is calculated from the 'relevant time' which can be calculated from Table A below (do not confuse the relevant time with the time from which reviews are due). The relevant time 'clock' will always start before, or at the same time as, the review 'clock'. This is because the review clock does not start until detention has been authorised, which clearly cannot happen until the person is brought before the custody officer which, as can be seen from the table below, is at the very latest the time the prisoner walks into the custody suite (with the exception of where the person has been under arrest for 24 hours but has not yet been taken to a police station).

This relevant time period (that is, the maximum period a person can be detained for) relates to the actual time spent in custody and not a 24-hour period in time. This means that every time the person is bailed the clock stops and usually continues from the time that the person returns to custody for the offence(s) for which he/she was bailed. Any time during which a person is on bail does not count when calculating how long a detained person has been in police detention (Police (Detention and Bail) Act 2011). This legislation applies retrospectively and therefore the changes to ss. 34 and 47 brought about by this Act are deemed always to have had effect.

Where a person has been released and re-arrested for an offence, it is possible that the relevant time will start again. This is covered by s. 47 of the 1984 Act:

(7) Where a person who was released on bail under this Part subject to a duty to attend at a police station is re-arrested, the provisions of this Part of this Act shall apply to him/her as they apply to a person arrested for the first time but this subsection does not apply to a person who is arrested under section 46A above or has attended a police station in accordance with the grant of bail (and who accordingly is deemed by section 34(7) above to have been arrested for an offence).

In cases where this subsection applies, the relevant time starts again and a fresh clock starts. This will apply where the person has been re-arrested for the same offence because of some new evidence (except at such time as when he/she is returning on bail at the appointed time) under s. 30C(4), 41(9) or 47(2).

Section 41 states:

(9) A person released under subsection (7) [i.e. where his/her relevant time period had expired] above shall not be re-arrested without a warrant for the offence for which he was previously arrested unless new evidence justifying a further arrest has come to light since his release; but this subsection does not prevent an arrest under section 46A below.

Section 47 states:

(2) Nothing in the Bail Act 1976 shall prevent the re-arrest without warrant of a person released on bail subject to a duty to attend at a police station if new evidence justifying a further arrest has come to light since his release.

Section 30C states:

(4) Nothing in section 30A or 30B or in this section prevents the re-arrest without warrant of a person released on bail under section 30A (bail by a constable elsewhere than a police station) if new evidence justifying a further arrest has come to light since his release.

The issue will be whether new evidence has come to light since the grant of bail and it will be a question of fact as to what the new evidence is. It is suggested that this must be evidence which was not available at the time the person was last in detention or which would not have been available even if all reasonable inquiries had been conducted.

It will always be important to check how much time is left on the person's 'relevant time' and when his/her next review is due.

For the purposes of Code C, paras 3.4(b) and 15.0; investigating officers are responsible for bringing to the attention of the officer who is responsible for authorising the suspect's continued detention (before or after charge), any documents and materials in their possession or control which appear to undermine the need to keep the suspect in custody. In accordance with part IV of PACE, this officer will be either the custody officer, the officer reviewing the need for detention before or after charge (PACE, s. 40), or the officer considering the need to extend detention without charge from 24 to 36 hours (PACE, s. 42). The authorising officer is then responsible for determining, which, if any, of those documents and materials are capable of undermining the need to detain the suspect and must therefore be made available to the suspect or their solicitor. It is not the case that documents need to be copied and provided to the suspect or their solicitor, the way in which documents and materials are 'made available' is a matter for the investigating officer to determine on a case-by-case basis and having regard to the nature and volume of the documents and materials involved. For example, they may be made available by supplying a copy or allowing supervised access to view. However, for view-only access, it will be necessary to demonstrate that sufficient time is allowed for the suspect and solicitor to view and consider the documents and materials in question.

2.8.16.4   **KEYNOTE**

The Three Stages of Pre-charge Detention

After the custody officer has authorised detention but before a person has been charged there are three distinct stages of detention. These are distinguished by the level at which authorisation for continuing detention is required.

The three stages of detention under the 1984 Act are:

- the basic period of detention, which is the period of detention up to 24 hours, as first authorised by the custody officer;
- those authorised by an officer of the rank of superintendent or above (s. 42) up to 36 hours (indictable offences only);
- those authorised by a magistrates' court (ss. 43 and 44) up to a maximum of 96 hours.

Each of these is examined in detail below.

2.8.16.5   **KEYNOTE**

The Basic Period of Detention

The majority of people detained by the police are detained for less than six hours; most other cases are dealt with within 24 hours. If a person's continued detention is not authorised beyond 24 hours and the person is not charged with an offence, he/she *must* be released (with or without bail) and cannot be re-arrested for the offence unless new evidence comes to light (s. 41(7) and (9) of the 1984 Act).

If a detained person is taken to hospital for medical treatment, the time at hospital and the period spent travelling to and from the hospital does not count towards the relevant time unless the person is asked questions for the purpose of obtaining evidence about an offence. Where questioning takes place, this period would count towards the relevant time and therefore the custody officer must be informed of it (s. 41(6)).

KEYNOTE

Detention Authorised by an Officer of the Rank of Superintendent or Above

Under s. 42(1) of the Police and Criminal Evidence Act 1984, detention can only be authorised beyond 24 hours and up to a maximum of 36 hours from the relevant time if:

- an offence being investigated is an 'indictable offence'; *and*
- an officer of the rank of superintendent or above is responsible for the station at which the person is detained (referred to here as the authorising officer); *and*
- that senior officer is satisfied that:
  - there is not sufficient evidence to charge; *and*
  - the investigation is being conducted diligently and expeditiously; *and*
  - the person's detention is necessary to secure or preserve evidence relating to the offence or to obtain such evidence by questioning that person.

The procedure under PACE, s. 42 must be done in person.

If the authorising officer considers that there is sufficient evidence to charge, he/she cannot authorise further detention beyond 24 hours unless the detained person is in custody for another indictable offence for which further detention can be authorised (*R* v *Samuel* [1988] QB 615 and Code H, para. 14.3). It is suggested that in considering the strength of evidence the authorising officer may wish to consult with any readily accessible CPS representative.

The grounds for this continuing detention are the same as those when the custody officer made the initial decision to detain, with the additional requirements that the case has been conducted diligently and expeditiously. To be able to satisfy the senior officer of this, it will be necessary for the custody record to be available for inspection and also details of what inquiries have been made and evidence that the investigation has been moving at a pace that will satisfy the senior officer that the inquiries should not already have been completed.

Although authorising officer can authorise detention up to a maximum of 36 hours from the 'relevant time' of detention, the period can be shorter than this. It can then be further authorised by that officer or any other officer of the rank of superintendent or above who is responsible for the station at which the person is detained to allow the period to be further extended up to the maximum 36-hour period (s. 42(2)). The officer responsible for the station holding the detainee includes a superintendent or above who, in accordance with their force operational policy or police regulations, is given that responsibility on a temporary basis whilst the appointed long-term holder is off duty or otherwise unavailable.

Section 42(5)–(8) mirrors the responsibility on the authorising officer at this stage with those of the review officer (see para. 2.8.16.12) during the 'general period' of detention with regard to allowing representations, informing the detained person of the decision to authorise further detention and the need to record the decision. The main difference here is that the authorising officer must look into how the case is being investigated and whether this is being done diligently and expeditiously. Consequently, the authorising officer must also consider any representations on these points and these points should also be covered in any record as to whether detention should continue. When considering whether to authorise further detention the authorising officer must check whether the detained person has exercised his/her right to have someone informed and to consult with a legal representative.

If it is proposed to transfer a detained person from one police area to another for the purpose of investigating the offences for which he/she is detained, the authorising officer may take into consideration the period it will take to get to the other police area when deciding whether detention can go beyond 24 hours (s. 42(3)).

Where a person has been arrested under s. 41 of the Terrorism Act 2000 he/she can be kept in police detention (in this case, this is generally from the time of the arrest) up to 48 hours without the court authorising an extension of time.

Table A Maximum Periods of Detention for Non-terrorism Act Offences

Arrest	Relevant time starts	Review clock relevant time	24 hours from detention	24 to 36 hours' detention	36 to 42 hours' detention	42 to 78 hours' detention	up to 96 hours
Arrested locally.	24 hours from arrest or arrival at police station, whichever earliest.		All offences other than indictable offences where the detention period has been extended by superintendent or above.	Only indictable offences.	Only indictable offences.	Only indictable offences.	Only indictable offences.
Arrested outside England and Wales.	Time first arrives at police station in police area where matter being investigated or 24 hours after first entered England or Wales, whichever is earliest.	Time custody officer authorises detention.	Release unless s. 41(1) applies.	Detention authorised by superintendent or above (s. 42).	Where delay in applying for warrant of further detention is reasonable (s. 43(5)).	First warrant for further detention issued by magistrates' court (s. 42).	Further warrants of detention issued by magistrates' court (s. 43).
Arrested for an offence in one police area in England or Wales then transferred to another police area for separate offence in that second police area, which is also in England or Wales. Arrested and bailed at a place other than a police station. Voluntarily attends police station or accompanies constable to station but not under arrest.	24 hours from time he/she leaves the police station in the first police area or the time he/she arrives at the first police station in second police area where the crime is being investigated, provided not interviewed about the offence while detained in the first police area, whichever is the earliest. Time of arrival at the police station to which the notice of bail states he/she must attend. Time of arrest.	This timing applies where the person was in detention for an offence in the first police area (s. 41(5)).			**see para. 2.8.16.10** for the dangers of not applying within the 36-hour period.	Remember the warrant can be applied for at any stage of detention.	
Arrested in one police area in England or Wales for an offence in another police area in England or Wales, there being no 'local' offence(s) for which he/she has been arrested.	From time the suspect arrives at the first police station in the area he/she is being sought or from 24 hours after the time he/she is arrested or if questioned about the offence while in the first police area, the relevant time starts from the time he/she first arrived at a police station in the first police area, whichever is the earliest.						

2.8.16.7 **KEYNOTE**

Warrants of Further Detention

Once the 36-hour limit has been reached, a person's detention can only continue with the authority of the courts through the issuing of a warrant of further detention.

Applications for warrants of further detention are made at the magistrates' court. Initially, the magistrates can issue a warrant for further detention for a period of up to 36 hours. This can be extended by the courts on further applications by police up to a maximum total period of detention of 96 hours. The warrant will specify what period of further detention the court has authorised.

The grounds on which the court must decide whether to grant a warrant authorising further detention are the same as those that must be considered by a 'superintendent's review'.

Should it be necessary to apply for a warrant, it is important that the time restraints are kept in mind at all times and the application procedure followed closely.

2.8.16.8 **KEYNOTE**

Warrants of Further Detention: Procedure

The application is made in the magistrates' court and both the detained person and the police must be in attendance (s. 43(1) and (2) of the Police and Criminal Evidence Act 1984). The application is made by laying an information before the court. The officer making the application does so on oath and is subject to cross-examination (see chapter 2.4). Under s. 43(14) the information must set out:

- the nature of the offence (this must be an indictable offence);
- the general nature of the evidence on which the person was arrested;
- what inquiries have been made;
- what further inquiries are proposed; and
- the reasons for believing that continuing detention is necessary for such further inquiries.

It will be important to be able to demonstrate why the person needs to remain in detention while additional inquiries are made, for instance that further facts need to be verified before further questioning of the suspect can continue and that this cannot be done effectively if the person is released. The detained person must be provided with a copy of the information before the matter can be heard (s. 43(2)). He/she is also entitled to be legally represented. If the person is not legally represented but then requests legal representation at court, the case must be adjourned to allow representation (s. 43(3)). In cases where the person is not represented it may be prudent to remind the person of his/her right to legal representation prior to the court hearing and to make a record of this in the custody record. Should the detained person choose to be legally represented at court, and thereby try to delay the police investigation, s. 43(3)(b) allows the person to be taken back into police detention during the adjournment.

2.8.16.9 **KEYNOTE**

Warrants of Further Detention: Timing of the Application

Officers should be mindful of whether a warrant for further detention may be required. If it appears likely that the investigation of the indictable offence requires the person's detention to go beyond 36 hours, then thought must be given as to when to make the application to the magistrates' court, and whether a court will be available to hear the application. If a court will not be available, then consideration should be given to making an earlier application. An application to a magistrates' court should be made between 10 am and 9 pm, and if possible during normal court hours. It will not usually be practicable to arrange for a court to sit specially outside the hours of 10 am to 9 pm. If it appears that a special sitting may be needed outside normal court hours but between 10 am and 9 pm, the clerk to the justices should be given notice and informed of this possibility, while the court is sitting if possible.

Section 43(5) allows the application to be made *before* the expiry of the 36-hour period (calculated from the relevant time) or, where it has not been practicable for the court to sit within the 36-hour period, the application can be made within the next six hours. There are dangers in applying outside the 36-hour period as if the court feels that it would have been reasonable to make the application within the 36-hour period it must refuse the application for the warrant regardless of the merits of the case (s. 43(7)). In *R v Slough Justices, ex parte Stirling* [1987] Crim LR 576, the 36-hour period expired at 12.53 pm. The case was not heard by the justices until 2.45 pm. The Divisional Court held that the police should have made their application between 10.30 am and 11.30 am, even though this was before the 36-hour time limit had been reached.

If the court is not satisfied that there are reasonable grounds for believing that further detention is justified, the court may either refuse the application or adjourn the hearing until such time as it specifies up to the end of the 36-hour period of detention (s. 43(8)). If the application is refused, the person must be charged or released with or without bail at the expiry of the current permissible period of detention (s. 43(15)).

The application for the warrant can be made at any time, *even before a superintendent's review has been carried out.* If the application is made within the 36-hour period and it is refused, it does not mean that the person must be released straight away. Section 43(16) allows the person to be detained until the end of the current detention period (24 hours or 36 hours). The benefit of an early application has to be set against the risk that, once the court has refused an application, it is not allowed to hear any further applications for a warrant of further detention unless new evidence has come to light since the application was refused (s. 43(17)).

2.8.16.10   KEYNOTE

Applying to Extend Warrants of Further Detention

Under s. 44 of the 1984 Act, the process for applying to extend the warrant follows the same procedure as for the initial warrant, with the exception that the application *must be* made before the expiry of the extension given in the previous warrant. Once the period of detention that has been authorised has expired, and no other applications have been made, the detained person must be charged or released with or without bail.

2.8.16.11   KEYNOTE

Terrorism Cases

The court can extend the period of detention of a person up to a total of 14 days. In the case of those arrested under s. 41 this starts at the time of arrest or, if the person was being detained under sch. 7 when he/she was arrested under s. 41, at the time his/her examination under that schedule began (Terrorism Act 2000, sch. 8, para. 36(3)).

A person detained in these circumstances may only be held for a maximum of 48 hours without charge before an application must be made to a court to issue or extend a warrant of further detention. At the end of that period, the detained person must either be released or an application to a court for a warrant for an extension to that detention must have been made and granted prior to the expiry of the initial 48-hour period. Extensions by the court will normally be for a seven-day period unless the application for a warrant of further detention requests a shorter period or the court is satisfied that it would be inappropriate for the period to be as long as seven days.

If detention is required beyond the first seven days, further applications are required to be made to the court as it is not possible for the court to issue a warrant authorising the full 14 days' detention on the first occasion a warrant for detention is sought (Code H, Note 14C).

The application to the court must be made by a superintendent or a Crown Prosecutor. Usually applications that cover a period of detention that does not extend beyond 14 days are heard by a district judge in the magistrates' court (unless an application in that case has already been considered by a High Court judge) and those that cover the period beyond 14 days are heard by a High Court judge. Paragraph 37 of sch. 8 to the

Terrorism Act 2000 states that if at any time the police officer or person in charge of the case considers that the grounds on which the warrant of further detention authorised by the court no longer apply the detained person must be released. Paragraph 33 of sch. 8 to the Terrorism Act 2000 allows for these applications to be conducted by live television links. The person who makes the application may also apply to the court for an order that specified information upon which he/she intends to rely should be withheld from the person to whom the application relates and anyone representing him/her. The order to withhold information can only be made if one of the following applies:

- evidence of an offence under any of the provisions mentioned in s. 40(1)(a) of the Terrorism Act 2000 would be interfered with or harmed;
- the recovery of property obtained as a result of an offence under any of those provisions would be hindered;
- the recovery of property in respect of which a forfeiture order could be made under s. 23 of the Terrorism Act 2000 would be hindered;
- the apprehension, prosecution or conviction of a person who is suspected of committing offences under the Terrorism Act 2000 would be made more difficult as a result of his/her being alerted;
- the prevention of an act of terrorism would be made more difficult as a result of the person being alerted;
- the gathering of information about the commission, preparation or instigation of an act of terrorism would be interfered with;
- a person would be interfered with or physically injured;
- the detained person has benefited from his criminal conduct and the recovery of the value of the property constituting the benefit would be hindered if the information were disclosed.

(sch. 8, part III to the Terrorism Act 2000)

Where a warrant is issued which authorises detention beyond a period of 14 days from the time of arrest the detainee must be transferred from detention in a police station to detention in a designated prison as soon as practicable, unless:

(a) the detainee specifically requests to remain in detention at a police station and that request can be accommodated; or
(b) there are reasonable grounds to believe that transferring a person to a prison would:
(i) significantly hinder a terrorism investigation;
(ii) delay charging of the detainee or his/her release from custody; or
(iii) otherwise prevent the investigation from being conducted diligently and expeditiously.

(Code H, para. 14.5)

If any of the grounds in (b)(i)–(iii) are relied upon, these must be presented to the judicial authority as part of the application for the warrant that would extend detention beyond a period of 14 days from the time of arrest. After grounds (b)(i)–(iii) cease to apply, the person must be transferred to a prison as soon as practicable.

2.8.16.12

KEYNOTE

The Review

This review acts as another safeguard to protect the detained person's right to be detained for only such periods as are necessary. Reviews of police detention are covered by s. 40 of the Police and Criminal Evidence Act 1984.

The Review Officer

The 'review officer' for the purposes of ss. 40, 40A and 45A of the 1984 Act means, in the case of a person arrested but not charged, an officer of at least *inspector* rank not directly involved in the investigation and, if a person has been arrested and charged, the *custody officer*.

It is important to understand the difference between the action of authorising an extension to the 'detention clock' and the role of the review officer. These are two distinct roles and both need to be carried out. When an officer of the rank of superintendent or above extends the 'relevant time' period, this is not automatically a review (although there is nothing to stop that officer from conducting the review). This means that the 're-viewing' officer may still have to conduct a review even though the relevant time has only recently been extended, unless the officer of the rank of superintendent or above extending the relevant time has shown the review as having been conducted in the custody record.

Timing of the Review

Section 40 sets out the times when reviews must be conducted:

> (3) Subject to subsection (4)…
> > (a) the first review shall be not later than six hours after the detention was first authorised;
> > (b) the second review shall be not later than nine hours after the first;
> > (c) subsequent reviews shall be at intervals of not more than nine hours.

The periods set out in s. 40(3) are the *maximum* periods that a review can be left; should the review officer wish to review before this time for operational reasons, etc. the review could be brought forward. The first review must be made within six hours of the custody officer authorising detention (this, it must be remembered, is not the time from which the 24-hour clock starts, i.e. the time the detainee came into the station, but the time at which the custody officer authorised detention). Thereafter, each review must be made within nine hours of the last review.

Method of the Review

Where a review is due under s. 40 and the detainee has not been charged, the review may be carried out by means of a discussion, conducted by telephone, with one or more persons at the police station where the arrested person is held. The provisions of s. 40A of the 1984 Act allowing telephone reviews do not apply to reviews of detention after charge by the custody officer.

Video conferencing facilities means any facilities (whether a live television link or other facilities) by means of which the review can be carried out with the review officer, the detainee concerned and the detainee's solicitor all being able to both see and hear each other. However, while s. 45A of the 1984 Act allows for pre-charge reviews to be conducted by video-conferencing facilities and provision for video conferencing is included within Code C, there are currently no regulations allowing such remote reviews.

Review Considerations

When reviewing the detention of a person the review officer goes through the same process as the custody officer did when detention was first authorised (ss. 40(8) and 37(1)–(6)), namely by asking:

- Is there sufficient evidence to charge? If 'yes', charge or release the person with or without bail. If 'no', then:
- Is detention necessary in order to secure or preserve evidence or is it necessary to detain the person in order to obtain such evidence by questioning him/her? If 'yes', authorise continued detention. If 'no', release the person with or without bail.

It is suggested that in order to consider whether there is sufficient evidence to charge, the review officer should have consideration for the Code for Crown Prosecutors and the Threshold Test. The situation may arise where the review officer considers that there is sufficient evidence to charge and only authorises continued detention to charge even though the custody officer disagrees. In this case, it is suggested that the custody officer must either charge or release the person with or without bail in line with s. 37B of the Police and Criminal Evidence Act 1984. Where bailed this may be in order to submit papers to the CPS in order for a decision to be made as to whether to charge and for what offence. There may also be situations where the custody officer has concluded that there is sufficient evidence to charge but the review officer disagrees; in these cases the review officer cannot overrule the custody officer's decision under s. 37(7). In any case where the decision has been made that there is sufficient evidence to charge, the review officer should confirm that the referral has been made, note the custody record to this effect and, thereafter, check to ensure that the decision is made within a *reasonable time*.

It is also suggested that the reviewing officer (or any other officer other than a superintendent or above) cannot tell the custody officer what he/she must do. The reviewing officer may wish to give advice but it will be for the custody officer to decide whether to take that advice. Clearly failure to do so could lead to internal criticism, but legally there is no requirement to follow that advice.

If there is not sufficient evidence to charge, the review officer may want to consider the question: 'If this person is bailed, what evidence will be lost?' If the answer is none, continued detention would seem unlawful.

In cases where it has been decided that a person should be charged but he/she has been detained because he/she is not in a fit state to be charged (s. 37(9)), the review officer must determine whether the person is yet in a fit state. If the detainee is in a fit state, the custody officer should be informed that the person should be charged or released. If the detainee is not in a fit state, detention can be authorised for a further period (s. 40(9)). In such cases, if the person is still unfit, it may be prudent to consider his/her welfare.

The detainee need not be woken for the review. However, if the detainee is likely to be asleep, e.g. during a period of rest, at the latest time a review or authorisation to extend detention may take place, the officer should, if the legal obligations and time constraints permit, bring forward the procedure to allow the detainee to make representations. A detainee not asleep during the review must be present when the grounds for his/her continued detention are recorded and must at the same time be informed of those grounds unless the review officer considers that the person is incapable of understanding what is said, is violent or likely to become violent or is in urgent need of medical attention. In relation to the detainee's solicitor or appropriate adult being 'available' to make representations, this includes being contactable in time to enable him/her to make representations remotely by telephone or other electronic means or in person by attending the station. Reasonable efforts should therefore be made to give the solicitor and appropriate adult sufficient notice of the time the decision is expected to be made so that they can make themselves available.

Delaying the Review

Section 40(4)(b) does allow reviews to be delayed if it is not practicable to carry out the review. Conducting late reviews should be avoided where at all possible. In *Roberts* v *Chief Constable of Cheshire Constabulary* [1999] 1 WLR 662, the defendant had his first review conducted 8 hours 20 minutes after his detention had been authorised. The Court of Appeal held that under s. 40(1)(b) of the 1984 Act a review of his detention should have been carried out by an officer of the rank of inspector or above six hours after detention was first authorised. Section 34(1) was mandatory and provided that a person must not be kept in police detention except in accordance with the relevant provisions of the Act. Therefore, the respondent's detention had been unlawful unless some event occurred to have made it lawful. The court made it clear that the 1984 Act existed in order to ensure that members of the public were not detained except in certain defined circumstances. In the absence of a review, the time spent in detention between 5.25 am and 7.45 am, meant that for that period the defendant's detention was unlawful and amounted to a false imprisonment.

Section 40(4) provides two other occasions where it may be justified to delay the review if at that time:

- the person in detention is being questioned by a police officer and the review officer is satisfied that an interruption of the questioning for the purpose of carrying out the review would prejudice the investigation in connection with which he/she is being questioned (s. 40(4)(b)(i));
- no review officer is readily available (s. 40(4)(b)(ii)).

It is likely that it will be necessary to justify why no review officer was available and that where it is known that a review may fall during an interview, the review is conducted prior to the interview where appropriate. With the ability to undertake reviews by telephone (or video link when regulations allow), a delay to a review is likely to need greater justification.

If the review is delayed, then it must still be conducted as soon as practicable and the reason for the delay must be recorded in the custody record by the review officer. In these circumstances the nine-hour period until the next review is calculated from the latest time the review should have been carried out and not from the time it was actually carried out. For instance, if the review was due at 3.15 pm and was delayed until 4 pm, the next review would have to be conducted no later than 12.15 am and not 1 am. When the review is conducted the review officer does not have to authorise detention for the full nine-hour period; he/she could decide that the case should be reviewed again within a shorter period and the review decision would reflect this.

Non-Statutory Reviews

The detention of persons in police custody not subject to the statutory review requirement in para. 15.1 should still be reviewed periodically as a matter of good practice. The purpose of such reviews is to check that the particular power under which a detainee is held continues to apply, any associated conditions are complied with, and to make sure that appropriate action is taken to deal with any changes. This includes the detainee's prompt release when the power no longer applies, or his/her transfer if the power requires the detainee be taken elsewhere as soon as the necessary arrangements are made. Examples include persons: arrested on warrant because they failed to answer bail to appear at court; arrested under the Bail Act 1976, s. 7(3) for breaching a condition of bail granted after charge and in police custody for specific purposes and periods under the Crime (Sentences) Act 1997, sch. 1; convicted or remand prisoners, held in police stations on behalf of the Prison Service under the Imprisonment (Temporary Provisions) Act 1980, s. 6; being detained to prevent them causing a breach of the peace; detained at police stations on behalf of Immigration Enforcement (formerly the UK Immigration Service); or detained by order of a magistrates' court under the Criminal Justice Act 1988, s. 152 (as amended by the Drugs Act 2005, s. 8) to facilitate the recovery of evidence after being charged with drug possession or drug trafficking and suspected of having swallowed drugs.

The detention of persons remanded into police detention by order of a court under the Magistrates' Courts Act 1980, s. 128 is subject to a statutory requirement to review that detention. This is to make sure that the detainee is taken back to court no later than the end of the period authorised by the court or when the need for his/her detention by police ceases, whichever is the sooner.

2.8.16.13

KEYNOTE

Terrorism Act Reviews

In cases where the person has been detained under the Terrorism Act 2000, the first review should be conducted as soon as reasonably practicable after his/her arrest and then at least every 12 hours; after 24 hours it must be conducted by an officer of the rank of superintendent or above. Once a warrant of further detention has been obtained there is no requirement to conduct further reviews. If an officer of higher rank than the review officer gives directions relating to the detained person, and those directions are at variance with the performance by the review officer of a duty imposed on him/her, then he/she must refer the matter at once to an officer of at least the rank of superintendent.

A review officer may only authorise a person's continued detention if he/she is satisfied that it is necessary:

- in order to obtain relevant evidence whether by questioning the person or otherwise;
- to preserve relevant evidence;
- pending a decision whether to apply to the Secretary of State for a deportation notice to be served on the detained person.

A review officer may authorise a person's continued detention if satisfied that detention is necessary:

(a) to obtain relevant evidence whether by questioning the person or otherwise;
(b) to preserve relevant evidence;
(c) while awaiting the result of an examination or analysis of relevant evidence;
(d) for the examination or analysis of anything with a view to obtaining relevant evidence;
(e) pending a decision to apply to the Secretary of State for a deportation notice to be served on the detainee, the making of any such application, or the consideration of any such application by the Secretary of State;
(f) pending a decision to charge the detainee with an offence.

Section 14 of Code H provides guidance on terrorism reviews and extensions of detention. In all cases the review officer must be satisfied that the matter is being dealt with diligently and expeditiously. Where the detained person's rights to a solicitor have been withheld or he/she is being held *incommunicado* at the time of the review, the review officer must consider whether the reason or reasons for which the delay was authorised continue to exist. If in his/her opinion the reason or reasons no longer exist, he/she must inform the officer who authorised the delay of his/her opinion. When recording the grounds for the review the officer must also include his/her conclusion on whether there is a continuing need to withhold the detained person's rights.

In cases where the person is detained under the Terrorism Act 2000 and the review officer does not authorise continued detention, the person does not have to be released if an application for a warrant for further detention is going to be applied for or if an application has been made and the result is pending (s. 41 and sch. 8).

2.8.17   16 Charging Detained Persons

(a) Action

16.1   When the officer in charge of the investigation reasonably believes there is sufficient evidence to provide a realistic prospect of conviction for the offence (see *paragraph 11.6*), they shall without delay, and subject to the following qualification, inform the custody officer who will be responsible for considering whether the detainee should be charged. When a person is detained in respect of more than one offence it is permissible to delay informing the custody officer until the above conditions are satisfied in respect of all the offences, but see *paragraph 11.6*. If the detainee is a juvenile, mentally disordered or otherwise mentally vulnerable, any resulting action shall be taken in the presence of the appropriate adult if they are present at the time.

Note: *Paragraph 1.5A* requires someone to fulfil the role of the appropriate adult to be present when the action applies to a 17-year-old detainee.

16.1A   Where guidance issued by the Director of Public Prosecutions under PACE, section 37A is in force the custody officer must comply with that Guidance in deciding how to act in dealing with the detainee.

16.1B   Where in compliance with the DPP's Guidance the custody officer decides that the case should be immediately referred to the CPS to make the charging decision, consultation should take place with a Crown Prosecutor as soon as is reasonably practicable. Where the Crown Prosecutor is unable to make the charging decision on the information available at that time, the detainee may be released without charge and on bail (with conditions if necessary) under section 37(7)(a). In such circumstances, the detainee should be informed that they are being released to enable the Director of Public Prosecutions to make a decision under section 37B.

16.2   When a detainee is charged with or informed they may be prosecuted for an offence, they shall, unless the restriction on drawing adverse inferences from silence applies, see *Annex C*, be cautioned as follows:

'You do not have to say anything. But it may harm your defence if you do not mention now something which you later rely on in court. Anything you do say may be given in evidence.'

Where the use of the Welsh Language is appropriate, a constable may provide the caution directly in Welsh in the following terms:

'Does dim rhaid i chi ddweud dim byd. Ond gall niweidio eich amddiffyniad os na fyddwch chi'n sôn, yn awr, am rywbeth y byddwch chi'n dibynnu arno nes ymlaen yn y llys. Gall unrhyw beth yr ydych yn ei ddweud gael ei roi fel tystiolaeth.'

Annex C, paragraph 2 sets out the alternative terms of the caution to be used when the restriction on drawing adverse inferences from silence applies.

16.3   When a detainee is charged they shall be given a written notice showing particulars of the offence and, subject to *paragraph 2.6A*, the officer's name and the case reference number. As far as possible the particulars of the charge shall be stated in simple terms, but they shall also show the precise offence in law with which the detainee is charged. The notice shall begin:

'You are charged with the offence(s) shown below.' Followed by the caution.

If the detainee is a juvenile, mentally disordered or otherwise mentally vulnerable, a copy of the notice should also be given to the appropriate adult.

Note: *Paragraph 1.5A* provides that a copy of the notice should be given to the person called to fulfil the role of the appropriate adult when a 17-year-old detainee is charged.

16.4 If, after a detainee has been charged with or informed they may be prosecuted for an offence, an officer wants to tell them about any written statement or interview with another person relating to such an offence, the detainee shall either be handed a true copy of the written statement or the content of the interview record brought to their attention. Nothing shall be done to invite any reply or comment except to:

(a) caution the detainee, *'You do not have to say anything, but anything you do say may be given in evidence.'*;

Where the use of the Welsh Language is appropriate, caution the detainee in the following terms:

'Does dim rhaid i chi ddweud dim byd, ond gall unrhyw beth yr ydych yn ei ddweud gael ei roi fel tystiolaeth' and

(b) remind the detainee about their right to legal advice.

16.4A If the detainee:

• cannot read, the document may be read to them

• is a juvenile, mentally disordered or otherwise mentally vulnerable, the appropriate adult shall also be given a copy, or the interview record shall be brought to their attention.

Note: *Paragraph 1.5A* requires a copy of the record to be given to, or brought to the attention of, the person called to fulfil the role of the appropriate adult for a 17-year-old detainee.

16.5 A detainee may not be interviewed about an offence after they have been charged with, or informed they may be prosecuted for it, unless the interview is necessary:

• to prevent or minimise harm or loss to some other person, or the public

• to clear up an ambiguity in a previous answer or statement

• in the interests of justice for the detainee to have put to them, and have an opportunity to comment on, information concerning the offence which has come to light since they were charged or informed they might be prosecuted.

Before any such interview, the interviewer shall:

(a) caution the detainee, *'You do not have to say anything, but anything you do say may be given in evidence.'*

Where the use of the Welsh Language is appropriate, the interviewer shall caution the detainee: *'Does dim rhaid i chi ddweud dim byd, ond gall unrhyw beth yr ydych yn ei ddweud gael ei roi fel tystiolaeth.'*

(b) remind the detainee about their right to legal advice.

16.6 The provisions of *paragraphs 16.2* to *16.5* must be complied with in the appropriate adult's presence if they are already at the police station. If they are not at the police station then these provisions must be complied with again in their presence when they arrive unless the detainee has been released.

Note: *Paragraph 1.5A* extends the requirement in this paragraph to 17-year-old detainees.

16.7 When a juvenile is charged with an offence and the custody officer authorises their continued detention after charge, the custody officer must make arrangements for the juvenile to be taken into the care of a local authority to be detained pending appearance in court unless the custody officer certifies in accordance with PACE, section 38(6), that:

(a) for any juvenile; it is impracticable to do so; or,

(b) in the case of a juvenile of at least 12 years old, no secure accommodation is available and other accommodation would not be adequate to protect the public from serious harm from that juvenile.

Note: The 16-year-old maximum age limit for transfer to local authority accommodation, the power of the local authority to detain the person transferred and take over responsibility for that person from the police are determined by section 38 of PACE. For this reason, this paragraph do not apply to detainees who appear to have attained the age of 17, see *paragraph 1.5A(a)*.

16.7A The requirement in *paragraph 3.4(b)* that documents and materials essential to effectively challenging the lawfulness of the detainee's arrest and detention must be made available to the detainee and, if they are represented, their solicitor, applies for the purposes of this section and a person's detention after charge. This means that the custody officer making the bail decision (PACE, s. 38) or reviewing the need for detention after charge (PACE, s. 40), is responsible for determining what, if any, documents or materials are essential and must be made available to the detainee or their solicitor.

(b) Documentation

16.8 A record shall be made of anything a detainee says when charged.

16.9 Any questions put in an interview after charge and answers given relating to the offence shall be recorded in full during the interview on forms for that purpose and the record signed by the detainee or, if they refuse, by the interviewer and any third parties present. If the questions are audibly recorded or visually recorded the arrangements in Code E or F apply.

16.10 If arrangements for a juvenile's transfer into local authority care as in *paragraph 16.7* are not made, the custody officer must record the reasons in a certificate which must be produced before the court with the juvenile.

2.8.17.1 **KEYNOTE**

Juveniles and Appropriate Adults

There is no power under PACE to detain a person and delay action under paras 16.2 to 16.5 solely to await the arrival of the appropriate adult. Reasonable efforts should therefore be made to give the appropriate adult sufficient notice of the time the decision (charge etc.) is to be implemented so that he/she can be present. If the appropriate adult is not, or cannot be, present at that time, the detainee should be released on bail to return for the decision to be implemented when the adult is present, unless the custody officer determines that the absence of the appropriate adult makes the detainee unsuitable for bail for this purpose. After charge, bail cannot be refused, or release on bail delayed, simply because an appropriate adult is not available, unless the absence of that adult provides the custody officer with the necessary grounds to authorise detention after charge under s. 38 of the 1984 Act.

Except as in para. 16.7, neither a juvenile's behaviour nor the nature of the offence provides grounds for the custody officer to decide it is impracticable to arrange the juvenile's transfer to local authority care. Impracticability concerns the transport and travel requirements, and the lack of secure accommodation which is provided for the purposes of restricting liberty does not make it impracticable to transfer the juvenile. The availability of secure accommodation is only a factor in relation to a juvenile aged 12 or over when other local authority accommodation would not be adequate to protect the public from serious harm from the juvenile. The obligation to transfer a juvenile to local authority accommodation applies as much to a juvenile charged during the daytime as to a juvenile to be held overnight, subject to a requirement to bring the juvenile before a court under s. 46 of the 1984 Act. It is important to note that, unlike a number of other changes to the Codes following the 2013 revision, this requirement does not apply to 17-year-olds.

2.8.17.2

KEYNOTE

Charging

The Decision Whether or Not to Charge

Section 37 of the Police and Criminal Evidence Act 1984 states:

(7) Subject to section 41(7) below [expiry of 24 hours after the relevant time], if the custody officer determines that he has before him sufficient evidence to charge the person arrested with the offence for which he was arrested, the person arrested—

    (a) shall be—

        (i) released without charge and on bail, or

        (ii) kept in police detention,

    for the purpose of enabling the Director of Public Prosecutions to make a decision under section 37B below,

    (b) shall be released without charge and on bail but not for that purpose,

    (c) shall be released without charge and without bail, or

    (d) shall be charged.

(7A) The decision as to how a person is to be dealt with under subsection (7) above shall be that of the custody officer.

(7B) Where a person is released under subsection (7)(a) above, it shall be the duty of the custody officer to inform him that he is being released or (as the case may be) detained, to enable the Director of Public Prosecutions to make a decision under section 37B below.

(8) Where—

    (a) a person is released under subsection (7)(b) or (c) above; and

    (b) at the time of his release a decision whether he should be prosecuted for the offence for which he was arrested has not been taken,

    it shall be the duty of the custody officer so to inform him/her.

Section 37A of the Police and Criminal Evidence Act 1984 states:

(1) The Director of Public Prosecutions may issue guidance—

    (a) for the purpose of enabling custody officers to decide how persons should be dealt with under section 37(7) above or 37(C) or 37CA(2) below, and

    (b) as to the information to be sent to the Director of Public Prosecutions under section 37B(1) below.

    …

(3) Custody officers are to have regard to guidance under this section in deciding how persons should be dealt with under section 37(7) above or 37C(2) or 37CA(2) below.

Unless officers are still investigating other offences for which the person is in police detention, s. 37(7) requires the custody officer to review the evidence in order to determine whether there is sufficient evidence to charge the detained person. If the custody officer decides that there is sufficient evidence to charge the detained person that person must be charged or, if not charged, released in relation to that matter, in any of the following ways:

- without charge on bail for the purpose of enabling the DPP to make a decision under s. 37B (in this case the custody officer must inform the person that he/she is being released to enable the DPP to make a decision as to case disposal);
- without charge on bail but not for the case to be referred to the DPP; or
- without charge and without bail (in either of these last two bullet points if at the time of his/her release a decision whether he/she should be prosecuted has not been made it shall be the duty of the custody officer to inform the detained person of this).

Under s. 37A(1) guidance has been issued to enable custody officers to decide whether there is sufficient evidence to charge and for which offences the police may charge without reference to the CPS. Where in accordance with the guidance the case is referred to the CPS for decision, the custody officer should ensure that an officer involved in the investigation sends to the CPS such information as is specified in the guidance. A detained person should not be kept in custody just for the sole purpose of seeking advice from the CPS as to what offences the offender should be charged with (*R (On the Application of G)* v *Chief Constable of West Yorkshire Police and DPP* [2008] EWCA Civ 28).

Charging decisions in cases will be made following a review of evidence and in accordance with the Code for Crown Prosecutors. This requires that the custody officer or Crown Prosecutor making the decision is satisfied that there is enough evidence for there to be a realistic prospect of conviction and that it is in the public interest to prosecute (Full Code Test). In order to allow the matter to have full consideration, often the time needed to consider the matter will require the detained person to be bailed. However, there will clearly be occasions when it will not be desirable to bail the detained person but the evidence required to permit the Full Code Test to be applied is not available. In such a case, the Threshold Test should be applied; this requires there to be reasonable suspicion that the suspect has committed an offence and it is in the public interest to charge that suspect. The evidential considerations include:

- there is insufficient evidence currently available to apply the evidential stage of the Full Code Test; and
- there are reasonable grounds for believing that further evidence will become available within a reasonable period; and
- the seriousness or the circumstances of the case justifies the making of an immediate charging decision; and
- there are continuing substantial grounds to object to bail in accordance with the Bail Act 1976 and in all the circumstances of the case it is proper to do so.

The Code for Crown Prosecutors advises that a prosecution will automatically take place once the evidential stage is met. A prosecution will usually take place unless the prosecutor is satisfied that there are public interest factors tending against prosecution which outweigh those tending in favour.

The public interest factors to be considered. These are:

- How serious is the offence committed?
- What is the level of culpability of the suspect?
- What are the circumstances of and the harm caused to the victim?
- Was the suspect under the age of 18 at the time of the offence?
- What is the impact on the community?
- Is prosecution a proportionate response?
- Do sources of information require protecting?

It is quite possible that one public interest factor alone may outweigh a number of other factors.

When a person is arrested under the provisions of the Criminal Justice Act 2003 which allow a person to be retried after being acquitted of a serious offence, provided a further prosecution has not been precluded by the Court of Appeal, an officer of the rank of superintendent or above who has not been directly involved in the investigation is responsible for determining whether the evidence is sufficient to charge.

2.8.17.3   **KEYNOTE**

Sufficient Evidence to Charge

Here the custody officer is looking at the evidence in order to satisfy him/herself that no further investigation is needed before the person can be charged. If this is the case, detention may be authorised for the purpose of charging the detained person. Where the custody officer is considering bail as in para. 16.7A, see para. 2.8.7.4.

Where Guidance issued by the DPP under s. 37B is in force, a custody officer who determines in accordance with that Guidance that there is sufficient evidence to charge the detainee may detain that person for no longer than is reasonably necessary to decide how that person is to be dealt with under PACE, s. 37(7)(a)–(d), including, where appropriate, consultation with the Duty Prosecutor. The period is subject to the maximum period of detention before charge determined by PACE, ss. 41 to 44. Where in accordance with the Guidance the case is referred to the CPS for decision, the custody officer should ensure that an officer involved in the investigation sends to the CPS such information as is specified in the Guidance.

Where there is sufficient evidence to charge, a delay in bringing charges may be seen to be unreasonable under Article 6 of the European Convention on Human Rights (*D v HM Advocate* [2000] HRLR 389). In deciding whether there is sufficient evidence to charge for the purposes of authorising detention or when a person's detention is reviewed, where there is a conflict between the detained person's account and victims' or witnesses' accounts it is reasonable to be in possession of at least one witness statement in the English language before preferring charges (*R (On the Application of Wiles)* v *Chief Constable of Hertfordshire* [2002] EWHC 387 (Admin)). There is no breach of PACE in keeping the detained person in police detention while a statement is translated. It is suggested that the translation needs to be completed expeditiously.

Under s. 37(9) of the 1984 Act release can be delayed if the person is not in a fit state to be released (e.g. he/she is drunk), until he/she is fit.

2.8.17.4 **KEYNOTE**

Insufficient Evidence to Charge

This creates two separate criteria for detention, that is to say, where detention is necessary to:

- secure and preserve evidence relating to an offence for which the person is arrested; or
- obtain such evidence by questioning the detained person.

If the custody officer has determined that there is not sufficient evidence to charge the person, the person must be released unless the custody officer has *reasonable grounds for believing* that the person's detention is necessary to preserve or obtain such evidence by questioning the person and the custody officer must be able to justify any decision not to release a person from detention.

When deciding if detention should be authorised in order to obtain evidence by questioning, the case of *R* v *McGuinness* [1999] Crim LR 318 should be considered. There the court held that the words 'sufficient evidence to prosecute' and 'sufficient evidence for a prosecution to succeed', in Code C, para. 16.1 (this was the wording under the previous PACE Code of Practice), had to involve some consideration of any explanation, or lack of one, from the suspect. While an interview may not be needed in all cases, questioning of detained people before they are charged may be necessary, particularly where intention or dishonesty is involved or where there may be a defence. It may also be important to put questions to the person about the offence or his/her explanation, as this may be important to negate any defence the person raises at court (see s. 34 of the Criminal Justice and Public Order Act 1994).

Where initial suspicion rests on several people, it may be appropriate to hold all suspects until they all are interviewed before deciding whether there is enough evidence to warrant a charge against any of them. Detention for questioning where there are reasonable grounds for suspecting that an offence has been committed is lawful so long as the suspicion has not been dispelled in the interim and the questioning is not unnecessarily delayed (*Clarke* v *Chief Constable of North Wales* [2000] Po LR 83).

The mere fact that a person needs to be interviewed about the offence is not of itself justification for authorising detention. The question that has to be asked is whether the person can be bailed prior to the interview or even bailed before being taken to the police station (s. 30A of the 1984 Act). Factors which might be relevant in making this decision include:

- whether the person may interfere with witnesses;
- whether he/she is likely to return if bailed;
- where there is more than one suspect, that they would have an opportunity to confer before their interviews;
- whether there is outstanding property;
- whether the person's name and address are verified.

The fact that the officers and any legal representative will be ready to start the interview shortly may also be relevant when making this decision.

KEYNOTE

Cases where the Detained Person is Bailed to Allow Consultation with the CPS

Section 37B of the Police and Criminal Evidence Act 1984 states:

(1) Where a person is dealt with under section 37(7)(a) above, an officer involved in the investigation of the offence shall, as soon as is practicable, send to the Director of Public Prosecutions such information as may be specified in guidance under section 37A above.

(2) The Director of Public Prosecutions shall decide whether there is sufficient evidence to charge the person with an offence.

(3) If he decides that there is sufficient evidence to charge the person with an offence, he shall decide—

(a) whether or not the person should be charged and, if so, the offence with which he should be charged, and

(b) whether or not the person should be given a caution and, if so, the offence in respect of which he should be given a caution.

(4) The Director of Public Prosecutions shall give notice of his decision to an officer involved in the investigation of the offence.

(4A) Notice under subsection (4) above shall be in writing, but in the case of a person kept in police detention under section 37(7)(a) above it may be given orally in the first instance and confirmed in writing subsequently.

(5) If his decision is—

(a) that there is not sufficient evidence to charge the person with an offence, or

(b) that there is sufficient evidence to charge the person with an offence but that the person should not be charged with an offence or given a caution in respect of an offence,

a custody officer shall give the person notice in writing that he is not to be prosecuted.

Where a person has been bailed under s. 37(7)(a) with or without bail conditions, the CPS must be consulted in order to determine what case disposal decision will be made (this may itself require further inquiries to gather further evidence). This referral should be made using forms MG3 (Report to Crown Prosecutor for a Charging Decision), and MG3A (Further Report to Crown Prosecutor for a Charging Decision). The pre-charge advice file can be a pre-charge expedited report (straightforward and guilty plea cases) or a pre-charge evidential report (contested/Crown Court cases) and must also include other relevant information, including:

Pre-charge Expedited Report

- MG3;
- MG11(s)—Witness statement or Index notes (if offence is witnessed by more than one officer and up to four, use the statement of one officer and summarise the others);
- MG15—Record of interview;
- Phoenix print of suspect(s)' previous convictions/cautions/reprimands/final warnings. If there is any other information that may be relevant, include it on form MG6—Case File Information.

Pre-charge Evidential Report

- MG3;
- MG5—Case summary (unless the statements cover all elements of the case);
- MG6—Case file information;
- MG11—Key witness statement(s), or Index notes (if offence is witnessed by police use the statement of one officer and summarise the others);
- MG12—Exhibit list;
- MG15—Interview record;
- Crime report and incident log;
- Unused material likely to undermine the case;
- Copies of key documentary exhibits;
- Phoenix print of suspect(s)' pre-cons/cautions/reprimands/final warnings.

The prosecutor will decide whether there is sufficient evidence to charge or caution the person and shall give written notice of the decision to an officer involved in the investigation of the details of the offence. This decision must be followed (s. 37B(6)) if the decision was for the person to be cautioned (this includes conditional cautions), and if the person refuses, or for some other reason a caution cannot be given, he/she must be charged with the offence (s. 37B(7)).

In cases where the prosecutor decides that there is not sufficient evidence to charge the person with an offence, or that there is sufficient evidence to charge the person with an offence but that the person should not be charged with an offence or given a caution in respect of an offence, the custody officer must inform the person in writing of the decision. Similarly the person must be informed of those cases where there is insufficient evidence to charge him/her, but if further evidence or information comes to light in the future the case may be reconsidered under the Code for Crown Prosecutors.

In cases where further time is needed to obtain evidence or for the prosecutor to make a case disposal decision, the person can be further bailed. In these cases the custody officer must give the person notice in writing. This does not affect any bail conditions that were included when the detained person was bailed (s. 37D(1)–(3)).

2.8.17.6

KEYNOTE

Bail to Allow Referral to the CPS

Section 47 of the Police and Criminal Evidence Act 1984 states:

(1A) The normal powers to impose conditions of bail shall be available to him where a custody officer releases a person on bail under section 37 above or section 38(1) above (including that subsection as applied by section 40(10) above) but not in any other cases.

In this subsection, 'the normal powers to impose conditions of bail' has the meaning given in s. 3(6) of the Bail Act 1976.

Where the person is bailed after charge or bailed without charge and on bail for the purpose of enabling the CPS to make a decision regarding case disposal, the custody officer may impose conditions on that bail (see para. 2.3.7). In cases where a person is bailed without being charged under s. 37(7)(b) or (c), that is to say bail is not given for the purposes of a CPS referral, the custody officer cannot impose conditions on that bail (s. 47(1A)).

2.8.17.7

KEYNOTE

Alternatives to Prosecution

The custody officer must take into account alternatives to prosecution under the Crime and Disorder Act 1998 applicable to persons under 18, and in national guidance on the cautioning of offenders applicable to persons aged 18 and over.

2.8.17.8

KEYNOTE

Police Caution

There are occasions where a person for whom there is sufficient evidence to charge may be cautioned as an alternative method of disposing with the case. *R v Chief Constable of Lancashire Constabulary, ex parte Atkinson* (1998) 162 JP 275 is a case which considered the level of evidence required before a caution can be considered. There the court said that, provided it was clear that there had been an admission of guilt, it was not necessary, for the purposes of administering a caution, to show that the admission had been obtained in circumstances which satisfied the Codes of Practice. However, police officers would be well advised to take precautions that would satisfy Code C. It would be both fairer and more reliable for a formal interview to take place.

Before making a case disposal decision it is essential that the matter has been fully investigated in order to reach an informed decision. In *Omar v Chief Constable of Bedfordshire Constabulary* [2002] EWHC 3060

(Admin), the Divisional Court quashed a caution that had been administered in order to allow a prosecution to be pursued. The court held that a number of reasonable lines of inquiry had not been made; for instance, the police had failed to take a statement from the victim's friend or obtain CCTV footage that was available or fully investigate the victim's injuries. Further, the length of time in custody (17 hours) should not have been a relevant consideration and also the suspect's admission was ambiguous. Therefore, it was in the public interest that a decision to caution rather than to charge should not prevent the subsequent pursuit of the prosecution of the offender.

While there is no general obligation on the police to disclose material prior to charge, there may be a need to make some disclosure to a suspect's legal representative in order that he/she can advise on whether a caution should be accepted (*DPP* v *Ara* [2001] EWHC Admin 493). In *Ara*, the suspect had been interviewed without a legal representative being present but the officers refused to disclose the terms of the interview.

Guidance as to the use of cautioning is provided by the Ministry of Justice's Simple Caution for Adult Offender guidance (MoJ Guidance): see <http://www.justice.gov.uk/out-of-court-disposals>. The MoJ Guidance applies to all decisions relating to simple cautions from the commencement date, regardless of when the offence was committed. Like the previous Home Office guidance (Home Office Circular 16/2008) the MoJ Guidance states that while simple cautions are available for any offence, they 'are generally intended for low level, mainly first time offending. An assessment of the seriousness of the offence is the starting point for considering whether a simple caution may be appropriate.' Officers are referred to the National Decision Model and the Association of Chief Police Officers (ACPO) *Gravity Factors Matrix* to assist them in reaching this decision. The guidelines should be considered carefully in all cases as any decision can be challenged by judicial review. It is important that the full implications of accepting a caution are made clear to suspects so that they are able to give informed consent or there is a risk that the courts may overturn the caution (*R (On the Application of Stratton)* v *Chief Constable of Thames Valley* [2013] EWHC 1561 (Admin)).

In cases where the case has been referred to the CPS under s. 37B of the 1984 Act and a decision has been made that the suspect should receive a caution, an officer involved in the investigation of the offence will be informed in writing. The notification will include the offence in respect of which a caution should be administered. If it is not possible to give the suspect such a caution then he/she must be charged with the offence (s. 37B(7)).

2.8.17.9 KEYNOTE

Young Offenders, Youth Cautions

Sections 66A to 66G, 66ZA and 66ZB of the Crime and Disorder Act 1998 make provisions for youth cautions and youth conditional cautions, which replace reprimands and warnings for children and young persons (see chapter 2.5). A reprimand or warning of a person under s. 65 of the Crime and Disorder Act 1998 is to be treated as a youth caution given to that person under s. 66ZA(1) of the 1998 Act.

2.8.17.10 KEYNOTE

Conditional Cautioning

Sections 22 to 27 of the Criminal Justice Act 2003 introduced conditional cautioning, the aim being to deal with offenders without the involvement of the usual court processes.

Section 24A of the Criminal Justice Act 2003 allows a constable to arrest without warrant any person whom the officer has reasonable grounds for believing has failed, without reasonable excuse, to comply with any of the conditions attached to the conditional caution. Certain provisions of the Police and Criminal Evidence Act 1984 relating to detention, reviews, searches, and searches and examinations to ascertain identity apply, with modifications, to a person arrested under s. 24A of the Criminal Justice Act 2003.

17 Testing Persons for the Presence of Specified Class A Drugs

(a) Action

17.1 This section of Code C applies only in selected police stations in police areas where the provisions for drug testing under section 63B of PACE (as amended by section 5 of the Criminal Justice Act 2003 and section 7 of the Drugs Act 2005) are in force and in respect of which the Secretary of State has given a notification to the relevant chief officer of police that arrangements for the taking of samples have been made. Such a notification will cover either a police area as a whole or particular stations within a police area. The notification indicates whether the testing applies to those arrested or charged or under the age of 18 as the case may be and testing can only take place in respect of the persons so indicated in the notification. Testing cannot be carried out unless the relevant notification has been given and has not been withdrawn.

17.2 A sample of urine or a non-intimate sample may be taken from a person in police detention for the purpose of ascertaining whether they have any specified Class A drug in their body only where they have been brought before the custody officer and:

(a) either the arrest condition, see *paragraph 17.3*, or the charge condition, see *paragraph 17.4* is met;

(b) the age condition see *paragraph 17.5*, is met;

(c) the notification condition is met in relation to the arrest condition, the charge condition, or the age condition, as the case may be. (Testing on charge and/or arrest must be specifically provided for in the notification for the power to apply. In addition, the fact that testing of under 18s is authorised must be expressly provided for in the notification before the power to test such persons applies.) See *paragraph 17.1*; and

(d) a police officer has requested the person concerned to give the sample (the request condition).

17.3 The arrest condition is met where the detainee:

(a) has been arrested for a trigger offence, but not charged with that offence; or

(b) has been arrested for any other offence but not charged with that offence and a police officer of inspector rank or above, who has reasonable grounds for suspecting that their misuse of any specified Class A drug caused or contributed to the offence, has authorised the sample to be taken.

17.4 The charge condition is met where the detainee:

(a) has been charged with a trigger offence, or

(b) has been charged with any other offence and a police officer of inspector rank or above, who has reasonable grounds for suspecting that the detainee's misuse of any specified Class A drug caused or contributed to the offence, has authorised the sample to be taken.

17.5 The age condition is met where:

(a) in the case of a detainee who has been arrested but not charged as in *paragraph 17.3*, they are aged 18 or over;

(b) in the case of a detainee who has been charged as in *paragraph 17.4*, they are aged 14 or over.

17.6 Before requesting a sample from the person concerned, an officer must:

(a) inform them that the purpose of taking the sample is for drug testing under PACE. This is to ascertain whether they have a specified Class A drug present in their body;

(b) warn them that if, when so requested, they fail without good cause to provide a sample they may be liable to prosecution;

(c) where the taking of the sample has been authorised by an inspector or above in accordance with *paragraph 17.3(b)* or *17.4(b)* above, inform them that the authorisation has been given and the grounds for giving it;

(d) remind them of the following rights, which may be exercised at any stage during the period in custody:

    (i) the right to have someone informed of their arrest [see *section 5*];

    (ii) the right to consult privately with a solicitor and that free independent legal advice is available [see *section 6*]; and

    (iii) the right to consult these Codes of Practice [see *section 3*].

17.7 In the case of a person who has not attained the age of 17—

    (a) the making of the request for a sample under *paragraph 17.2(d)* above;

    (b) the giving of the warning and the information under *paragraph 17.6* above; and

    (c) the taking of the sample, may not take place except in the presence of an appropriate adult.

Note: *Paragraph 1.5A* requires someone to fulfil the role of the appropriate adult to be present if the person to be tested appears to be under the age of 18.

17.8 Authorisation by an officer of the rank of inspector or above within *paragraph 17.3(b)* or *17.4(b)* may be given orally or in writing but, if it is given orally, it must be confirmed in writing as soon as practicable.

17.9 If a sample is taken from a detainee who has been arrested for an offence but not charged with that offence as in *paragraph 17.3*, no further sample may be taken during the same continuous period of detention. If during that same period the charge condition is also met in respect of that detainee, the sample which has been taken shall be treated as being taken by virtue of the charge condition, see *paragraph 17.4*, being met.

17.10 A detainee from whom a sample may be taken may be detained for up to six hours from the time of charge if the custody officer reasonably believes the detention is necessary to enable a sample to be taken. Where the arrest condition is met, a detainee whom the custody officer has decided to release on bail without charge may continue to be detained, but not beyond 24 hours from the relevant time (as defined in section 41(2) of PACE), to enable a sample to be taken.

17.11 A detainee in respect of whom the arrest condition is met, but not the charge condition, see *paragraphs 17.3* and *17.4*, and whose release would be required before a sample can be taken had they not continued to be detained as a result of being arrested for a further offence which does not satisfy the arrest condition, may have a sample taken at any time within 24 hours after the arrest for the offence that satisfies the arrest condition.

(b) Documentation

17.12 The following must be recorded in the custody record:

    (a) if a sample is taken following authorisation by an officer of the rank of inspector or above, the authorisation and the grounds for suspicion;

    (b) the giving of a warning of the consequences of failure to provide a sample;

    (c) the time at which the sample was given; and

    (d) the time of charge or, where the arrest condition is being relied upon, the time of arrest and, where applicable, the fact that a sample taken after arrest but before charge is to be treated as being taken by virtue of the charge condition, where that is met in the same period of continuous detention. See *paragraph 17.9*.

(c) General

17.13 A sample may only be taken by a prescribed person.

17.14 Force may not be used to take any sample for the purpose of drug testing.

17.15 The terms "Class A drug" and "misuse" have the same meanings as in the Misuse of Drugs Act 1971. "Specified" (in relation to a Class A drug) and "trigger offence" have the same meanings as in Part III of the Criminal Justice and Court Services Act 2000.

17.16 Any sample taken:

(a) may not be used for any purpose other than to ascertain whether the person concerned has a specified Class A drug present in his body; and

(b) can be disposed of as clinical waste unless it is to be sent for further analysis in cases where the test result is disputed at the point when the result is known, including on the basis that medication has been taken, or for quality assurance purposes.

(d) Assessment of misuse of drugs

17.17 Under the provisions of Part 3 of the Drugs Act 2005, where a detainee has tested positive for a specified Class A drug under section 63B of PACE a police officer may, at any time before the person's release from the police station, impose a requirement on the detainee to attend an initial assessment of their drug misuse by a suitably qualified person and to remain for its duration. Where such a requirement is imposed, the officer must, at the same time, impose a second requirement on the detainee to attend and remain for a follow-up assessment. The officer must inform the detainee that the second requirement will cease to have effect if, at the initial assessment they are informed that a follow-up assessment is not necessary These requirements may only be imposed on a person if:

(a) they have reached the age of 18

(b) notification has been given by the Secretary of State to the relevant chief officer of police that arrangements for conducting initial and follow-up assessments have been made for those from whom samples for testing have been taken at the police station where the detainee is in custody.

17.18 When imposing a requirement to attend an initial assessment and a follow-up assessment the police officer must:

(a) inform the person of the time and place at which the initial assessment is to take place;

(b) explain that this information will be confirmed in writing; and

(c) warn the person that they may be liable to prosecution if they fail without good cause to attend the initial assessment and remain for its duration and if they fail to attend the follow-up assessment and remain for its duration (if so required).

17.19 Where a police officer has imposed a requirement to attend an initial assessment and a follow-up assessment in accordance with *paragraph 17.17*, he must, before the person is released from detention, give the person notice in writing which:

(a) confirms their requirement to attend and remain for the duration of the assessments; and

(b) confirms the information and repeats the warning referred to in *paragraph 17.18*.

17.20 The following must be recorded in the custody record:

(a) that the requirement to attend an initial assessment and a follow-up assessment has been imposed; and

(b) the information, explanation, warning and notice given in accordance with *paragraphs 17.17* and *17.19*.

17.21 Where a notice is given in accordance with *paragraph 17.19*, a police officer can give the person a further notice in writing which informs the person of any change to the time or place at which the initial assessment is to take place and which repeats the warning referred to in *paragraph 17.18(c)*.

17.22 Part 3 of the Drugs Act 2005 also requires police officers to have regard to any guidance issued by the Secretary of State in respect of the assessment provisions.

KEYNOTE

The power to take samples is subject to notification by the Secretary of State that appropriate arrangements for the taking of samples have been made for the police area as a whole or for the particular police station concerned for whichever of the following is specified in the notification: persons in respect of whom the arrest condition is met; persons in respect of whom the charge condition is met; and/or persons who have not attained the age of 18.

A sample has to be sufficient and suitable. A sufficient sample is sufficient in quantity and quality to enable drug-testing analysis to take place. A suitable sample is one which by its nature is suitable for a particular form of drug analysis. It can only be taken by a prescribed person as defined in regulations made by the Secretary of State under s. 63B(6) of the Police and Criminal Evidence Act 1984. The regulations are currently contained in the Police and Criminal Evidence Act 1984 (Drug Testing Persons in Police Detention) (Prescribed Persons) Regulations 2001 (SI 2001/2645). Samples, and the information derived from them, may not subsequently be used in the investigation of any offence or in evidence against the persons from whom they were taken.

When warning a person who is asked to provide a urine or non-intimate sample in accordance with para. 17.6(b), the following form of words may be used:

> You do not have to provide a sample, but I must warn you that if you fail or refuse without good cause to do so, you will commit an offence for which you may be imprisoned, or fined, or both.

Where the Welsh language is appropriate, the following form of words may be used:

> Does dim rhaid i chi roi sampl, ond mae'n rhaid i mi eich rhybuddio y byddwch chi'n cyflawni trosedd os byddwch chi'n methu neu yn gwrthod gwneud hynny heb reswm da, ac y gellir, oherwydd hynny, eich carcharu, eich dirwyo, neu'r ddau.

The trigger offences referred to in the section are:

1. Offences under the following provisions of the Theft Act 1968:

section 1	(theft)
section 8	(robbery)
section 9	(burglary)
section 10	(aggravated burglary)
section 12	(taking a motor vehicle or other conveyance without authority)
section 12A	(aggravated vehicle-taking)
section 22	(handling stolen goods)
section 25	(going equipped for stealing, etc.)

2. Offences under the following provisions of the Misuse of Drugs Act 1971, if committed in respect of a specified Class A drug:

section 4	(restriction on production and supply of controlled drugs)
section 5(2)	(possession of a controlled drug)
section 5(3)	(possession of a controlled drug with intent to supply)

3. Offences under the following provisions of the Fraud Act 2006:

section 1	(fraud)
section 6	(possession, etc. of articles for use in frauds)
section 7	(making or supplying articles for use in frauds)

3A. An offence under s. 1(1) of the Criminal Attempts Act 1981 if committed in respect of an offence under:
   (a) any of the following provisions of the Theft Act 1968:

section 1	(theft)
section 8	(robbery)
section 9	(burglary)
section 22	(handling stolen goods)

(b) s. 1 of the Fraud Act 2006 (fraud)

4. Offences under the following provisions of the Vagrancy Act 1824:

section 3	(begging)
section 4	(persistent begging)

For the purposes of needing the presence of an appropriate adult for Code C, para. 17.7, an appropriate adult in para. 17.7 means the person's:

(a) parent or guardian or, if he/she is in the care of a local authority or voluntary organisation, a person representing that authority or organisation; or

(b) a social worker of a local authority; or

(c) if no person falling within (a) or (b) above is available, any responsible person aged 18 or over who is not a police officer or a person employed by the police.

Again this provision to provide an appropriate adult applies to 17-year-olds.

2.8.19   ## Annex A—Intimate and Strip Searches

A Intimate search

1. An intimate search consists of the physical examination of a person's body orifices other than the mouth. The intrusive nature of such searches means the actual and potential risks associated with intimate searches must never be underestimated.

(a) Action

2. Body orifices other than the mouth may be searched only:

    (a) if authorised by an officer of inspector rank or above who has reasonable grounds for believing that the person may have concealed on themselves:

        (i) anything which they could and might use to cause physical injury to themselves or others at the station; or

        (ii) a Class A drug which they intended to supply to another or to export;

        and the officer has reasonable grounds for believing that an intimate search is the only means of removing those items; and

    (b) if the search is under *paragraph 2(a)(ii)* (a drug offence search), the detainee's appropriate consent has been given in writing.

2A. Before the search begins, a police officer or designated detention officer, must tell the detainee:

    (a) that the authority to carry out the search has been given;

    (b) the grounds for giving the authorisation and for believing that the article cannot be removed without an intimate search.

    Note: *Paragraph 1.5A* of this Code requires someone to fulfil the role of the appropriate adult to be present when a 17-year-old is told about the authority and grounds for an intimate search.

2B. Before a detainee is asked to give appropriate consent to a search under *paragraph 2(a) (ii)* (a drug offence search) they must be warned that if they refuse without good cause their refusal may harm their case if it comes to trial. This warning may be given by a police officer or member of police staff. In the case of juveniles, mentally vulnerable or mentally disordered suspects, the seeking and giving of consent must take place in the presence of the appropriate adult. A juvenile's consent is only valid if their parent's or guardian's consent is also obtained unless the juvenile is under 14, when their parent's or guardian's consent is sufficient in its own right. A detainee who is not legally represented must be reminded of their entitlement to have free legal advice, see Code C, *paragraph 6.5*, and the reminder noted in the custody record.

Note: *Paragraph 1.5A* of this Code requires someone to fulfil the role of the appropriate adult to be present when the warning is given to a 17-year-old and their consent to a drug offence search is sought and given but the consent of their parent or guardian is not required.

3. An intimate search may only be carried out by a registered medical practitioner or registered nurse, unless an officer of at least inspector rank considers this is not practicable and the search is to take place under *paragraph 2(a)(i)*, in which case a police officer may carry out the search.

3A. Any proposal for a search under *paragraph 2(a)(i)* to be carried out by someone other than a registered medical practitioner or registered nurse must only be considered as a last resort and when the authorising officer is satisfied the risks associated with allowing the item to remain with the detainee outweigh the risks associated with removing it.

4. An intimate search under:
   - *paragraph 2(a)(i)* may take place only at a hospital, surgery, other medical premises or police station;
   - *paragraph 2(a)(ii)* may take place only at a hospital, surgery or other medical premises and must be carried out by a registered medical practitioner or a registered nurse.

5. An intimate search at a police station of a juvenile or mentally disordered or otherwise mentally vulnerable person may take place only in the presence of an appropriate adult of the same sex (see *Annex L*), unless the detainee specifically requests a particular adult of the opposite sex who is readily available. In the case of a juvenile, the search may take place in the absence of the appropriate adult only if the juvenile signifies in the presence of the appropriate adult they do not want the adult present during the search and the adult agrees. A record shall be made of the juvenile's decision and signed by the appropriate adult.

   Note: *Paragraph 1.5A* of this Code extends the requirement in this paragraph to an intimate search of a 17-year-old.

6. When an intimate search under *paragraph 2(a)(i)* is carried out by a police officer, the officer must be of the same sex as the detainee (see *Annex L*). A minimum of two people, other than the detainee, must be present during the search. Subject to *paragraph 5*, no person of the opposite sex who is not a medical practitioner or nurse shall be present, nor shall anyone whose presence is unnecessary. The search shall be conducted with proper regard to the sensitivity and vulnerability of the detainee.

(b) Documentation

7. In the case of an intimate search, the following shall be recorded as soon as practicable in the detainee's custody record:
   (a) for searches under *paragraphs 2(a)(i)* and *(ii)*:
      - the authorisation to carry out the search;
      - the grounds for giving the authorisation;
      - the grounds for believing the article could not be removed without an intimate search;
      - which parts of the detainee's body were searched;
      - who carried out the search;
      - who was present;
      - the result.
   (b) for searches under *paragraph 2(a)(ii)*:
      - the giving of the warning required by *paragraph 2B*;
      - the fact that the appropriate consent was given or (as the case may be) refused, and if refused, the reason given for the refusal (if any).

8. If an intimate search is carried out by a police officer, the reason why it was impracticable for a registered medical practitioner or registered nurse to conduct it must be recorded.

KEYNOTE

Before authorising any intimate search, the authorising officer must make every reasonable effort to persuade the detainee to hand the article over without a search. If the detainee agrees, a registered medical practitioner or registered nurse should whenever possible be asked to assess the risks involved and, if necessary, attend to assist the detainee.

If the detainee does not agree to hand the article over without a search, the authorising officer must carefully review all the relevant factors before authorising an intimate search. In particular, the officer must consider whether the grounds for believing that an article may be concealed are reasonable.

If authority is given for a search for anything which the detained person could and might use to cause physical injury to him/herself or others at the station, a registered medical practitioner or registered nurse shall be consulted whenever possible. The presumption should be that the search will be conducted by the registered medical practitioner or registered nurse and the authorising officer must make every reasonable effort to persuade the detainee to allow the medical practitioner or nurse to conduct the search. A constable should only be authorised to carry out a search as a last resort and when all other approaches have failed. In these circumstances, the authorising officer must be satisfied that the detainee might use the article to cause physical injury to him/herself and/or others at the station and the physical injury likely to be caused is sufficiently severe to justify authorising a constable to carry out the search. If an officer has any doubts whether to authorise an intimate search by a constable, the officer should seek advice from an officer of superintendent rank or above. Annex L should be referred to for guidance when establishing the gender of persons for the purpose of searching.

The following form of words should be used when asking a detained person to consent to an intimate drug offence search:

You do not have to allow yourself to be searched, but I must warn you that if you refuse without good cause, your refusal may harm your case if it comes to trial.

Where the use of the Welsh language is appropriate, the following form of words may be used:

Nid oes rhaid i chi roi caniatâd i gael eich archwilio, ond mae'n rhaid i mi eich rhybuddio os gwrthodwch heb reswm da, y gallai eich penderfyniad i wrthod wneud niwed i'ch achos pe bai'n dod gerbron llys.

B Strip search

9. A strip search is a search involving the removal of more than outer clothing. In this Code, outer clothing includes shoes and socks.

(a) Action

10. A strip search may take place only if it is considered necessary to remove an article which a detainee would not be allowed to keep and the officer reasonably considers the detainee might have concealed such an article. Strip searches shall not be routinely carried out if there is no reason to consider that articles are concealed.

The conduct of strip searches

11. When strip searches are conducted:
    (a) a police officer carrying out a strip search must be the same sex as the detainee (see *Annex L*);
    (b) the search shall take place in an area where the detainee cannot be seen by anyone who does not need to be present, nor by a member of the opposite sex (see *Annex L*) except an appropriate adult who has been specifically requested by the detainee;

(c) except in cases of urgency, where there is risk of serious harm to the detainee or to others, whenever a strip search involves exposure of intimate body parts, there must be at least two people present other than the detainee, and if the search is of a juvenile or mentally disordered or otherwise mentally vulnerable person, one of the people must be the appropriate adult. Except in urgent cases as above, a search of a juvenile may take place in the absence of the appropriate adult only if the juvenile signifies in the presence of the appropriate adult that they do not want the adult to be present during the search and the adult agrees. A record shall be made of the juvenile's decision and signed by the appropriate adult. The presence of more than two people, other than an appropriate adult, shall be permitted only in the most exceptional circumstances;

Note: *Paragraph 1.5A* of this Code extends the requirement in this sub-paragraph to a strip search of a 17-year-old.

(d) the search shall be conducted with proper regard to the sensitivity and vulnerability of the detainee in these circumstances and every reasonable effort shall be made to secure the detainee's co-operation and minimise embarrassment. Detainees who are searched shall not normally be required to remove all their clothes at the same time, e.g. a person should be allowed to remove clothing above the waist and redress before removing further clothing;

(e) if necessary to assist the search, the detainee may be required to hold their arms in the air or to stand with their legs apart and bend forward so a visual examination may be made of the genital and anal areas provided no physical contact is made with any body orifice;

(f) if articles are found, the detainee shall be asked to hand them over. If articles are found within any body orifice other than the mouth, and the detainee refuses to hand them over, their removal would constitute an intimate search, which must be carried out as in *Part A*;

(g) a strip search shall be conducted as quickly as possible, and the detainee allowed to dress as soon as the procedure is complete.

(b) Documentation

12. A record shall be made on the custody record of a strip search including the reason it was considered necessary, those present and any result.

2.8.19.3   **KEYNOTE**

Annex A, para. 11 applies to all the powers given to custody officers under s. 54 of the 1984 Act, including the power to remove and seize clothing under s. 54(4). In *Davies* v *Chief Constable of Merseyside and Others* [2015] EWCA Civ 114 the Court held that Annex A, para. 11 applied to any strip search, not just those strip searches carried out in compliance with para. 10. For example it would apply where the custody officer determines that a detained person is a suicide risk and orders the removal of their clothing under s. 54 so they can be dressed in a safety gown.

2.8.20   ## Annex B—Delay in Notifying Arrest or Allowing Access to Legal Advice

A Persons detained under PACE

1. The exercise of the rights in *Section 5* or *Section 6*, or both, may be delayed if the person is in police detention, as in PACE, section 118(2), in connection with an indictable offence, has not yet been charged with an offence and an officer of superintendent rank or above, or inspector

rank or above only for the rights in *Section 5*, has reasonable grounds for believing their exercise will:

(i) lead to:
- interference with, or harm to, evidence connected with an indictable offence; or
- interference with, or physical harm to, other people; or

(ii) lead to alerting other people suspected of having committed an indictable offence but not yet arrested for it; or

(iii) hinder the recovery of property obtained in consequence of the commission of such an offence.

2. These rights may also be delayed if the officer has reasonable grounds to believe that:

(i) the person detained for an indictable offence has benefited from their criminal conduct (decided in accordance with Part 2 of the Proceeds of Crime Act 2002); and

(ii) the recovery of the value of the property constituting that benefit will be hindered by the exercise of either right.

3. Authority to delay a detainee's right to consult privately with a solicitor may be given only if the authorising officer has reasonable grounds to believe the solicitor the detainee wants to consult will, inadvertently or otherwise, pass on a message from the detainee or act in some other way which will have any of the consequences specified under *paragraphs 1* or *2*. In these circumstances, the detainee must be allowed to choose another solicitor.

4. If the detainee wishes to see a solicitor, access to that solicitor may not be delayed on the grounds they might advise the detainee not to answer questions or the solicitor was initially asked to attend the police station by someone else. In the latter case, the detainee must be told the solicitor has come to the police station at another person's request, and must be asked to sign the custody record to signify whether they want to see the solicitor.

5. The fact the grounds for delaying notification of arrest may be satisfied does not automatically mean the grounds for delaying access to legal advice will also be satisfied.

6. These rights may be delayed only for as long as grounds exist and in no case beyond 36 hours after the relevant time as in PACE, section 41. If the grounds cease to apply within this time, the detainee must, as soon as practicable, be asked if they want to exercise either right, the custody record must be noted accordingly, and action taken in accordance with the relevant section of the Code.

7. A detained person must be permitted to consult a solicitor for a reasonable time before any court hearing.

B Not used

C Documentation

13. The grounds for action under this Annex shall be recorded and the detainee informed of them as soon as practicable.

14. Any reply given by a detainee under *paragraphs 6* or *11* must be recorded and the detainee asked to endorse the record in relation to whether they want to receive legal advice at this point.

D Cautions and special warnings

15. When a suspect detained at a police station is interviewed during any period for which access to legal advice has been delayed under this Annex, the court or jury may not draw adverse inferences from their silence.

KEYNOTE

Even if Annex B applies in the case of a juvenile, 17-year-old, or a person who is mentally disordered or otherwise mentally vulnerable, action to inform the appropriate adult and the person responsible for a juvenile's welfare if that is a different person, must nevertheless be taken as in paras 3.13 and 3.15. Similarly, for detained persons who are citizens of independent Commonwealth countries or foreign nationals the exercise of the rights in Code C, section 7 may not be interfered with.

In cases where the person is detained under the Terrorism Act 2000 an officer of the rank of superintendent or above may delay the exercise of either right or both if he/she has reasonable grounds for believing that the exercise of the right will lead to any of the consequences of:

- interference with or harm to evidence of a serious offence;
- interference with or physical injury to any person;
- the alerting of persons who are suspected of having committed a serious offence but who have not been arrested for it;
- the hindering of the recovery of property obtained as a result of a serious offence or in respect of which a forfeiture order could be made under s. 23;
- interference with the gathering of information about the commission, preparation or instigation of acts of terrorism;
- the alerting of a person and thereby making it more difficult to prevent an act of terrorism;
- the alerting of a person and thereby making it more difficult to secure a person's apprehension, prosecution or conviction in connection with the commission, preparation or instigation of an act of terrorism;
- the detained person having benefited from his/her criminal conduct, and the recovery of the value of the property constituting the benefit will be hindered by informing the named person of the detained person's detention or access to legal advice. For these purposes whether a person has benefited from his/her criminal conduct is to be decided in accordance with part 2 of the Proceeds of Crime Act 2002. Briefly, criminal conduct is conduct which constitutes an offence in England and Wales, or would constitute such an offence if it occurred in England and Wales. A person benefits from conduct if he/she obtains property as a result of or in connection with the conduct (Code H, Annex B, paras 1 and 2).

When considering the delay of access to a solicitor the authorising officer must bear in mind that access to a solicitor is 'a fundamental right of a citizen' (*R* v *Samuel* [1988] QB 615). The authorising officer must actually believe that by allowing access to the solicitor he/she will intentionally or inadvertently alert other suspects.

Occasions where delay will be authorised in such circumstances will be rare and only when it can be shown that the suspect is capable of misleading that particular solicitor and there is more than a substantial risk that the suspect will succeed in causing information to be conveyed which will lead to one or more of the specified consequences. In deciding whether such an interview will be admissible the court will consider how reliable it is and will consider how the refusal to allow that particular detained person access to a solicitor affected his/her decision to make a confession. One such case where the confession was excluded is *R* v *Sanusi* [1992] Crim LR 43, where a person from another country was denied access to a solicitor and the court held that his right to advice was particularly significant due to his lack of familiarity with police procedures.

Annex C—Restriction on Drawing Adverse Inferences from Silence and Terms of the Caution when the Restriction Applies (see chapter 2.10)

Annex D—Written Statements Under Caution (see chapter 2.10)

Annex E—Summary of Provisions Relating to Mentally Disordered and Otherwise Mentally Vulnerable People

1. If an officer has any suspicion, or is told in good faith, that a person of any age may be mentally disordered or otherwise mentally vulnerable, or mentally incapable of understanding the

significance of questions or their replies that person shall be treated as mentally disordered or otherwise mentally vulnerable for the purposes of this Code. See *paragraph 1.4.*

2. In the case of a person who is mentally disordered or otherwise mentally vulnerable, 'the appropriate adult' means:

    (a) a relative, guardian or other person responsible for their care or custody;

    (b) someone experienced in dealing with mentally disordered or mentally vulnerable people but who is not a police officer or employed by the police;

    (c) failing these, some other responsible adult aged 18 or over who is not a police officer or employed by the police. See *paragraph 1.7(b).*

3. If the custody officer authorises the detention of a person who is mentally vulnerable or appears to be suffering from a mental disorder, the custody officer must as soon as practicable inform the appropriate adult of the grounds for detention and the person's whereabouts, and ask the adult to come to the police station to see them. If the appropriate adult:

    • is already at the station when information is given as in *paragraphs 3.1* to *3.5* the information must be given in their presence;

    • is not at the station when the provisions of *paragraph 3.1* to *3.5* are complied with these provisions must be complied with again in their presence once they arrive.

    See *paragraphs 3.15* to *3.17.*

4. If the appropriate adult, having been informed of the right to legal advice, considers legal advice should be taken, the provisions of *section 6* apply as if the mentally disordered or otherwise mentally vulnerable person had requested access to legal advice. See *paragraph 3.19.*

5. The custody officer must make sure a person receives appropriate clinical attention as soon as reasonably practicable if the person appears to be suffering from a mental disorder or in urgent cases immediately call the nearest appropriate healthcare professional or an ambulance. It is not intended these provisions delay the transfer of a detainee to a place of safety under the Mental Health Act 1983, section 136 if that is applicable. If an assessment under that Act is to take place at a police station, the custody officer must consider whether an appropriate healthcare professional should be called to conduct an initial clinical check on the detainee. See *paragraph 9.5* and *9.6.*

6. It is imperative a mentally disordered or otherwise mentally vulnerable person detained under the Mental Health Act 1983, section 136 be assessed as soon as possible. A police station should only be used as a place of safety as a last resort but if that assessment is to take place at the police station, an approved social worker and registered medical practitioner shall be called to the station as soon as possible to carry it out. Once the detainee has been assessed and suitable arrangements been made for their treatment or care, they can no longer be detained under section 136. A detainee should be immediately discharged from detention if a registered medical practitioner having examined them, concludes they are not mentally disordered within the meaning of the Act. See *paragraph 3.16.*

7. If a mentally disordered or otherwise mentally vulnerable person is cautioned in the absence of the appropriate adult, the caution must be repeated in the appropriate adult's presence. See *paragraph 10.12.*

8. A mentally disordered or otherwise mentally vulnerable person must not be interviewed or asked to provide or sign a written statement in the absence of the appropriate adult unless the provisions of *paragraphs 11.1* or *11.18* to *11.20* apply. Questioning in these circumstances may not continue in the absence of the appropriate adult once sufficient information to avert the risk has been obtained. A record shall be made of the grounds for any decision to begin an interview in these circumstances. See *paragraphs 11.1, 11.15* and *11.18* to *11.20.*

9. If the appropriate adult is present at an interview, they shall be informed they are not expected to act simply as an observer and the purposes of their presence are to:

    • advise the interviewee;

    • observe whether or not the interview is being conducted properly and fairly;

    • facilitate communication with the interviewee.

    See *paragraph 11.17.*

10. If the detention of a mentally disordered or otherwise mentally vulnerable person is reviewed by a review officer or a superintendent, the appropriate adult must, if available at the time, be given an opportunity to make representations to the officer about the need for continuing detention. See *paragraph 15.3*.

11. If the custody officer charges a mentally disordered or otherwise mentally vulnerable person with an offence or takes such other action as is appropriate when there is sufficient evidence for a prosecution this must be carried out in the presence of the appropriate adult if they are at the police station. A copy of the written notice embodying any charge must also be given to the appropriate adult. See *paragraphs 16.1* to *16.4A*.

12. An intimate or strip search of a mentally disordered or otherwise mentally vulnerable person may take place only in the presence of the appropriate adult of the same sex, unless the detainee specifically requests the presence of a particular adult of the opposite sex. A strip search may take place in the absence of an appropriate adult only in cases of urgency when there is a risk of serious harm to the detainee or others. See *Annex A, paragraphs 5* and *11(c)*.

13. Particular care must be taken when deciding whether to use any form of approved restraints on a mentally disordered or otherwise mentally vulnerable person in a locked cell. See *paragraph 8.2*.

2.8.21.1

KEYNOTE

The purpose of allowing the detained person's appropriate adult on the detainee's behalf to ask for a solicitor to be called to give legal advice is to protect the rights of a mentally disordered or otherwise mentally vulnerable detained person who does not understand the significance of what is said to him/her. If the detained person wants to exercise the right to legal advice, the appropriate action should be taken and not delayed until the appropriate adult arrives. A mentally disordered or otherwise mentally vulnerable detained person should always be given an opportunity, when an appropriate adult is called to the police station, to consult privately with a solicitor in the absence of the appropriate adult if he/she wants.

Although people who are mentally disordered or otherwise mentally vulnerable are often capable of providing reliable evidence, they may, without knowing or wanting to do so, be particularly prone in certain circumstances to provide information that may be unreliable, misleading or self-incriminating. Special care should always be taken when questioning such a person, and the appropriate adult should be involved if there is any doubt about a person's mental state or capacity. Because of the risk of unreliable evidence, it is important to obtain corroboration of any facts admitted whenever possible. For these reasons officers of superintendent rank or above should exercise their discretion to authorise the commencement of an interview in the appropriate adult's absence only in exceptional cases, if it is necessary to avert an immediate risk of serious harm.

There is no requirement for an appropriate adult to be present if a person is detained under s. 136 of the Mental Health Act 1983 for assessment.

2.8.22 ## Annex F—No longer in use, see Code C, section 7

2.8.23 ## Annex G—Fitness to be Interviewed

1. This Annex contains general guidance to help police officers and healthcare professionals assess whether a detainee might be at risk in an interview.

2. A detainee may be at risk in a interview if it is considered that:
   (a) conducting the interview could significantly harm the detainee's physical or mental state;
   (b) anything the detainee says in the interview about their involvement or suspected involvement in the offence about which they are being interviewed might be considered unreliable in subsequent court proceedings because of their physical or mental state.

3. In assessing whether the detainee should be interviewed, the following must be considered:

(a) how the detainee's physical or mental state might affect their ability to understand the nature and purpose of the interview, to comprehend what is being asked and to appreciate the significance of any answers given and make rational decisions about whether they want to say anything;

(b) the extent to which the detainee's replies may be affected by their physical or mental condition rather than representing a rational and accurate explanation of their involvement in the offence;

(c) how the nature of the interview, which could include particularly probing questions, might affect the detainee.

4. It is essential healthcare professionals who are consulted consider the functional ability of the detainee rather than simply relying on a medical diagnosis, e.g. it is possible for a person with severe mental illness to be fit for interview.

5. Healthcare professionals should advise on the need for an appropriate adult to be present, whether reassessment of the person's fitness for interview may be necessary if the interview lasts beyond a specified time, and whether a further specialist opinion may be required.

6. When healthcare professionals identify risks they should be asked to quantify the risks. They should inform the custody officer:

- whether the person's condition:
    ~ is likely to improve;
    ~ will require or be amenable to treatment; and
- indicate how long it may take for such improvement to take effect.

7. The role of the healthcare professional is to consider the risks and advise the custody officer of the outcome of that consideration. The healthcare professional's determination and any advice or recommendations should be made in writing and form part of the custody record.

8. Once the healthcare professional has provided that information, it is a matter for the custody officer to decide whether or not to allow the interview to go ahead and if the interview is to proceed, to determine what safeguards are needed. Nothing prevents safeguards being provided in addition to those required under the Code. An example might be to have an appropriate healthcare professional present during the interview, in addition to an appropriate adult, in order constantly to monitor the person's condition and how it is being affected by the interview.

2.8.24   Annex H—Detained Person: Observation List

1. If any detainee fails to meet any of the following criteria, an appropriate healthcare professional or an ambulance must be called.

2. When assessing the level of rousability, consider:
Rousability–can they be woken?
- go into the cell
- call their name
- shake gently

Response to questions–can they give appropriate answers to questions such as:
- What's your name?
- Where do you live?
- Where do you think you are?

Response to commands–can they respond appropriately to commands such as:
- Open your eyes!
- Lift one arm, now the other arm!

3. Remember to take into account the possibility or presence of other illnesses, injury, or mental condition; a person who is drowsy and smells of alcohol may also have the following:
- Diabetes
- Epilepsy

- Head injury
- Drug intoxication or overdose
- Stroke

Annex I—NOT USED

Annex J—NOT USED

2.8.25

Annex K—X-rays and Ultrasound Scans

(a) Action

1. PACE, section 55A allows a person who has been arrested and is in police detention to have an X-ray taken of them or an ultrasound scan to be carried out on them (or both) if:
   (a) authorised by an officer of inspector rank or above who has reasonable grounds for believing that the detainee:
      (i) may have swallowed a Class A drug; and
      (ii) was in possession of that Class A drug with the intention of supplying it to another or to export; and
   (b) the detainee's appropriate consent has been given in writing.
2. Before an x-ray is taken or an ultrasound scan carried out, a police officer or designated detention officer must tell the detainee:
   (a) that the authority has been given; and
   (b) the grounds for giving the authorisation.
   Note: *Paragraph 1.5A* in this Code requires someone to fulfil the role of the appropriate adult to be present when a 17-year-old is told about the authority and grounds for an x-ray and ultra sound scan.
3. Before a detainee is asked to give appropriate consent to an x-ray or an ultrasound scan, they must be warned that if they refuse without good cause their refusal may harm their case if it comes to trial. This warning may be given by a police officer or member of police staff. In the case of juveniles, mentally vulnerable or mentally disordered suspects the seeking and giving of consent must take place in the presence of the appropriate adult. A juvenile's consent is only valid if their parent's or guardian's consent is also obtained unless the juvenile is under 14, when their parent's or guardian's consent is sufficient in its own right. A detainee who is not legally represented must be reminded of their entitlement to have free legal advice, see Code C, *paragraph 6.5*, and the reminder noted in the custody record.
   Note: *Paragraph 1.5A* in this Code requires someone to fulfil the role of the appropriate adult to be present when the warning is given to a 17-year-old and their consent to an x-ray or ultra sound scan is sought and given but the consent of their parent or guardian is not required.
4. An x-ray may be taken, or an ultrasound scan may be carried out, only by a registered medical practitioner or registered nurse, and only at a hospital, surgery or other medical premises.

(b) Documentation

5. The following shall be recorded as soon as practicable in the detainee's custody record:
   (a) the authorisation to take the x-ray or carry out the ultrasound scan (or both);
   (b) the grounds for giving the authorisation;
   (c) the giving of the warning required by paragraph 3; and
   (d) the fact that the appropriate consent was given or (as the case may be) refused, and if refused, the reason given for the refusal (if any); and
   (e) if an x-ray is taken or an ultrasound scan carried out:

- where it was taken or carried out;
- who took it or carried it out;
- who was present;
- the result.

6. *Not used.*

<hr>

2.8.25.1

KEYNOTE

If authority is given for an x-ray to be taken or an ultrasound scan to be carried out (or both), consideration should be given to asking a registered medical practitioner or registered nurse to explain to the detainee what is involved and to allay any concerns that the detainee might have about the effect on him/her of taking an x-ray or carrying out an ultrasound scan. If appropriate consent is not given, evidence of the explanation may, if the case comes to trial, be relevant to determining whether the detainee had a good cause for refusing.

The following form of words may be used to warn a detainee who is asked to consent to an X-ray being taken or an ultrasound scan being carried out (or both):

You do not have to allow an x-ray of you to be taken or an ultrasound scan to be carried out on you, but I must warn you that if you refuse without good cause, your refusal may harm your case if it comes to trial.

Where the use of the Welsh language is appropriate, the following form of words may be provided in Welsh:

Does dim rhaid i chi ganiatáu cymryd sgan uwchsain neu belydr-x (neu'r ddau) arnoch, ond mae'n rhaid i mi eich rhybuddio os byddwch chi'n gwrthod gwneud hynny heb reswm da, fe allai hynny niweidio eich achos pe bai'n dod gerbron llys.

<hr>

2.8.26   Annex L—Establishing Gender of Persons for the Purpose of Searching

1. Certain provisions of this and other PACE Codes explicitly state that searches and other procedures may only be carried out by, or in the presence of, persons of the same sex as the person subject to the search or other procedure.

2. All searches and procedures must be carried out with courtesy, consideration and respect for the person concerned. Police officers should show particular sensitivity when dealing with transgender individuals (including transsexual persons) and transvestite persons.

(a) Consideration

3. In law, the gender (and accordingly the sex) of an individual is their gender as registered at birth unless they have been issued with a Gender Recognition Certificate (GRC) under the Gender Recognition Act 2004 (GRA), in which case the person's gender is their acquired gender. This means that if the acquired gender is the male gender, the person's sex becomes that of a man and, if it is the female gender, the person's sex becomes that of a woman and they must be treated as their acquired gender.

4. When establishing whether the person concerned should be treated as being male or female for the purposes of these searches and procedures, the following approach which is designed to minimise embarrassment and secure the person's co-operation should be followed:
   (a) The person must not be asked whether they have a GRC (see *paragraph 8*);
   (b) If there is no doubt as to as to whether the person concerned should be treated as being male or female, they should be dealt with as being of that sex.
   (c) If at any time (including during the search or carrying out the procedure) there is doubt as to whether the person should be treated, or continue to be treated, as being male or female:
   (i) the person should be asked what gender they consider themselves to be. If they express a preference to be dealt with as a particular gender, they should be asked to indicate and confirm their preference by signing the custody record or, if a custody

record has not been opened, the search record or the officer's notebook. Subject to (ii) below, the person should be treated according to their preference;

    (ii) if there are grounds to doubt that the preference in (i) accurately reflects the person's predominant lifestyle, for example, if they ask to be treated as a woman but documents and other information make it clear that they live predominantly as a man, or vice versa, they should be treated according to what appears to be their predominant lifestyle and not their stated preference;

    (iii) If the person is unwilling to express a preference as in (i) above, efforts should be made to determine their predominant lifestyle and they should be treated as such. For example, if they appear to live predominantly as a woman, they should be treated as being female; or

    (iv) if none of the above apply, the person should be dealt with according to what reasonably appears to have been their sex as registered at birth.

5. Once a decision has been made about which gender an individual is to be treated as, each officer responsible for the search or procedure should where possible be advised before the search or procedure starts of any doubts as to the person's gender and the person informed that the doubts have been disclosed. This is important so as to maintain the dignity of the person and any officers concerned.

(b) Documentation

6. The person's gender as established under *paragraph 4(c)(i)* to *(iv)* above must be recorded in the person's custody record or, if a custody record has not been opened, on the search record or in the officer's notebook.

7. Where the person elects which gender they consider themselves to be under *paragraph 4(b)(i)* but, following *4(b)(ii)* is not treated in accordance with their preference, the reason must be recorded in the search record, in the officer's notebook or, if applicable, in the person's custody record.

(c) Disclosure of information

8. Section 22 of the GRA defines any information relating to a person's application for a GRC or to a successful applicant's gender before it became their acquired gender as 'protected information'. Nothing in this Annex is to be read as authorising or permitting any police officer or any police staff who has acquired such information when acting in their official capacity to disclose that information to any other person in contravention of the GRA. Disclosure includes making a record of 'protected information' which is read by others.

2.8.26.1

KEYNOTE

Provisions to which paragraph 1 applies include:

- in Code C: para. 4.1 and Annex A, paras 5, 6 and 11 (searches, strip and intimate searches of detainees under ss. 54 and 55 of the 1984 Act);
- in Code A: paras 2.8 and 3.6 and Note 4;
- in Code D: para. 5.5 and Note 5F (searches, examinations and photographing of detainees under s. 54A of the 1984 Act) and para. 6.9 (taking samples);
- in Code H: para. 4.1 and Annex A, paras 6, 7 and 12 (searches, strip and intimate searches under ss. 54 and 55 of the 1984 Act of persons arrested under s. 41 of the Terrorism Act 2000).

While there is no agreed definition of transgender (or trans), it is generally used as an umbrella term to describe people whose gender identity (self-identification as being a woman, man, neither or both) differs from the sex they were registered as at birth. The term includes, but is not limited to, transsexual people. Transsexual means a person who is proposing to undergo, is undergoing or has undergone a process (or part of a process) for the purpose of gender reassignment which is a protected characteristic under the Equality Act 2010 by changing physiological or other attributes of their sex. This includes aspects of gender such as dress and title. It would apply to a woman making the transition to being a man and a man making the transition to being a woman, as well as to a person who has only just started out on the process of gender reassignment and to a person who has completed the process. Both would share the characteristic of gender reassignment with each having the characteristics of one sex, but with certain characteristics of the other sex. Transvestite means a person of one gender who dresses in the clothes of a person of the opposite gender. However, transvestites do not live permanently in the gender opposite to their birth sex.

It is important to check the force guidance and instructions for the deployment of transgender officers and staff under their direction and control to duties which involve carrying out, or being present at, any of the searches and procedures described in para. 1. Force guidance which must be provided by each force's Chief Officer must comply with the Equality Act 2010.

2.8.27 Annex M—Documents and Records to be Translated

1. For the purposes of Directive 2010/64/EU of the European Parliament and of the Council of 20 October 2010 and this Code, essential documents comprise records required to be made in accordance with this Code which are relevant to decisions to deprive a person of their liberty, to any charge and to any record considered necessary to enable a detainee to defend themselves in criminal proceedings and to safeguard the fairness of the proceedings. Passages of essential documents which are not relevant need not be translated.

2. The table below lists the documents considered essential for the purposes of this Code and when (subject to *paragraphs 3 to 7*) written translations must be created and provided.

Table of essential documents:

	Essential documents for the purposes of this Code	When Translation to be created	When Translation to be Provided
(i)	The grounds for each of the following authorisations to keep the person in custody as they are described and referred to in the custody record: (a) Authorisation for detention before and after charge given by the custody officer and by the review officer, see *Code C paragraphs 3.4* and *15.16(a)*. (b) Authorisation to extend detention without charge beyond 24 hours given by a superintendent, see *Code C paragraph 15.16(b)*. (c) A warrant of further detention issued by a magistrates' court and any extension(s) of the warrant, see *Code C paragraph 15.16(c)*. An authority to detain in accordance with the directions in a warrant of arrest issued in connection with criminal proceedings including the court issuing the warrant.	As soon as practicable after each authorisation has been recorded in the custody record.	As soon as practicable after the translation has been created, whilst the person is detained or after they have been released (see *Note M3*).

(ii)	Written notice showing particulars of the offence charged required by *Code C paragraph 16.3* or the offence for which the suspect has been told they may be prosecuted.		As soon as practicable after the person has been charged or reported.
(iii)	Written interview records: *Code C11.11, 13.3, 13.4 & Code E4.7.* Written statement under caution: *Code C Annex D.*	To be created contemporaneously by the interpreter for the person to check and sign.	As soon as practicable after the person has been charged or told they may be prosecuted.

3. The custody officer may authorise an oral translation or oral summary of documents (i) to (ii) in the table (but not (iii)) to be provided (through an interpreter) instead of a written translation. Such an oral translation or summary may only be provided if it would not prejudice the fairness of the proceedings by in any way adversely affecting or otherwise undermining or limiting the ability of the suspect in question to understand their position and to communicate effectively with police officers, interviewers, solicitors and appropriate adults with regard to their detention and the investigation of the offence in question and to defend themselves in the event of criminal proceedings. The quantity and complexity of the information in the document should always be considered and specific additional consideration given if the suspect is mentally disordered or otherwise mentally vulnerable or is a juvenile or a 17-year-old (see *Code C paragraph 1.5A*). The reason for the decision must be recorded (see *paragraph 13.11(e)*)

4. Subject to *paragraphs 5* to *7* below, a suspect may waive their right to a written translation of the essential documents described in the table but only if they do so voluntarily after receiving legal advice or having full knowledge of the consequences and give their unconditional and fully informed consent in writing (see *paragraph 9*).

5. The suspect may be asked if they wish to waive their right to a written translation and before giving their consent, they must be reminded of their right to legal advice and asked whether they wish to speak to a solicitor.

6. No police officer or police staff should do or say anything with the intention of persuading a suspect who is entitled to a written translation of an essential document to waive that right.

7. For the purpose of the waiver:
   (a) the consent of a person who is mentally disordered or otherwise mentally vulnerable person is only valid if the information about the circumstances under which they can waive the right and the reminder about their right to legal advice mentioned in *paragraphs 3* to *5* and their consent is given in the presence of the appropriate adult.

   Note: *Paragraph 1.5A* in Code C requires someone to fulfil the role of the appropriate adult to be present when a 17-year-old is given the information and reminder mentioned in sub-paragraph (a) above and gives their consent to waive their right. The consent of their parent or guardian is not required.

   (b) the consent of a juvenile is only valid if their parent's or guardian's consent is also obtained unless the juvenile is under 14, when their parent's or guardian's consent is sufficient in its own right and the information and reminder mentioned in sub paragraph (a) above and their consent is also given in the presence of the appropriate adult (who may or may not be a parent or guardian).

8. The detainee, their solicitor or appropriate adult may make representations to the custody officer that a document which is not included in the table is essential and that a translation should be provided. The request may be refused if the officer is satisfied that the translation requested is not essential for the purposes described in *paragraph 1* above.

9. If the custody officer has any doubts about
    - providing an oral translation or summary of an essential document instead of a written translation (see *paragraph 3*);
    - whether the suspect fully understands the consequences of waiving their right to a written translation of an essential document (see *paragraph 4*), or
    - about refusing to provide a translation of a requested document (see *paragraph 7*), the officer should seek advice from an inspector or above.

Documentation

10. Action taken in accordance with this Annex shall be recorded in the detainee's custody record or interview record as appropriate (see *Code C paragraph 13.11(e)*).

2.8.27.1

KEYNOTE

This Annex lists the essential documents and the requirements to provide translations to reflect the terms of EU Directive 2010/64. It is not necessary to disclose information in any translation which is capable of undermining or otherwise adversely affecting any investigative processes, for example, by enabling the suspect to fabricate an innocent explanation or to conceal lies from the interviewer. No police officer or police staff shall indicate to any suspect, except to answer a direct question, whether the period for which they are liable to be detained or if not detained, the time taken to complete the interview, might be reduced:

- if they do not ask for legal advice before deciding whether they wish to waive their right to a written translation of an essential document; or
- if they decide to waive their right to a written translation of an essential document.

There is no power under PACE to detain a person or to delay their release solely to create and provide a written translation of any essential document.

2.9 | Identification

PACE Code of Practice for the Identification of Persons by Police Officers (Code D)

> A thick grey line down the margin denotes text that is an extract of the PACE Code itself (i.e. the actual wording of the legislation). This material is examinable for both Sergeants and Inspectors.

2.9.1 Introduction

A critical issue in the investigation and prosecution of offences is the identification of the offender. Many different methods of identification exist but the main feature which must be considered in relation to each is its *reliability*.

The visual identification of suspects by witnesses is one of the most common forms of identification; it is also one of the most unreliable. Even under research conditions, the recall of eye witnesses is inconsistent; where the witness sees or experiences the spontaneous commission of a crime, that reliability is reduced even further.

It was for these reasons that the *Turnbull* guidelines were set out, together with the provisions of Code D. If there is no identification evidence, the *Turnbull* guidelines will not apply. It should be remembered that a witness who does not identify the suspect may still be able to provide other valuable evidence to the case, for instance a description of the person who committed the offence, or a description of what he/she was wearing. Again it is not uncommon for witnesses to qualify their identification of the suspect by indicating that they 'cannot be quite certain'. While a defendant cannot be convicted on such a qualified identification alone, it may be admissible to support the case where other evidence is also available (*R v George* [2002] EWCA Crim 1923).

A lot will depend on the individual circumstances of each case, but it is essential that these issues are covered in any interview or other evidence-gathering process.

'Dock identifications', where the witness's first identification of the accused involves pointing out the person in the dock, are often dramatised by filmmakers but, in practice, are generally disallowed as being unreliable and unfair.

The Police and Criminal Evidence Act 1984 Code of Practice, Code D provides guidance for the identification of persons by police officers. This chapter sets out the actual Codes of Practice with keynotes which incorporate the notes of guidance to the Code.

Generally, the methods of identification covered by Code D can be divided into two:

- occasions where the identity of the suspect is known; and
- occasions where the identity of the suspect is not known.

Where the identity of the suspect is known this can be further divided into those cases where the suspect is available and those where he/she is not available.

Although a breach of Code D (or any of the other Codes of Practice) will not automatically result in the evidence being excluded (*R v Khan* (1999) 19 July, CA, unreported), the judge or magistrate(s) will consider the effects of any breach on the fairness of any subsequent proceedings. The Codes are intended to provide protection to suspects and, if it is felt that the breach of Code D has resulted in unfairness or other prejudicial effect on the defendant, the court may exclude the related evidence under s. 78 of the Police and Criminal Evidence Act 1984 (**see chapter 2.6**).

The Police Reform Act 2002 has introduced designated support staff who have some of the powers that police officers have (**see chapter 2.8**).

2.9.2 PACE Code of Practice for the Identification of Persons by Police Officers (Code D)

This code has effect in relation to any identification procedure carried out after midnight on 06 March 2011.

1 Introduction

1.1 This Code of Practice concerns the principal methods used by police to identify people in connection with the investigation of offences and the keeping of accurate and reliable criminal records. The powers and procedures in this code must be used fairly, responsibly, with respect for the people to whom they apply and without unlawful discrimination. The Equality Act 2010 makes it unlawful for police officers to discriminate against, harass or victimise any person on the grounds of the 'protected characteristics' of age, disability, gender reassignment, race, religion or belief, sex and sexual orientation, marriage and civil partnership, pregnancy and maternity when using their powers. When police forces are carrying out their functions they also have a duty to have regard to the need to eliminate unlawful discrimination, harassment and victimisation and to take steps to foster good relations.

1.2 Identification by witnesses arises, e.g., if the offender is seen committing the crime and a witness is given an opportunity to identify the suspect in a video identification, identification parade or similar procedure. The procedures are designed to:
- test the witness' ability to identify the person they saw on a previous occasion
- provide safeguards against mistaken identification.

While this Code concentrates on visual identification procedures, it does not preclude the police making use of aural identification procedures such as a 'voice identification parade', where they judge that appropriate.

1.2A In this code, separate provisions in Part B of *section 3* below apply when any person, including a police officer, is asked if they recognise anyone they see in an image as being someone they know and to test their claim that they recognise that person as someone who is known to them. Except where stated, these separate provisions are not subject to the eye-witnesses identification procedures described in *paragraph 1.2*.

1.3 Identification by fingerprints applies when a person's fingerprints are taken to:
- compare with fingerprints found at the scene of a crime
- check and prove convictions
- help to ascertain a person's identity.

1.3A Identification using footwear impressions applies when a person's footwear impressions are taken to compare with impressions found at the scene of a crime.

1.4 Identification by body samples and impressions includes taking samples such as blood or hair to generate a DNA profile for comparison with material obtained from the scene of a crime, or a victim.

1.5 Taking photographs of arrested people applies to recording and checking identity and locating and tracing persons who:
- are wanted for offences
- fail to answer their bail.

1.6 Another method of identification involves searching and examining detained suspects to find, e.g., marks such as tattoos or scars which may help establish their identity or whether they have been involved in committing an offence.

1.7 The provisions of the Police and Criminal Evidence Act 1984 (PACE) and this Code are designed to make sure fingerprints, samples, impressions and photographs are taken, used and retained, and identification procedures carried out, only when justified and necessary for preventing, detecting or investigating crime. If these provisions are not observed, the application of the relevant procedures in particular cases may be open to question.

2.9.3 2 General

2.1 This Code must be readily available at all police stations for consultation by:
- police officers and police staff
- detained persons
- members of the public

2.2 The provisions of this Code:
- include the *Annexes*
- do not include the Notes for guidance.

2.3 Code C, *paragraph 1.4*, regarding a person who may be mentally disordered or otherwise mentally vulnerable and the *Notes for guidance* applicable to those provisions apply to this Code.

2.4 Code C, *paragraph 1.5*, regarding a person who appears to be under the age of 17 applies to this Code.

2.5 Code C, *paragraph 1.6*, regarding a person who appears blind, seriously visually impaired, deaf, unable to read or speak or has difficulty orally because of a speech impediment applies to this Code.

2.6 In this Code:
- 'appropriate adult' means the same as in Code C, *paragraph 1.7*,
- 'solicitor' means the same as in Code C, *paragraph 6.12* and the *Notes for guidance* applicable to those provisions apply to this Code.
- where a search or other procedure under this code may only be carried out or observed by a person of the same sex as the person to whom the search or procedure applies, the gender of the detainee and other persons present should be established and recorded in line with *Annex F* of Code A.

2.7 References to custody officers include those performing the functions of custody officer, see *paragraph 1.9* of Code C.

2.8 When a record of any action requiring the authority of an officer of a specified rank is made under this Code, subject to *paragraph 2.18*, the officer's name and rank must be recorded.

2.9 When this Code requires the prior authority or agreement of an officer of at least inspector or superintendent rank, that authority may be given by a sergeant or chief inspector who has been authorised to perform the functions of the higher rank under PACE, section 107.

2.10 Subject to *paragraph 2.18*, all records must be timed and signed by the maker.

2.11 Records must be made in the custody record, unless otherwise specified. References to 'pocket book' include any official report book issued to police officers or police staff.

2.12 If any procedure in this Code requires a person's consent, the consent of a:
- mentally disordered or otherwise mentally vulnerable person is only valid if given in the presence of the appropriate adult
- juvenile, is only valid if their parent's or guardian's consent is also obtained unless the juvenile is under 14, when their parent's or guardian's consent is sufficient in its own right. If the only obstacle to an identification procedure in section 3 is that a juvenile's parent or guardian refuses consent or reasonable efforts to obtain it have failed, the identification officer may apply the provisions of *paragraph 3.21*.

2.13　If a person is blind, seriously visually impaired or unable to read, the custody officer or identification officer shall make sure their solicitor, relative, appropriate adult or some other person likely to take an interest in them and not involved in the investigation is available to help check any documentation. When this Code requires written consent or signing, the person assisting may be asked to sign instead, if the detainee prefers. This paragraph does not require an appropriate adult to be called solely to assist in checking and signing documentation for a person who is not a juvenile, or mentally disordered or otherwise mentally vulnerable (see Code C, *paragraph 3.15*).

2.14　If any procedure in this Code requires information to be given to or sought from a suspect, it must be given or sought in the appropriate adult's presence if the suspect is mentally disordered, otherwise mentally vulnerable or a juvenile. If the appropriate adult is not present when the information is first given or sought, the procedure must be repeated in the presence of the appropriate adult when they arrive. If the suspect appears deaf or there is doubt about their hearing or speaking ability or ability to understand English, and effective communication cannot be established, the information must be given or sought through an interpreter.

2.15　Any procedure in this Code involving the participation of a suspect who is mentally disordered, otherwise mentally vulnerable or a juvenile must take place in the presence of the appropriate adult. See Code C, *paragraph 1.4*.

2.15A　Any procedure in this Code involving the participation of a witness who is or appears to be mentally disordered, otherwise mentally vulnerable or a juvenile should take place in the presence of a pre-trial support person. However, the support-person must not be allowed to prompt any identification of a suspect by a witness.

2.16　References to:
- 'taking a photograph', include the use of any process to produce a single, still or moving, visual image
- 'photographing a person', should be construed accordingly
- 'photographs', 'films', 'negatives' and 'copies' include relevant visual images recorded, stored, or reproduced through any medium
- 'destruction' includes the deletion of computer data relating to such images or making access to that data impossible.

2.17　Except as described, nothing in this Code affects the powers and procedures:
(i) for requiring and taking samples of breath, blood and urine in relation to driving offences, etc, when under the influence of drink, drugs or excess alcohol under the:
- Road Traffic Act 1988, sections 4 to 11
- Road Traffic Offenders Act 1988, sections 15 and 16
- Transport and Works Act 1992, sections 26 to 38;

(ii) under the Immigration Act 1971, Schedule 2, paragraph 18, for taking photographs and fingerprints from persons detained under that Act, Schedule 2, paragraph 16 (Administrative Controls as to Control on Entry etc.); for taking fingerprints in accordance with the Immigration and Asylum Act 1999; sections 141 and 142(3), or other methods for collecting information about a person's external physical characteristics provided for by regulations made under that Act, section 144;

(iii) under the Terrorism Act 2000, Schedule 8, for taking photographs, fingerprints, skin impressions, body samples or impressions from people:
- arrested under that Act, section 41,
- detained for the purposes of examination under that Act, Schedule 7, and to whom the Code of Practice issued under that Act, Schedule 14, paragraph 6, applies ('the terrorism provisions')

(iv) for taking photographs, fingerprints, skin impressions, body samples or impressions from people who have been:
- arrested on warrants issued in Scotland, by officers exercising powers under the Criminal Justice and Public Order Act 1994, section 136(2)

- arrested or detained without warrant by officers from a police force in Scotland exercising their powers of arrest or detention under the Criminal Justice and Public Order Act 1994, section 137(2), (Cross Border powers of arrest etc.).

Note: In these cases, police powers and duties and the person's rights and entitlements whilst at a police station in England and Wales are the same as if the person had been arrested in Scotland by a Scottish police officer.

2.18 Nothing in this Code requires the identity of officers or police staff to be recorded or disclosed:

(a) in the case of enquiries linked to the investigation of terrorism;

(b) if the officers or police staff reasonably believe recording or disclosing their names might put them in danger.

In these cases, they shall use warrant or other identification numbers and the name of their police station.

2.19 In this Code:

(a) 'designated person' means a person other than a police officer, designated under the Police Reform Act 2002, Part 4, who has specified powers and duties of police officers conferred or imposed on them;

(b) any reference to a police officer includes a designated person acting in the exercise or performance of the powers and duties conferred or imposed on them by their designation.

2.20 If a power conferred on a designated person:

(a) allows reasonable force to be used when exercised by a police officer, a designated person exercising that power has the same entitlement to use force;

(b) includes power to use force to enter any premises, that power is not exercisable by that designated person except:

(i) in the company, and under the supervision, of a police officer; or

(ii) for the purpose of:

- saving life or limb; or
- preventing serious damage to property.

2.21 Nothing in this Code prevents the custody officer, or other officer given custody of the detainee, from allowing police staff who are not designated persons to carry out individual procedures or tasks at the police station if the law allows. However, the officer remains responsible for making sure the procedures and tasks are carried out correctly in accordance with the Codes of Practice. Any such person must be:

(a) a person employed by a police authority maintaining a police force and under the control and direction of the Chief Officer of that force;

(b) employed by a person with whom a police authority has a contract for the provision of services relating to persons arrested or otherwise in custody.

2.22 Designated persons and other police staff must have regard to any relevant provisions of the Codes of Practice.

2.9.3.1 **KEYNOTE**

Examples of when it would not be practicable to obtain a detainee's consent, under para. 2.12 to a search, examination or the taking of a phonograph of an identifying mark include

- when the person is drunk or otherwise unfit to give consent;
- when there are reasonable grounds to suspect that if the person became aware that a search or examination was to take place or an identifying mark was to be photographed, he/she would take to steps to prevent this happening, e g, by violently resisting, covering or concealing the mark, etc. and it would not otherwise be possible to carry out the search or examination or to photograph any identifying mark:
- in the case of a juvenile, if the parent or guardian cannot be contacted in sufficient time to allow the search or examination to be carried out or the photograph to be taken.

Examples of when it would not be practicable to obtain the person's consent to a photograph being taken include:

- when the person is drunk or otherwise unfit to give consent;
- when there are reasonable grounds to suspect that if the person became aware a photograph suitable to be used or disclosed for the use and disclosure described in para. 5.6 was to be taken, he/she would take steps to prevent it being taken, e.g. by violently resisting, covering or distorting his/her face etc., and it would not otherwise be possible to take a suitable photograph;
- when, in order to obtain a suitable photograph, it is necessary to take it covertly; and
- in the case of a juvenile, if the parent or guardian cannot be contacted in sufficient time to allow the photograph to be taken.

People who are seriously visually impaired or unable to read may be unwilling to sign police documents. The alternative, i.e. The representative signing on his/her behalf, seeks to protect the interests of both police and suspects.

For the purposes of any procedures within this Code which require an appropriate adult's consent, where a juvenile is in the care of a local authority or voluntary organisation the consent may be given by that authority or organisation. Where a parent, guardian or representative of a local authority or voluntary organisation is not acting as the appropriate adult under para. 2.14 or 2.15 he/she does not have to be present to give consent. However, it is important that a parent or guardian not present is fully informed before being asked to consent. He/she must be given the same information about the procedure and the juvenile's suspected involvement in the offence as the juvenile and appropriate adult. The parent or guardian must also be allowed to speak to the juvenile and the appropriate adult if he/she wishes. Provided the consent is fully informed and is not withdrawn, it may be obtained at any time before the procedure takes place.

The Youth Justice and Criminal Evidence Act 1999 guidance 'Achieving Best Evidence in Criminal Proceedings; Guidance on interviewing victims and witnesses; and guidance on using special measures' indicates that a pre-trial support person should accompany a vulnerable witness during any identification procedure. It states that this support person should not be (or not be likely to be) a witness in the investigation.

The purpose of using warrant or identification numbers instead of names referred to in Code D, para. 2.18(b) is to protect those involved in serious organised crime investigations or arrest of particularly violent suspects when there is reliable information that those arrested or their associates may threaten or cause harm to those involved. In cases of doubt, an officer of inspector rank or above should be consulted.

In relation to terrorism cases, photographs, fingerprints, samples and impressions may be taken from a person defined under the terrorism provisions to help determine whether he/she is, or has been, involved in terrorism, as well as when there are reasonable grounds for suspecting his/her involvement in a particular offence (see Code H in **appendix 2.1**).

2.9.4   ▌ 3 Identification by Witnesses

2.9.4.1   KEYNOTE

Section 3 of Code D is split into Parts A and B, thereby distinguishing eyewitness identification procedures such as video identification from procedures for obtaining recognition evidence by viewing CCTV or similar images.

2.9.4.2   (A) Identification of a suspect by an eye-witness

3.0 This part applies when an eye-witness has seen the offender committing the crime or in any other circumstances which tend to prove or disprove the involvement of the person they saw in the crime, for example, close to the scene of the crime, immediately before or immediately after it was committed. It sets out the procedures to be used to test the ability of that eye-witness to identify a person suspected of involvement in the offence as the person they saw on the previous occasion. Except where stated, this part does not apply to the procedures described in Part B and *Note 3AA*.

3.1 A record shall be made of the suspect's description as first given by a potential witness. This record must:

(a) be made and kept in a form which enables details of that description to be accurately produced from it, in a visible and legible form, which can be given to the suspect or the suspect's solicitor in accordance with this Code; and

(b) unless otherwise specified, be made before the witness takes part in any identification procedures under *paragraphs 3.5 to 3.10, 3.21 or 3.23.*

A copy of the record shall where practicable, be given to the suspect or their solicitor before any procedures under *paragraphs 3.5 to 3.10, 3.21* or *3.23* are carried out.

(a) Cases when the suspect's identity is not known

3.2 In cases when the suspect's identity is not known, a witness may be taken to a particular neighbourhood or place to see whether they can identify the person they saw. Although the number, age, sex, race, general description and style of clothing of other people present at the location and the way in which any identification is made cannot be controlled, the principles applicable to the formal procedures under *paragraphs 3.5 to 3.10* shall be followed as far as practicable. For example:

(a) where it is practicable to do so, a record should be made of the witness' description of the suspect, as in *paragraph 3.1(a)*, before asking the witness to make an identification;

(b) care must be taken not to direct the witness' attention to any individual unless, taking into account all the circumstances, this cannot be avoided. However, this does not prevent a witness being asked to look carefully at the people around at the time or to look towards a group or in a particular direction, if this appears necessary to make sure that the witness does not overlook a possible suspect simply because the witness is looking in the opposite direction and also to enable the witness to make comparisons between any suspect and others who are in the area;

(c) where there is more than one witness, every effort should be made to keep them separate and witnesses should be taken to see whether they can identify a person independently;

(d) once there is sufficient information to justify the arrest of a particular individual for suspected involvement in the offence, e.g., after a witness makes a positive identification, the provisions set out from *paragraph 3.4* onwards shall apply for any other witnesses in relation to that individual. Subject to *paragraphs 3.12* and *3.13*, it is not necessary for the witness who makes such a positive identification to take part in a further procedure;

(e) the officer or police staff accompanying the witness must record, in their pocket book, the action taken as soon as, and in as much detail, as possible. The record should include: the date, time and place of the relevant occasion the witness claims to have previously seen the suspect; where any identification was made; how it was made and the conditions at the time (e.g., the distance the witness was from the suspect, the weather and light); if the witness's attention was drawn to the suspect; the reason for this; and anything said by the witness or the suspect about the identification or the conduct of the procedure.

3.3 A witness must not be shown photographs, computerised or artist's composite likenesses or similar likenesses or pictures (including 'E-fit' images) if the identity of the suspect is known to the police and the suspect is available to take part in a video identification, an identification parade or a group identification. If the suspect's identity is not known, the showing of such images to a witness to obtain identification evidence must be done in accordance with *Annex E.*

2.9.4.3 **KEYNOTE**

Identification at the Scene

The need for 'scene identifications' was recognised by Lord Lane CJ in *R* v *Oscar* [1991] Crim LR 778 and by the Court of Appeal in *R* v *Rogers* [1993] Crim LR 386.

In *Oscar*, the court held that there had been no requirement for an identity parade in that case and Lord Lane pointed out that, in any case, a later parade where the suspect was dressed differently would be of no value at all. In *Rogers*, the suspect was found near a crime scene and was confronted by a witness who positively identified him. The court held that the identification in that case was necessary for an arrest to be made, although the court considered that a later parade could have been carried out.

The admissibility of identification evidence obtained when carrying out a 'scene identification' may be compromised if, before a person is identified, the witness's attention is specifically drawn to that person.

Careful consideration must be given before a decision to identify a suspect in this manner is used. If there is sufficient evidence to arrest the suspect without using a witness's identification, then it is likely that the courts will find that an identification method outlined at Code D, para. 3.4 should have been used and the evidence may be excluded. Confrontations between witnesses and suspects on the street can be useful at times, but where this takes place it defeats the formal identification process and needs to be carefully considered. The reason for this is that, even if the suspect is picked out on the identification parade by that witness, the defence will be able to argue that the identification was from the confrontation after the incident and not at the time of the commission of the offence. If there is more than one witness available and a decision is taken to use a witness to try to identify a suspect at the scene, other witnesses should be moved away, so as to reduce the possibility of a chance encounter with the suspect. Where possible, these witnesses should be kept apart until the identification parade and ideally should not discuss the matter between themselves.

An example where a street identification was appropriate is *R* v *El-Hinnachi* [1998] 2 Cr App R 226. Here an affray took place in the car park of a public house. A witness had seen the man earlier in the pub and she had had an unobstructed view in good light before the attack. The witness described the attacker's clothing to the police and then identified a group of men who had been stopped by other officers a short distance away. The court accepted that this was the correct approach. The defendants were not known suspects when they were stopped by the police prior to the witness's identification. The court also accepted that it had not been practicable for a record to have been made of the witness's description, as required by Code D, para. 3.1, prior to the identification.

A not uncommon situation is where police officers chase a suspect who is arrested by other officers on the description circulated by the chasing officer, who then attends the scene to confirm the person's identity. The case of *R* v *Nunes* [2001] EWCA Crim 2283, covers this point and points out the dangers of this practice. The facts of the case were that a police officer saw a man inside a house and circulated a description on his radio. A person fitting the description was seen and arrested. The first officer arrived on the scene and identified the arrested person as the man he had earlier seen in the house. The Court of Appeal held that on the particular facts of this case the identification amounted to a breach of the Code. By the time of the identification, the man had been arrested for suspected involvement in the offence and, on his arrest, the identity of the suspect was known to the police. Therefore, by the time the witnessing officer arrived on the scene, the case involved 'disputed identification evidence' because the suspect had said that he had not done anything while the police had told him he matched the description of a suspected burglar. That said, the court did go on to hold that the judge had the discretion to allow the identification evidence to be adduced notwithstanding the breach of the Codes, but a full and careful direction regarding the breaches, together with a warning about the shortcomings in the procedure, would have been necessary.

Where a suspect is identified by witnesses, other evidence should still be sought to strengthen the case (or to prove the person's innocence) as identification evidence is often challenged at court. Such supporting evidence may include admissions by the suspect that links him/her to the identification evidence; e.g. that he/she owns the vehicle that was driven at the time of the offence (*R* v *Ward* [2001] Crim LR 316).

2.9.4.4

(b) Cases when the suspect is known and available

3.4   If the suspect's identity is known to the police and they are available, the identification procedures set out in *paragraphs 3.5* to *3.10* may be used. References in this section to a suspect being 'known' mean there is sufficient information known to the police to justify the arrest of a particular person for suspected involvement in the offence. A suspect being 'available' means they are immediately available or will be within a reasonably short time and willing to take an effective part in at least one of the following which it is practicable to arrange:

- video identification;
- identification parade; or
- group identification.

Video identification

3.5 A 'video identification' is when the witness is shown moving images of a known suspect, together with similar images of others who resemble the suspect. Moving images must be used unless:

- the suspect is known but not available (see *paragraph 3.21* of this Code); or
- in accordance with *paragraph 2A of Annex A* of this Code, the identification officer does not consider that replication of a physical feature can be achieved or that it is not possible to conceal the location of the feature on the image of the suspect.

The identification officer may then decide to make use of video identification but using still images.

3.6 Video identifications must be carried out in accordance with *Annex A*.

Identification parade

3.7 An 'identification parade' is when the witness sees the suspect in a line of others who resemble the suspect.

3.8 Identification parades must be carried out in accordance with *Annex B*.

Group identification

3.9 A 'group identification' is when the witness sees the suspect in an informal group of people.

3.10 Group identifications must be carried out in accordance with *Annex C*.

Arranging eye-witness identification procedures

3.11 Except for the provisions in *paragraph 3.19*, the arrangements for, and conduct of, the identification procedures in *paragraphs 3.5* to *3.10* and circumstances in which an identification procedure must be held shall be the responsibility of an officer not below inspector rank who is not involved with the investigation, 'the identification officer'. Unless otherwise specified, the identification officer may allow another officer or police staff, see *paragraph 2.21*, to make arrangements for, and conduct, any of these identification procedures. In delegating these procedures, the identification officer must be able to supervise effectively and either intervene or be contacted for advice. No officer or any other person involved with the investigation of the case against the suspect, beyond the extent required by these procedures, may take any part in these procedures or act as the identification officer. This does not prevent the identification officer from consulting the officer in charge of the investigation to determine which procedure to use. When an identification procedure is required, in the interest of fairness to suspects and witnesses, it must be held as soon as practicable.

Circumstances in which an eye-witness identification procedure must be held

3.12 Whenever:

(i) a witness has identified a suspect or purported to have identified them prior to any identification procedure set out in *paragraphs 3.5* to *3.10* having been held; or

(ii) there is a witness available, who expresses an ability to identify the suspect, or where there is a reasonable chance of the witness being able to do so, and they have not been given an opportunity to identify the suspect in any of the procedures set out in *paragraphs 3.5* to *3.10*, and the suspect disputes being the person the witness claims to have seen, an identification procedure shall be held unless it is not practicable or it would serve no useful purpose in proving or disproving whether the suspect was involved in committing the offence, for example:

- where the suspect admits being at the scene of the crime and gives an account of what took place and the eye-witness does not see anything which contradicts that;
- when it is not disputed that the suspect is already known to the witness who claims to have recognised them when seeing them commit the crime.

3.13 An eye-witness identification procedure may also be held if the officer in charge of the investigation considers it would be useful.

2.9.4.5

KEYNOTE

When Must an Identification Procedure be Held?

Identification procedures should be held for the benefit of the defence as well as the prosecution (*R* v *Wait* [1998] Crim LR 68). The key factor to consider when deciding whether to hold an identification parade is whether *a failure to hold a parade could be a matter of genuine potential prejudice to the suspect*. In *R* v *SBC (A Juvenile)* [2001] EWCA Crim 885 the defence was one of duress but the appeal was based on the failure of the police to hold identification parades. The Court of Appeal stated that this was not a case about identification, as none of the defendants denied their presence at the scene. What they denied was their criminal participation in the activities that took place. It followed, therefore, that Code D did not apply. Other examples would be where it is not in dispute that the suspect is already well known to the witness who claims to have seen the suspect commit the crime or where there is no reasonable possibility that a witness would be able to make an identification.

Any decision to proceed without an identification parade must be capable of justification later to the relevant court. The courts have taken different approaches to justification based on practical difficulties. In an early case, the submissions of the identification officer that it was impracticable to find enough people who sufficiently resembled the defendant were treated fairly dismissively by the trial judge (*R* v *Gaynor* [1988] Crim LR 242). In later cases, however, the courts have been more lenient, accepting that the timescales involved in arranging identification parades may render them 'impracticable' (see *R* v *Jamel* [1993] Crim LR 52, where the court refused an objection by the defence to a group identification). A group identification was used in *Jamel* because a parade using mixed-race volunteers would have taken too long to arrange. All reasonable steps must be taken to investigate the possibility of one identification option before moving on to an alternative, and an offer from a suspect's solicitor to find volunteers to stand on a parade is such a 'reasonable' step (*R* v *Britton & Richards* [1989] Crim LR 144).

There have been a number of Court of Appeal cases concerning the requirement to hold identification parades. It is suggested that these should be applied to the Code regardless of which form of identification procedure is used. The leading case is *R* v *Forbes* [2001] 1 AC 473, which was based on earlier versions of the Code of Practice. The House of Lords held that if the police are in possession of sufficient evidence to justify the arrest of a suspect, and that suspect's identification depends on eye-witness identification evidence, even in part, then if the identification is disputed, the Code requires that an identification parade should be held with the suspect's consent, unless one of the exceptions applies.

The House of Lords went on to say that this mandatory obligation to hold an identification parade ('parade' at the time of judgment was right, but this applies equally to any identification procedure) applies even if there has been a 'fully satisfactory', 'actual and complete' or 'unequivocal' identification of the suspect.

Despite the wording of Code D, it has been held that a suspect's right to have an identification [procedure] is not confined to cases where a dispute over identity has already arisen; that right also applies where such a dispute might reasonably be anticipated (*R* v *Rutherford and Palmer* (1994) 98 Cr App R 191). Similarly, a suspect's failure to request an identification [procedure] does not mean that the police may proceed without one (*R* v *Graham* [1994] Crim LR 212).

It is important to consider the distinction between identification of a suspect and the suspect's clothing or other features. In *D* v *DPP* (1998) *The Times*, 7 August, a witness had observed two youths for a continuous period of five to six minutes and then informed the police of what he had seen, describing the age of the youths and the clothes that they were wearing. The court held that there had not been an identification within the terms of the Codes of Practice because the witness had at no stage identified the defendant or the co-accused. He had described only their clothing and their approximate ages, and the police, acting on that information, had made the arrests. An identification parade could have served no useful purpose, since the clothing would have been changed and those persons used for the parade would have been the same approximate age. This point was further supported in *R* v *Haynes* [2004] EWCA Crim 390, where the Court of Appeal held that as a practical point the identification parade, whether or not the suspect was regarded as a known or unknown suspect, was of little value where the witness identified the suspect by clothing and not by recognition of the suspect's features. An identification parade would have provided little assistance.

The question for the court will be whether it is fair to admit the identification evidence. When looking at this issue the court will consider how reliable that identification evidence is.

2.9.4.6   Selecting an eye-witness identification procedure

3.14   If, because of *paragraph 3.12*, an identification procedure is to be held, the suspect shall initially be offered a video identification unless:

(a) a video identification is not practicable; or

(b) an identification parade is both practicable and more suitable than a video identification; or

(c) *paragraph 3.16* applies.

The identification officer and the officer in charge of the investigation shall consult each other to determine which option is to be offered. An identification parade may not be practicable because of factors relating to the witnesses, such as their number, state of health, availability and travelling requirements. A video identification would normally be more suitable if it could be arranged and completed sooner than an identification parade. Before an option is offered the suspect must also be reminded of their entitlement to have free legal advice, see Code C, *paragraph 6.5*.

3.15   A suspect who refuses the identification procedure first offered shall be asked to state their reason for refusing and may get advice from their solicitor and/or if present, their appropriate adult. The suspect, solicitor and/or appropriate adult shall be allowed to make representations about why another procedure should be used. A record should be made of the reasons for refusal and any representations made. After considering any reasons given, and representations made, the identification officer shall, if appropriate, arrange for the suspect to be offered an alternative which the officer considers suitable and practicable. If the officer decides it is not suitable and practicable to offer an alternative identification procedure, the reasons for that decision shall be recorded.

3.16   A group identification may initially be offered if the officer in charge of the investigation considers it is more suitable than a video identification or an identification parade and the identification officer considers it practicable to arrange.

Notice to suspect

3.17 Unless *paragraph 3.20* applies, before a video identification, an identification parade or group identification is arranged, the following shall be explained to the suspect:

(i) the purposes of the video identification, identification parade or group identification;

(ii) their entitlement to free legal advice; see Code C, *paragraph 6.5*;

(iii) the procedures for holding it, including their right to have a solicitor or friend present;

(iv) that they do not have to consent to or co-operate in a video identification, identification parade or group identification;

(v) that if they do not consent to, and co-operate in, a video identification, identification parade or group identification, their refusal may be given in evidence in any subsequent trial and police may proceed covertly without their consent or make other arrangements to test whether a witness can identify them, see *paragraph 3.21*;

(vi) whether, for the purposes of the video identification procedure, images of them have previously been obtained, see *paragraph 3.20*, and if so, that they may co-operate in providing further, suitable images to be used instead;

(vii) if appropriate, the special arrangements for juveniles;

(viii) if appropriate, the special arrangements for mentally disordered or otherwise mentally vulnerable people;

(ix) that if they significantly alter their appearance between being offered an identification procedure and any attempt to hold an identification procedure, this may be given in evidence if the case comes to trial, and the identification officer may then consider other forms of identification, see *paragraph 3.21*;

(x) that a moving image or photograph may be taken of them when they attend for any identification procedure;

(xi) whether, before their identity became known, the witness was shown photographs, a computerised or artist's composite likeness or similar likeness or image by the police;

(xii) that if they change their appearance before an identification parade, it may not be practicable to arrange one on the day or subsequently and, because of the appearance change, the identification officer may consider alternative methods of identification;

(xiii) that they or their solicitor will be provided with details of the description of the suspect as first given by any witnesses who are to attend the video identification, identification parade, group identification or confrontation, see par*agraph 3.1*.

3.18 This information must also be recorded in a written notice handed to the suspect. The suspect must be given a reasonable opportunity to read the notice, after which, they should be asked to sign a second copy to indicate if they are willing to co-operate with the making of a video or take part in the identification parade or group identification. The signed copy shall be retained by the identification officer.

3.19 The duties of the identification officer under *paragraphs 3.17* and *3.18* may be performed by the custody officer or other officer not involved in the investigation if:

(a) it is proposed to release the suspect in order that an identification procedure can be arranged and carried out and an inspector is not available to act as the identification officer, see *paragraph 3.11*, before the suspect leaves the station; or

(b) it is proposed to keep the suspect in police detention whilst the procedure is arranged and carried out and waiting for an inspector to act as the identification officer, see *paragraph 3.11*, would cause unreasonable delay to the investigation.

The officer concerned shall inform the identification officer of the action taken and give them the signed copy of the notice.

3.20 If the identification officer and officer in charge of the investigation suspect, on reasonable grounds that if the suspect was given the information and notice as in *paragraphs 3.17* and *3.18*, they would then take steps to avoid being seen by a witness in any identification procedure, the identification officer may arrange for images of the suspect suitable for use in a video identification procedure to be obtained before giving the information and notice. If suspects' images are obtained in these circumstances, the suspect may, for the purposes of a video identification procedure, co-operate in providing new images which if suitable, would be used instead, see *paragraph 3.17(vi)*.

2.9.4.7

KEYNOTE

The purpose of allowing the custody officer or other officer not involved in the investigation to undertake the role of the identification officer at Code D, paras 3.17 and 3.18 is to avoid or reduce delays in arranging identification procedures by enabling the required information and warning to be given at the earliest opportunity.

2.9.4.8

(c) Cases when the suspect is known but not available

3.21 When a known suspect is not available or has ceased to be available, see *paragraph 3.4*, the identification officer may make arrangements for a video identification (see *Annex A*). If necessary, the identification officer may follow the video identification procedures but using *still* images. Any suitable moving or still images may be used and these may be obtained covertly if necessary. Alternatively, the identification officer may make arrangements for a group identification. These provisions may also be applied to juveniles where the consent of their parent or guardian is either refused or reasonable efforts to obtain that consent have failed (see *paragraph 2.12*).

3.22 Any covert activity should be strictly limited to that necessary to test the ability of the witness to identify the suspect.

3.23 The identification officer may arrange for the suspect to be confronted by the witness if none of the options referred to in *paragraphs 3.5 to 3.10* or *3.21* are practicable. A 'confrontation' is when the suspect is directly confronted by the witness. A confrontation does not require the suspect's consent. Confrontations must be carried out in accordance with *Annex D*.

3.24 Requirements for information to be given to, or sought from, a suspect or for the suspect to be given an opportunity to view images before they are shown to a witness, do not apply if the suspect's lack of co-operation prevents the necessary action.

2.9.4.9

KEYNOTE

Which Identification Procedure should be Used?

Code D, para. 3.21 also apples where a suspect refuses or fails to take part in a video identification, an identification parade or a group identification, or refuses or fails to take part in the only practicable options from that list. It enables any suitable images of the suspect, moving or still, which are available or can be obtained, to be used in an identification procedure. Examples include images from custody and other CCTV systems and from visually recorded interview records.

It is only if none of the other options are practicable that the identification officer may arrange for the suspect to be confronted by the witness. A confrontation does not require the suspect's consent. In *R v McCulloch, Smith & Wheeler* (1999) 6 May, unreported, the Court of Appeal made it clear that confrontations between suspects and witnesses should only be carried out if no other identification procedure is practicable.

2.9.4.10

(d) Documentation

3.25 A record shall be made of the video identification, identification parade, group identification or confrontation on forms provided for the purpose.

3.26 If the identification officer considers it is not practicable to hold a video identification or identification parade requested by the suspect, the reasons shall be recorded and explained to the suspect.

3.27 A record shall be made of a person's failure or refusal to co-operate in a video identification, identification parade or group identification and, if applicable, of the grounds for obtaining images in accordance with *paragraph 3.20*.

(e) Showing films and photographs of incidents and information released to the media

3.28 Nothing in this Code inhibits showing films, photographs or other images to the public through the national or local media, or to police officers for the purposes of recognition and tracing suspects. However, when such material is shown to obtain evidence of recognition, the procedures in Part B will apply.

3.29 When a broadcast or publication is made, see *paragraph 3.28*, a copy of the relevant material released to the media for the purposes of recognising or tracing the suspect, shall be kept. The suspect or their solicitor shall be allowed to view such material before any eye-witness identification procedures under *paragraphs 3.5* to *3.10, 3.21* or *3.23* of Part A are carried out, provided it is practicable and would not unreasonably delay the investigation. Each eye-witness involved in the procedure shall be asked, after they have taken part, whether they have seen any film, photograph or image relating to the offence or any description of the suspect which has been broadcast or published in any national or local media or on any social networking site and if they have, they should be asked to give details of the circumstances, such as the date and place, as relevant. Their replies shall be recorded. This paragraph does not affect any separate requirement under the Criminal Procedure and Investigations Act 1996 to retain material in connection with criminal investigations.

(f) Destruction and retention of photographs taken or used in eye-witness identification procedures

3.30 PACE, section 64A, see *paragraph 5.12*, provides powers to take photographs of suspects and allows these photographs to be used or disclosed only for purposes related to the prevention or detection of crime, the investigation of offences or the conduct of prosecutions by, or on behalf of, police or other law enforcement and prosecuting authorities inside and outside the United Kingdom or the enforcement of a sentence. After being so used or disclosed, they may be retained but can only be used or disclosed for the same purposes.

3.31 Subject to *paragraph 3.33*, the photographs (and all negatives and copies), of suspects not taken in accordance with the provisions in *paragraph 5.12* which are taken for the purposes of, or in connection with, the identification procedures in *paragraphs 3.5* to *3.10, 3.21* or *3.23* must be destroyed unless the suspect:

(a) is charged with, or informed they may be prosecuted for, a recordable offence;

(b) is prosecuted for a recordable offence;

(c) is cautioned for a recordable offence or given a warning or reprimand in accordance with the Crime and Disorder Act 1998 for a recordable offence; or

(d) gives informed consent, in writing, for the photograph or images to be retained for purposes described in *paragraph 3.30*.

3.32 When *paragraph 3.31* requires the destruction of any photograph, the person must be given an opportunity to witness the destruction or to have a certificate confirming the destruction if they request one within five days of being informed that the destruction is required.

3.33 Nothing in *paragraph 3.31* affects any separate requirement under the Criminal Procedure and Investigations Act 1996 to retain material in connection with criminal investigations.

(B) Evidence of recognition by showing films, photographs and other images

3.34 This Part of this section applies when, for the purposes of obtaining evidence of recognition, any person, including a police officer:

(a) views the image of an individual in a film, photograph or any other visual medium; and

(b) is asked whether they recognise that individual as someone who is known to them.

3.35 The films, photographs and other images shall be shown on an individual basis to avoid any possibility of collusion and to provide safeguards against mistaken recognition, the showing shall as far as possible follow the principles for video identification if the suspect is known, see *Annex A*, or identification by photographs if the suspect is not known, see *Annex E*.

3.36 A record of the circumstances and conditions under which the person is given an opportunity to recognise the individual must be made and the record must include:

(a) Whether the person knew or was given information concerning the name or identity of any suspect.

(b) What the person has been told *before* the viewing about the offence, the person(s) depicted in the images or the offender and by whom.

(c) How and by whom the witness was asked to view the image or look at the individual.

(d) Whether the viewing was alone or with others and if with others, the reason for it.

(e) The arrangements under which the person viewed the film or saw the individual and by whom those arrangements were made.

(f) Whether the viewing of any images was arranged as part of a mass circulation to police and the public or for selected persons.

(g) The date time and place images were viewed or further viewed or the individual was seen.

(h) The times between which the images were viewed or the individual was seen.

(i) How the viewing of images or sighting of the individual was controlled and by whom.

(j) Whether the person was familiar with the location shown in any images or the place where they saw the individual and if so, why.

(k) Whether or not on this occasion, the person claims to recognise any image shown, or any individual seen, as being someone known to them, and if they do:

(i) the reason

(ii) the words of recognition

(iii) any expressions of doubt

(iv) what features of the image or the individual triggered the recognition.

3.37 The record under *paragraph 3.36* may be made by:

• the person who views the image or sees the individual and makes the recognition.

• the officer or police staff in charge of showing the images to the person or in charge of the conditions under which the person sees the individual.

2.9.4.11

KEYNOTE

Photographs, Image and Sound Reproduction Generally

The use of photographic and computer-generated images (such as E-Fit) to identify suspects has increased considerably over the past few years. Although the courts will exercise considerable caution when admitting such evidence (see *R v Blenkinsop* [1995] 1 Cr App R 7), these methods of identification are particularly useful. Expert evidence may be admitted to interpret images on film (see e.g. *R v Stockwell* (1993) 97 Cr App R 260) and police officers who are very familiar with a particular film clip (e.g. of crowd violence at a football match) may be allowed to assist the court in interpreting and explaining events shown within it (see *R v Clare* [1995] 2 Cr App R 333).

Logically E-Fit and other witness-generated images would be treated as 'visual statements', in that they represent the witness's recollection of what he/she saw. However, the Court of Appeal has decided that they are not to be so treated (*R v Cook* [1987] QB 417) and therefore the restrictions imposed by the rule against hearsay will not apply (see also *R v Constantinou* (1990) 91 Cr App R 74, where this ruling was followed in relation to a photofit image).

KEYNOTE

Recognition Cases

Recognition cases, that is to say, those cases where the witness states that he/she knows the person who committed the offence as opposed to only being able to give a description, need to be carefully considered and Part B of this section of the Code adhered to. The eye-witness identification procedures in Part A should not be used to test whether a witness can recognise a person as someone he/she knows and would be able to give evidence of recognition along the lines of 'On (describe date, time location) I saw an image of an individual who I recognised as XY'. In these cases, the procedures in Part B shall apply. The admissibility and value of evidence of recognition obtained when carrying out the procedures in Part B may be compromised if before the person is recognised, the witness who has claimed to know him/her is given or is made, or becomes, aware of, information about the person which was not previously known to the witness personally but which he/she has purported to rely on to support his/her claim that the person is in fact known to him/her.

In *R v Ridley* (1999) *The Times*, 13 October, the Court of Appeal stated that there has never been a rule that an identification parade had to be held in all recognition cases and that it will be a question of fact in each case whether or not there is a need to do so. The view that an identification procedure is not required in these cases is supported by para. 3.12(ii).

The facts in *Ridley*, which it is suggested are not uncommon among patrolling officers, were that two police officers in a marked police vehicle noticed a car, which had been stolen earlier that day, drive past them. Both officers said that they recognised the defendant driving the car. The officers gave chase and gave evidence that the car was speeding and being driven dangerously. They decided that it was unsafe to continue pursuit, but arrested the suspect six days later. One of the officers claimed to have recognised the suspect because she had interviewed him for some 20 minutes five months previously and had seen him about town. She gave evidence that she had a view of the suspect in the car for about nine seconds. The other officer said that he recognised the suspect from a photograph but could not say when he had seen that photograph. He said that he had seen the suspect in the car for about two seconds. The court found that the female police officer's identification had been complete and there was no requirement for her to have further identified the suspect.

Ridley can be contrasted with *R v Conway* (1990) 91 Cr App R 143, where the witnesses' evidence was not as strong. There the witnesses stated that they recognised the accused simply because they knew him. The defence argument was that the witnesses did not actually know the accused and so could not have recognised him at the time of the offence. His conviction was quashed because of the prejudice caused by the absence of a parade. In *R v Davies* [2004] EWCA Crim 2521 a witness identified a masked attacker from his voice and eyes. The court in this case held that this identification evidence coupled with other circumstantial evidence was sufficient for a conviction.

A case can still amount to one of recognition, even where the witness does not know the name of the suspect but later obtained those details from a third party, for example where the witness and the suspect went to the same school and the witness became aware of the suspect's full names from other pupils at the school (*R v C; R v B* [2003] EWCA Crim 718).

In *R (On the Application of H) v DPP* [2003] EWHC 133 (Admin), the court accepted that it was reasonable for the police not to undertake an identification procedure. In the circumstances of the case the police had every reason to believe that the claimant and the victim were well known to each other. The claimant had accepted that the victim knew her. There was no question of doubt as to the victim's ability to recognise the claimant and as such this was a case of pure recognition where it was futile to hold an identification parade.

Care must be taken in cases where it is believed that the case is one of recognition not requiring an identification procedure. In *R v Harris* [2003] EWCA Crim 174 the witness stated that he recognised the suspect as being someone he went to school with. The suspect gave a prepared statement in which he disputed the suggestion that he was well known to the witness. Here the court held that an identification procedure should have been undertaken, as the circumstances of the case did not fall within the general exception of the Code, i.e. that an identification procedure would serve no useful purpose in proving or disproving whether the suspect had been involved in committing the offence. It is suggested therefore that where a suspect disputes that a witness knows him/her, an identification procedure should be considered.

When a suspect is filmed committing an offence, it may be admissible to give evidence of identification by way of recognition from a witness not present at the scene. In *Attorney-General's Ref (No. 2 of 2002)* [2002] EWCA Crim 2373 the Court reviewed the previous case law and concluded that there are at least four circumstances in which a jury could be invited to conclude that a defendant committed an offence on the basis of photographic evidence from the scene:

- where the photographic image was sufficiently clear the jury could compare it with the defendant sitting in the dock;
- where a witness knew the defendant sufficiently well to recognise him as the offender depicted in the photographic image;
- where a witness who did not know the defendant spent substantial time viewing and analysing photographic images from the scene, thereby acquiring special knowledge which the jury did not have, evidence of identification based on comparison between them and a reasonably contemporary photo of the defendant could be given so long as the image and photograph were available to the jury. Further, in *R v Savalia* [2011] EWCA Crim 1334 the Court held that this did not just apply to facial features but could properly be extended to apply to identification of a defendant from closed-circuit television footage based on a combination of factors, including build and gait;
- a suitably qualified expert with facial mapping skills giving opinion evidence of identification based on a comparison between images from the scene and a reasonably contemporary photograph of the defendant could be given so long as the image and photograph were available to the jury.

R v McCullough [2011] EWCA Crim 1413 is a case where the victim of a robbery identified the suspect from a photograph on Facebook and then later identified the suspect on a video identification parade. The Court of Appeal found that the Facebook identification was far from ideal and it was capable of having a substantial effect on the weight of the witness's subsequent identification of the defendant in the formal identification procedure. The key here is that the formal identification procedure is still required.

2.9.4.13   KEYNOTE

Voice Identification

The Codes do not preclude the police making use of aural identification procedures such as a 'voice identification parade', where they judge that appropriate.

Generally, a witness may give evidence identifying the defendant's voice (*R v Robb* (1991) 93 Cr App R 161), while expert testimony may be admitted in relation to tape recordings of a voice which is alleged to belong to the defendant. In the latter case, the jury should be allowed to hear the recording(s) so that they can draw their own conclusions (*R v Bentum* (1989) 153 JP 538).

In *R v Flyn; R v St John* [2008] EWCA Crim 970 the Court of Appeal held that where the voice identification is from a recording a prerequisite for making a speaker identification was that there should be a sample of an adequate size from the disputed recording that could confidently be attributed to a single speaker. The court also recognised that expert evidence showed that lay listeners with considerable familiarity with a voice and listening to a clear recording could still make mistakes. It is therefore suggested that other supporting evidence will be needed for a conviction to succeed.

Home Office Circular 57/2003, *Advice on the Use of Voice Identification Parades*, provides guidance on the use of voice identification parades.

2.9.4.14   KEYNOTE

Identification of Disqualified Drivers

Another common identification problem is that of disqualified drivers and being able to satisfy the court that the person charged with disqualified driving is the same person who was disqualified by the court. This is because s. 73 of the Police and Criminal Evidence Act 1984 requires proof that the person named in a certificate of conviction as having been convicted is the person whose conviction is to be proved. There has been some guidance from the courts as to how this can be achieved. In *R v Derwentside Justices, ex parte Heaviside* [1996] RTR 384, the court stated that this could be done by:

- fingerprints under s. 39 of the Criminal Justice Act 1948;
- the evidence of a person who was present in court when the disqualification order was made;
- admission of the defendant (preferably in interview) (*DPP v Mooney* (1997) RTR 434);
- requiring the suspect's solicitor who was present when he/she was disqualified on the earlier occasion to give evidence (such a summons is a last resort when there was no other means of identifying whether an individual had been disqualified from driving) (*R (On the Application of Howe) and Law Society (Interested Party) v South Durham Magistrates' Court and CPS (Interested Party)* [2004] EWHC 362 (Admin)).

The methods outlined in *Heaviside* are not exhaustive, but just suggested methods (*DPP v Mansfield* [1997] RTR 96).

2.9.5   4 Identification by Fingerprints and Footwear Impressions

(A) Taking fingerprints in connection with a criminal investigation

(a) General

4.1 References to 'fingerprints' means any record, produced by any method, of the skin pattern and other physical characteristics or features of a person's:
(i) fingers; or
(ii) palms.

(b) Action

4.2 A person's fingerprints may be taken in connection with the investigation of an offence only with their consent or if *paragraph 4.3* applies. If the person is at a police station consent must be in writing.

4.3 PACE, section 61, provides powers to take fingerprints without consent from any person over the age of ten years:
   (a) under section 61(3), from a person detained at a police station in consequence of being arrested for a recordable offence, if they have not had their fingerprints taken in the course of the investigation of the offence unless those previously taken fingerprints are not a complete set or some or all of those fingerprints are not of sufficient quality to allow satisfactory analysis, comparison or matching;
   (b) under section 61(4), from a person detained at a police station who has been charged with a recordable offence, or informed they will be reported for such an offence if they have not had their fingerprints taken in the course of the investigation of or all of those fingerprints are not of sufficient quality to allow satisfactory analysis, comparison or matching;
   (c) under section 61(4A), from a person who has been bailed to appear at a court or police station if the person:
      (i) has answered to bail for a person whose fingerprints were taken previously and there are reasonable grounds for believing they are not the same person; or
      (ii) who has answered to bail claims to be a different person from a person whose fingerprints were previously taken;

and in either case, the court or an officer of inspector rank or above, authorises the fingerprints to be taken at the court or police station (an inspector's authority may be given in writing or orally and confirmed in writing as soon as practicable);

(ca) under section 61(5A) from a person who has been arrested for a recordable offence and released if the person:

(i) is on bail and has not had their fingerprints taken in the course of the investigation of the offence, or;

(ii) has had their fingerprints taken in the course of the investigation of the offence, but they do not constitute a complete set or some, or all, of the fingerprints are not of sufficient quality to allow satisfactory analysis, comparison or matching;

(cb) under section 61(5B) from a person not detained at a police station who has been charged with a recordable offence or informed they will be reported for such an offence if they have not had their fingerprints taken in the course of the investigation or their fingerprints have been taken in the course of the investigation of the offence, but they do not constitute a complete set or some, or all, of the fingerprints are not of sufficient quality to allow satisfactory analysis, comparison or matching.

(d) under section 61(6), from a person who has been:

(i) convicted of a recordable offence;

(ii) given a caution in respect of a recordable offence which, at the time of the caution, the person admitted; or

(iii) warned or reprimanded under the Crime and Disorder Act 1998, section 65, for a recordable offence,

if, since their conviction, caution, warning or reprimand their fingerprints have not been taken or their fingerprints which have been taken since then do not constitute a complete set or some, or all, of the fingerprints are not of sufficient quality to allow satisfactory analysis, comparison or matching, and in either case, an officer of inspector rank or above, is satisfied that taking the fingerprints is necessary to assist in the prevention or detection of crime and authorises the taking;

(e) under section 61(6A) from a person a constable reasonably suspects is committing or attempting to commit, or has committed or attempted to commit, any offence if either:

• the person's name is unknown and cannot be readily ascertained by the constable; or

• the constable has reasonable grounds for doubting whether a name given by the person is their real name.

Note: fingerprints taken under this power are not regarded as having been taken in the course of the investigation of an offence.

(f) under section 61(6D) from a person who has been convicted outside England and Wales of an offence which if committed in England and Wales would be a qualifying offence as defined by PACE, section 65A if:

(i) the person's fingerprints have not been taken previously under this power or their fingerprints have been so taken on a previous occasion but they do not constitute a complete set or some, or all, of the fingerprints are not of sufficient quality to allow satisfactory analysis, comparison or matching; and

(ii) a police officer of inspector rank or above is satisfied that taking fingerprints is necessary to assist in the prevention or detection of crime and authorises them to be taken.

4.4 PACE, section 63A(4) and Schedule 2A provide powers to:

(a) make a requirement (in accordance with *Annex G*) for a person to attend a police station to have their fingerprints taken in the exercise of certain powers in *paragraph 4.3* above when that power applies at the time the fingerprints would be taken in accordance with the requirement. Those powers are:

(i) section 61(5A) – Persons arrested for a recordable offence and released, see *paragraph 4.3(ca)*: The requirement may not be made more than six months from the day the investigating officer was informed that the fingerprints previously taken were incomplete or below standard.

(ii) section 61(5B) – Persons charged etc. with a recordable offence, see *paragraph 4.3(cb)*: The requirement may not be made more than six months from:
- the day the person was charged or reported if fingerprints have not been taken since then; or
- the day the investigating officer was informed that the fingerprints previously taken were incomplete or below standard.

(iii) section 61(6) – Person convicted, cautioned, warned or reprimanded for a recordable offence in England and Wales, see *paragraph 4.3(d)*: Where the offence for which the person was convicted etc is also a qualifying offence, there is no time limit for the exercise of this power. Where the conviction etc. is for a recordable offence which is not a qualifying offence, the requirement may not be made more than two years from:
- the day the person was convicted, cautioned, warned or reprimanded, or the day Schedule 2A comes into force (if later), if fingerprints have not been taken since then; or
- the day an officer from the force investigating the offence was informed that the fingerprints previously taken were incomplete or below standard or the day Schedule 2A comes into force (if later).

(iv) section 61(6D) – A person who has been convicted of a qualifying offence outside England and Wales, see *paragraph 4.3(g)*: There is no time limit for making the requirement.

Note: A person who has had their fingerprints taken under any of the powers in section 61 mentioned in *paragraph 4.3* on two occasions in relation to any offence may not be required under Schedule 2A to attend a police station for their fingerprints to be taken again under section 61 in relation to that offence, unless authorised by an officer of inspector rank or above. The fact of the authorisation and the reasons for giving it must be recorded as soon as practicable.

(b) arrest, without warrant, a person who fails to comply with the requirement.

4.5 A person's fingerprints may be taken, as above, electronically.

4.6 Reasonable force may be used, if necessary, to take a person's fingerprints without their consent under the powers as in *paragraphs 4.3* and *4.4*.

4.7 Before any fingerprints are taken:
(a) without consent under any power mentioned in *paragraphs 4.3* and *4.4* above, the person must be informed of:
  (i) the reason their fingerprints are to be taken;
  (ii) the power under which they are to be taken; and
  (iii) the fact that the relevant authority has been given if any power mentioned in *paragraph 4.3(c), (d)* or *(f)* applies;
(b) with or without consent at a police station or elsewhere, the person must be informed:
  (i) that their fingerprints may be subject of a speculative search against other fingerprints and
  (ii) that their fingerprints may be retained in accordance with *Annex F, Part (a)* unless they were taken under the power mentioned in *paragraph 4.3(e)* when they must be destroyed after they have being checked.

(c) Documentation

4.8A A record must be made as soon as practicable after the fingerprints are taken, of:
- the matters in *paragraph 4.7(a)(i)* to *(iii)* and the fact that the person has been informed of those matters; and
- the fact that the person has been informed of the matters in *paragraph 4.7(b)(i)* and *(ii)*.

The record must be made in the person's custody record if they are detained at a police station when the fingerprints are taken.

4.8 If force is used, a record shall be made of the circumstances and those present.

4.9 *Not used*

2.9.5.1

KEYNOTE

The power under s. 61(6A) of the 1984 Act described in para. 4.3(e) allows fingerprints of a suspect who has not been arrested to be taken in connection with any offence (whether recordable or not) using a mobile device and then checked on the street against the database containing the national fingerprint collection. Fingerprints taken under this power cannot be retained after they have been checked. The results may make an arrest for the suspected offence based on the name condition unnecessary (see Code G, para. 2.9(a)) and enable the offence to be disposed of without arrest, e.g. by summons/charging by post, penalty notice or words of advice. If arrest for a non-recordable offence is necessary for any other reasons, this power may also be exercised at the station. Before the power is exercised, the officer should:

- inform the person of the nature of the suspected offence and why he/she is suspected of committing it;
- give the person a reasonable opportunity to establish his/her real name before deciding that his/her name is unknown and cannot be readily ascertained or that there are reasonable grounds to doubt that a name that he/she has given is his/her real name;
- as applicable, inform the person of the reason why his/her name is not known and cannot be readily ascertained or of the grounds for doubting that a name he/she has given is his/her real name, including, for example, the reason why a particular document the person has produced to verify his/her real name is not sufficient.

Speculative Search

Paragraph 4.7(b) makes reference to a 'speculative search'. Fingerprints, footwear impressions or a DNA sample (and the information derived from it) taken from a person arrested on suspicion of being involved in a recordable offence, or charged with such an offence, or informed they will be reported for such an offence, may be the subject of a speculative search. This means that the fingerprints, footwear impressions or DNA sample may be checked against other fingerprints, footwear impressions and DNA records held by, or on behalf of, the police and other law enforcement authorities in, or outside, the United Kingdom, or held in connection with, or as a result of, an investigation of an offence inside or outside the United Kingdom. Fingerprints, footwear impressions and samples taken from a person suspected of committing a recordable offence but not arrested, charged or informed that he/she will be reported for it, may be subject to a speculative search only if the person consents in writing. The following is an example of a basic form of words:

I consent to my fingerprints/DNA sample and information derived from it being retained and used only for purposes related to the prevention and detection of a crime, the investigation of an offence or the conduct of a prosecution either nationally or internationally.

I understand that this sample may be checked against other fingerprint/DNA records held by or on behalf of relevant law enforcement authorities, either nationally or internationally.

I understand that once I have given my consent for the sample to be retained and used I cannot withdraw this consent.

2.9.5.2

(B) Taking fingerprints in connection with immigration enquiries

Action

4.10 A person's fingerprints may be taken and retained for the purposes of immigration law enforcement and control in accordance with powers and procedures other than under PACE and for which the UK Border Agency (not the police) are responsible. Details of these powers and procedures which are under the Immigration Act 1971, Schedule 2 and Immigration and Asylum Act 1999, section 141, including modifications to the PACE Codes of Practice are contained in Chapter 24 of the Operational Instructions and Guidance manual which is published by the UK Border Agency.

4.11   *Not used*
4.12   *Not used*
4.13   *Not used*
4.14   *Not used*
4.15   *Not used*

2.9.5.3

KEYNOTE

Powers to take fingerprints without consent for immigration purposes are given to police and immigration officers under the:

(a) Immigration Act 1971, sch. 2, para. 18(2), when it is reasonably necessary for the purposes of identifying a person detained under the Immigration Act 1971, sch. 2, para. 16 (Detention of person liable to examination or removal); and

(b) Immigration and Asylum Act 1999, s. 141(7) when a person:
- fails without reasonable excuse to produce, on arrival, a valid passport with a photograph or some other document satisfactorily establishing his/her identity and nationality;
- is refused entry to the United Kingdom but is temporarily admitted if an immigration officer reasonably suspects that the person might break a residence or reporting condition;
- is subject to directions for removal from the United Kingdom;
- has been arrested under the Immigration Act 1971, sch. 2, para. 17;
- has made a claim for asylum;
- is a dependant of any of the above.

The Immigration and Asylum Act 1999, s. 142(3) also gives police and immigration officers power to arrest without warrant a person who fails to comply with a requirement imposed by the Secretary of State to attend a specified place for fingerprinting.

2.9.5.4

(C) Taking footwear impressions in connection with a criminal investigation

(a) Action

4.16   Impressions of a person's footwear may be taken in connection with the investigation of an offence only with their consent or if *paragraph 4.17* applies. If the person is at a police station consent must be in writing.

4.17   PACE, section 61A, provides power for a police officer to take footwear impressions without consent from any person over the age of ten years who is detained at a police station:

(a) in consequence of being arrested for a recordable offence or if the detainee has been charged with a recordable offence, or informed they will be reported for such an offence; and

(b) the detainee has not had an impression of their footwear taken in the course of the investigation of the offence unless the previously taken impression is not complete or is not of sufficient quality to allow satisfactory analysis, comparison or matching (whether in the case in question or generally).

4.18   Reasonable force may be used, if necessary, to take a footwear impression from a detainee without consent under the power in *paragraph 4.17*.

4.19   Before any footwear impression is taken with, or without, consent as above, the person must be informed:

(a) of the reason the impression is to be taken;

(b) that the impression may be retained and may be subject of a speculative search against other impressions, unless destruction of the impression is required in accordance with *Annex F, Part (a)*; and

(c) that if their footwear impressions are required to be destroyed, they may witness their destruction as provided for in *Annex F, Part (a)*.

(b) Documentation

4.20 A record must be made as soon as possible, of the reason for taking a person's footwear impressions without consent. If force is used, a record shall be made of the circumstances and those present.

4.21 A record shall be made when a person has been informed under the terms of *paragraph 4.19(b)*, of the possibility that their footwear impressions may be subject of a speculative search.

2.9.5.5

KEYNOTE

Recordable Offences

References to 'recordable offences' in this Code relate to those offences for which convictions, cautions, reprimands and warnings may be recorded in national police records. See the Police and Criminal Evidence Act 1984, s. 27(4). The recordable offences current at the time when this Code was prepared are any offences which carry a sentence of imprisonment on conviction (irrespective of the period, or the age of the offender or actual sentence passed) as well as the non-imprisonable offences under the Vagrancy Act 1824, ss. 3 and 4 (begging and persistent begging), the Street Offences Act 1959, s. 1 (loitering or soliciting for purposes of prostitution), the Road Traffic Act 1988, s. 25 (tampering with motor vehicles), the Criminal Justice and Public Order Act 1994, s. 167 (touting for hire car services) and others listed in the National Police Records (Recordable Offences) Regulations 2000 (SI 2000/1139) as amended.

Qualifying Offences

When dealing with a person convicted of an offence outside England and Wales, a qualifying offence is one of the offences specified in s. 65A of the 1984 Act. These indictable offences which concern the use or threat of violence or unlawful force against persons, sexual offences and offences against children include, for example, murder, manslaughter, false imprisonment, kidnapping and other offences such as:

- ss. 4, 16, 18, 20 to 24 or 47 of the Offences Against the Person Act 1861;
- ss. 16 to 18 of the Firearms Act 1968;
- ss. 9 or 10 of the Theft Act 1968 or under s. 12A of that Act involving an accident which caused a person's death;
- s. 1 of the Criminal Damage Act 1971 required to be charged as arson;
- s. 1 of the Protection of Children Act 1978;
- ss. 1 to 19, 25, 26, 30 to 41, 47 to 50, 52, 53, 57 to 59, 61 to 67, 69 to 70 of the Sexual Offences Act 2003;

It should be noted that this list is not exhaustive.

Whether fingerprint evidence is admissible as evidence tending to prove guilt, depends on:

- the experience and expertise of the witness: this requires at least three years' experience;
- the number of similar ridge characteristics (if there are fewer than eight ridge characteristics matching the fingerprints of the accused with those found by the police, it is unlikely that a judge would exercise his/her discretion to admit such evidence);
- whether there are dissimilar characteristics;
- the size of print relied on; and
- the quality and clarity of print relied on.

The jury should be warned that expert evidence is not conclusive in itself and that guilt has to be proved in the light of all evidence (*R* v *Buckley* [1999] EWCA Crim 1191).

2.9.5.6

KEYNOTE

Power to Require Persons to Attend a Police Station to Provide Samples

Code D, Annex G deals with the requirement for a person to attend a police station for fingerprints and samples.

2.9.5.7

KEYNOTE

Retention of Fingerprints

Code D, Annex F deals with the destruction and the speculative searches of fingerprints and samples and speculative searches of footwear impressions. It is important that the Annex is followed particularly in relation to obtaining consent and explaining to volunteers what they are consenting to.

2.9.5.8

KEYNOTE

Criminal Record and Conviction Certificates

Under s. 118 of the Police Act 1997, in certain circumstances the Secretary of State issues certificates concerning an individual's previous convictions. In some cases the Secretary of State will not do this until it has been possible to verify the person's identity, which can be done through the taking of his/her fingerprints. Where this is the case, the Secretary of State may require the police officer in charge of the specified police station, or any other police station the Secretary of State reasonably determines, to take the applicant's fingerprints at the specified station at such reasonable time as the officer may direct and notify the applicant.

If fingerprints are taken in these circumstances they must be destroyed as soon as is practicable after the identity of the applicant is established to the satisfaction of the Secretary of State. The destruction can be witnessed by the person giving the fingerprints if he/she requests and/or the person can ask for a certificate stating that the fingerprints have been destroyed. The certificate must be issued within three months of the request.

In the case of an individual under the age of 18 years the consent of the applicant's parent or guardian to the taking of the applicant's fingerprints is also required.

2.9.5.9

KEYNOTE

Other Body Prints

While the more established and convincing body marks are fingerprints it is possible for other body prints to be used as evidence to identify a suspect. In *R* v *Kempster* [2008] EWCA Crim 975 the police recovered an ear print from the fixed window pane to the side of the window that had been forced in order to gain entry to the property. In this case the conviction was not successful, but it was recognised that an ear print comparison was capable of providing information that could identify a person who had left an ear print on a surface. This would only be achieved with certainty where the minutiae of the ear structure could be identified and matched.

Fingerprints etc. and non-intimate samples may be taken from an arrested or detained person with the authority of an officer of a rank no lower than inspector.

2.9.6

5 Examinations to Establish Identity and the Taking of Photographs

(A) Detainees at police stations

(a) Searching or examination of detainees at police stations

5.1 PACE, section 54A(1), allows a detainee at a police station to be searched or examined or both, to establish:

(a) whether they have any marks, features or injuries that would tend to identify them as a person involved in the commission of an offence and to photograph any identifying marks, see *paragraph 5.5*; or

(b) their identity.

A person detained at a police station to be searched under a stop and search power, see Code A, is not a detainee for the purposes of these powers.

5.2 A search and/or examination to find marks under section 54A(1)(a) may be carried out without the detainee's consent, see *paragraph 2.12*, only if authorised by an officer of at least inspector rank when consent has been withheld or it is not practicable to obtain consent.

5.3 A search or examination to establish a suspect's identity under section 54A(1)(b) may be carried out without the detainee's consent, see *paragraph 2.12*, only if authorised by an officer of at least inspector rank when the detainee has refused to identify themselves or the authorising officer has reasonable grounds for suspecting the person is not who they claim to be.

5.4 Any marks that assist in establishing the detainee's identity, or their identification as a person involved in the commission of an offence, are identifying marks. Such marks may be photographed with the detainee's consent, see *paragraph 2.12*; or without their consent if it is withheld or it is not practicable to obtain it.

5.5 A detainee may only be searched, examined and photographed under section 54A, by a police officer of the same sex.

5.6 Any photographs of identifying marks, taken under section 54A, may be used or disclosed only for purposes related to the prevention or detection of crime, the investigation of offences or the conduct of prosecutions by, or on behalf of, police or other law enforcement and prosecuting authorities inside, and outside, the UK. After being so used or disclosed, the photograph may be retained but must not be used or disclosed except for these purposes.

5.7 The powers, as in *paragraph 5.1*, do not affect any separate requirement under the Criminal Procedure and Investigations Act 1996 to retain material in connection with criminal investigations.

5.8 Authority for the search and/or examination for the purposes of *paragraphs 5.2* and *5.3* may be given orally or in writing. If given orally, the authorising officer must confirm it in writing as soon as practicable. A separate authority is required for each purpose which applies.

5.9 If it is established a person is unwilling to co-operate sufficiently to enable a search and/or examination to take place or a suitable photograph to be taken, an officer may use reasonable force to:

(a) search and/or examine a detainee without their consent; and

(b) photograph any identifying marks without their consent.

5.10 The thoroughness and extent of any search or examination carried out in accordance with the powers in section 54A must be no more than the officer considers necessary to achieve the required purpose. Any search or examination which involves the removal of more than the person's outer clothing shall be conducted in accordance with Code C, *Annex A, paragraph 11*.

5.11 An intimate search may not be carried out under the powers in section 54A.

(b) Photographing detainees at police stations and other persons elsewhere than at a police station

5.12 Under PACE, section 64A, an officer may photograph:

(a) any person whilst they are detained at a police station; and

(b) any person who is elsewhere than at a police station and who has been:

(i) arrested by a constable for an offence;

(ii) taken into custody by a constable after being arrested for an offence by a person other than a constable;

(iii) made subject to a requirement to wait with a community support officer under paragraph 2(3) or (3B) of Schedule 4 to the Police Reform Act 2002;

(iiia) given a direction by a constable under section 27 of the Violent Crime Reduction Act 2006;

(iv) given a penalty notice by a constable in uniform under Chapter 1 of Part 1 of the Criminal Justice and Police Act 2001, a penalty notice by a constable under section 444A of the Education Act 1996, or a fixed penalty notice by a constable in uniform under section 54 of the Road Traffic Offenders Act 1988;

(v) given a notice in relation to a relevant fixed penalty offence (within the meaning of paragraph 1 of Schedule 4 to the Police Reform Act 2002) by a community support officer by virtue of a designation applying that paragraph to him;

(vi) given a notice in relation to a relevant fixed penalty offence (within the meaning of paragraph 1 of Schedule 5 to the Police Reform Act 2002) by an accredited person by virtue of accreditation specifying that that paragraph applies to him; or

(vii) given a direction to leave and not return to a specified location for up to 48 hours by a police constable (under section 27 of the Violent Crime Reduction Act 2006).

5.12A   Photographs taken under PACE, section 64A:

(a) may be taken with the person's consent, or without their consent if consent is withheld or it is not practicable to obtain their consent, and

(b) may be used or disclosed only for purposes related to the prevention or detection of crime, the investigation of offences or the conduct of prosecutions by, or on behalf of, police or other law enforcement and prosecuting authorities inside and outside the United Kingdom or the enforcement of any sentence or order made by a court when dealing with an offence. After being so used or disclosed, they may be retained but can only be used or disclosed for the same purposes.

5.13   The officer proposing to take a detainee's photograph may, for this purpose, require the person to remove any item or substance worn on, or over, all, or any part of, their head or face. If they do not comply with such a requirement, the officer may remove the item or substance.

5.14   If it is established the detainee is unwilling to co-operate sufficiently to enable a suitable photograph to be taken and it is not reasonably practicable to take the photograph covertly, an officer may use reasonable force:

(a) to take their photograph without their consent; and

(b) for the purpose of taking the photograph, remove any item or substance worn on, or over, all, or any part of, the person's head or face which they have failed to remove when asked.

5.15   For the purposes of this Code, a photograph may be obtained without the person's consent by making a copy of an image of them taken at any time on a camera system installed anywhere in the police station.

(c)   Information to be given

5.16   When a person is searched, examined or photographed under the provisions as in *paragraph 5.1* and *5.12*, or their photograph obtained as in *paragraph 5.15*, they must be informed of the:

(a) purpose of the search, examination or photograph;

(b) grounds on which the relevant authority, if applicable, has been given; and

(c) purposes for which the photograph may be used, disclosed or retained.

This information must be given before the search or examination commences or the photograph is taken, except if the photograph is:

(i) to be taken covertly;

(ii) obtained as in *paragraph 5.15*, in which case the person must be informed as soon as practicable after the photograph is taken or obtained.

(d) Documentation

5.17 A record must be made when a detainee is searched, examined, or a photograph of the person, or any identifying marks found on them, are taken. The record must include the:
   (a) identity, subject to *paragraph 2.18*, of the officer carrying out the search, examination or taking the photograph;
   (b) purpose of the search, examination or photograph and the outcome;
   (c) detainee's consent to the search, examination or photograph, or the reason the person was searched, examined or photographed without consent;
   (d) giving of any authority as in *paragraphs 5.2* and *5.3*, the grounds for giving it and the authorising officer.
5.18 If force is used when searching, examining or taking a photograph in accordance with this section, a record shall be made of the circumstances and those present.

(B) Persons at police stations not detained

5.19 When there are reasonable grounds for suspecting the involvement of a person in a criminal offence, but that person is at a police station **voluntarily** and not detained, the provisions of *paragraphs 5.1* to *5.18* should apply, subject to the modifications in the following paragraphs.
5.20 References to the 'person being detained' and to the powers mentioned in *paragraph 5.1* which apply only to detainees at police stations shall be omitted.
5.21 Force may not be used to:
   (a) search and/or examine the person to:
      (i) discover whether they have any marks that would tend to identify them as a person involved in the commission of an offence; or
      (ii) establish their identity;
   (b) take photographs of any identifying marks, see *paragraph 5.4*; or
   (c) take a photograph of the person.
5.22 Subject to *paragraph 5.24*, the photographs of persons or of their identifying marks which are not taken in accordance with the provisions mentioned in *paragraphs 5.1* or *5.12*, must be destroyed (together with any negatives and copies) unless the person:
   (a) is charged with, or informed they may be prosecuted for, a recordable offence;
   (b) is prosecuted for a recordable offence;
   (c) is cautioned for a recordable offence or given a warning or reprimand in accordance with the Crime and Disorder Act 1998 for a recordable offence; or
   (d) gives informed consent, in writing, for the photograph or image to be retained as in *paragraph 5.6*.
5.23 When *paragraph 5.22* requires the destruction of any photograph, the person must be given an opportunity to witness the destruction or to have a certificate confirming the destruction provided they so request the certificate within five days of being informed the destruction is required.
5.24 Nothing in *paragraph 5.22* affects any separate requirement under the Criminal Procedure and Investigations Act 1996 to retain material in connection with criminal investigations.

2.9.6.1   **KEYNOTE**

The conditions under which fingerprints may be taken to assist in establishing a person's identity, are described in s. 4.

A photograph taken under s. 54A of the Police and Criminal Evidence Act 1984 may be used by, or disclosed to, any person for any purpose related to the prevention or detection of crime, the investigation of an offence or the conduct of a prosecution. The use of the photograph is for any conduct which constitutes a criminal offence (whether under UK law or in another country). Examples of purposes related to the prevention or detection of crime, the investigation of offences or the conduct of prosecutions include:

- checking the photograph against other photographs held in records or in connection with, or as a result of, an investigation of an offence to establish whether the person is liable to arrest for other offences;
- when the person is arrested at the same time as other people, or at a time when it is likely that other people will be arrested, using the photograph to help establish who was arrested, at what time and where;
- when the real identity of the person is not known and cannot be readily ascertained or there are reasonable grounds for doubting that a name and other personal details given by the person, are his/her real name and personal details. In these circumstances, using or disclosing the photograph to help to establish or verify the person's real identity or determine whether he/she is liable to arrest for some other offence, e.g. by checking it against other photographs held in records or in connection with, or as a result of, an investigation of an offence;
- when it appears that any identification procedure in section 3 may need to be arranged for which the person's photograph would assist;
- when the person's release without charge may be required, and if the release is:
  (i) on bail to appear at a police station, using the photograph to help verify the person's identity when he/she answers bail and if the person does not answer bail, to assist in arresting him/her; or
  (ii) without bail, using the photograph to help verify the person's identity or assist in locating him/her for the purposes of serving him/her with a summons to appear at court in criminal proceedings;
- when the person has answered to bail at a police station and there are reasonable grounds for doubting that he/she is the person who was previously granted bail, using the photograph to help establish or verify his/her identity;
- when the person has been charged with, reported for, or convicted of, a recordable offence and his/her photograph is not already on record as a result of any of the circumstances set out in the bullet points above or his/her photograph is on record but his/her appearance has changed since it was taken and the person has not yet been released or brought before a court;
- when the person arrested on a warrant claims to be a different person from the person named on the warrant and a photograph would help to confirm or disprove this claim.

There is no power to arrest a person convicted of a recordable offence solely to take his/her photograph. The power to take photographs in this section applies only where the person is in custody as a result of the exercise of another power, e.g. arrest for fingerprinting under s. 27 of the 1984 Act.

The use of reasonable force to take the photograph of a suspect elsewhere than at a police station must be carefully considered. In order to obtain a suspect's consent and co-operation to remove an item of religious headwear to take his/her photograph, a constable should consider whether in the circumstances of the situation the removal of the headwear and the taking of the photograph should be by an officer of the same sex as the person. It would be appropriate for these actions to be conducted out of public view.

2.9.7 | 6 Identification by Body Samples and Impressions

(A) General

6.1 References to:
  (a) an 'intimate sample' mean a dental impression or sample of blood, semen or any other tissue fluid, urine, or pubic hair, or a swab taken from any part of a person's genitals or from a person's body orifice other than the mouth;
  (b) a 'non-intimate sample' means:
    (i) a sample of hair, other than pubic hair, which includes hair plucked with the root;

(ii) a sample taken from a nail or from under a nail;

(iii) a swab taken from any part of a person's body other than a part from which a swab taken would be an intimate sample;

(iv) saliva;

(v) a skin impression which means any record, other than a fingerprint, which is a record, in any form and produced by any method, of the skin pattern and other physical characteristics or features of the whole, or any part of, a person's foot or of any other part of their body.

2.9.7.1 KEYNOTE

Intimate and Non-intimate Samples - General

The analysis of intimate and non-intimate samples may provide essential evidence in showing or refuting a person's involvement in an offence. However, the courts have made it clear that DNA evidence alone will not be sufficient for a conviction and that there needs to be supporting evidence to link the suspect to the crime.

The purpose behind the taking of many samples is to enable the process of DNA profiling. Very basically, this involves an analysis of the sample taken from the suspect (the first sample), an analysis of samples taken from the crime scene or victim (the second sample) and then a comparison of the two. Both the process and the conclusions which might be drawn from the results are set out by Lord Taylor CJ in *R v Deen* (1994) *The Times*, 10 January.

The matching process involves creating 'bands' from each sample and then comparing the number of those bands which the two samples share. The more 'matches' that exist between the first and second samples, the less probability there is of that happening by pure chance. A 'good match' between the two samples does not of itself prove that the second sample came from the defendant. In using such samples to prove identification the prosecution will give evidence of:

- the *probability* of such a match happening by chance; and
- the *likelihood* that the person responsible was in fact the defendant.

While DNA evidence is often portrayed in the media as conclusive evidence of guilt, the question for the courts remains 'How reliable is this piece of evidence in proving or disproving the person's involvement in the offence?'

In most cases there will be other evidence against the defendant which clearly increases the likelihood of his/her having committed the offence. Such evidence may include confessions, or may show that the suspect was near the crime scene at the time of the offence or that the suspect lived in the locality or had connections in the area.

It will be for the prosecution to produce other facts to the court which reduce the 'chance' of the DNA sample belonging to someone other than the defendant. This may require further inquiries linking the suspect to the area or circumstances of the crime or may come from questions put to the suspect during interview. In *R v Lashley* (2000) 25 February, unreported, the sole evidence against the defendant for a robbery was DNA evidence from a half-smoked cigarette found behind the counter of the post office. The DNA matched a sample obtained from the suspect and would have matched the profile of seven to 10 other males in the United Kingdom. The court held that the significance of DNA evidence depended critically upon what else was known about the suspect. Had there been evidence that the suspect was in the area, or normally lived there, or had connections there, at the material time, then the jury could have found that the case was compelling. This, the court said, would be because it may have been almost incredible that two out of seven men in the United Kingdom were in the vicinity at the relevant time. The courts are willing to allow the jury to consider partial or incomplete DNA profiles in some circumstances. In *R v Bates* [2006] EWCA Crim 1395, DNA evidence at the scene produced a partial profile that was interpreted as providing a 1 in 610,000 probability that Bates was the killer. The Court of Appeal held that there was no reason why partial-profile DNA evidence should not be admissible provided that the jury were made aware of its inherent limitations and were given a sufficient explanation to enable them to evaluate it.

If there is a decision to charge on partial DNA profile basis of such a match, the supporting evidence needs to be all the stronger. The amount of supporting evidence required will depend on the value of the DNA evidence in the context of the case. A scientist should be consulted where the value of the DNA evidence requires clarification.

It is also important to ensure that there is no cross-contamination of DNA evidence between crime scenes, victims and suspects, as was seen in the infamous American case of OJ Simpson's murder trial. It will be important to ensure that any allegations that officers may have contaminated evidence through handling/being present at several crime scenes can be successfully challenged. It is suggested that the best evidence here will be through records of crime scene logs and, where suspects have been or are being held in custody, records of who visited the custody suite. It will also be important that suspects and victims are kept apart. The integrity and continuity of DNA samples will be important evidence and likely to be challenged by the defence if not managed properly.

Speculative searches may be carried out of the National DNA Database and a suspect may now be charged on the basis of a match between a profile from DNA from the scene of the crime and a profile on the National DNA Database from an individual, so long as there is further supporting evidence (Home Office Circular 58/2004, *Charges on Basis of Speculative Search Match on the National DNA Database*).

It should also be noted that the databases can also now be used for the purpose of identifying a deceased person or a person from whom a body part came (Serious Organised Crime and Police Act 2005, s. 117(7) amending s. 64 of the 1984 Act).

An insufficient sample is one which is not sufficient either in quantity or quality to provide information for a particular form of analysis, such as DNA analysis. A sample may also be insufficient if enough information cannot be obtained from it by analysis because of loss, destruction, damage or contamination of the sample or as a result of an earlier, unsuccessful attempt at analysis. An unsuitable sample is one which, by its nature, is not suitable for a particular form of analysis.

2.9.7.2

(B) Action

(a) Intimate samples

6.2   PACE, section 62, provides that intimate samples may be taken under:
(a) section 62(1), from a person in police detention only:
(i) if a police officer of inspector rank or above has reasonable grounds to believe such an impression or sample will tend to confirm or disprove the suspect's involvement in a recordable offence, and gives authorisation for a sample to be taken; and
(ii) with the suspect's written consent;
(b) section 62(1A), from a person not in police detention but from whom two or more non-intimate samples have been taken in the course of an investigation of an offence and the samples, though suitable, have proved insufficient if:
(i) a police officer of inspector rank or above authorises it to be taken; and
(ii) the person concerned gives their written consent;
(c) section 62(2A), from a person convicted outside England and Wales of an offence which if committed in England and Wales would be qualifying offence as defined by PACE, section 65A from whom two or more non intimate samples taken under section 63(3E) (see *paragraph 6.6(h)*) have proved insufficient if:
(i) a police officer of inspector rank or above is satisfied that taking the sample is necessary to assist in the prevention or detection of crime and authorises it to be taken; and
(ii) the person concerned gives their written consent.
6.2A PACE, section 63A(4) and Schedule 2A provide powers to:
(a) make a requirement (in accordance with *Annex G*) for a person to attend a police station to have an intimate sample taken in the exercise of one of the following powers in

paragraph 6.2 when that power applies at the time the sample is to be taken in accordance with the requirement or after the person's arrest if they fail to comply with the requirement:

    (i) section 62(1A) – Persons from whom two or more non-intimate samples have been taken and proved to be insufficient, see *paragraph 6.2(b)*: There is no time limit for making the requirement.

    (ii) section 62(2A) – Persons convicted outside England and Wales from whom two or more non-intimate samples taken under section 63(3E) (see *paragraph 6.6(h)*) have proved insufficient, see *paragraph 6.2(c)*: There is no time limit for making the requirement.

6.3   Before a suspect is asked to provide an intimate sample, they must be:

    (a) informed:

        (i) of the reason, including the nature of the suspected offence (except if taken under *paragraph 6.2(c)* from a person convicted outside England and Wales;

        (ii) that authorisation has been given and the provisions under which given;

        (iii) that a sample taken at a police station may be subject of a speculative search;

    (b) warned that if they refuse without good cause their refusal may harm their case if it comes to trial. If the suspect is in police detention and not legally represented, they must also be reminded of their entitlement to have free legal advice, see Code C, *paragraph 6.5*, and the reminder noted in the custody record. If *paragraph 6.2(b)* applies and the person is attending a station voluntarily, their entitlement to free legal advice as in Code C, *paragraph 3.21* shall be explained to them.

6.4   Dental impressions may only be taken by a registered dentist. Other intimate samples, except for samples of urine, may only be taken by a registered medical practitioner or registered nurse or registered paramedic.

2.9.7.3   **KEYNOTE**

Intimate Samples

Taking a sample without the relevant authority may amount to inhuman or degrading treatment under Article 3 of the European Convention on Human Rights (as to which, **see** *General Police Duties*, **chapter 4.4**). It may also amount to a criminal offence of assault (**see** *Crime*, **chapter 1.9**) and give rise to liability at civil law.

    Nothing in para. 6.2 prevents intimate samples being taken for elimination purposes with the consent of the person concerned, but the provisions of para. 2.12, relating to the role of the appropriate adult, should be applied. Paragraph 6.2(b) does not, however, apply where the non-intimate samples were previously taken under the Terrorism Act 2000, sch. 8, para. 10.

    In warning a person who is asked to provide an intimate sample, the following form of words may be used:

You do not have to provide this sample/allow this swab or impression to be taken, but I must warn you that if you refuse without good cause, your refusal may harm your case if it comes to trial.

2.9.7.4   **(b) Non-intimate samples**

6.5   A non-intimate sample may be taken from a detainee only with their written consent or if *paragraph 6.6* applies.

6.6   a non-intimate sample may be taken from a person without the appropriate consent in the following circumstances:

    (a) Under section 63(2A) from a person who is in police detention as a consequence of being arrested for a recordable offence and who has not had a non-intimate sample of the same type and from the same part of the body taken in the course of the investigation of the offence by the police or they have had such a sample taken but it proved insufficient.

(b) Under section 63(3) from a person who is being held in custody by the police on the authority of a court if an officer of at least the rank of inspector authorises it to be taken. An authorisation may be given:

(i) if the authorising officer has reasonable grounds for suspecting the person of involvement in a recordable offence and for believing that the sample will tend to confirm or disprove that involvement, and

(ii) in writing or orally and confirmed in writing, as soon as practicable;

but an authorisation may not be given to take from the same part of the body a further non-intimate sample consisting of a skin impression unless the previously taken impression proved insufficient.

(c) Under section 63(3ZA) from a person who has been arrested for a recordable offence and released if the person:

(i) is on bail and has not had a sample of the same type and from the same part of the body taken in the course of the investigation of the offence, or;

(ii) has had such a sample taken in the course of the investigation of the offence, but it proved unsuitable or insufficient.

(d) Under section 63(3A), from a person (whether or not in police detention or held in custody by the police on the authority of a court) who has been charged with a recordable offence or informed they will be reported for such an offence if the person:

(i) has not had a non-intimate sample taken from them in the course of the investigation of the offence;

(ii) has had a sample so taken, but it proved unsuitable or insufficient or

(iii) has had a sample taken in the course of the investigation of the offence and the sample has been destroyed and in proceedings relating to that offence there is a dispute as to whether a DNA profile relevant to the proceedings was derived from the destroyed sample.

(e) Under section 63(3B), from a person who has been:

(i) convicted of a recordable offence;

(ii) given a caution in respect of a recordable offence which, at the time of the caution, the person admitted; or

(iii) warned or reprimanded under the Crime and Disorder Act 1998, section 65, for a recordable offence,

if, since their conviction, caution, warning or reprimand a non-intimate sample has not been taken from them or a sample which has been taken since then has proved to be unsuitable or insufficient and in either case, an officer of inspector rank or above, is satisfied that taking the fingerprints is necessary to assist in the prevention or detection of crime and authorises the taking.

(f) Under section 63(3C) from a person to whom section 2 of the Criminal Evidence (Amendment) Act 1997 applies (persons detained following acquittal on grounds of insanity or finding of unfitness to plead).

(g) Under section 63(3E) from a person who has been convicted outside England and Wales of an offence which if committed in England and Wales would be a qualifying offence as defined by PACE, section 65A if:

(i) a non-intimate sample has not been taken previously under this power or unless a sample was so taken but was unsuitable or insufficient; and

(ii) a police officer of inspector rank or above is satisfied that taking a sample is necessary to assist in the prevention or detection of crime and authorises it to be taken.

6.6A PACE, section 63A(4) and Schedule 2A provide powers to:

(a) make a requirement (in accordance with *Annex G*) for a person to attend a police station to have a non-intimate sample taken in the exercise of one of the following powers in *paragraph 6.6* when that power applies at the time the sample would be taken in accordance with the requirement:

    (i) section 63(3ZA) – Persons arrested for a recordable offence and released, see *paragraph 6.6(c)*: The requirement may not be made more than six months from the day the investigating officer was informed that the sample previously taken was unsuitable or insufficient.

    (ii) section 63(3A) – Persons charged etc. with a recordable offence, see *paragraph 6.6(d)*: The requirement may not be made more than six months from:

- the day the person was charged or reported if a sample has not been taken since then; or
- the day the investigating officer was informed that the sample previously taken was unsuitable or insufficient.

    (iii) section 63(3B) – Person convicted, cautioned, warned or reprimanded for a recordable offence in England and Wales, *see paragraph 6.6(e)*: Where the offence for which the person was convicted etc is also a qualifying offence, there is no time limit for the exercise of this power. Where the conviction etc was for a recordable offence that is not a qualifying offence, the requirement may not be made more than two years from:

- the day the person was convicted, cautioned, warned or reprimanded, or the day Schedule 2A comes into force (if later), if a samples has not been taken since then; or
- the day an officer from the force investigating the offence was informed that the sample previously taken was unsuitable or insufficient or the day Schedule 2A comes into force (if later).

    (iv) section 63(3E) – A person who has been convicted of qualifying offence outside England and Wales, *see paragraph 6.6(h)*: There is no time limit for making the requirement.

Note: A person who has had a non-intimate sample taken under any of the powers in section 63 mentioned in *paragraph 6.6* on two occasions in relation to any offence may not be required under Schedule 2A to attend a police station for a sample to be taken again under section 63 in relation to that offence, unless authorised by an officer of inspector rank or above. The fact of the authorisation and the reasons for giving it must be recorded as soon as practicable.

(b) arrest, without warrant, a person who fails to comply with the requirement.

6.7   Reasonable force may be used, if necessary, to take a non-intimate sample from a person without their consent under the powers mentioned in *paragraph 6.6*.

6.8   Before any non-intimate sample is taken:

(a) without consent under any power mentioned in *paragraphs 6.6* and *6.6A*, the person must be informed of:

    (i) the reason for taking the sample;

    (ii) the power under which the sample is to be taken;

    (iii) the fact that the relevant authority has been given if any power mentioned in *paragraph 6.6(b), (e)* or *(h)* applies;

(b) with or without consent at a police station or elsewhere, the person must be informed:

    (i) that their sample or information derived from it may be subject of a speculative search against other samples and information derived from them; and

    (ii) that their sample and the information derived from it may be retained in accordance with *Annex F, Part (a)*.

(c) Removal of clothing

6.9   When clothing needs to be removed in circumstances likely to cause embarrassment to the person, no person of the opposite sex who is not a registered medical practitioner or registered health care professional shall be present (unless in the case of a juvenile, mentally disordered or mentally vulnerable person, that person specifically requests the presence of an appropriate adult of the opposite sex who is readily available) nor shall anyone whose presence is unnecessary. However, in the case of a juvenile, this is subject to the overriding proviso that such a removal of clothing may take place in the absence of the appropriate adult only if the juvenile signifies, in their presence, that they prefer the adult's absence and they agree.

(C) Documentation

6.10   A record of the reasons for taking a sample or impression and, if applicable, of its destruction must be made as soon as practicable. If force is used, a record shall be made of the circumstances and those present. If written consent is given to the taking of a sample or impression, the fact must be recorded in writing.

6.11   A record must be made of a warning given as required by *paragraph 6.3*.

6.12   *Not used.*

2.9.7.5

KEYNOTE

Taking a Non-intimate Sample

Where a non-intimate sample consisting of a skin impression is taken electronically from a person, it must be taken only in such manner, and using such devices, as the Secretary of State has approved for the purpose of the electronic taking of such an impression (s. 63(9A) of PACE). No such devices are currently approved.

When hair samples are taken for the purpose of DNA analysis (rather than for other purposes, such as making a visual match), the suspect should be permitted a reasonable choice as to what part of the body the hairs are taken from. When hairs are plucked, they should be plucked individually, unless the suspect prefers otherwise and no more should be plucked than the person taking them reasonably considers necessary for a sufficient sample.

Fingerprints or a DNA sample and the information derived from it taken from a person arrested on suspicion of being involved in a recordable offence, or charged with such an offence, or informed that he/she will be reported for such an offence, may be the subject of a speculative search. This means that they may be checked against other fingerprints and DNA records held by, or on behalf of, the police and other law enforcement authorities in or outside the United Kingdom or held in connection with, or as a result of, an investigation of an offence inside or outside the United Kingdom. Fingerprints and samples taken from any other person, e.g. a person suspected of committing a recordable offence but who has not been arrested, charged or informed that he/she will be reported for it, may be subject to a speculative search only if the person consents in writing to his/her fingerprints being the subject of such a search. The following is an example of a basic form of words:

I consent to my fingerprints, footwear impressions and DNA sample and information derived from it being retained and used only for purposes related to the prevention and detection of a crime, the investigation of an offence or the conduct of a prosecution either nationally or internationally.

I understand that my fingerprints, footwear impressions or DNA sample may be checked against other fingerprint, footwear impressions and DNA records held by or on behalf of relevant law enforcement authorities, either nationally or internationally.

I understand that once I have given my consent for my fingerprints, footwear impressions or DNA sample to be retained and used I cannot withdraw this consent.

Urine and non-intimate samples and the information derived from testing detained persons for the presence of specified Class A drugs, may not be subsequently used in the investigation of any offence or in evidence against the persons from whom they were taken.

2.9.7.6

KEYNOTE

Power to Require Persons to Attend a Police Station to Provide Samples

Code D, Annex G deals with the requirement for a person to attend a police station for fingerprints and samples.

KEYNOTE

Destruction of Samples

Code D, Annex F deals with the destruction and the speculative searches of fingerprints and samples and speculative searches of footwear impressions. It is important that the Annex is followed, particularly in relation to obtaining consent and explaining to volunteers what they are consenting to.

2.9.8 Annex A—Video Identification

(a) General

1. The arrangements for obtaining and ensuring the availability of a suitable set of images to be used in a video identification must be the responsibility of an identification officer, who has no direct involvement with the case.

2. The set of images must include the suspect and at least eight other people who, so far as possible, resemble the suspect in age, general appearance and position in life. Only one suspect shall appear in any set unless there are two suspects of roughly similar appearance, in which case they may be shown together with at least twelve other people.

2A. If the suspect has an unusual physical feature, e.g., a facial scar, tattoo or distinctive hairstyle or hair colour which does not appear on the images of the other people that are available to be used, steps may be taken to:
   (a) conceal the location of the feature on the images of the suspect and the other people; or
   (b) replicate that feature on the images of the other people.
   For these purposes, the feature may be concealed or replicated electronically or by any other method which it is practicable to use to ensure that the images of the suspect and other people resemble each other. The identification officer has discretion to choose whether to conceal or replicate the feature and the method to be used. If an unusual physical feature has been described by the witness, the identification officer should, if practicable, have that feature replicated. If it has not been described, concealment may be more appropriate.

2B. If the identification officer decides that a feature should be concealed or replicated, the reason for the decision and whether the feature was concealed or replicated in the images shown to any witness shall be recorded.

2C. If the witness requests to view an image where an unusual physical feature has been concealed or replicated without the feature being concealed or replicated, the witness may be allowed to do so.

3. The images used to conduct a video identification shall, as far as possible, show the suspect and other people in the same positions or carrying out the same sequence of movements. They shall also show the suspect and other people under identical conditions unless the identification officer reasonably believes:
   (a) because of the suspect's failure or refusal to co-operate or other reasons, it is not practicable for the conditions to be identical; and
   (b) any difference in the conditions would not direct a witness' attention to any individual image.

4. The reasons identical conditions are not practicable shall be recorded on forms provided for the purpose.

5. Provision must be made for each person shown to be identified by number.

6. If police officers are shown, any numerals or other identifying badges must be concealed. If a prison inmate is shown, either as a suspect or not, then either all, or none of, the people shown should be in prison clothing.

7. The suspect or their solicitor, friend, or appropriate adult must be given a reasonable opportunity to see the complete set of images before it is shown to any witness. If the suspect has a

reasonable objection to the set of images or any of the participants, the suspect shall be asked to state the reasons for the objection. Steps shall, if practicable, be taken to remove the grounds for objection. If this is not practicable, the suspect and/or their representative shall be told why their objections cannot be met and the objection, the reason given for it and why it cannot be met shall be recorded on forms provided for the purpose.

8. Before the images are shown in accordance with *paragraph 7*, the suspect or their solicitor shall be provided with details of the first description of the suspect by any witnesses who are to attend the video identification. When a broadcast or publication is made, as in *paragraph 3.28*, the suspect or their solicitor must also be allowed to view any material released to the media by the police for the purpose of recognising or tracing the suspect, provided it is practicable and would not unreasonably delay the investigation.

9. The suspect's solicitor, if practicable, shall be given reasonable notification of the time and place the video identification is to be conducted so a representative may attend on behalf of the suspect. If a solicitor has not been instructed, this information shall be given to the suspect. The suspect may not be present when the images are shown to the witness(es). In the absence of the suspect's representative, the viewing itself shall be recorded on video. No unauthorised people may be present.

(b) Conducting the video identification

10. The identification officer is responsible for making the appropriate arrangements to make sure, before they see the set of images, witnesses are not able to communicate with each other about the case, see any of the images which are to be shown, see, or be reminded of, any photograph or description of the suspect or be given any other indication as to the suspect's identity, or overhear a witness who has already seen the material. There must be no discussion with the witness about the composition of the set of images and they must not be told whether a previous witness has made any identification.

11. Only one witness may see the set of images at a time. Immediately before the images are shown, the witness shall be told that the person they saw on a specified earlier occasion may, or may not, appear in the images they are shown and that if they cannot make a positive identification, they should say so. The witness shall be advised that at any point, they may ask to see a particular part of the set of images or to have a particular image frozen for them to study. Furthermore, it should be pointed out to the witness that there is no limit on how many times they can view the whole set of images or any part of them. However, they should be asked not to make any decision as to whether the person they saw is on the set of images until they have seen the whole set at least twice.

12. Once the witness has seen the whole set of images at least twice and has indicated that they do not want to view the images, or any part of them, again, the witness shall be asked to say whether the individual they saw in person on a specified earlier occasion has been shown and, if so, to identify them by number of the image. The witness will then be shown that image to confirm the identification, see paragraph 17.

13. Care must be taken not to direct the witness' attention to any one individual image or give any indication of the suspect's identity. Where a witness has previously made an identification by photographs, or a computerised or artist's composite or similar likeness, the witness must not be reminded of such a photograph or composite likeness once a suspect is available for identification by other means in accordance with this Code. Nor must the witness be reminded of any description of the suspect.

14. After the procedure, each witness shall be asked whether they have seen any broadcast or published films or photographs, or any descriptions of suspects relating to the offence and their reply shall be recorded.

(c) Image security and destruction

15. Arrangements shall be made for all relevant material containing sets of images used for specific identification procedures to be kept securely and their movements accounted for. In particular, no-one involved in the investigation shall be permitted to view the material prior to it being shown to any witness.

16. As appropriate, *paragraph 3.30* or *3.31* applies to the destruction or retention of relevant sets of images.

(d) Documentation

17. A record must be made of all those participating in, or seeing, the set of images whose names are known to the police.

18. A record of the conduct of the video identification must be made on forms provided for the purpose. This shall include anything said by the witness about any identifications or the conduct of the procedure and any reasons it was not practicable to comply with any of the provisions of this Code governing the conduct of video identifications.

2.9.9 Annex B—Identification Parades

(a) General

1. A suspect must be given a reasonable opportunity to have a solicitor or friend present, and the suspect shall be asked to indicate on a second copy of the notice whether or not they wish to do so.

2. An identification parade may take place either in a normal room or one equipped with a screen permitting witnesses to see members of the identification parade without being seen. The procedures for the composition and conduct of the identification parade are the same in both cases, subject to *paragraph 8* (except that an identification parade involving a screen may take place only when the suspect's solicitor, friend or appropriate adult is present or the identification parade is recorded on video).

3. Before the identification parade takes place, the suspect or their solicitor shall be provided with details of the first description of the suspect by any witnesses who are attending the identification parade. When a broadcast or publication is made as in *paragraph 3.28*, the suspect or their solicitor should also be allowed to view any material released to the media by the police for the purpose of recognising or tracing the suspect, provided it is practicable to do so and would not unreasonably delay the investigation.

(b) Identification parades involving prison inmates

4. If a prison inmate is required for identification, and there are no security problems about the person leaving the establishment, they may be asked to participate in an identification parade or video identification.

5. An identification parade may be held in a Prison Department establishment but shall be conducted, as far as practicable under normal identification parade rules. Members of the public shall make up the identification parade unless there are serious security, or control, objections to their admission to the establishment. In such cases, or if a group or video identification is arranged within the establishment, other inmates may participate. If an inmate is the suspect, they are not required to wear prison clothing for the identification parade unless the other

people taking part are other inmates in similar clothing, or are members of the public who are prepared to wear prison clothing for the occasion.

(c) Conduct of the identification parade

6. Immediately before the identification parade, the suspect must be reminded of the procedures governing its conduct and cautioned in the terms of Code C, *paragraphs 10.5 or 10.6*, as appropriate.

7. All unauthorised people must be excluded from the place where the identification parade is held.

8. Once the identification parade has been formed, everything afterwards, in respect of it, shall take place in the presence and hearing of the suspect and any interpreter, solicitor, friend or appropriate adult who is present (unless the identification parade involves a screen, in which case everything said to, or by, any witness at the place where the identification parade is held, must be said in the hearing and presence of the suspect's solicitor, friend or appropriate adult or be recorded on video).

9. The identification parade shall consist of at least eight people (in addition to the suspect) who, so far as possible, resemble the suspect in age, height, general appearance and position in life. Only one suspect shall be included in an identification parade unless there are two suspects of roughly similar appearance, in which case they may be paraded together with at least twelve other people. In no circumstances shall more than two suspects be included in one identification parade and where there are separate identification parades, they shall be made up of different people.

10. If the suspect has an unusual physical feature, e.g., a facial scar, tattoo or distinctive hairstyle or hair colour which cannot be replicated on other members of the identification parade, steps may be taken to conceal the location of that feature on the suspect and the other members of the identification parade if the suspect and their solicitor, or appropriate adult, agree. For example, by use of a plaster or a hat, so that all members of the identification parade resemble each other in general appearance.

11. When all members of a similar group are possible suspects, separate identification parades shall be held for each unless there are two suspects of similar appearance when they may appear on the same identification parade with at least twelve other members of the group who are not suspects. When police officers in uniform form an identification parade any numerals or other identifying badges shall be concealed.

12. When the suspect is brought to the place where the identification parade is to be held, they shall be asked if they have any objection to the arrangements for the identification parade or to any of the other participants in it and to state the reasons for the objection. The suspect may obtain advice from their solicitor or friend, if present, before the identification parade proceeds. If the suspect has a reasonable objection to the arrangements or any of the participants, steps shall, if practicable, be taken to remove the grounds for objection. When it is not practicable to do so, the suspect shall be told why their objections cannot be met and the objection, the reason given for it and why it cannot be met, shall be recorded on forms provided for the purpose.

13. The suspect may select their own position in the line, but may not otherwise interfere with the order of the people forming the line. When there is more than one witness, the suspect must be told, after each witness has left the room, that they can, if they wish, change position in the line. Each position in the line must be clearly numbered, whether by means of a number laid on the floor in front of each identification parade member or by other means.

14. Appropriate arrangements must be made to make sure, before witnesses attend the identification parade, they are not able to:
    (i) communicate with each other about the case or overhear a witness who has already seen the identification parade;

(ii) see any member of the identification parade;

(iii) see, or be reminded of, any photograph or description of the suspect or be given any other indication as to the suspect's identity; or

(iv) see the suspect before or after the identification parade.

15. The person conducting a witness to an identification parade must not discuss with them the composition of the identification parade and, in particular, must not disclose whether a previous witness has made any identification.

16. Witnesses shall be brought in one at a time. Immediately before the witness inspects the identification parade, they shall be told the person they saw on a specified earlier occasion may, or may not, be present and if they cannot make a positive identification, they should say so. The witness must also be told they should not make any decision about whether the person they saw is on the identification parade until they have looked at each member at least twice.

17. When the officer or police staff (see *paragraph 3.11*) conducting the identification procedure is satisfied the witness has properly looked at each member of the identification parade, they shall ask the witness whether the person they saw on a specified earlier occasion is on the identification parade and, if so, to indicate the number of the person concerned, see *paragraph 28*.

18. If the witness wishes to hear any identification parade member speak, adopt any specified posture or move, they shall first be asked whether they can identify any person(s) on the identification parade on the basis of appearance only. When the request is to hear members of the identification parade speak, the witness shall be reminded that the participants in the identification parade have been chosen on the basis of physical appearance only. Members of the identification parade may then be asked to comply with the witness' request to hear them speak, see them move or adopt any specified posture.

19. If the witness requests that the person they have indicated remove anything used for the purposes of *paragraph 10* to conceal the location of an unusual physical feature, that person may be asked to remove it.

20. If the witness makes an identification after the identification parade has ended, the suspect and, if present, their solicitor, interpreter or friend shall be informed. When this occurs, consideration should be given to allowing the witness a second opportunity to identify the suspect.

21. After the procedure, each witness shall be asked whether they have seen any broadcast or published films or photographs or any descriptions of suspects relating to the offence and their reply shall be recorded.

22. When the last witness has left, the suspect shall be asked whether they wish to make any comments on the conduct of the identification parade.

(d) Documentation

23. A video recording must normally be taken of the identification parade. If that is impracticable, a colour photograph must be taken. A copy of the video recording or photograph shall be supplied, on request, to the suspect or their solicitor within a reasonable time.

24. As appropriate, *paragraph 3.30* or *3.31*, should apply to any photograph or video taken as in *paragraph 23*.

25. If any person is asked to leave an identification parade because they are interfering with its conduct, the circumstances shall be recorded.

26. A record must be made of all those present at an identification parade whose names are known to the police.

27. If prison inmates make up an identification parade, the circumstances must be recorded.

28. A record of the conduct of any identification parade must be made on forms provided for the purpose. This shall include anything said by the witness or the suspect about any identifications or the conduct of the procedure, and any reasons it was not practicable to comply with any of this Code's provisions.

KEYNOTE

Conduct of Identification Parades

Identification evidence can be crucial to the success of a prosecution. There are clear guidelines that must be followed. Where such guidelines are not followed it is likely that the defence will argue strongly to have the identification evidence excluded. In *R* v *Jones* (1999) *The Times*, 21 April, identification evidence was excluded as the officers told the suspect that if he did not comply with the procedure, force would be used against him.

Annexes A to F of Code D set out in detail the procedures and requirements which must be followed in conducting identification procedures.

Although the courts are aware of the many practical difficulties involved in organising and running identification procedures (see e.g. *R* v *Jamel* [1993] Crim LR 52), any flaws in the procedure will be considered in the light of their potential impact on the defendant's trial. Serious or deliberate breaches (such as the showing of photographs to witnesses before the parade), will invariably lead to any evidence so gained being excluded (*R* v *Finley* [1993] Crim LR 50). The key question for the court will be whether the breach of the Codes is likely to have made the identification less reliable.

Breaches which appear to impact on the safeguards imposed by Annexes A–F to separate the functions of investigation and identification (e.g. where the investigating officer becomes involved with the running of the parade in a way which allows him/her to talk to the witnesses (*R* v *Gall* (1990) 90 Cr App R 64)) will also be treated seriously by the court.

The case of *R* v *Marrin* [2002] EWCA Crim 251, provides some guidance as to methods that could be used to get a suitable pool of participants for an identification parade. The court held that there was nothing inherently unfair or objectionable in some colouring or dye being used on the facial stubble of some volunteers to make them look more like the suspect. However, care needed to be taken with such measures because the procedure would be undermined if it was obvious to the witness that make-up had been used. Another point raised was that it may sometimes be appropriate for those on parade to wear hats, but if possible the wearing of hats should be avoided if hats had not been worn during the offence because this would make it more difficult for a witness to make an identification. However, there could be circumstances where the wearing of hats could help to achieve a resemblance and might be desirable to minimise differences. Finally, an identification of a suspect was not invalidated by the witness's request for the removal of a hat. There was nothing unfair in that taking place and there was no breach of any Code either.

It is important to follow the guidance in the Codes regardless of what agreement is obtained from the suspect or his/her solicitor. In *R* v *Hutton* [1999] Crim LR 74, at the suggestion of the suspect's solicitor, all the participants in the identification parade wore back-to-front baseball caps and had the lower part of their faces obscured by material. That identification was the only evidence against the defendant on that count. The court excluded the evidence and did not accept the fact that the decision had been agreed by the defence.

It will be essential that any photographs, photofits or other such material is stored securely in a manner that restricts access so as to be able to demonstrate to the court that the material cannot have been viewed by any of the witnesses and that copies have not been made that have not been accounted for. Where a witness attending an identification procedure has previously been shown photographs, or been shown or provided with computerised or artist's composite likenesses, or similar likenesses or pictures, it is the officer in charge of the investigation's responsibility to make the identification officer aware of this.

2.9.10 Annex C—Group Identification

(a) General

1. The purpose of this Annex is to make sure, as far as possible, group identifications follow the principles and procedures for identification parades so the conditions are fair to the suspect in the way they test the witness' ability to make an identification.

2. Group identifications may take place either with the suspect's consent and cooperation or covertly without their consent.

3. The location of the group identification is a matter for the identification officer, although the officer may take into account any representations made by the suspect, appropriate adult, their solicitor or friend.

4. The place where the group identification is held should be one where other people are either passing by or waiting around informally, in groups such that the suspect is able to join them and be capable of being seen by the witness at the same time as others in the group. For example people leaving an escalator, pedestrians walking through a shopping centre, passengers on railway and bus stations, waiting in queues or groups or where people are standing or sitting in groups in other public places.

5. If the group identification is to be held covertly, the choice of locations will be limited by the places where the suspect can be found and the number of other people present at that time. In these cases, suitable locations might be along regular routes travelled by the suspect, including buses or trains or public places frequented by the suspect.

6. Although the number, age, sex, race and general description and style of clothing of other people present at the location cannot be controlled by the identification officer, in selecting the location the officer must consider the general appearance and numbers of people likely to be present. In particular, the officer must reasonably expect that over the period the witness observes the group, they will be able to see, from time to time, a number of others whose appearance is broadly similar to that of the suspect.

7. A group identification need not be held if the identification officer believes, because of the unusual appearance of the suspect, none of the locations it would be practicable to use satisfy the requirements of *paragraph 6* necessary to make the identification fair.

8. Immediately after a group identification procedure has taken place (with or without the suspect's consent), a colour photograph or video should be taken of the general scene, if practicable, to give a general impression of the scene and the number of people present. Alternatively, if it is practicable, the group identification may be video recorded.

9. If it is not practicable to take the photograph or video in accordance with *paragraph 8*, a photograph or film of the scene should be taken later at a time determined by the identification officer if the officer considers it practicable to do so.

10. An identification carried out in accordance with this Code remains a group identification even though, at the time of being seen by the witness, the suspect was on their own rather than in a group.

11. Before the group identification takes place, the suspect or their solicitor shall be provided with details of the first description of the suspect by any witnesses who are to attend the identification. When a broadcast or publication is made, as in *paragraph 3.28*, the suspect or their solicitor should also be allowed to view any material released by the police to the media for the purposes of recognising or tracing the suspect, provided that it is practicable and would not unreasonably delay the investigation.

12. After the procedure, each witness shall be asked whether they have seen any broadcast or published films or photographs or any descriptions of suspects relating to the offence and their reply recorded.

(b) Identification with the consent of the suspect

13. A suspect must be given a reasonable opportunity to have a solicitor or friend present. They shall be asked to indicate on a second copy of the notice whether or not they wish to do so.

14. The witness, the person carrying out the procedure and the suspect's solicitor, appropriate adult, friend or any interpreter for the witness, may be concealed from the sight of the individuals in the group they are observing, if the person carrying out the procedure considers this assists the conduct of the identification.

15. The person conducting a witness to a group identification must not discuss with them the forthcoming group identification and, in particular, must not disclose whether a previous witness has made any identification.

16. Anything said to, or by, the witness during the procedure about the identification should be said in the presence and hearing of those present at the procedure.

17. Appropriate arrangements must be made to make sure, before witnesses attend the group identification, they are not able to:

    (i) communicate with each other about the case or overhear a witness who has already been given an opportunity to see the suspect in the group;

    (ii) see the suspect; or

    (iii) see, or be reminded of, any photographs or description of the suspect or be given any other indication of the suspect's identity.

18. Witnesses shall be brought one at a time to the place where they are to observe the group. Immediately before the witness is asked to look at the group, the person conducting the procedure shall tell them that the person they saw may, or may not, be in the group and that if they cannot make a positive identification, they should say so. The witness shall be asked to observe the group in which the suspect is to appear. The way in which the witness should do this will depend on whether the group is moving or stationary.

Moving group

19. When the group in which the suspect is to appear is moving, e.g. leaving an escalator, the provisions of *paragraphs 20* to *24* should be followed.

20. If two or more suspects consent to a group identification, each should be the subject of separate identification procedures. These may be conducted consecutively on the same occasion.

21. The person conducting the procedure shall tell the witness to observe the group and ask them to point out any person they think they saw on the specified earlier occasion.

22. Once the witness has been informed as in *paragraph 21* the suspect should be allowed to take whatever position in the group they wish.

23. When the witness points out a person as in *paragraph 21* they shall, if practicable, be asked to take a closer look at the person to confirm the identification. If this is not practicable, or they cannot confirm the identification, they shall be asked how sure they are that the person they have indicated is the relevant person.

24. The witness should continue to observe the group for the period which the person conducting the procedure reasonably believes is necessary in the circumstances for them to be able to make comparisons between the suspect and other individuals of broadly similar appearance to the suspect as in *paragraph 6*.

Stationary groups

25. When the group in which the suspect is to appear is stationary, e.g. people waiting in a queue, the provisions of *paragraphs 26* to *29* should be followed.

26. If two or more suspects consent to a group identification, each should be subject to separate identification procedures unless they are of broadly similar appearance when they may appear in the same group. When separate group identifications are held, the groups must be made up of different people.

27. The suspect may take whatever position in the group they wish. If there is more than one witness, the suspect must be told, out of the sight and hearing of any witness, that they can, if they wish, change their position in the group.

28. The witness shall be asked to pass along, or amongst, the group and to look at each person in the group at least twice, taking as much care and time as possible according to the circumstances, before making an identification. Once the witness has done this, they shall be asked whether the person they saw on the specified earlier occasion is in the group and to indicate any such person by whatever means the person conducting the procedure considers appropriate in the circumstances. If this is not practicable, the witness shall be asked to point out any person they think they saw on the earlier occasion.

29. When the witness makes an indication as in *paragraph 28*, arrangements shall be made, if practicable, for the witness to take a closer look at the person to confirm the identification. If this is not practicable, or the witness is unable to confirm the identification, they shall be asked how sure they are that the person they have indicated is the relevant person.

All cases

30. If the suspect unreasonably delays joining the group, or having joined the group, deliberately conceals themselves from the sight of the witness, this may be treated as a refusal to co-operate in a group identification.

31. If the witness identifies a person other than the suspect, that person should be informed what has happened and asked if they are prepared to give their name and address. There is no obligation upon any member of the public to give these details. There shall be no duty to record any details of any other member of the public present in the group or at the place where the procedure is conducted.

32. When the group identification has been completed, the suspect shall be asked whether they wish to make any comments on the conduct of the procedure.

33. If the suspect has not been previously informed, they shall be told of any identifications made by the witnesses.

(c) Identification without the suspect's consent

34. Group identifications held covertly without the suspect's consent should, as far as practicable, follow the rules for conduct of group identification by consent.

35. A suspect has no right to have a solicitor, appropriate adult or friend present as the identification will take place without the knowledge of the suspect.

36. Any number of suspects may be identified at the same time.

(d) Identifications in police stations

37. Group identifications should only take place in police stations for reasons of safety, security or because it is not practicable to hold them elsewhere.

38. The group identification may take place either in a room equipped with a screen permitting witnesses to see members of the group without being seen, or anywhere else in the police station that the identification officer considers appropriate.

39. Any of the additional safeguards applicable to identification parades should be followed if the identification officer considers it is practicable to do so in the circumstances.

(e) Identifications involving prison inmates

40. A group identification involving a prison inmate may only be arranged in the prison or at a police station.

41. When a group identification takes place involving a prison inmate, whether in a prison or in a police station, the arrangements should follow those in *paragraphs 37* to *39*. If a group identification takes place within a prison, other inmates may participate. If an inmate is the suspect, they do not have to wear prison clothing for the group identification unless the other participants are wearing the same clothing.

(f) Documentation

42. When a photograph or video is taken as in *paragraph 8* or *9*, a copy of the photograph or video shall be supplied on request to the suspect or their solicitor within a reasonable time.
43. *Paragraph 3.30* or *3.31*, as appropriate, shall apply when the photograph or film taken in accordance with *paragraph 8* or *9* includes the suspect.
44. A record of the conduct of any group identification must be made on forms provided for the purpose. This shall include anything said by the witness or suspect about any identifications or the conduct of the procedure and any reasons why it was not practicable to comply with any of the provisions of this Code governing the conduct of group identifications.

2.9.11   ## Annex D—Confrontation by a Witness

1. Before the confrontation takes place, the witness must be told that the person they saw may, or may not, be the person they are to confront and that if they are not that person, then the witness should say so.
2. Before the confrontation takes place the suspect or their solicitor shall be provided with details of the first description of the suspect given by any witness who is to attend. When a broadcast or publication is made, as in *paragraph 3.28*, the suspect or their solicitor should also be allowed to view any material released to the media for the purposes of recognising or tracing the suspect, provided it is practicable to do so and would not unreasonably delay the investigation.
3. Force may not be used to make the suspect's face visible to the witness.
4. Confrontation must take place in the presence of the suspect's solicitor, interpreter or friend unless this would cause unreasonable delay.
5. The suspect shall be confronted independently by each witness, who shall be asked 'Is this the person?'. If the witness identifies the person but is unable to confirm the identification, they shall be asked how sure they are that the person is the one they saw on the earlier occasion.
6. The confrontation should normally take place in the police station, either in a normal room or one equipped with a screen permitting a witness to see the suspect without being seen. In both cases, the procedures are the same except that a room equipped with a screen may be used only when the suspect's solicitor, friend or appropriate adult is present or the confrontation is recorded on video.
7. After the procedure, each witness shall be asked whether they have seen any broadcast or published films or photographs or any descriptions of suspects relating to the offence and their reply shall be recorded.

2.9.12   ## Annex E—Showing Photographs

(a) Action

1. An officer of sergeant rank or above shall be responsible for supervising and directing the showing of photographs. The actual showing may be done by another officer or police staff, see *paragraph 3.11*.

2. The supervising officer must confirm the first description of the suspect given by the witness has been recorded before they are shown the photographs. If the supervising officer is unable to confirm the description has been recorded they shall postpone showing the photographs.

3. Only one witness shall be shown photographs at any one time. Each witness shall be given as much privacy as practicable and shall not be allowed to communicate with any other witness in the case.

4. The witness shall be shown not less than twelve photographs at a time, which shall, as far as possible, all be of a similar type.

5. When the witness is shown the photographs, they shall be told the photograph of the person they saw may, or may not, be amongst them and if they cannot make a positive identification, they should say so. The witness shall also be told they should not make a decision until they have viewed at least twelve photographs. The witness shall not be prompted or guided in any way but shall be left to make any selection without help.

6. If a witness makes a positive identification from photographs, unless the person identified is otherwise eliminated from enquiries or is not available, other witnesses shall not be shown photographs. But both they, and the witness who has made the identification, shall be asked to attend a video identification, an identification parade or group identification unless there is no dispute about the suspect's identification.

7. If the witness makes a selection but is unable to confirm the identification, the person showing the photographs shall ask them how sure they are that the photograph they have indicated is the person they saw on the specified earlier occasion.

8. When the use of a computerised or artist's composite or similar likeness has led to there being a known suspect who can be asked to participate in a video identification, appear on an identification parade or participate in a group identification, that likeness shall not be shown to other potential witnesses.

9. When a witness attending a video identification, an identification parade or group identification has previously been shown photographs or computerised or artist's composite or similar likeness (and it is the responsibility of the officer in charge of the investigation to make the identification officer aware that this is the case), the suspect and their solicitor must be informed of this fact before the identification procedure takes place.

10. None of the photographs shown shall be destroyed, whether or not an identification is made, since they may be required for production in court. The photographs shall be numbered and a separate photograph taken of the frame or part of the album from which the witness made an identification as an aid to reconstituting it.

(b) Documentation

11. Whether or not an identification is made, a record shall be kept of the showing of photographs on forms provided for the purpose. This shall include anything said by the witness about any identification or the conduct of the procedure, any reasons it was not practicable to comply with any of the provisions of this Code governing the showing of photographs and the name and rank of the supervising officer.

12. The supervising officer shall inspect and sign the record as soon as practicable.

2.9.12.1   **KEYNOTE**

Identification Where there is No Suspect

Where the police have no suspect, Code D provides for witnesses (including police officers) to be shown photographs. If photographs are to be shown, the procedure set out at Annex E must be followed. When it is proposed to show photographs to a witness in accordance with Annex E, it is the responsibility of the officer in charge of the investigation to confirm to the officer responsible for supervising and directing the showing, that the first description of the suspect given by that witness has been recorded. If this description has not been recorded, the procedure under Annex E must be postponed. Except for the provisions of Annex E, para. 1, a police officer who is a witness for the purposes of this part of the Code is subject to the same principles and procedures as a civilian witness.

Using photographs from police criminal records can affect the judgment of a jury and nothing should be done to draw their attention to the fact that the defendant's photograph was already held by the police (*R* v *Lamb* (1980) 71 Cr App R 198). This rule does not apply if the jury are already aware of the defendant's previous convictions (*R* v *Allen* [1996] Crim LR 426).

CCTV

CCTV to identify suspects is becoming more common and the Court of Appeal in *R* v *Spencer* [2014] EWCA Crim 933 recognised that the widespread use of CCTV for investigating crime had not been foreseen when Code D was drafted, and suggested that a reconsideration of the Code would be worthwhile. This was a case where suspects were caught on CCTV, and a local newspaper carried photographs captured from the CCTV footage. About a month later, Spencer was arrested for unrelated matters. A police officer spent about an hour and a half with him. Thinking that he recognised Spencer from somewhere, the officer searched the police computer, found the newspaper's CCTV stills, and recognised Spencer as one of the men therein. A witness subsequently picked Spencer out at a video identification parade. The Court held that it was important to note that the witness had not been asked to look at the newspaper's CCTV images and say whether he recognised anybody on the basis that the police had identified a suspect. The officer had searched the computer not for images of Spencer, but for the image that was imprinted in his memory, and he had done so to see if there was a link between that image and Spencer. That was not an identification of a known suspect as envisaged by Code D.

It is important that where pictures or film are shown to specific police officers to try to identify suspects this must be done in a controlled way. In *R* v *Smith (Dean)* [2008] EWCA Crim 1342, the court held that a police officer who was asked to view a CCTV recording to see if he could recognise any suspects involved in a robbery was not in the same shoes as a witness asked to identify someone he/she had seen committing a crime. However, safeguards that Code D was designed to put in place were equally important in cases where a police officer was asked to see whether he/she could recognise anyone in a CCTV recording. Whether or not Code D applied, there had to be in place some record that assisted in gauging the reliability of the assertion that the police officer recognised an individual. It was important that a police officer's initial reactions to viewing a CCTV recording were set out and available for scrutiny. Thus if the police officer failed to recognise anyone on first viewing but did so subsequently, those circumstances ought to be noted. If a police officer failed to pick anybody else out, that also should be recorded, as should any words of doubt. Furthermore, it was necessary that if recognition took place a record was made of what it was about the image that was said to have triggered the recognition. The case of *R* v *JD* [2012] EWCA Crim 2637 further highlights the need to keep records and comply with the Codes. As there was no record of how the police officer in this case viewed the CCTV, the court held that the defence could not test the officer's account that he watched the footage alone and no records had been made as to what features of the image triggered the recognition and other aspects of the recognition. It had been highly suggestive of the investigating constable to tell C that she believed D to feature in the CCTV footage rather than simply asking him to watch it and waiting to see if he recognised anybody. Another case is *R* v *McCook* [2012] EWCA Crim 2817 where the court commented on some of the process required by Code D, for example, the witness's statement did not reveal the nature of the viewing equipment, the number of times the footage was played, how the viewing arrangements were made, what the witness had been told prior to the viewing and whether or not he was alone.

If a film which has been shown to a witness is later lost or unavailable, the witness may give evidence of what he/she saw on that film but the court will have to consider all the relevant circumstances in deciding whether to admit that evidence and what weight to attach to it. (*Taylor* v *Chief Constable of Cheshire* [1986] 1 WLR 1479.)

Facebook

Other types of identification are also coming before the courts. In *R* v *Alexander and McGill* [2012] EWCA Crim 2768 the victim identified the suspects through their Facebook account pictures. The court observed that identifications done in this way, through the use of Facebook, were likely to rise and it was therefore incumbent upon investigators to take steps to obtain, in as much detail as possible, evidence in relation to the initial identification. In this case, before trial requests were made by the defence for photographs of the other Facebook pages that had been considered by victim and his sister so that defendants could consider how their identifications might have been made.

2.9.13 Annex F—Fingerprints, Footwear Impressions and Samples—Destruction and Speculative Searches

Please read keynote to see changes in legislation which make references to s. 64 of PACE out of date.

(a) Fingerprints, footwear impressions and samples taken in connection with a criminal investigation from a person suspected of committing the offence under investigation

1. The retention and destruction of fingerprints, footwear impressions and samples taken in connection with a criminal investigation from a person suspected of committing the offence under investigation is subject to PACE, section 64. (*Please now see PACE, s. 63D.*)

(b) Fingerprints, footwear impressions and samples taken in connection with a criminal investigation from a person not suspected of committing the offence under investigation

2. When fingerprints, footwear impressions or DNA samples are taken from a person in connection with an investigation and the person is not suspected of having committed the offence, they must be destroyed as soon as they have fulfilled the purpose for which they were taken unless:
   (a) they were taken for the purposes of an investigation of an offence for which a person has been convicted; and
   (b) fingerprints, footwear impressions or samples were also taken from the convicted person for the purposes of that investigation.
   However, subject to *paragraph 2*, the fingerprints, footwear impressions and samples, and the information derived from samples, may not be used in the investigation of any offence or in evidence against the person who is, or would be, entitled to the destruction of the fingerprints, footwear impressions and samples.
3. The requirement to destroy fingerprints, footwear impressions and DNA samples, and information derived from samples, and restrictions on their retention and use in *paragraph 1* do not apply if the person gives their written consent for their fingerprints, footwear impressions or sample to be retained and used after they have fulfilled the purpose for which they were taken.
4. When a person's fingerprints, footwear impressions or sample are to be destroyed:
   (a) any copies of the fingerprints and footwear impressions must also be destroyed;
   (b) the person may witness the destruction of their fingerprints, footwear impressions or copies if they ask to do so within five days of being informed destruction is required;
   (c) access to relevant computer fingerprint data shall be made impossible as soon as it is practicable to do so and the person shall be given a certificate to this effect within three months of asking; and
   (d) neither the fingerprints, footwear impressions, the sample, or any information derived from the sample, may be used in the investigation of any offence or in evidence against the person who is, or would be, entitled to its destruction.
5. Fingerprints, footwear impressions or samples, and the information derived from samples, taken in connection with the investigation of an offence which are not required to be des-

troyed, may be retained after they have fulfilled the purposes for which they were taken but may be used only for purposes related to the prevention or detection of crime, the investigation of an offence or the conduct of a prosecution in, as well as outside, the UK and may also be subject to a speculative search. This includes checking them against other fingerprints, footwear impressions and DNA records held by, or on behalf of, the police and other law enforcement authorities in, as well as outside, the UK.

(c) Fingerprints taken in connection with Immigration Service enquiries

6. See *paragraph 4.10*.

2.9.13.1

KEYNOTE

The rules around the retention and use of DNA samples, fingerprints and associated data have changed since the Protection of Freedoms Act 2012 came into force. However Code D has not been amended in line with these changes.

The Criminal Justice and Police Act 2001 amended PACE to provide the police with the power to retain DNA and fingerprints relating to persons following acquittal at court or discontinuance of a case. The Criminal Justice Act 2003 further amended PACE to provide the police in England and Wales with additional powers to take and retain DNA and fingerprints from all persons detained at a police station having been arrested for a recordable offence. The Protection of Freedoms Act 2012, which came into force on 31 October 2013, has created a number of situations whereby police are no longer able to retain fingerprints and DNA. In these circumstances the material will be deleted automatically. The police can still retain the fingerprints and DNA of convicted individuals indefinitely, but the amendments have introduced 'retention periods' for other circumstances, whereby DNA and fingerprints can be retained by police only for specified periods prior to being automatically deleted.

DNA and fingerprints can be retained in the following circumstances:

*   DNA profiles and fingerprints of convicted individuals may be retained indefinitely, except in some situations involving offenders under 18. The early deletion procedure is not intended to interfere with the lawful retention of material from convicted persons. In such cases the applicant would have to appeal the conviction itself. Under PACE, 'conviction' includes cautions, reprimands and warnings.
*   DNA profiles and fingerprints of individuals arrested, or arrested and charged, but not convicted of minor offences are deleted when proceedings conclude. There is no need for these individuals to apply for early deletion as their material will be deleted automatically.
*   DNA profiles and fingerprints of individuals arrested but not charged with a qualifying offence are deleted, unless the force applies to the Biometrics Commissioner for retention for three years. In these cases, the individual's representations should be made to the Biometrics Commissioner, and not via the early deletion process.

Applications for early deletion of DNA and fingerprints can be made in two specific circumstances where individuals may apply for early deletion of such lawfully held material, providing they also satisfy the grounds for early deletion:

*   Individuals with no prior convictions whose material is held after they have been given a Penalty Notice for Disorder (PND). A PND is not a conviction under PACE and does not involve any admission of guilt. It is expected to be very rare that the grounds for deletion are also met in these circumstances.
*   Individuals with no prior convictions whose material is held as a result of being arrested and charged with a qualifying (serious) offence, but where they were not subsequently convicted. PACE allows for the lawful retention of DNA and fingerprints for three years in these circumstances.

Fingerprints, footwear impressions and samples given voluntarily for the purposes of elimination play an important part in many police investigations. It is, therefore, important to make sure that innocent volunteers are not deterred from participating and their consent to their fingerprints, footwear impressions and DNA being used for the purposes of a specific investigation is fully informed and voluntary. If the police seek to have the fingerprints, footwear impressions or samples of a volunteer retained for use after the specific investigation ends, it is important that the volunteer's consent to this is also fully informed and voluntary.

The two types of consent are to allow DNA/fingerprints/footwear impressions to be used only for the purposes of a specific investigation or for specific investigation *and* retained by the police for future use.

To minimise the risk of confusion, each consent should be physically separate and the volunteer should be asked to sign *each consent*. For example:

For a DNA sample taken for the purposes of elimination or as part of an intelligence-led screening and to be used only for the purposes of that investigation and destroyed afterwards:

> I consent to my DNA/mouth swab being taken for forensic analysis. I understand that the sample will be destroyed at the end of the case and that my profile will only be compared to the crime stain profile from this enquiry. I have been advised that the person taking the sample may be required to give evidence and/or provide a written statement to the police in relation to the taking of it.

Where the person agrees to the DNA sample to be retained on the National DNA database and used in the future:

> I consent to my DNA sample and information derived from it being retained and used only for purposes related to the prevention and detection of a crime, the investigation of an offence or the conduct of a prosecution either nationally or internationally.
> I understand that this sample may be checked against other DNA records held by, or on behalf of, relevant law enforcement authorities, either nationally or internationally.
> I understand that once I have given my consent for the sample to be retained and used I cannot withdraw this consent.

For fingerprints taken for the purposes of elimination or as part of an intelligence-led screening and to be used only for the purposes of that investigation and destroyed afterwards:

> I consent to my fingerprints being taken for elimination purposes. I understand that the fingerprints will be destroyed at the end of the case and that my fingerprints will only be compared to the fingerprints from this enquiry. I have been advised that the person taking the fingerprints may be required to give evidence and/or provide a written statement to the police in relation to the taking of it.

For cases where the person agrees to fingerprints to be retained for future use:

> I consent to my fingerprints being retained and used only for purposes related to the prevention and detection of a crime, the investigation of an offence or the conduct of a prosecution either nationally or internationally.
> I understand that my fingerprints may be checked against other records held by, or on behalf of, relevant law enforcement authorities, either nationally or internationally.
> I understand that once I have given my consent for my fingerprints to be retained and used I cannot withdraw this consent.

For footwear impressions taken for the purposes of elimination or as part of an intelligence-led screening and to be used only for the purposes of that investigation and destroyed afterwards:

> I consent to my footwear impressions being taken for elimination purposes. I understand that the footwear impressions will be destroyed at the end of the case and that my footwear impressions will only be compared to the footwear impressions from this enquiry. I have been advised that the person taking the footwear impressions may be required to give evidence and/or provide a written statement to the police in relation to the taking of it.

For cases where the person agrees to footwear impressions to be retained for future use:

> I consent to my footwear impressions being retained and used only for purposes related to the prevention and detection of a crime, the investigation of an offence or the conduct of a prosecution, either nationally or internationally.
> I understand that my footwear impressions may be checked against other records held by, or on behalf of, relevant law enforcement authorities, either nationally or internationally.
> I understand that once I have given my consent for my footwear impressions to be retained and used I cannot withdraw this consent.

The provisions for the retention of fingerprints, footwear impressions and samples taken from a person in connection to an investigation need to be retained to allow all fingerprints, footwear impressions and samples in a case to be available for any subsequent miscarriage of justice investigation.

Annex G—Requirement for a Person to Attend a Police Station for Fingerprints and Samples

1. A requirement under Schedule 2A for a person to attend a police station to have fingerprints or samples taken:
   (a) must give the person a period of at least seven days within which to attend the police station; and
   (b) may direct them to attend at a specified time of day or between specified times of day.
2. When specifying the period and times of attendance, the officer making the requirements must consider whether the fingerprints or samples could reasonably be taken at a time when the person is required to attend the police station for any other reason.
3. An officer of the rank of inspector or above may authorise a period shorter than 7 days if there is an urgent need for person's fingerprints or sample for the purposes of the investigation of an offence. The fact of the authorisation and the reasons for giving it must be recorded as soon as practicable.
4. The constable making a requirement and the person to whom it applies may agree to vary it so as to specify any period within which, or date or time at which, the person is to attend. However, variation shall not have effect for the purposes of enforcement, unless it is confirmed by the constable in writing.

2.9.14.1

KEYNOTE

The specified period within which the person is to attend need not fall within the period allowed (if applicable) for making the requirement. To justify the arrest without warrant of a person who fails to comply with a requirement (Code D, para. 4.4, see para. 2.9.5), the officer making the requirement, or confirming a variation, should be prepared to explain how, when and where the requirement was made or the variation was confirmed and what steps were taken to ensure that the person understood what to do and the consequences of not complying with the requirement.

Following the correct procedure for requesting samples is crucial. In *R (On the Application of R) v A Chief Constable* [2013] EWHC 2864 (Admin) R had been convicted of unlawful act manslaughter in 1984. Twenty years after a kidnap conviction in 1993, R was asked to provide a non-intimate sample to be placed on the police national DNA database. R refused to provide a sample and was handed a letter informing him that he had seven days to attend the police station to provide the sample, and if he failed to do so he would be arrested and a sample would be forcibly taken from him pursuant to the Police and Criminal Evidence Act 1984, s. 63(3B)(a). When the letter was served authority had not been given by an inspector. The court held that a requirement to attend a police station to provide a non-intimate sample under the 1984 Act could not be made to a person who did not consent to providing a sample unless an officer of the rank of inspector or above had first given authorisation for the taking of the sample under s. 63(3B)(b). The letter handed to R constituted a demand that he attend a police station to provide a sample within seven days. That demand was unlawful because it was made without prior authorisation by an inspector or an officer of higher rank.

The second point in this case related to the authority that was eventually given by the inspector and the historic nature of the conviction; the court held that the inspector was fully justified in concluding that the public interest in the detection of crime outweighed the limited interference with R's private life. The absence of specific grounds for suspicion of R did not render the requirement to provide a sample disproportionate. The conclusion that R might have committed other offences during the period of his admitted offending and after 1995 was justified. While there was a theoretical deterrent effect in the knowledge by R that police were in possession of his DNA profile, it was the objective of solving crime which provided the legitimate justification for the requirement in the instant case. The requirement that R attend the police station to give a sample was proportionate.

2.10 Interviews

PACE Code of Practice for the Detention, Treatment and Questioning of Persons by Police Officers (Code C)

PACE Code of Practice on Audio Recording Interviews with Suspects (Code E)

PACE Code of Practice on Visual Recording with Sound of Interviews with Suspects (Code F)

> A thick grey line down the margin denotes text that is an extract of the PACE Code itself (i.e. the actual wording of the legislation). This material is examinable for both Sergeants and Inspectors.

2.10.1 Introduction

The PACE Codes of Practice C, E and F are intended to provide some protection to people being interviewed by the police and lay down guidelines as to how interviews should be conducted. This chapter examines the treatment of suspects when they are interviewed. The chapter includes the relevant sections of Code C and all of Code E and F. The chapter sets out the actual Codes of Practice with keynotes, which incorporate the notes of guidance to the Code, relevant legislation and case law.

See **chapter 2.8** regarding designated officers carrying out some functions of police officers.

Code C was amended on 27 October 2013. Code H applies to persons detained for the purposes of a terrorist investigation; references to terrorism matters, where appropriate, are included in the keynotes to this chapter.

2.10.2 PACE Code of Practice for the Detention, Treatment and Questioning of Persons by Police Officers (Code C)

10 Cautions

(a) When a caution must be given

10.1 A person whom there are grounds to suspect of an offence, must be cautioned before any questions about an offence, or further questions if the answers provide the grounds for suspicion, are put to them if either the suspect's answers or silence, (i.e. failure or refusal to *answer* or *answer* satisfactorily) may be given in evidence to a court in a prosecution. A person need not be cautioned if questions are for other necessary purposes, e.g.:

(a) solely to establish their identity or ownership of any vehicle;

(b) to obtain information in accordance with any relevant statutory requirement, see *paragraph 10.9*;

(c) in furtherance of the proper and effective conduct of a search, e.g. to determine the need to search in the exercise of powers of stop and search or to seek co-operation while carrying out a search; or

(d) to seek verification of a written record as in *paragraph 11.13*.

(e) *Not used.*

10.2 Whenever a person not under arrest is initially cautioned, or reminded they are under caution, that person must at the same time be told they are not under arrest and informed of the provisions of *paragraph 3.21* which explain how they may obtain legal advice according to whether they are at a police station or elsewhere.

10.3 A person who is arrested, or further arrested, must be informed at the time if practicable or, if not, as soon as it becomes practicable thereafter, that they are under arrest and of the grounds and reasons for their arrest, see *paragraph 3.4* and Code G, *paragraphs 2.2* and *4.3*.

10.4 As required by Code G, *section 3*, a person who is arrested, or further arrested, must also be cautioned unless:

(a) it is impracticable to do so by reason of their condition or behaviour at the time;

(b) they have already been cautioned immediately prior to arrest as in *paragraph 10.1*.

2.10.2.1

KEYNOTE

In considering whether there are grounds to suspect a person of committing an offence there must be some reasonable, objective grounds for the suspicion, based on known facts or information which are/is relevant to the likelihood that the offence has been committed and that the person to be questioned committed it.

An arrested person must be given sufficient information to enable him/her to understand that he/she has been deprived of his/her liberty and the reason for the arrest, e.g. when a person is arrested on suspicion of committing an offence he/she must be informed of the suspected offence's nature, and when and where it was committed. The suspect must also be informed of the reason or reasons why the arrest is considered necessary. Vague or technical language should be avoided. If it appears that a person does not understand the caution, the person giving it should explain it in his/her own words.

2.10.2.2

(b) Terms of the cautions

10.5 The caution which must be given on:

(a) arrest; or

(b) all other occasions before a person is charged or informed they may be prosecuted; see *section 16*,

should, unless the restriction on drawing adverse inferences from silence applies, see *Annex C*, be in the following terms:

'*You do not have to say anything. But it may harm your defence if you do not mention when questioned something which you later rely on in Court. Anything you do say may be given in evidence.*'

Where the use of the Welsh Language is appropriate, a constable may provide the caution directly in Welsh in the following terms:

'*Does dim rhaid i chi ddweud dim byd. Ond gall niweidio eich amddiffyniad os na fyddwch chi'n sôn, wrth gael eich holi, am rywbeth y byddwch chi'n dibynnu arno nes ymlaen yn y Llys. Gall unrhyw beth yr ydych yn ei ddweud gael ei roi fel tystiolaeth.*'

10.6 *Annex C, paragraph 2* sets out the alternative terms of the caution to be used when the restriction on drawing adverse inferences from silence applies.

10.7 Minor deviations from the words of any caution given in accordance with this Code do not constitute a breach of this Code, provided the sense of the relevant caution is preserved.

10.8 After any break in questioning under caution, the person being questioned must be made aware they remain under caution. If there is any doubt the relevant caution should be given again in full when the interview resumes.

10.9 When, despite being cautioned, a person fails to co-operate or to answer particular questions which may affect their immediate treatment, the person should be informed of any relevant consequences and that those consequences are not affected by the caution. Examples are when a person's refusal to provide:

- their name and address when charged may make them liable to detention;
- particulars and information in accordance with a statutory requirement, e.g. under the Road Traffic Act 1988, may amount to an offence or may make the person liable to a further arrest.

2.10.2.3 **KEYNOTE**

As well as considering whether to administer the caution again after a break in questioning or at the beginning of a subsequent interview, the interviewing officer should summarise the reason for the break and confirm this with the suspect. This may help to show to the court that nothing occurred during an interview break or between interviews which influenced the suspect's recorded evidence.

Nothing in this Code requires a caution to be given or repeated when informing a person not under arrest that he/she may be prosecuted for an offence. However, a court will not be able to draw any inferences under the Criminal Justice and Public Order Act 1994, s. 34, if the person was not cautioned.

The giving of a warning or the service of the Notice of Intended Prosecution required by the Road Traffic Offenders Act 1988, s. 1 does not amount to informing a detainee that he/she may be prosecuted for an offence and so does not preclude further questioning in relation to that offence.

Section 34 of the Criminal Justice and Public Order Act 1994

Section 34 of the Criminal Justice and Public Order Act 1994 provides that inferences can be drawn if, when questioned by the police under caution, charged or officially informed that he/she may be prosecuted, the accused fails to mention a fact on which he/she later relies in his/her defence, and which he/she could reasonably have been expected to mention at the time.

Section 34 states:

(1) Where, in any proceedings against a person for an offence, evidence is given that the accused—
  (a) at any time before he was charged with the offence, on being questioned under caution by a constable trying to discover whether or by whom the offence had been committed, failed to mention any fact relied on in his defence in those proceedings; or
  (b) on being charged with the offence or officially informed that he might be prosecuted for it, failed to mention any such fact, or
  (c) at any time after being charged with the offence, on being questioned under section 22 of the Counter-Terrorism Act 2008 (post-charge questioning), failed to mention any such fact,
  being a fact which in the circumstances existing at the time the accused could reasonably have been expected to mention when so questioned, charged or informed, as the case may be, subsection (2) below applies.

(2) Where this subsection applies—
  (a) magistrates' court inquiring into the offence as examining justices;
  (b) a judge, in deciding whether to grant an application made by the accused under paragraph 2 of Schedule 3 to the Crime and Disorder Act 1998;
  (c) the court, in determining whether there is a case to answer; and
  (d) the court or jury, in determining whether the accused is guilty of the offence charged,
  may draw such inferences from the failure as appear proper.

(2A) Where the accused was at an authorised place of detention at the time of the failure, subsections (1) and (2) above do not apply if he had not been allowed an opportunity to consult a solicitor prior to being questioned, charged or informed as mentioned in subsection (1) above.

(3) Subject to any directions by the court, evidence tending to establish the failure may be given before or after evidence tending to establish the fact which the accused is alleged to have failed to mention.

(4)   This section applies in relation to questioning by persons (other than constables) charged with the duty of investigating offences or charging offenders as it applies in relation to questioning by constables; and in subsection (1) above 'officially informed' means informed by a constable or any such person.

(5)   This section does not—

(a)   prejudice the admissibility in evidence of the silence or other reaction of the accused in the face of anything said in his presence relating to the conduct in respect of which he is charged, in so far as evidence thereof would be admissible apart from this section; or

(b)   preclude the drawing of any inference from any such silence or other reaction of the accused which could properly be drawn apart from this section.

Although judges have discretion in individual cases it has been recommended that in relation to s. 34 they should closely follow the Judicial Studies Board specimen direction. This direction was followed in *Beckles* v *United Kingdom* (2003) 36 EHRR 13 and accepted by the European Court of Human Rights. However, failure to give proper direction does not necessarily involve a breach of Article 6 (right to a fair trial).

Section 34 deals with the 'failure to mention any fact' and the word 'fact' is given its normal dictionary definition of 'something that is actually the case' (*R* v *Milford* [2001] Crim LR 330). Where an accused alleges that he/she did mention the relevant fact when being questioned it is for the prosecution to prove the contrary before any adverse inference can be drawn.

There have been numerous domestic and European case decisions about failure to advance facts following legal advice to remain silent, and more recent cases have attempted to unravel the difficulties experienced in this area. These cases have accepted that a genuine reliance by a defendant on his/her solicitor's advice to remain silent is not in itself enough to preclude adverse comment. The real question to be answered is whether the defendant remained silent, not because of legal advice, but because there was no satisfactory explanation to give (*R* v *Beckles* [2004] EWCA Crim 2766, *R* v *Bresa* [2005] EWCA Crim 1414 and *R* v *Loizou* [2006] EWCA Crim 1719).

In assessing whether to draw an inference from a failure to mention facts later relied on as part of the defence, the court may look at the validity of the waiver to legal advice. In *R* v *Saunders* [2012] EWCA Crim 1380, the suspect declined the offer of legal representation, and in interview she either made no comment or denied the allegations put to her. At trial she blamed her cousin who she said had been staying at her flat at the time. The prosecution sought to rely on her interview to show that she had made no mention of her cousin at that stage. In accepting the prosecution's submission the court considered the extent of her knowledge and the extent to which her decision caused her disadvantage. As to the first factor, S had particular experience and understanding of the interview procedure having experienced it before and was well-fitted to decide whether she wanted legal advice. She was neither unintelligent nor vulnerable and could be expected to be well aware of the benefit of legal advice.

In relation to s. 34, the accused cannot be convicted solely on an inference drawn from silence. The European Court of Human Rights, although accepting that there are cases which clearly call for an accused to provide an explanation, stated that the court is required to apply 'particular caution' before invoking the accused's silence against him (*Condron* v *United Kingdom* (2001) 31 EHRR 1). In *R* v *Miah* [2009] EWCA Crim 2368, Hughes LJ said: 'Section 34 bites not on silence in interview but upon the late advancing of a case which could have been made earlier. What it does is to permit the jury to ask why, if there is an explanation for the evidence, or a defence to the accusation, the defendant did not advance it when he could have done, providing only that it was reasonable to expect him to have done so then.'

In *R* v *Argent* [1997] 2 Cr App R 27, the court stated that personal factors which might be relevant to an assessment of what an individual could reasonably have been expected to mention were age, experience, mental capacity, state of health, sobriety, tiredness and personality.

In *R* v *Flynn* [2001] EWCA Crim 1633, the court held that the police are entitled to conduct a second interview with a suspect, having obtained evidence from their witnesses which was not available in the first interview, and adverse inference could be drawn from the suspect's silence.

Where an accused, following legal advice, fails to answer questions during interview but presents a prepared statement, no adverse inference can be drawn where the accused's defence does not rely on any facts not mentioned in the interview (*R* v *Campbell* [2005] EWCA Crim 1249). However, this would not be the case when evidence of facts relied on during the trial was not contained within the pre-prepared statement (*R* v *Turner* [2003] EWCA Crim 3108).

Section 34 differs from the other 'inference' sections in that the questioning need not occur at a police station and therefore the presence of a legal representative is not required. However, it appears clear that, should the prosecution seek to draw any inferences of an accused's silence where such questioning has occurred, the questions would need to be asked of the suspect again once he/she had access to legal advice.

A requirement to caution the person is contained in s. 34(1)(a) in order to make clear the risks connected with a failure to mention facts which later form part of the defence.

In certain justice areas the Criminal Justice Act 2003 repeals s. 34(2)(a) and (b)(i) and (ii) and replaces them with sch. 3, para. 2 to the Crime and Disorder Act 1998 (these amendments are not yet in force in other areas). Section 22(9) of the Counter Terrorism Act 2008 adds s. 34(1)(c) to the Criminal Justice and Public Order Act 1994, which extends inferences from silence to post-charge questioning which has been authorised by a judge of the Crown Court if the offence is a terrorism offence or it appears to the judge that the offence has a terrorist connection. The post-charge questioning provisions of the 2008 Act require the issue of a mandatory Code for the video recording with sound of such questioning (**see appendix 2.1**).

2.10.2.4 (c) Special warnings under the Criminal Justice and Public Order Act 1994, sections 36 and 37

10.10 When a suspect interviewed at a police station or authorised place of detention after arrest fails or refuses to answer certain questions, or to answer satisfactorily, after due warning, a court or jury may draw such inferences as appear proper under the Criminal Justice and Public Order Act 1994, sections 36 and 37. Such inferences may only be drawn when:

(a) the restriction on drawing adverse inferences from silence, *see Annex C*, does not apply; and

(b) the suspect is arrested by a constable and fails or refuses to account for any objects, marks or substances, or marks on such objects found:
- on their person;
- in or on their clothing or footwear;
- otherwise in their possession; or
- in the place they were arrested;

(c) the arrested suspect was found by a constable at a place at or about the time the offence for which that officer has arrested them is alleged to have been committed, and the suspect fails or refuses to account for their presence there.

When the restriction on drawing adverse inferences from silence applies, the suspect may still be asked to account for any of the matters in (b) or (c) but the special warning described in *paragraph 10.11* will not apply and must not be given.

10.11 For an inference to be drawn when a suspect fails or refuses to answer a question about one of these matters or to answer it satisfactorily, the suspect must first be told in ordinary language:

(a) what offence is being investigated;

(b) what fact they are being asked to account for;

(c) this fact may be due to them taking part in the commission of the offence;

(d) a court may draw a proper inference if they fail or refuse to account for this fact; and

(e) a record is being made of the interview and it may be given in evidence if they are brought to trial.

KEYNOTE

Sections 36 and 37 of the Criminal Justice and Public Order Act 1994

The Criminal Justice and Public Order Act 1994, ss. 36 and 37 apply only to suspects who have been arrested by a constable or an officer of Revenue and Customs and are given the relevant warning by the police or customs officer who made the arrest or who is investigating the offence. They do not apply to any interviews with suspects who have not been arrested. Further, a person who is not in police detention is not prevented from seeking legal advice if he/she wants; therefore the restrictions on drawing inferences from silence set out in Code C, Annex C, para. 1, do not apply.

Inferences from Silence: Failure to Account for Objects, Substances and Marks

Section 36 of the Criminal Justice and Public Order Act 1994 provides that inferences can be drawn from an accused's failure to give evidence or refusal to answer any question about any object, substance or mark which may be attributable to the accused in the commission of an offence.

Section 36 states:

(1) Where—
  (a) a person is arrested by a constable, and there is—
     (i) on his person; or
     (ii) in or on his clothing or footwear; or
     (iii) otherwise in his possession; or
     (iv) in any place in which he is at the time of his arrest,
     any object, substance or mark, or there is any mark on any such object; and
  (b) that or another constable investigating the case reasonably believes that the presence of the object, substance or mark may be attributable to the participation of the person arrested in the commission of an offence specified by the constable; and
  (c) the constable informs the person arrested that he so believes, and requests him to account for the presence of the object, substance or mark; and
  (d) the person fails or refuses to do so,
  then if, in any proceedings against the person for the offence so specified, evidence of those matters is given, subsection (2) below applies.
(2) Where this subsection applies—
  (a) a magistrates' court inquiring into the offence as examining justices; in deciding whether to grant an application for dismissal made by the accused under section 6 of the Magistrates' Courts Act 1980 (application for dismissal of charge in course of proceedings with a view to transfer for trial);
  (b) a judge, in deciding whether to grant an application made by the accused under—
     (i) section 6 of the Criminal Justice Act 1987 (application for dismissal of charge of serious fraud in respect of which notice of transfer has been given under section 4 of that Act); or
     (ii) paragraph 5 of schedule 6 to the Criminal Justice Act 1991 (application for dismissal of charge of violent or sexual offence involving a child in respect of which notice of transfer has been given under section 53 of that Act);
  (c) the court, in determining whether there is a case to answer; and
  (d) the court or jury, in determining whether the accused is guilty of the offence charged, may draw such inferences from the failure or refusal as appear proper.
(3) Subsections (1) and (2) above apply to the condition of clothing or footwear as they apply to a substance or mark thereon.
(4) Subsections (1) and (2) above do not apply unless the accused was told in ordinary language by the constable when making the request mentioned in subsection (1)(c) above what the effect of this section would be if he failed or refused to comply with the request.
(4A) Where the accused was at an authorised place of detention at the time of the failure or refusal, subsections (1) and (2) do not apply if he had not been allowed an opportunity to consult a solicitor prior to the request being made.
(5) This section applies in relation to officers of customs and excise as it applies in relation to constables.
(6) This section does not preclude the drawing of any inference from a failure or refusal of the accused to account for the presence of an object, substance or mark or from the condition of clothing or footwear which could properly be drawn apart from this section.

As with s. 37 below, an inference may only be drawn where four conditions are satisfied:

- the accused has been arrested;
- a constable reasonably believes that the object, substance or mark (or the presence of the accused (s. 37)) may be attributable to the accused's participation in a crime (s. 36 (an offence 'specified by the constable') or s. 37 (the offence for which he/she was arrested));
- the constable informs the accused of his/her belief and requests an explanation (by giving a special warning (see below));
- the constable tells the suspect (in ordinary language) the effect of a failure or refusal to comply with the request.

The request for information under both s. 36 and s. 37 is a form of questioning and should be undertaken during the interview at the police station. The request for such information prior to this would be an exception to the rule.

The interviewing officer is required to give the accused a 'special warning' for an inference to be drawn from a suspect's failure or refusal to answer a question about one of these matters or to answer it satisfactorily. This 'special warning' is provided by PACE Code C, para. 10.11 which states that the interviewing officer must first tell the suspect *in ordinary language*:

- what offence is being investigated;
- what fact the suspect is being asked to account for;
- that the interviewing officer believes this fact may be due to the suspect's taking part in the commission of the offence in question;
- that a court may draw a proper inference if the suspect fails or refuses to account for the fact about which he/she is being questioned;
- that a record is being made of the interview and that it may be given in evidence at any subsequent trial.

Section 36 considers the circumstances of the suspect at the time of arrest; it is suggested therefore that in relation to items that are *otherwise in the possession of the suspect* under s. 36(1)(a) there must be some link to the suspect at the time of arrest and this would not for instance include items found sometime later at a search of the suspect's home address some distance away.

As with s. 34, in relation to s. 36 the accused cannot be convicted solely on an inference drawn from a failure or refusal (s. 38(3)).

When the provisions of the Criminal Justice Act 2003 are in force s. 36(2)(a) and (2)(b)(i) and (ii) will be repealed and replaced by sch. 3, para. 2 to the Crime and Disorder Act 1998.

Inferences from Silence: Failure to Account for Presence

Section 37 of the Criminal Justice and Public Order Act 1994 provides that inferences can be drawn from an accused's failure to give evidence or refusal to answer any question about his/her presence at a place or time when the offence for which he/she was arrested was committed.

Section 37 states:

(1) Where—
    (a) a person arrested by a constable was found by him at a place at or about the time the offence for which he was arrested is alleged to have been committed; and
    (b) that or another constable investigating the offence reasonably believes that the presence of the person at that place and at that time may be attributable to his participation in the commission of the offence; and
    (c) the constable informs the person that he so believes, and requests him to account for that presence; and
    (d) the person fails or refuses to do so,
    then if, in any proceedings against the person for the offence, evidence of those matters is given, subsection (2) below applies.
(2) Where this subsection applies—
    (a) a magistrates' court inquiring into the offence as examining justices; in deciding whether to grant an application for dismissal made by the accused under section 6 of the Magistrates' Courts Act 1980 (application for dismissal of charge in course of proceedings with a view to transfer for trial);
    (b) a judge, in deciding whether to grant an application made by the accused under—
        (i) section 6 of the Criminal Justice Act 1987 (application for dismissal of charge of serious fraud in respect of which notice of transfer has been given under section 4 of that Act); or
        (ii) paragraph 5 of schedule 6 to the Criminal Justice Act 1991 (application for dismissal of charge of violent or sexual offence involving child in respect of which notice of transfer has been given under section 53 of that Act);

(c) the court, in determining whether there is a case to answer; and

(d) the court or jury, in determining whether the accused is guilty of the offence charged,

may draw such inferences from the failure or refusal as appear proper.

(3) Subsections (1) and (2) do not apply unless the accused was told in ordinary language by the constable when making the request mentioned in subsection (1)(c) above what the effect of this section would be if he failed or refused to comply with the request.

(3A) Where the accused was at an authorised place of detention at the time of the failure or refusal, subsections (1) and (2) do not apply if he had not been allowed an opportunity to consult a solicitor prior to the request being made.

(4) This section applies in relation to officers of customs and excise as it applies in relation to constables.

(5) This section does not preclude the drawing of any inference from a failure or refusal of the accused to account for his presence at a place which could properly be drawn apart from this section.

Section 37 appears somewhat restrictive in that it is only concerned with the suspect's location at the time of arrest and applies only when he/she was found at that location at or about the time of the offence.

PACE Code C also applies to s. 37 in relation to the 'special warning' required to be given by the interviewing officer.

Unlike s. 36, here the officer that sees the person at or near the scene of the alleged offence must be the arresting officer.

As with ss. 34 and 36, in relation to s. 37 the accused cannot be convicted solely on an inference drawn from a failure or refusal (s. 38(3)).

When the provisions of the Criminal Justice Act 2003 are in force s. 37(2)(a) and (2)(b)(i) and (ii) will be repealed and replaced by sch. 3, para. 2 to the Crime and Disorder Act 1998.

2.10.2.6 KEYNOTE

Inferences from Silence at Trial

Section 35 of the Criminal Justice and Public Order Act 1994 provides that inferences can be drawn from an accused's failure to give evidence or refusal to answer any question, without good cause, where the person has been sworn. Section 35 states:

(1) At the trial of any person for an offence, subsections (2) and (3) below apply unless—

(a) the accused's guilt is not in issue; or

(b) it appears to the court that the physical or mental condition of the accused makes it undesirable for him to give evidence; but subsection (2) below does not apply if, at the conclusion of the evidence for the prosecution, his legal representative informs the court that the accused will give evidence or, where he is unrepresented, the court ascertains from him that he will give evidence.

(2) Where this subsection applies, the court shall, at the conclusion of the evidence for the prosecution, satisfy itself (in the case of proceedings on indictment with a jury, in the presence of the jury) that the accused is aware that the stage has been reached at which evidence can be given for the defence and that he can, if he wishes, give evidence and that, if he chooses not to give evidence, or having been sworn, without good cause refuses to answer any question, it will be permissible for the court or jury to draw such inferences as appear proper from his failure to give evidence or his refusal, without good cause, to answer any question.

(3) Where this subsection applies, the court or jury, in determining whether the accused is guilty of the offence charged, may draw such inferences as appear proper from the failure of the accused to give evidence or his refusal, without good cause, to answer any question.

(4) This section does not render the accused compellable to give evidence on his own behalf, and he shall accordingly not be guilty of contempt of court by reason of a failure to do so.

(5) For the purposes of this section a person who, having been sworn, refuses to answer any question shall be taken to do so without good cause unless—

(a) he is entitled to refuse to answer the question by virtue of any enactment, whenever passed or made, or on the ground of privilege; or

(b) the court in the exercise of its general discretion excuses him from answering it.

(6) [repealed]

In R v Friend [1997] 1 WLR 1433 (in considering s. 35(1)(b) of the Act), the accused was aged 15 with a mental age of nine and an IQ of 63. It was held that the accused's mental condition did not make it 'undesirable' for him to give evidence and it was right that inferences be drawn under s. 35(3).

As with s. 34, in relation to s. 35 the accused cannot be convicted solely on an inference drawn from a failure or refusal (s. 38(3)).

It must be made clear to the accused that when the prosecution case has finished he/she may give evidence if he/she so wishes. The court must inform the accused that if he/she fails to give evidence or, being sworn, refuses to answer any question without good cause, then the jury may infer such inferences that appear proper from such a failure to give evidence or a refusal to answer any question. In *R* v *Gough* [2001] EWCA Crim 2545, it was held that it is mandatory for the court to inform the accused of his/her right to give or not to give evidence even where the accused has absconded.

In *Murray* v *United Kingdom* (1996) 22 EHRR 29 it was held that it would be incompatible with the rights of an accused to base a conviction 'solely or mainly' on their silence, or on their refusal to answer questions or give evidence in person. The Court of Appeal also held that in cases involving directions under s. 34, the burden of proof remained on the Crown despite the fact that the accused chose to make no comment (*R* v *Gowland-Wynn* [2001] EWCA Crim 2715).

2.10.2.7

(d) Juveniles and persons who are mentally disordered or otherwise mentally vulnerable

10.11A The information required in *paragraph 10.11* must not be given to a suspect who is a juvenile or who is mentally disordered or otherwise mentally vulnerable unless the appropriate adult is present.

10.12 If a juvenile or a person who is mentally disordered or otherwise mentally vulnerable is cautioned in the absence of the appropriate adult, the caution must be repeated in the adult's presence.

10.12A *Paragraph 1.5A* extends the requirements in *paragraphs 10.11A* and *10.12* to 17-year-old detainees.

(e) Documentation

10.13 A record shall be made when a caution is given under this section, either in the interviewer's pocket book or in the interview record.

2.10.3

11 Interviews—General

(a) Action

11.1A An interview is the questioning of a person regarding their involvement or suspected involvement in a criminal offence or offences which, under *paragraph 10.1*, must be carried out under caution. Before a person is interviewed, they and, if they are represented, their solicitor must be given sufficient information to enable them to understand the nature of any such offence, and why they are suspected of committing it (see *paragraphs 3.4(a)* and *10.3*), in order to allow for the effective exercise of the rights of the defence. However, whilst the information must always be sufficient for the person to understand the nature of any offence, this does not require the disclosure of details at a time which might prejudice the criminal investigation. The decision about what needs to be disclosed for the purpose of this requirement therefore rests with the investigating officer who has sufficient knowledge of the case to make that decision. The officer who discloses the information shall make a record of the information disclosed and when it was disclosed. This record may be made in the interview record, in the officer's pocket book or other form provided for this purpose. Procedures under the Road Traffic Act 1988, s. 7 or the Transport and Works Act 1992, s. 31 do not constitute interviewing for the purpose of this Code.

11.1   Following a decision to arrest a suspect, they must not be interviewed about the relevant offence except at a police station or other authorised place of detention, unless the consequent delay would be likely to:

(a) lead to:
- interference with, or harm to, evidence connected with an offence;
- interference with, or physical harm to, other people; or
- serious loss of, or damage to, property;

(b) lead to alerting other people suspected of committing an offence but not yet arrested for it; or

(c) hinder the recovery of property obtained in consequence of the commission of an offence.

Interviewing in any of these circumstances shall cease once the relevant risk has been averted or the necessary questions have been put in order to attempt to avert that risk.

11.2   Immediately prior to the commencement or re-commencement of any interview at a police station or other authorised place of detention, the interviewer should remind the suspect of their entitlement to free legal advice and that the interview can be delayed for legal advice to be obtained, unless one of the exceptions in *paragraph 6.6* applies. It is the interviewer's responsibility to make sure all reminders are recorded in the interview record.

11.3   *Not used.*

11.4   At the beginning of an interview the interviewer, after cautioning the suspect, see *section 10*, shall put to them any significant statement or silence which occurred in the presence and hearing of a police officer or other police staff before the start of the interview and which have not been put to the suspect in the course of a previous interview. The interviewer shall ask the suspect whether they confirm or deny that earlier statement or silence and if they want to add anything.

11.4A   A significant statement is one which appears capable of being used in evidence against the suspect, in particular a direct admission of guilt. A significant silence is a failure or refusal to answer a question or answer satisfactorily when under caution, which might, allowing for the restriction on drawing adverse inferences from silence, see *Annex C*, give rise to an inference under the Criminal Justice and Public Order Act 1994, Part III.

11.5   No interviewer may try to obtain answers or elicit a statement by the use of oppression. Except as in *paragraph 10.9*, no interviewer shall indicate, except to answer a direct question, what action will be taken by the police if the person being questioned answers questions, makes a statement or refuses to do either. If the person asks directly what action will be taken if they answer questions, make a statement or refuse to do either, the interviewer may inform them what action the police propose to take provided that action is itself proper and warranted.

11.6   The interview or further interview of a person about an offence with which that person has not been charged or for which they have not been informed they may be prosecuted, must cease when:

(a) the officer in charge of the investigation is satisfied all the questions they consider relevant to obtaining accurate and reliable information about the offence have been put to the suspect, this includes allowing the suspect an opportunity to give an innocent explanation and asking questions to test if the explanation is accurate and reliable, e.g. to clear up ambiguities or clarify what the suspect said;

(b) the officer in charge of the investigation has taken account of any other available evidence; and

(c) the officer in charge of the investigation, or in the case of a detained suspect, the custody officer, *see paragraph 16.1*, reasonably believes there is sufficient evidence to provide a realistic prospect of conviction for that offence. This paragraph does not prevent officers in revenue cases or acting under the confiscation provisions of the Criminal Justice Act 1988 or the Drug Trafficking Act 1994 from inviting suspects to complete a formal question and answer record after the interview is concluded.

KEYNOTE

Code C, para. 11.1 deals with when an interview should be held. By itself this might suggest that an interview is not needed when there is other strong evidence. However, the Criminal Procedure and Investigations Act 1996 Code of Practice, para. 3.4 states: 'In conducting an investigation, the investigator should pursue all reasonable lines of enquiry, whether these point towards or away from the suspect. What is reasonable will depend on the particular circumstances.' Interviewers should keep this in mind when deciding what questions to ask in an interview. Although juveniles, 17-year-olds or people who are mentally disordered or otherwise mentally vulnerable are often capable of providing reliable evidence, they may, without knowing or wishing to do so, be particularly prone in certain circumstances to provide information that may be unreliable, misleading or self-incriminating. Special care should always be taken when questioning such a person, and the appropriate adult should be involved if there is any doubt about a person's age, mental state or capacity. Because of the risk of unreliable evidence it is also important to obtain corroboration of any facts admitted whenever possible.

Significant Statement/Silence

At the start of the interview the investigating officer should put to the suspect any significant statement or silence which occurred before his/her arrival at the police station.

Significant statements/silence described in paras 11.4 and 11.4A will always be relevant to the offence and must be recorded. When a suspect agrees to read records of interviews and other comments and sign them as correct, he/she should be asked to endorse the record with, for example, 'I agree that this is a correct record of what was said' and add his/her signature. If the suspect does not agree with the record, the interviewer should record the details of any disagreement and ask the suspect to read these details and sign them to the effect that they accurately reflect his/her disagreement. Any refusal to sign should be recorded. Even where, as required by para. 11.4, at the beginning of an interview the interviewer puts to the detainee any significant statement or silence which occurred in the presence and hearing of a police officer or other police staff, this does not prevent the interviewer from putting significant statements and silences to a suspect again at a later stage or a further interview as the interviewer may wish to go through any significant statement or silence again if during earlier interviews adverse inferences could not be drawn.

This aspect of the interview is very important in terms of establishing whether the facts are disputed. If they are not disputed at this stage, it is unlikely that they will be challenged at any later court hearing and, if challenged, the defence will have to explain why this was not done at the time of the interview.

The courts may view a failure to put the statement to the suspect in a sinister light. In *R v Allen* [2001] EWCA Crim 1607, the court was concerned that the police failed to put the admission to the suspect in interview, despite thorough questioning, which it felt clearly placed a question mark over the admission's reliability.

If the suspect remains silent in relation to a 'significant silence', that silence may give rise to an adverse inference being drawn under s. 34 of the Criminal Justice and Public Order Act 1994 if the person raises it in his/her defence at court (as this is a very important issue, it may be necessary to delay the interview until the arrest notes are completed or the officers witnessing the offence/arrest have been consulted to ensure that all matters are put to the suspect at this stage.) Consideration should be given to putting questions to a suspect who makes no comment, or even where the legal representative has stated that the suspect will make no comment, as this may allow the court to draw inferences against a defence that the suspect raises at court.

(b) Interview records

11.7

    (a) An accurate record must be made of each interview, whether or not the interview takes place at a police station.

    (b) The record must state the place of interview, the time it begins and ends, any interview breaks and, subject to *paragraph 2.6A*, the names of all those present; and must be made on the forms provided for this purpose or in the interviewer's pocket book or in accordance with Codes of Practice E or F.

(c) Any written record must be made and completed during the interview, unless this would not be practicable or would interfere with the conduct of the interview, and must constitute either a verbatim record of what has been said or, failing this, an account of the interview which adequately and accurately summarises it.

11.8 If a written record is not made during the interview it must be made as soon as practicable after its completion.

11.9 Written interview records must be timed and signed by the maker.

11.10 If a written record is not completed during the interview the reason must be recorded in the interview record.

11.11 Unless it is impracticable, the person interviewed shall be given the opportunity to read the interview record and to sign it as correct or to indicate how they consider it inaccurate. If the person interviewed cannot read or refuses to read the record or sign it, the senior interviewer present shall read it to them and ask whether they would like to sign it as correct or make their mark or to indicate how they consider it inaccurate. The interviewer shall certify on the interview record itself what has occurred.

11.12 If the appropriate adult or the person's solicitor is present during the interview, they should also be given an opportunity to read and sign the interview record or any written statement taken down during the interview.

Note: *Paragraph 1.5A* extends the requirement in this paragraph to interviews of 17-year-old suspects.

11.13 A written record shall be made of any comments made by a suspect, including unsolicited comments, which are outside the context of an interview but which might be relevant to the offence. Any such record must be timed and signed by the maker. When practicable the suspect shall be given the opportunity to read that record and to sign it as correct or to indicate how they consider it inaccurate.

11.14 Any refusal by a person to sign an interview record when asked in accordance with this Code must itself be recorded.

(c) Juveniles and mentally disordered or otherwise mentally vulnerable people

11.15 A juvenile or person who is mentally disordered or otherwise mentally vulnerable must not be interviewed regarding their involvement or suspected involvement in a criminal offence or offences, or asked to provide or sign a written statement under caution or record of interview, in the absence of the appropriate adult unless *paragraphs 11.1, 11.18 to 11.20* apply.

Note: *Paragraph 1.5A* extends the requirement in this paragraph to 17-year-old suspects.

11.16 Juveniles may only be interviewed at their place of education in exceptional circumstances and only when the principal or their nominee agrees. Every effort should be made to notify the parent(s) or other person responsible for the juvenile's welfare and the appropriate adult, if this is a different person, that the police want to interview the juvenile and reasonable time should be allowed to enable the appropriate adult to be present at the interview. If awaiting the appropriate adult would cause unreasonable delay, and unless the juvenile is suspected of an offence against the educational establishment, the principal or their nominee can act as the appropriate adult for the purposes of the interview.

Note: *Paragraph 1.5A* extends the requirement in this paragraph to 17-year-old suspects.

11.17 If an appropriate adult is present at an interview, they shall be informed:
- that they are not expected to act simply as an observer; and
- that the purpose of their presence is to:
  - ~ advise the person being interviewed;
  - ~ observe whether the interview is being conducted properly and fairly; and
  - ~ facilitate communication with the person being interviewed.

(d) Vulnerable suspects—urgent interviews at police stations

11.18 The following interviews may take place only if an officer of superintendent rank or above considers delaying the interview will lead to the consequences in *paragraph 11.1(a)* to *(c)*, and is satisfied the interview would not significantly harm the person's physical or mental state (see *Annex G*):

(a) an interview of a juvenile or person who is mentally disordered or otherwise mentally vulnerable without the appropriate adult being present;

Note: *Paragraph 1.5A* extends this requirement to 17-year-old detainees.

(b) an interview of anyone other than in (a) who appears unable to:
- appreciate the significance of questions and their answers; or
- understand what is happening because of the effects of drink, drugs or any illness, ailment or condition;

(c) an interview, without an interpreter being present, of a person whom the custody officer has determined requires an interpreter (see *paragraphs 3.5(c)(ii)* and *3.12*) which is carried out by an interviewer speaking the suspect's own language or (as the case may be) otherwise establishing effective communication which is sufficient to enable the necessary questions to be asked and answered in order to avert the consequences. See *paragraphs 13.2* and *13.5*.

11.19 These interviews may not continue once sufficient information has been obtained to avert the consequences in *paragraph 11.1(a)* to *(c)*.

11.20 A record shall be made of the grounds for any decision to interview a person under *paragraph 11.18*.

2.10.3.3

KEYNOTE

Whether an interaction between a police officer and a member of the public is defined as an interview by the court can be crucial as to whether it will be admissible in evidence. It is therefore essential to understand the definition of an interview for the purposes of the Police and Criminal Evidence Act 1984 and when a caution must be given and which caution must be given.

If a person is asked questions for reasons *other than obtaining evidence about his/her involvement or suspected involvement in an offence*, this is not an interview (and a caution need not be given). This point is confirmed in the case of *R* v *McGuinness* [1999] Crim LR 318, where the court confirmed that it was only when a person was suspected of an offence that the caution must be administered before questioning. Consequently, in *R* v *Miller* [1998] Crim LR 209 the court held that asking a person the single question, 'Are these ecstasy tablets?' criminally implicated the person and therefore the conversation was an interview (i.e. it would not be necessary to ask such a question if there were no suspicion that the tablets were a controlled substance).

Guidance on when questions do not amount to an interview is given by Code C, para. 10.1.

This is not an exhaustive list, and officers may have other valid reasons to speak to a person before it becomes an interview.

Before a person can be interviewed about his/her involvement in an offence, that person must be cautioned. So it might be said that an interview is any questioning of a person after such time as a caution has been or should have been administered. Where a person is arrested for an offence, he/she must also be cautioned, as any questioning will amount to an interview.

The requirement in para. 11.1A for a suspect to be given sufficient information about the offence applies prior to the interview and whether or not they are legally represented. What is sufficient will depend on the circumstances of the case, but it should normally include, as a minimum, a description of the facts relating to the suspected offence that are known to the officer, including the time and place in question. This aims to avoid suspects being confused or unclear about what they are supposed to have done and to help an innocent suspect to clear the matter up more quickly.

If a person has not been arrested then he/she can be interviewed almost anywhere (but an officer intending to interview a person on private property must consider whether he/she is trespassing). If the interview with a person not under arrest takes place in a police station, Code C, para. 3.21 applies. Juveniles should not be arrested at their place of education unless this is unavoidable. When a juvenile is arrested at his/her place of education, the principal or his/her nominee must be informed; this also applies to 17-year-olds.

Paragraph 11.18(c) is worthy of note; this requires urgent interviews authorised by a superintendent under para. 11.18 which would have had an interpreter to be carried out by an interviewer who can speak the suspect's own language or in some other way establish effective communication to allow the questions to be asked and answered.

2.10.3.4

KEYNOTE

Statements from Suspects

Statements made by an accused under caution to the police, whether in writing or verbally are confidential in the sense that they may be used against the suspect in proceedings, not that they could be used for any purpose of the police. It is clearly implicit in the relationship between the police and the accused that the information, before being used in open court, is used only for the purposes for which it is provided and not for extraneous purposes, such as the media. However, the obligation of confidentiality (which is now included in the Police Standards of Professional Behaviour) in respect of such a statement will be brought to an end where the contents of the statement are already in the public domain (*Bunn* v *British Broadcasting Corporation* [1998] 3 All ER 552).

2.10.4

12 Interviews in Police Stations

(a) Action

12.1 If a police officer wants to interview or conduct enquiries which require the presence of a detainee, the custody officer is responsible for deciding whether to deliver the detainee into the officer's custody. An investigating officer who is given custody of a detainee takes over responsibility for the detainee's care and safe custody for the purposes of this Code until they return the detainee to the custody officer when they must report the manner in which they complied with the Code whilst having custody of the detainee.

12.2 Except as below, in any period of 24 hours a detainee must be allowed a continuous period of at least 8 hours for rest, free from questioning, travel or any interruption in connection with the investigation concerned. This period should normally be at night or other appropriate time which takes account of when the detainee last slept or rested. If a detainee is arrested at a police station after going there voluntarily, the period of 24 hours runs from the time of their arrest and not the time of arrival at the police station. The period may not be interrupted or delayed, except:

  (a) when there are reasonable grounds for believing not delaying or interrupting the period would:

    (i) involve a risk of harm to people or serious loss of, or damage to, property;

    (ii) delay unnecessarily the person's release from custody; or

    (iii) otherwise prejudice the outcome of the investigation;

  (b) at the request of the detainee, their appropriate adult or legal representative;

  (c) when a delay or interruption is necessary in order to:

    (i) comply with the legal obligations and duties arising under *section 15*; or

    (ii) to take action required under *section 9* or in accordance with medical advice.

If the period is interrupted in accordance with (a), a fresh period must be allowed. Interruptions under (b) and (c) do not require a fresh period to be allowed.

12.3 Before a detainee is interviewed the custody officer, in consultation with the officer in charge of the investigation and appropriate healthcare professionals as necessary, shall assess whether the detainee is fit enough to be interviewed. This means determining and considering the risks to the detainee's physical and mental state if the interview took place and determining what safeguards are needed to allow the interview to take place. See *Annex G.* The custody officer shall not allow a detainee to be interviewed if the custody officer considers it would cause significant harm to the detainee's physical or mental state. Vulnerable suspects listed at *paragraph 11.18* shall be treated as always being at some risk during an interview and these persons may not be interviewed except in accordance with *paragraphs 11.18* to *11.20.*

12.4 As far as practicable interviews shall take place in interview rooms which are adequately heated, lit and ventilated.

12.5 A suspect whose detention without charge has been authorised under PACE because the detention is necessary for an interview to obtain evidence of the offence for which they have been arrested may choose not to answer questions but police do not require the suspect's consent or agreement to interview them for this purpose. If a suspect takes steps to prevent themselves being questioned or further questioned, e.g. by refusing to leave their cell to go to a suitable interview room or by trying to leave the interview room, they shall be advised their consent or agreement to interview is not required. The suspect shall be cautioned as in *section 10,* and informed if they fail or refuse to co-operate, the interview may take place in the cell and that their failure or refusal to co-operate may be given in evidence. The suspect shall then be invited to co-operate and go into the interview room.

12.6 People being questioned or making statements shall not be required to stand.

12.7 Before the interview commences each interviewer shall, subject to *paragraph 2.6A,* identify themselves and any other persons present to the interviewee.

12.8 Breaks from interviewing should be made at recognised meal times or at other times that take account of when an interviewee last had a meal. Short refreshment breaks shall be provided at approximately two hour intervals, subject to the interviewer's discretion to delay a break if there are reasonable grounds for believing it would:

(i) involve a:
  - risk of harm to people;
  - serious loss of, or damage to, property;

(ii) unnecessarily delay the detainee's release; or

(iii) otherwise prejudice the outcome of the investigation.

12.9 If during the interview a complaint is made by or on behalf of the interviewee concerning the provisions of any of the Codes, or it comes to the interviewer's notice that the interviewee may have been treated improperly, the interviewer should:

(i) record the matter in the interview record; and

(ii) inform the custody officer, who is then responsible for dealing with it as in *section 9.*

(b) Documentation

12.10 A record must be made of the:
  - time a detainee is not in the custody of the custody officer, and why
  - reason for any refusal to deliver the detainee out of that custody.

12.11 A record shall be made of:

(a) the reasons it was not practicable to use an interview room; and

(b) any action taken as in *paragraph 12.5.*

The record shall be made on the custody record or in the interview record for action taken whilst an interview record is being kept, with a brief reference to this effect in the custody record.

12.12 Any decision to delay a break in an interview must be recorded, with reasons, in the interview record.

12.13 All written statements made at police stations under caution shall be written on forms provided for the purpose.

12.14 All written statements made under caution shall be taken in accordance with *Annex D*. Before a person makes a written statement under caution at a police station, they shall be reminded about the right to legal advice.

2.10.4.1

KEYNOTE

When deciding whether to hand over a detained person to the interviewing officer under para. 12.1 the custody officer should be mindful of whether there is sufficient relevant time remaining for the detained person to be interviewed (see Code C, para. 15).

Statements under caution, particularly of a detained person, are less common than interviews. If a person has been interviewed and it has been audio or visually recorded or an interview has been recorded contemporaneously in writing, statements under caution should normally be taken in these circumstances only at the person's express wish. See Code C, Annex C for restrictions on drawing inferences and Annex D for the variable declarations the person must include in his/her statements.

Meal breaks should normally last at least 45 minutes and shorter breaks after two hours should last at least 15 minutes. If the interviewer prolongs the interview to avoid the risk of harm to people, serious loss of, or damage to, property, to delay the detainee's release or otherwise prejudice the outcome of the investigation, a longer break should be provided. If there is a short interview, and another short interview is contemplated, the length of the break may be reduced if there are reasonable grounds to believe that this is necessary to avoid any of the consequences in para. 12.8(i)–(iii).

2.10.4.2

KEYNOTE

Solicitors and Legal Advice

Code C, section 6 provides guidance with regard to legal advice and access to solicitors during interview. Where a solicitor is available at the time the interview begins or while it is in progress, the solicitor must be allowed to be present while the person is interviewed (Code C, para. 6.8).

If the investigating officer considers that a solicitor is acting in such a way that he/she is unable properly to put questions to the suspect, he/she will stop the interview and consult an officer not below the rank of superintendent, if one is readily available, otherwise an officer not below the rank of inspector who is not connected with the investigation, to decide whether that solicitor should be excluded from the interview. The interview may also have to be stopped in order to allow another solicitor to be instructed (Code C, para. 6.10).

If a request for legal advice is made during an interview, the interviewing officer must stop the interview immediately and arrange for legal advice to be provided. If the suspect changes his/her mind again, the interview can continue provided Code C, para. 6.6 is complied with.

2.10.4.3

KEYNOTE

What should be Disclosed to the Solicitor?

It is important not to confuse the duty of disclosure to a person once charged with the need to disclose evidence to suspects before interviewing them. After a person has been charged, and before trial, the rules of disclosure are clear (see chapter 2.7) and almost all material must be disclosed to the defence.

However, this is not necessarily the case at the interview stage of the investigation. There is no specific provision within the Police and Criminal Evidence Act 1984 or the Codes of Practice for the disclosure of any information by the police at the police station, *with the exception of the custody record* and, generally in identification procedures, the initial description given by the witnesses. In respect of the provision of a copy of the 'first description' of a suspect it should be noted that Code D (para. 3.1) states that a copy of the 'first description' shall, where practicable, be given to the suspect or his/her solicitor before any procedures under paras 3.5 to 3.10, 3.21 or 3.23 are carried out. In other words, the disclosure requirement is that a copy of the 'first description' shall, where practicable, be given to the suspect or his/her solicitor before a video identification, an identification parade, a group identification or confrontation takes place. Therefore, an officer disclosing information to a solicitor at the interview stage (which is taking place in advance of any identification procedures) need not provide the 'first description' of a suspect at that time.

Further, there is nothing within the Criminal Justice and Public Order Act 1994 that states that information must be disclosed before an inference from silence can be made. Indeed, in *R* v *Imran* [1997] Crim LR 754, the court held that it is totally wrong to submit that a defendant should be prevented from lying by being presented with the whole of the evidence against him/her prior to the interview.

In *R* v *Argent* [1997] Crim LR 346, the court dismissed the argument that an inference could not be drawn under s. 34 of the Criminal Justice and Public Order Act 1994 because there had not been full disclosure at the interview. However, the court did recognise that it may be a factor to take into for the jury to decide whether the failure to answer questions was reasonable.

In *R* v *Roble* [1997] Crim LR 449, the court suggested that an inference would not be drawn where a solicitor gave advice to remain silent where, for example, the interviewing officer had disclosed too little of the case for the solicitor usefully to advise his/her client, or where the nature of the offence, or the material in the hands of the police, was so complex or related to matters so long ago that no sensible immediate response was feasible.

It was not uncommon in the past for solicitors to advise on no comment interviews and this has been relied on by defendants to avoid adverse inferences being drawn from their silence. The courts and legal advisers are now very aware of the consequences of advising a suspect to offer no comment. In *R* v *Morgan* [2001] EWCA Crim 445, the Court of Appeal stated that a court was entitled to assume that a solicitor would advise his/her client about the adverse inferences rule. In *R* v *Ali* [2001] EWCA Crim 683, the court stated that the question was not whether the advice to remain silent was good advice but whether it provided an adequate reason for failing to answer questions.

In *R* v *Hoare* [2004] EWCA Crim 784, the Court of Appeal held that the purpose of s. 34 was to qualify a defendant's right to silence, rather than to exclude a jury from drawing an adverse inference against a defendant merely because he/she had been advised by his/her solicitor to remain silent, whether or not he/she genuinely or reasonably relied on that advice. Where a defendant had an explanation to give that was consistent with his/her innocence it was not 'reasonable', within the meaning of s. 34(1), for him/her to fail to give that explanation in interview even where he/she had been advised by his/her solicitor to remain silent. Legal advice by itself could not preclude the drawing of an adverse inference.

There is a balance to be struck between providing the solicitor with enough information to understand the nature of the case against his/her client and keeping back material which, if disclosed, may allow the suspect the opportunity to avoid implicating him/herself. For instance in *R* v *Thirlwell* [2002] EWCA Crim 286, the Court of Appeal agreed that the solicitor had not been entitled to provisional medical evidence as to possible causes of death in a murder case.

Useful guidance is provided in the ACPO National Policing Position Statement: Pre-Interview Briefings With Legal Advisers and Information to be Supplied to Unrepresented Detainees; this can be found at <http://library.college.police.uk/docs/APPREF/National-Policing-Position-Statement-Pre-Interview-Briefings-2014.pdf>.

Annex C—Restriction on Drawing Adverse Inferences from Silence and Terms of the Caution when the Restriction Applies

(a) The restriction on drawing adverse inferences from silence

1. The Criminal Justice and Public Order Act 1994, sections 34, 36 and 37 as amended by the Youth Justice and Criminal Evidence Act 1999, section 58 describe the conditions under which adverse inferences may be drawn from a person's failure or refusal to say anything about their involvement in the offence when interviewed, after being charged or informed they may be prosecuted. These provisions are subject to an overriding restriction on the ability of a court or jury to draw adverse inferences from a person's silence. This restriction applies:

   (a) to any detainee at a police station, who, before being interviewed, see *section 11* or being charged or informed they may be prosecuted, see *section 16*, has:

     (i) asked for legal advice, see *section 6, paragraph 6.1*;

     (ii) not been allowed an opportunity to consult a solicitor, including the duty solicitor, as in this Code; and

     (iii) not changed their mind about wanting legal advice, see *section 6, paragraph 6.6(d)*. Note the condition in (ii) will:

     ~ apply when a detainee who has asked for legal advice is interviewed before speaking to a solicitor as in *section 6, paragraph 6.6(a)* or *(b)*;

     ~ not apply if the detained person declines to ask for the duty solicitor, see *section 6, paragraphs 6.6(c)* and *(d)*.

   (b) to any person charged with, or informed they may be prosecuted for, an offence who:

     (i) has had brought to their notice a written statement made by another person or the content of an interview with another person which relates to that offence, see *section 16, paragraph 16.4*;

     (ii) is interviewed about that offence, see *section 16, paragraph 16.5*; or

     (iii) makes a written statement about that offence, see *Annex D, paragraphs 4* and *9*.

(b) Terms of the caution when the restriction applies

2. When a requirement to caution arises at a time when the restriction on drawing adverse inferences from silence applies, the caution shall be:

   '*You do not have to say anything, but anything you do say may be given in evidence.*'

   Where the use of the Welsh Language is appropriate, the caution may be used directly in Welsh in the following terms:

   '*Does dim rhaid i chi ddweud dim byd, ond gall unrhyw beth yr ydych chi'n ei ddweud gael ei roi fel tystiolaeth.*'

3. Whenever the restriction either begins to apply or ceases to apply after a caution has already been given, the person shall be re-cautioned in the appropriate terms. The changed position on drawing inferences and that the previous caution no longer applies shall also be explained to the detainee in ordinary language.

2.10.5.1

KEYNOTE

The restriction on drawing inferences from silence does not apply to a person who has not been detained and who therefore cannot be prevented from seeking legal advice if he/she wants to (see Code C, paras 10.2 and 3.15).

The following is suggested as a framework to help explain changes in the position on drawing adverse inferences if the restriction on drawing adverse inferences from silence applies. Annex C, para. 2 sets out the alternative terms of the caution to be used when the restriction on drawing adverse inferences from silence applies. The situation is likely to occur during a detainee's detention where it will be necessary to administer both of these cautions at various times during his/her detention. As there is a significant difference between them in relation to the right to silence, it will be important to make it clear which caution applies to the detainee during any interview or charge procedure. Guidance as to what the detainee should be told is provided by Code C, Annex C, Note C2; this paragraph gives sample explanations that need to be explained to the detainee before the change in caution is given.

Full caution already given (in most cases given when arrested)	→ Detainee's access to legal advice restricted as per Code C, Annex C, para. 1. Need to give alternative caution.	→ Explain change in caution as set out at Code C, Annex C, Note C2(a)(i).	→ Give caution as set out at Annex C, para. 2.
Full caution already given	→ Detainee has been charged but is further interviewed (Code C, Annex C, para. 1). Need to give alternative caution.	→ Explain change in caution as set out at Code C, Annex C, Note C2(a)(ii).	→ Give caution as set out at Annex C, para. 2.
Caution as set out at Annex C, para. 2, given	→ Detainee has now had access to a solicitor or changed his/her mind. Need to give alternative caution.	→ Explain change in caution as set out at Code C, Annex C, Note C2(b).	→ Give caution as set out at Code C, para. 10.5.

Where Code C, Annex C, para. 1 applies (i.e. the detainee has not been given access to a solicitor) and the detainee is charged with an offence or informed that he/she may be prosecuted, the caution at Annex C, para. 2 should be used; on all other occasions the caution at Code C, para. 16.2 should be used.

When the circumstances of the detained person change and restrictions on drawing adverse inferences now apply, the following form of words, where applicable, can be used:

The caution you were previously given no longer applies. This is because after that caution:
(i) you asked to speak to a solicitor but have not yet been allowed an opportunity to speak to a solicitor; or
(ii) you have been charged with/informed you may be prosecuted.

See para. 1(b).
Followed by:

This means that from now on, adverse inferences cannot be drawn at court and your defence will not be harmed just because you choose to say nothing. Please listen carefully to the caution I am about to give you because it will apply from now on. You will see that it does not say anything about your defence being harmed.

The following form of words should be used where the circumstances set out in Annex C, para. 1(a) that a restriction on drawing adverse inferences ceases to apply before or at the time the person is charged or informed that he/she may be prosecuted apply:

The caution you were previously given no longer applies. This is because after that caution you have been allowed an opportunity to speak to a solicitor. Please listen carefully to the caution I am about to give you because it will apply from now on. It explains how your defence at court may be affected if you choose to say nothing.

2.10.6 Annex D—Written Statements under Caution

(a) Written by a person under caution

1. A person shall always be invited to write down what they want to say.
2. A person who has not been charged with, or informed they may be prosecuted for, any offence to which the statement they want to write relates, shall:

(a) unless the statement is made at a time when the restriction on drawing adverse inferences from silence applies, see *Annex C*, be asked to write out and sign the following before writing what they want to say:

'*I make this statement of my own free will. I understand that I do not have to say anything but that it may harm my defence if I do not mention when questioned something which I later rely on in court. This statement may be given in evidence.*';

(b) if the statement is made at a time when the restriction on drawing adverse inferences from silence applies, be asked to write out and sign the following before writing what they want to say;

'*I make this statement of my own free will. I understand that I do not have to say anything. This statement may be given in evidence.*'

3. When a person, on the occasion of being charged with or informed they may be prosecuted for any offence, asks to make a statement which relates to any such offence and wants to write it they shall:

(a) unless the restriction on drawing adverse inferences from silence, see *Annex C*, applied when they were so charged or informed they may be prosecuted, be asked to write out and sign the following before writing what they want to say:

'*I make this statement of my own free will. I understand that I do not have to say anything but that it may harm my defence if I do not mention when questioned something which I later rely on in court. This statement may be given in evidence.*';

(b) if the restriction on drawing adverse inferences from silence applied when they were so charged or informed they may be prosecuted, be asked to write out and sign the following before writing what they want to say:

'*I make this statement of my own free will. I understand that I do not have to say anything. This statement may be given in evidence.*'

4. When a person who has already been charged with or informed they may be prosecuted for any offence asks to make a statement which relates to any such offence and wants to write it, they shall be asked to write out and sign the following before writing what they want to say:

'*I make this statement of my own free will. I understand that I do not have to say anything. This statement may be given in evidence.*';

5. Any person writing their own statement shall be allowed to do so without any prompting except a police officer or other police staff may indicate to them which matters are material or question any ambiguity in the statement.

(b) Written by a police officer or other police staff

6. If a person says they would like someone to write the statement for them, a police officer, or other police staff shall write the statement.

7. If the person has not been charged with, or informed they may be prosecuted for, any offence to which the statement they want to make relates they shall, before starting, be asked to sign, or make their mark, to the following:

(a) unless the statement is made at a time when the restriction on drawing adverse inferences from silence applies, see *Annex C*:

'*I, ..., wish to make a statement. I want someone to write down what I say. I understand that I do not have to say anything but that it may harm my defence if I do not mention when questioned something which I later rely on in court. This statement may be given in evidence.'*;

(b) if the statement is made at a time when the restriction on drawing adverse inferences from silence applies:

'I, ..., wish to make a statement. I want someone to write down what I say. I understand that I do not have to say anything. This statement may be given in evidence.'

8. If, on the occasion of being charged with or informed they may be prosecuted for any offence, the person asks to make a statement which relates to any such offence they shall before starting be asked to sign, or make their mark to, the following:

(a) unless the restriction on drawing adverse inferences from silence applied, see *Annex C*, when they were so charged or informed they may be prosecuted:

'I, ..., wish to make a statement. I want someone to write down what I say. I understand that I do not have to say anything but that it may harm my defence if I do not mention when questioned something which I later rely on in court. This statement may be given in evidence.';

(b) if the restriction on drawing adverse inferences from silence applied when they were so charged or informed they may be prosecuted:

'I, ..., wish to make a statement. I want someone to write down what I say. I understand that I do not have to say anything. This statement may be given in evidence.'

9. If, having already been charged with or informed they may be prosecuted for any offence, a person asks to make a statement which relates to any such offence they shall before starting, be asked to sign, or make their mark to:

'I, ..., wish to make a statement. I want someone to write down what I say. I understand that I do not have to say anything. This statement may be given in evidence.'

10. The person writing the statement must take down the exact words spoken by the person making it and must not edit or paraphrase it. Any questions that are necessary, e.g. to make it more intelligible, and the answers given must be recorded at the same time on the statement form.

11. When the writing of a statement is finished the person making it shall be asked to read it and to make any corrections, alterations or additions they want. When they have finished reading they shall be asked to write and sign or make their mark on the following certificate at the end of the statement:

'I have read the above statement, and I have been able to correct, alter or add anything I wish. This statement is true. I have made it of my own free will.'

12. If the person making the statement cannot read, or refuses to read it, or to write the above mentioned certificate at the end of it or to sign it, the person taking the statement shall read it to them and ask them if they would like to correct, alter or add anything and to put their signature or make their mark at the end. The person taking the statement shall certify on the statement itself what has occurred.

2.10.6.1 **KEYNOTE**

The sections of Code C above need to be read in conjunction with Code E where the interview of a suspect is to be audio recorded.

2.10.7 PACE Code of Practice on Audio Recording Interviews with Suspects (Code E)

This Code applies to interviews carried out after 00.00 on 27 October 2013 notwithstanding that the interview may have commenced before that time.

1 General

1.0 The procedures in this Code must be used fairly, responsibly, with respect for the people to whom they apply and without unlawful discrimination. Under the Equality Act 2010, section 149, when police officers are carrying out their functions, they also have a duty to have due regard to the need to eliminate unlawful discrimination, harassment and victimisation, to advance equality of opportunity between people who share a relevant protected characteristic and people who do not share it, and to take steps to foster good relations between those persons.

1.1 This Code of Practice must be readily available for consultation by:
- police officers
- police staff
- detained persons
- members of the public.

1.2 The *Notes for Guidance* included are not provisions of this Code.

1.3 Nothing in this Code shall detract from the requirements of Code C, the Code of Practice for the detention, treatment and questioning of persons by police officers.

1.4 The interviews to which this Code applies are described in *section 3*.

1.5 The term:
- 'appropriate adult' has the same meaning as in Code C, *paragraph 1.7* and in the case of a 17-year-old suspect, includes the person called to fulfil that role in accordance with C *paragraph 1.5A* of Code C.
- 'solicitor' has the same meaning as in Code C, *paragraph 6.12*.
- 'interview' has the same meaning as in Code C, *paragraph 11.1A*.

1.5A Recording of interviews shall be carried out openly to instil confidence in its reliability as an impartial and accurate record of the interview.

1.6 In this Code:
- (aa) 'recording media' means any removable, physical audio recording medium (such as magnetic tape, optical disc or solid state memory) which can be played and copied;
- (a) 'designated person' means a person other than a police officer, designated under the Police Reform Act 2002, Part 4 who has specified powers and duties of police officers conferred or imposed on them;
- (b) any reference to a police officer includes a designated person acting in the exercise or performance of the powers and duties conferred or imposed on them by their designation; and
- (c) 'secure digital network' is a computer network system which enables an original interview recording to be stored as a digital multi media file or a series of such files, on a secure file server which is accredited by the National Accreditor for Police Information Systems in accordance with the UK Government Protective Marking Scheme. (See *section 7* of this Code.)

1.7 *Sections 2* to *6* of this Code set out the procedures and requirements which apply to all interviews together with the provisions which apply only to interviews recorded using removable media. *Section 7* sets out the provisions which apply to interviews recorded using a secure digital network and specifies the provisions in *sections 2* to *6* which do not apply to secure digital network recording.

1.8   Nothing in this Code prevents the custody officer, or other officer given custody of the detainee, from allowing police staff who are not designated persons to carry out individual procedures or tasks at the police station if the law allows. However, the officer remains responsible for making sure the procedures and tasks are carried out correctly in accordance with this Code. Any such police staff must be:

   (a)   a person employed by a police force and under the control and direction of the chief officer of that force; or

   (b)   employed by a person with whom a police force has a contract for the provision of services relating to persons arrested or otherwise in custody.

1.9   Designated persons and other police staff must have regard to any relevant provisions of the Codes of Practice.

1.10   References to pocket book include any official report book issued to police officers or police staff.

1.11   References to a custody officer include those performing the functions of a custody officer as in *paragraph 1.9* of Code C.

1.12   In the application of this Code to the conduct and recording of an interview of a suspect who has not been arrested:

   (a)   references to the 'custody officer' include references to an officer of the rank of sergeant or above who is not directly involved in the investigation of the offence(s);

   (b)   if the interview takes place elsewhere than at a police station, references to 'interview room' include any place or location which the interviewer is satisfied will enable the interview to be conducted and recorded in accordance with this Code and where the suspect is present voluntarily; and

   (c)   provisions in addition to those which expressly apply to these interviews shall be followed insofar as they are relevant and can be applied in practice.

2.10.7.1   **KEYNOTE**

The Codes recognise the importance that detained persons are treated in accordance with the Equality Act 2010; for these Codes relevant protected characteristic' includes: age, disability, gender reassignment, pregnancy and maternity, race, religion or belief, sex and sexual orientation.

It is important to ensure interviews are conducted at appropriate locations; an interviewer who is not sure, or has any doubt, about the suitability of a place or location of an interview to be carried out elsewhere than at a police station, should consult an officer of the rank of sergeant or above for advice.

The Code includes provisions for the conduct and recording of voluntary interviews of suspects who are not under arrest. These take account of provisions in Code G (arrest) and Code C, paras 3.21 and 3.22 which support the use of voluntary interviews to ensure that voluntary interviews are subject to Code E and distinguish them from custody cases. Paragraph 1.12(c) avoids the need to distinguish the voluntary option in detail in every paragraph in this Code. The Code provides for a sergeant to be responsible for voluntary, non-custodial cases and for giving authority not to make an audio recording similar to the arrangements in place for those in custody.

2.10.8   **2 Recording and Sealing Master Recordings**

2.1   *Not used.*

2.2   One recording, the master recording, will be sealed in the suspect's presence. A second recording will be used as a working copy. The master recording is any of the recordings made by a multi-deck/drive machine or the only recording made by a single deck/drive machine. The working copy is one of the other recordings made by a multi-deck/drive machine or a copy of the master recording made by a single deck/drive machine.

(*This paragraph does not apply to interviews recorded using a secure digital network, see paragraphs 7.4 to 7.6.*)

2.3   Nothing in this Code requires the identity of officers or police staff conducting interviews to be recorded or disclosed:

(a) *Not used.*

(b) if the interviewer reasonably believes recording or disclosing their name might put them in danger.

In these cases interviewers should use warrant or other identification numbers and the name of their police station. Such instances and the reasons for them shall be recorded in the custody record or the interviewer's pocket book.

2.10.8.1

KEYNOTE

The purpose of sealing the master recording in the suspect's presence is to show that the recording's integrity is preserved. If a single deck/drive machine is used, the working copy of the master recording must be made in the suspect's presence and without the master recording leaving his/her sight. The working copy shall be used for making further copies if needed.

The reason for the interviewer using his/her warrant number or other identification numbers and the name of his/her police station is to protect those involved in serious organised crime investigations or arrests of particularly violent suspects when there is reliable information that those arrested or their associates may threaten or cause harm to those involved. In cases of doubt, an officer of inspector rank or above should be consulted.

2.10.9

3 Interviews to be Audio Recorded

3.1   Subject to *paragraphs 3.3* and *3.4*, audio recording shall be used for any interview:

(a) with a person cautioned under Code C, *section 10* in respect of any indictable offence, which includes any offence triable either way, except where that person has been arrested and the interview takes place elsewhere than at a police station in accordance with Code C, *paragraph 11.1* for which a written record would be required.

(b) which takes place as a result of an interviewer exceptionally putting further questions to a suspect about an offence described in *paragraph 3.1(a)* after they have been charged with, or told they may be prosecuted for, that offence, see Code C, *paragraph 16.5*.

(c) when an interviewer wants to tell a person, after they have been charged with, or informed they may be prosecuted for, an offence described in *paragraph 3.1(a)*, about any written statement or interview with another person, see Code C, *paragraph 16.4*.

3.2   The Terrorism Act 2000 and the Counter-Terrorism Act 2008 make separate provisions for a Code of Practice for the video recording with sound of:

• interviews of persons detained under section 41 of, or Schedule 7 to, the 2000 Act; and

• post-charge questioning of persons authorised under section 22 or 23 of the 2008 Act.

The provisions of this Code do not apply to such interviews.

3.3   If the conditions in *paragraph 3.3A* are satisfied, authority not to audio record an interview to which *paragraph 3.1* applies may be given by:

(a) the custody officer in the case of a detained suspect, or

(b) an officer of the rank of sergeant or above in the case of a suspect who has not been arrested and to whom *paragraphs 3.21* and *3.22* of Code C (Persons attending a police station or elsewhere voluntarily) apply.

3.3A The conditions referred to in *paragraph 3.3* are:

(a) it is not reasonably practicable to audio record, or as the case may be, continue to audio record, the interview because of equipment failure or the unavailability of a suitable interview room or recording equipment; and

(b) the authorising officer considers, on reasonable grounds, that the interview or continuation of the interview should not be delayed until the failure has been rectified or until a suitable room or recording equipment becomes available.

In these cases:

- the interview must be recorded or continue to be recorded in writing in accordance with Code C, *section 11*; and
- the authorising officer shall record the specific reasons for not audio recording and the interviewer is responsible for ensuring that the written interview record shows the date and time of the authority, the authorising officer and where the authority is recorded.

3.4 If a detainee refuses to go into or remain in a suitable interview room, see Code C, *paragraph 12.5*, and the custody officer considers, on reasonable grounds, that the interview should not be delayed the interview may, at the custody officer's discretion, be conducted in a cell using portable recording equipment or, if none is available, recorded in writing as in Code C, *section 11*. The reasons for this shall be recorded.

3.5 The whole of each interview shall be audio recorded, including the taking and reading back of any statement.

3.6 A sign or indicator which is visible to the suspect must show when the recording equipment is recording.

2.10.9.1 **KEYNOTE**

The requirements of Code E do not preclude other interviews being audio recorded. Investigators may well be advised to audio record interviews concerning summary only offences as it may be more difficult for the defence to suggest that any confession was fabricated.

A decision not to audio record an interview for any reason may be the subject of comment in court. The authorising officer should be prepared to justify that decision.

If, during the course of an interview under this Code, it becomes apparent that the interview should be conducted under one of the terrorism Codes for video recording of interviews, the interview should only continue in accordance with the relevant Code.

For cases where:

- a person detained under s. 41 of the Terrorism Act 2000 is interviewed in a police station in England, Wales or Scotland; or
- any questioning by a constable of a person detained for examination under sch. 7 to the Terrorism Act 2000 takes place in a police station in England, Wales or Scotland;
- any interview by a constable of a person takes place in accordance with an authorisation under s. 22 of the Counter-Terrorism Act 2008 (post-charge questioning) anywhere in England and Wales; and
- any interview by a constable of a person takes place in accordance with an authorisation under s. 23 of the Counter-Terrorism Act 2008 (post-charge questioning) anywhere in Scotland,

the Code of Practice for the video recording with sound of interviews of persons detained under s. 41 of, or sch. 7 to, the Terrorism Act 2000 and post-charge questioning of persons authorised under ss. 22 or 23 of the Counter-Terrorism Act 2008 must be followed.

Consideration of Code C remains important when interviewing detained persons; attention is drawn to the provisions set out in Code C about the matters to be considered when deciding whether a detained person is fit to be interviewed.

Code C also sets out the circumstances in which a suspect may be questioned about an offence after being charged with it and sets out the procedures to be followed when a person's attention is drawn, after charge, to a statement made by another person. One method of bringing the content of an interview with another person to the notice of a suspect may be to play them a recording of that interview.

4 The Interview

(a) General

4.1 The provisions of Code C:
- *sections 10* and *11*, and the applicable *Notes for Guidance* apply to the conduct of interviews to which this Code applies.
- *paragraphs 11.7* to *11.14* apply only when a written record is needed.

4.2 Code C, *paragraphs 10.10, 10.11* and *Annex C* describe the restriction on drawing adverse inferences from an arrested suspect's failure or refusal to say anything about their involvement in the offence when interviewed or after being charged or informed they may be prosecuted, and how it affects the terms of the caution and determines if and by whom a special warning under sections 36 and 37 of the Criminal Justice and Public Order Act 1994 can be given.

KEYNOTE

Preparation before Interview at Police Station

Preparation is essential before any interview (indeed it is the first step in the PEACE interviewing model). This preparation should include the following points:

- Decide where the interview will be conducted. Consider the availability of a room and the timing of the interview.
- The location must have a seat for the person being interviewed (Code C, para. 12.6) and should be adequately lit, heated and ventilated (Code C, para. 12.4). The detained person must also have clothing of a reasonable standard of comfort and cleanliness (Code C, para. 8.5). (It will be a question of fact as to what amounts to adequate clothing and it is suggested that if the clothing is such as to degrade the detained person or make him/her uncomfortable, it may lead to the confession being held to be unreliable.)
- If the interview is being audio recorded (this is not relevant to interviews being recorded on a secure digital network), ensure that there are sufficient recording media for the anticipated length of the interview (or at least until the first break period). If the interview is being recorded in writing, ensure that there are enough forms.
- In deciding the timing of the interview, consideration must be given to the detainee's rest period, which should not be interrupted or delayed unless Code C, para. 12.2 applies. Where the interview goes ahead during the rest period under Code C, para. 12.2(a), a fresh rest period must be allowed. Before a detainee is interviewed, the custody officer, in consultation with the officer in charge of the investigation and appropriate health care professionals as necessary, shall assess whether the detainee is fit enough to be interviewed (Code C, para. 12.3 and Annex G).
- If legal advice has been requested you must arrange for the legal representative to be present at the interview unless Code C, para. 6.6 applies.
- If a person has asked for legal advice and an interview is initiated in the absence of a legal adviser (e.g. where the person has agreed to be interviewed without his/her legal adviser being present or because of the urgent need to interview under Code C, para. 11.1), a record must be made in the interview record (Code C, para. 6.17).
- If an appropriate adult should be present, arrange for his/her attendance. (For the definition of appropriate adult, see Code C, para. 1.7.)
- If an interpreter is needed for the interview, arrange for his/her attendance. The provisions of Code C, section 13 on interpreters for deaf persons or for interviews with suspects who have difficulty understanding English apply to these interviews.
- The reason for the interviewer making a written note of the interview where a person is deaf or has impaired hearing is to give the equivalent rights of access to the full interview record as far as this is possible using audio recording. The interview notes must be in accordance with Code C.

- It is also important to draw up an interview plan and to include any relevant areas that may provide a general or specific defence.
- Look at the evidence available and identify any significant statement or silence by the suspect in order that it can be put to him/her in interview (Code C, para. 11.4).

(b) Commencement of interviews

4.3 When the suspect is brought into the interview room the interviewer shall, without delay but in the suspect's sight, load the recorder with new recording media and set it to record. The recording media must be unwrapped or opened in the suspect's presence.
(This paragraph does not apply to interviews recorded using a secure digital network, see paragraphs 7.4 and 7.5.)

4.4 The interviewer should tell the suspect about the recording process and point out the sign or indicator which shows that the recording equipment is activated and recording. (See *paragraph 3.6.*) The interviewer shall:
    (a) explain that the interview is being audibly recorded;
    (b) subject to *paragraph 2.3*, give their name and rank and that of any other interviewer present;
    (c) ask the suspect and any other party present, e.g. the appropriate adult, a solicitor or interpreter, to identify themselves;
    (d) state the date, time of commencement and place of the interview; and
    (e) state the suspect will be given a notice about what will happen to the recording. (This sub-paragraph does not apply to interviews recorded using a secure digital network, see *paragraphs 7.4 and 7.6 to 7.7.*)

4.4A Any person entering the interview room after the interview has commenced shall be invited by the interviewer to identify themselves for the purpose of the audio recording and state the reason why they have entered the interview room.

4.5 The interviewer shall:
- caution the suspect, see Code C, *section 10*; and
- if they are detained, remind them of their entitlement to free legal advice, see Code C, *paragraph 11.2*; or
- if they are not detained under arrest, explain this and their entitlement to free legal advice, see Code C, *paragraph 3.21.*

4.6 The interviewer shall put to the suspect any significant statement or silence, see Code C, *paragraph 11.4.*

(c) Interviews with suspects who appear to have a hearing impediment

4.7 If the suspect appears to have a hearing impediment, the interviewer shall make a written note of the interview in accordance with Code C, at the same time as audio recording it in accordance with this Code.

KEYNOTE

Special Groups

As a confession can be very damning evidence against a defendant, it is important to provide safeguards that give all suspects the same level of protection. The PACE Codes of Practice recognise certain groups as being in need of additional protection. These groups include juveniles, 17-year-olds, people who do not speak

English, those suffering from a mental impairment and those who are deaf. Such suspects must not be interviewed without the relevant person being present. See Code C, section 13.

The Criminal Justice Act 2003 introduces a Code of Practice for police officers interviewing a witness notified by the accused (which would include an alibi witness), see para. 2.7.10.7.

2.10.10.4 (d) Objections and complaints by the suspect

4.8 If the suspect or an appropriate adult on their behalf, objects to the interview being audibly recorded either at the outset, during the interview or during a break, the interviewer shall explain that the interview is being audibly recorded and that this Code requires the objections to be recorded on the audio recording. When any objections have been audibly recorded or the suspect or appropriate adult have refused to have their objections recorded, the interviewer shall say they are turning off the recorder, give their reasons and turn it off. The interviewer shall then make a written record of the interview as in Code C, *section 11.* If, however, the interviewer reasonably considers they may proceed to question the suspect with the audio recording still on, the interviewer may do so. This procedure also applies in cases where the suspect has previously objected to the interview being visually recorded, see Code F, *paragraph 4.8*, and the investigating officer has decided to audibly record the interview.

4.9 If in the course of an interview a complaint is made by or on behalf of the person being questioned concerning the provisions of this or any other Codes, or it comes to the interviewer's notice that the person may have been treated improperly, the interviewer shall act as in Code C, *paragraph 12.9.*

4.10 If the suspect indicates they want to tell the interviewer about matters not directly connected with the offence of which they are suspected and they are unwilling for these matters to be audio recorded, the suspect should be given the opportunity to tell the interviewer about these matter after the conclusion of the formal interview.

2.10.10.5 KEYNOTE

If the suspect asks for the audio recording to be stopped and the interviewer decides to continue recording against the wishes of the suspect the decision may be the subject of comment in court. That said, it should be noted that in any case where the custody officer, or, in the case of a person who has not been arrested, a sergeant, is called to deal with the complaint, the recorder should, if possible, be left on until the custody officer has entered the room and spoken to the person being interviewed. Continuation or termination of the interview should be at the interviewer's discretion pending action by an inspector under Code C, para. 9.2. If the complaint is about a matter not connected with this Code or Code C, the decision to continue is at the interviewer's discretion. When the interviewer decides to continue the interview, he/she shall tell the suspect that the complaint will be brought to the custody officer's attention at the conclusion of the interview. When the interview is concluded the interviewer must, as soon as practicable, inform the custody officer or, as the case may be, the sergeant, about the existence and nature of the complaint made.

2.10.10.6 (e) Changing recording media

4.11 When the recorder shows the recording media only has a short time left to run, the interviewer shall so inform the person being interviewed and round off that part of the interview. If the interviewer leaves the room for a second set of recording media, the suspect shall not be left unattended. The interviewer will remove the recording media from the recorder and insert the new recording media which shall be unwrapped or opened in the suspect's presence. The recorder should be set to record on the new media. To avoid confusion between the recording media, the interviewer shall mark the media with an identification number immediately after it is removed from the recorder.

(This paragraph does not apply to interviews recorded using a secure digital network as this does not use removable media, see paragraphs 1.6(c), 7.4 and 7.14 to 7.15.)

(f) Taking a break during interview

4.12 When a break is taken, the fact that a break is to be taken, the reason for it and the time shall be recorded on the audio recording.

4.12A When the break is taken and the interview room vacated by the suspect, the recording media shall be removed from the recorder and the procedures for the conclusion of an interview followed, see *paragraph 4.18.*

4.13 When a break is a short one and both the suspect and an interviewer remain in the interview room, the recording may be stopped. There is no need to remove the recording media and when the interview recommences the recording should continue on the same recording media. The time the interview recommences shall be recorded on the audio recording.

4.14 After any break in the interview the interviewer must, before resuming the interview, remind the person being questioned of their right to legal advice if they have not exercised it and that they remain under caution or, if there is any doubt, give the caution in full again. *(Paragraphs 4.12 to 4.14 do not apply to interviews recorded using a secure digital network, see paragraphs 7.4 and 7.8 to 7.10.)*

2.10.10.7

KEYNOTE

The interviewer should remember that it may be necessary to show to the court that nothing occurred during a break or between interviews which influenced the suspect's recorded evidence. After a break or at the beginning of a subsequent interview, the interviewer should consider summarising on the record the reason for the break and confirming this with the suspect. The interviewer should also consider whether to administer the caution again after a break; the interviewer should bear in mind that they may have to satisfy a court that the person understood that they were still under caution when the interview resumed.

2.10.10.8

(g) Failure of recording equipment

4.15 If there is an equipment failure which can be rectified quickly, e.g. by inserting new recording media, the interviewer shall follow the appropriate procedures as in *paragraph 4.11.* When the recording is resumed the interviewer shall explain what happened and record the time the interview recommences. If, however, it will not be possible to continue recording on that recorder and no replacement recorder is readily available, the interview may continue without being audibly recorded. If this happens, the interviewer shall seek the authority as in *paragraph 3.3* of the custody officer, or as applicable, a sergeant or above. *(This paragraph does not apply to interviews recorded using a secure digital network, see paragraphs 7.4 and 7.11.)*

2.10.10.9

KEYNOTE

Where the interview is being recorded and the media or the recording equipment fails, the officer conducting the interview should stop the interview immediately. Where part of the interview is unaffected by the error and is still accessible on the media, that media shall be copied and sealed in the suspect's presence and the interview recommenced using new equipment/media as required. Where the content of the interview has been lost in its entirety the media should be sealed in the suspect's presence and the interview begun again. If the recording equipment cannot be fixed or no replacement is immediately available the interview should be recorded in accordance with Code C, section 11.

2.10.10.10

(h) Removing recording media from the recorder

4.16 Recording media which is removed from the recorder during the interview shall be retained and the procedures in *paragraph 4.18* followed.

(This paragraph does not apply to interviews recorded using a secure digital network as this does not use removable media, see paragraphs 1.6(c), 7.4 and 7.14 to 7.15.)

(i) Conclusion of interview

4.17 At the conclusion of the interview, the suspect shall be offered the opportunity to clarify anything they have said and asked if there is anything they want to add.

4.18 At the conclusion of the interview, including the taking and reading back of any written statement, the time shall be recorded and the recording shall be stopped. The interviewer shall seal the master recording with a master recording label and treat it as an exhibit in accordance with force standing orders. The interviewer shall sign the label and ask the suspect and any third party present during the interview to sign it. If the suspect or third party refuse to sign the label an officer of at least the rank of inspector, or if not available the custody officer, or if the suspect has not been arrested, a sergeant, shall be called into the interview room and asked, subject to *paragraph 2.3*, to sign it.

4.19 The suspect shall be handed a notice which explains:

- how the audio recording will be used;
- the arrangements for access to it;
- that if they are charged or informed they will be prosecuted, a copy of the audio recording will be supplied as soon as practicable or as otherwise agreed between the suspect and the police or on the order of a court.

(Paragraphs 4.17 to 4.19 do not apply to interviews recorded using a secure digital network, see paragraphs 7.4 and 7.12 to 7.13.)

2.10.10.11

KEYNOTE

Guidance is provided by Code C, para. 11.6 as to when an interview should be concluded. It is important to remember that the interview should not be concluded at the point when there is sufficient evidence to prosecute but when there is sufficient evidence to provide a realistic prospect of conviction. (In *Prouse* v *DPP* [1999] All ER (D) 748 the question was said to be not how much evidence there is but the quality of it.) Once there is enough evidence to prosecute, it may still be necessary to cover those other points in the interview that may be relevant to the defence case (see *Crime*, chapter 1.4).

2.10.11

5 After the Interview

5.1 The interviewer shall make a note in their pocket book that the interview has taken place and that it was audibly recorded, the time it commenced, its duration and date and identification number of the master recording.

5.2 If no proceedings follow in respect of the person whose interview was recorded, the recording media must be kept securely as in paragraph 6.1.

(This section (paragraphs 5.1, 5.2) does not apply to interviews recorded using a secure digital network, see paragraphs 7.4 and 7.14 to 7.15.)

2.10.11.1

KEYNOTE

Any written record of an audio recorded interview should be made in accordance with current national guidelines for police officers, police staff and CPS prosecutors concerned with the preparation, processing and submission of prosecution files.

6 Master Recording Security

(a) General

6.1   The officer in charge of each police station at which interviews with suspects are recorded or as the case may be, where recordings of interviews carried out elsewhere than at a police station are held, shall make arrangements for master recordings to be kept securely and their movements accounted for on the same basis as material which may be used for evidential purposes, in accordance with force standing orders.

(b) Breaking master recording seal for criminal proceedings

6.2   A police officer has no authority to break the seal on a master recording which is required for criminal trial or appeal proceedings. If it is necessary to gain access to the master recording, the police officer shall arrange for its seal to be broken in the presence of a representative of the Crown Prosecution Service. The defendant or their legal adviser should be informed and given a reasonable opportunity to be present. If the defendant or their legal representative is present they shall be invited to re-seal and sign the master recording. If either refuses or neither is present this should be done by the representative of the Crown Prosecution Service.

(c) Breaking master recording seal: other cases

6.3   The chief officer of police is responsible for establishing arrangements for breaking the seal of the master copy where no criminal proceedings result, or the criminal proceedings to which the interview relates, have been concluded and it becomes necessary to break the seal. These arrangements should be those which the chief officer considers are reasonably necessary to demonstrate to the person interviewed and any other party who may wish to use or refer to the interview record that the master copy has not been tampered with and that the interview record remains accurate.

6.3A   Subject to *paragraph 6.3C*, a representative of each party must be given a reasonable opportunity to be present when the seal is broken and the master recording copied and re-sealed.

6.3B   If one or more of the parties is not present when the master copy seal is broken because they cannot be contacted or refuse to attend or *paragraph 6.6* applies, arrangements should be made for an independent person such as a custody visitor, to be present. Alternatively, or as an additional safeguard, arrangement should be made for a film or photographs to be taken of the procedure.

6.3C   *Paragraph 6.3A* does not require a person to be given an opportunity to be present when:
   (a)   it is necessary to break the master copy seal for the proper and effective further investigation of the original offence or the investigation of some other offence; and
   (b)   the officer in charge of the investigation has reasonable grounds to suspect that allowing an opportunity might prejudice any such an investigation or criminal proceedings which may be brought as a result or endanger any person.

(d) Documentation

6.4   When the master recording seal is broken, a record must be made of the procedure followed, including the date, time, place and persons present.
       (This section (paragraphs 6.1 to 6.4) does not apply to interviews recorded using a secure digital network, see paragraphs 7.4 and 7.14 to 7.15.)

2.10.12.1

KEYNOTE

This section is concerned with the security of the master recording sealed at the conclusion of the interview. Care must be taken of working copies of recordings because their loss or destruction may lead to the need to access master recordings.

The most common reasons for needing access to master copies that are not required for criminal proceedings arise from civil actions and complaints against police and civil actions between individuals arising out of allegations of crime investigated by police. Examples of outcomes or likely outcomes of the investigation that might help the officer in charge of the investigation to decide whether a representative of each party needs to be present when the seal is broken and the master recording copied and re-sealed might be: (i) the prosecution of one or more of the original suspects; (ii) the prosecution of someone previously not suspected, including someone who was originally a witness; and (iii) any original suspect being treated as a prosecution witness and when premature disclosure of any police action, particularly through contact with any parties involved, could lead to a real risk of compromising the investigation and endangering witnesses.

If the recording has been delivered to the Crown Court for its keeping after committal for trial the Crown Prosecutor will apply to the Chief Clerk of the Crown Court centre for the release of the recording for unsealing by the Crown Prosecutor.

Reference to the CPS or to the Crown Prosecutor in this part of the Code should be taken to include any other body or person with a statutory responsibility for the proceedings for which the police recorded interview is required.

2.10.13

7 Recording of Interviews by Secure Digital Network

7.1 A secure digital network does not use removable media and this section specifies the provisions which will apply when a secure digital network is used.

7.2 *Not used.*

7.3 The following requirements are solely applicable to the use of a secure digital network for the recording of interviews.

(a) Application of sections 1 to 6 of Code E

7.4 *Sections 1 to 6* of Code E above apply except for the following paragraphs:
   - *Paragraph 2.2* under 'Recording and sealing of master recordings';
   - *Paragraph 4.3* under '(b) Commencement of interviews';
   - *Paragraph 4.4(e)* under '(b) Commencement of interviews';
   - *Paragraphs 4.11* to *4.19* under '(e) Changing recording media', '(f) Taking a break during interview', '(g) Failure of recording equipment', '(h) Removing recording media from the recorder' and '(i) Conclusion of interview'; and
   - *Paragraphs 6.1* to *6.4* under 'Media security'

(b) Commencement of interviews

7.5 When the suspect is brought into the interview room, the interviewer shall without delay and in the sight of the suspect, switch on the recording equipment and enter the information necessary to log on to the secure network and start recording.

7.6 The interviewer must then inform the suspect that the interview is being recorded using a secure digital network and that recording has commenced.

7.7 In addition to the requirements of *paragraph 4.4 (a)* to *(d)* above, the interviewer must inform the person that:

- they will be given access to the recording of the interview in the event that they are charged or informed that they will be prosecuted but if they are not charged or informed that they will be prosecuted they will only be given access as agreed with the police or on the order of a court; and
- they will be given a written notice at the end of the interview setting out their rights to access the recording and what will happen to the recording.

(c) Taking a break during interview

7.8   When a break is taken, the fact that a break is to be taken, the reason for it and the time shall be recorded on the audio recording. The recording shall be stopped and the procedures in *paragraphs 7.12* and *7.13* for the conclusion of an interview followed.

7.9   When the interview recommences the procedures in *paragraphs 7.5* to *7.7* for commencing an interview shall be followed to create a new file to record the continuation of the interview. The time the interview recommences shall be recorded on the audio recording.

7.10   After any break in the interview the interviewer must, before resuming the interview, remind the person being questioned that they remain under caution or, if there is any doubt, give the caution in full again.

(d) Failure of recording equipment

7.11   If there is an equipment failure which can be rectified quickly, e.g. by commencing a new secure digital network recording, the interviewer shall follow the appropriate procedures as in *paragraphs 7.8* to *7.10*. When the recording is resumed the interviewer shall explain what happened and record the time the interview recommences. If, however, it is not possible to continue recording on the secure digital network the interview should be recorded on removable media as in *paragraph 4.3* unless the necessary equipment is not available. If this happens the interview may continue without being audibly recorded and the interviewer shall seek the authority of the custody officer or a sergeant as in *paragraph 3.3(a)* or *(b)*.

(e) Conclusion of interview

7.12   At the conclusion of the interview, the suspect shall be offered the opportunity to clarify anything he or she has said and asked if there is anything they want to add.

7.13   At the conclusion of the interview, including the taking and reading back of any written statement:
   (a) the time shall be orally recorded.
   (b) the suspect shall be handed a notice which explains:
      - how the audio recording will be used
      - the arrangements for access to it
      - that if they are charged or informed that they will be prosecuted, they will be given access to the recording of the interview either electronically or by being given a copy on removable recording media, but if they are not charged or informed that they will prosecuted, they will only be given access as agreed with the police or on the order of a court.
   (c) the suspect must be asked to confirm that he or she has received a copy of the notice at sub-paragraph (b) above. If the suspect fails to accept or to acknowledge receipt of the notice, the interviewer will state for the recording that a copy of the notice has been provided to the suspect and that he or she has refused to take a copy of the notice or has refused to acknowledge receipt.

       (d) the time shall be recorded and the interviewer shall notify the suspect that the recording is being saved to the secure network. The interviewer must save the recording in the presence of the suspect. The suspect should then be informed that the interview is terminated.

(f) After the interview

7.14   The interviewer shall make a note in their pocket book that the interview has taken place and, that it was audibly recorded, the time it commenced, its duration and date and the identification number of the original recording.

7.15   If no proceedings follow in respect of the person whose interview was recorded, the recordings must be kept securely as in *paragraphs 7.16* and *7.17*.

(g) Security of secure digital network interview records

7.16   Interview record files are stored in read only format on non-removable storage devices, for example, hard disk drives, to ensure their integrity. The recordings are first saved locally to a secure non-removable device before being transferred to the remote network device. If for any reason the network connection fails, the recording remains on the local device and will be transferred when the network connections are restored.

7.17   Access to interview recordings, including copying to removable media, must be strictly controlled and monitored to ensure that access is restricted to those who have been given specific permission to access for specified purposes when this is necessary. For example, police officers and CPS lawyers involved in the preparation of any prosecution case, persons interviewed if they have been charged or informed they may be prosecuted and their legal representatives.

2.10.13.1

KEYNOTE

The notice given to the suspect at the conclusion of the interview (see Code E, para. 7.13) should provide a brief explanation of the secure digital network and how access is strictly limited to the recording. The notice should also explain the access rights of the suspect, his or her legal representative, the police and the prosecutor to the recording of the interview. Space should be provided on the form to insert the date and the file reference number for the interview.

2.10.14

PACE Code of Practice on Visual Recording with Sound of Interviews with Suspects (Code F)

The contents of this Code should be considered if an interviewer decides to make a visual recording with sound of an interview with a suspect after 00.00 on 27 October 2013.

There is no statutory requirement under PACE to visually record interviews [however s. 25 of the Counter-Terrorism Act 2008 requires all interviews to be video recorded with sound in accordance with the separate Code of Practice issued under the video recording with sound of post-charge questioning authorised under s. 22 of the Counter-Terrorism Act 2008 (see Code H, para. 15.3 and *appendix 2.1*)].

1 General

1.0   The procedures in this Code must be used fairly, responsibly, with respect for the people to whom they apply and without unlawful discrimination. Under the Equality Act 2010, section 149, when police officers are carrying out their functions, they also have a duty to have due regard to the need to eliminate unlawful discrimination, harassment and victimisation, to advance equality of opportunity between people who share a relevant protected characteristic and people who do not share it, and to take steps to foster good relations between those persons.

1.1   This Code of practice must be readily available for consultation by police officers and other police staff, detained persons and members of the public.

1.2   The Notes for Guidance included are not provisions of this Code. They form guidance to police officers and others about its application and interpretation.

1.3   Nothing in this Code shall be taken as detracting in any way from the requirements of the Code of Practice for the Detention, Treatment and Questioning of Persons by Police Officers (Code C).

1.4   The interviews to which this Code applies are described in *section 3*.

1.5   In this Code, the term 'appropriate adult', 'solicitor' and 'interview' have the same meaning as those set out in Code C and in the case of a 17 year old suspect, 'appropriate adult' includes the person called to fulfil that role in accordance with C *paragraph 1.5A* of Code C. The corresponding provisions and Notes for Guidance in Code C applicable to those terms shall also apply where appropriate.

1.5A   The visual recording of interviews shall be carried out openly to instil confidence in its reliability as an impartial and accurate record of the interview.

1.6   Any reference in this Code to visual recording shall be taken to mean visual recording with sound and in this Code:

(aa) 'recording media' means any removable, physical audio recording medium (such as magnetic tape, optical disc or solid state memory) which can be played and copied.

(a) 'designated person' means a person other than a police officer, designated under the Police Reform Act 2002, Part 4 who has specified powers and duties of police officers conferred or imposed on them;

(b) any reference to a police officer includes a designated person acting in the exercise or performance of the powers and duties conferred or imposed on them by their designation.

(c) 'secure digital network' is a computer network system which enables an original interview recording to be stored as a digital multi media file or a series of such files, on a secure file server which is accredited by the National Accreditor for Police Information Systems in accordance with the UK Government Protective Marking Scheme. See *paragraph 1.6A* and *section 7* of this Code. [N.B. the UK Government Protective Marking Scheme has been replaced by the Government Security Classification Scheme.]

1.6A   *Section 7* below sets out the provisions which apply to interviews visually recorded using a secure digital network by reference to Code E and by excluding provisions of *sections 1* to *6* of this Code which relate or apply only to removable media.

1.7   References to 'pocket book' in this Code include any official report book issued to police officers.

1.8   In the application of this Code to the conduct and visual recording of an interview of a suspect who has not been arrested:

(a) references to the 'custody officer' include references to an officer of the rank of sergeant or above who is not directly involved in the investigation of the offence(s);

(b) if the interview takes place elsewhere than at a police station, references to 'interview room' include any place or location which the interviewer is satisfied will enable the interview to be conducted and recorded in accordance with this Code and where the suspect is present voluntarily; and

(c) provisions in addition to those which expressly apply to these interviews shall be followed insofar as they are relevant and can be applied in practice.

2.10.14.1

KEYNOTE

The Codes recognise the importance that detained persons are treated in accordance with the Equality Act 2010; for these Codes 'relevant protected characteristic' includes: age, disability, gender reassignment, pregnancy and maternity, race, religion or belief, sex and sexual orientation.

As in para. 1.9 of Code C, references to custody officers include those carrying out the functions of a custody officer.

The Code includes provisions for the conduct and recording of voluntary interviews of suspects who are not under arrest. These take account Code G (arrest) and Code C, paras 3.21 and 3.22 which support the use of voluntary interviews to ensure that voluntary interviews are subject to Code E and distinguish them from custody cases. Paragraph 1.8(c) avoids the need to distinguish the voluntary option in detail in every paragraph in this Code. The Code provides for a sergeant to be responsible for giving authority not to make an audio/visual recording similar to the arrangements in place for those in custody. An interviewer who is not sure, or has any doubt, about the suitability of a place or location of an interview to be carried out elsewhere than at a police station, should consult an officer of the rank of sergeant or above for advice.

2.10.15

2 Recording and Sealing of Master Recordings

2.1 *Not used.*

2.2 The camera(s) shall be placed in the interview room so as to ensure coverage of as much of the room as is practically possible whilst the interviews are taking place.

2.3 When the recording medium is placed in the recorder and it is switched on to record, the correct date and time, in hours, minutes and seconds, will be superimposed automatically, second by second, during the whole recording. See *section 7* regarding the use of a secure digital network to record the interview.

2.4 One recording, referred to in this Code as the master recording copy, will be sealed before it leaves the presence of the suspect. A second recording will be used as a working copy.

2.5 Nothing in this Code requires the identity of an officer or police staff to be recorded or disclosed:

 (a) *Not used.*

 (b) if the interviewer reasonably believes that recording or disclosing their name might put them in danger.

 In these cases, the interviewer will have their back to the camera and shall use their warrant or other identification number and the name of the police station to which they are attached. Such instances and the reasons for them shall be recorded in the custody record or the interviewer's pocket book.

2.10.15.1

KEYNOTE

The certified recording media should be capable of having an image of the date and time superimposed upon them as they record the interview. Interviewing officers will wish to arrange that, as far as possible, visual recording arrangements are unobtrusive. It must be clear to the suspect, however, that there is no opportunity to interfere with the recording equipment or the recording media. The purpose of sealing the master copy before it leaves the presence of the suspect is to establish his/her confidence that the integrity of the copy is preserved.

In cases where a suspect is not available for an identification as set out in Code D, para. 3.21, the recording of the interview may be used for identification procedures.

The purpose of the interviewer having his/her back to the camera and using his/her warrant number or other identification numbers and the name of his/her police station is to protect police officers and others involved in the investigation of serious organised crime or the arrest of particularly violent suspects when there is reliable information that those arrested or their associates may threaten or cause harm to the officers, their families or their personal property. In cases of doubt, an officer of inspector rank should be consulted.

3 Interviews to be Visually Recorded

3.1 Subject to *paragraph 3.2* below, when an interviewer is deciding whether to make a visual recording, these are the areas where it might be appropriate:

(a) with a suspect in respect of an indictable offence (including an offence triable either way);

(b) which takes place as a result of an interviewer exceptionally putting further questions to a suspect about an offence described in sub-paragraph (a) above after they have been charged with, or informed they may be prosecuted for, that offence

(c) in which an interviewer wishes to bring to the notice of a person, after that person has been charged with, or informed they may be prosecuted for an offence described in sub-paragraph (a) above, any written statement made by another person, or the content of an interview with another person;

(d) with, or in the presence of, a deaf or deaf/blind or speech impaired person who uses sign language to communicate;

(e) with, or in the presence of anyone who requires an appropriate adult, or

(f) in any case where the suspect or their representative requests that the interview be recorded visually.

3.2 The Terrorism Act 2000 and the Counter-Terrorism Act 2008 make separate provisions for a Code of Practice for the video recording with sound of:

- interviews of persons detained under section 41 of, or Schedule 7 to, the 2000 Act; and

- post-charge questioning of persons authorised under section 22 or 23 of the 2008 Act. The provisions of this Code do not therefore apply to such interviews.

3.3 Following a decision by an interviewer to visually record any interview mentioned in *paragraph 3.1* above, the custody officer in the case of a detained person, or a sergeant in the case of a suspect who has not been arrested, may authorise the interviewer not to make a visual record and for the purpose of this Code (F), the provisions of Code E, *paragraphs 3.1, 3.2, 3.3, 3.3A* and *3.4* shall apply as appropriate. However, authority not to make a visual recording does not detract in any way from the requirement for audio recording. This would require a further authorisation not to make in accordance with Code E.

3.5 The whole of each interview shall be recorded visually, including the taking and reading back of any statement.

3.6 A sign or indicator which is visible to the suspect must show when the visual recording equipment is recording.

KEYNOTE

A decision not to record an interview visually for any reason may be the subject of comment in court. The authorising officer should therefore be prepared to justify his/her decision in each case. Nothing in the Code is intended to preclude visual recording at police discretion of interviews at police stations with people cautioned in respect of offences not covered by para. 3.1, or responses made by interviewees after they have been charged or informed they may be prosecuted for an offence, provided that this Code is complied with.

As stated, Code F needs to be read in conjunction with the relevant sections of Code C. For instance, attention is drawn to the provisions set out in Code C about the matters to be considered when deciding whether a detained person is fit to be interviewed. Code C also sets out the circumstances in which a suspect may be questioned about an offence after being charged with it, as well as the procedures to be followed when a person's attention is drawn, after charge, to a statement made by another person. One method of bringing the content of an interview with another person to the notice of a suspect may be to play him/her a recording of that interview.

If, during the course of an interview under this Code, it becomes apparent that the interview should be conducted under one of the terrorism Codes for video recording of interviews, the interview should only continue in accordance with the relevant Code (see Code H, and **appendix 2.1**).

4 The Interview

(a) General

4.1 The provisions of Code C in relation to cautions and interviews and the Notes for Guidance applicable to those provisions shall apply to the conduct of interviews to which this Code applies.

4.2 Particular attention is drawn to those parts of Code C that describe the restrictions on drawing adverse inferences from an arrested suspect's failure or refusal to say anything about their involvement in the offence when interviewed, or after being charged or informed they may be prosecuted and how those restrictions affect the terms of the caution and determine whether a special warning under Sections 36 and 37 of the Criminal Justice and Public Order Act 1994 can be given.

KEYNOTE

For 'Preparation before Interview at Police Station', see para. 2.10.10.1.

(b) Commencement of interviews

4.3 When the suspect is brought into the interview room the interviewer shall without delay, but in sight of the suspect, load the recording equipment and set it to record. The recording media must be unwrapped or otherwise opened in the presence of the suspect.

4.4 The interviewer shall then tell the suspect formally about the visual recording and point out the sign or indicator which shows that the recording equipment is activated and recording (see *paragraph 3.6*). The interviewer shall:

(a) explain that the interview is being visually recorded;

(b) subject to *paragraph 2.5*, give their name and rank, and that of any other interviewer present;

(c) ask the suspect and any other party present (e.g. the appropriate adult, a solicitor or interpreter) to identify themselves;

(d) state the date, time of commencement and place of the interview, and

(e) state that the suspect will be given a notice about what will happen to the recording.

4.4A Any person entering the interview room after the interview has commenced shall be invited by the interviewer to identify themselves for the purpose of the recording and state the reason why they have entered the interview room.

4.5 The interviewer shall then caution the suspect, see Code C, *section 10* and:

- if they are detained, remind them of their entitlement to free legal advice, see Code C *paragraph 11.2*, or

- if they are not detained under arrest, explain this and their entitlement to free legal advice, see Code C, *paragraph 3.21*.

4.6 The interviewer shall then put to the suspect any significant statement or silence, see Code C, *paragraph 11.4*.

(c) Interviews suspects who appear to require an interpreter

4.7 The provisions of Code C on interpreters for suspects who do not appear to speak or understand English, or who appear to have a hearing or speech impediment, continue to apply.

(d) Objections and complaints by the suspect

4.8 If the suspect or an appropriate adult on their behalf, objects to the interview being visually recorded either at the outset or during the interview or during a break in the interview the interviewer shall explain that the interview is being visually recorded and that this Code requires that the objections to be recorded on the visual recording. When any objections have been recorded or the suspect or the appropriate adult have refused to have their objections recorded, the interviewer shall say that they are turning off the visual recording, give their reasons and turn it off. If a separate audio recording is being maintained, the interviewer shall ask the person to record the reasons for refusing to agree to the interview being visually recorded. *Paragraph 4.8* of Code E will apply if the person also objects to the interview being audio recorded. If the interviewer reasonably considers they may proceed to question the suspect with the visual recording still on, the interviewer may do so.

4.9 If in the course of an interview a complaint is made by the person being questioned, or on their behalf, concerning the provisions of this or any other Code, or it comes to the interviewer's notice that the person may have been treated improperly, then the interviewer shall act as in Code C, *paragraph 12.9.*

4.10 If the suspect indicates that they wish to tell the interviewer about matters not directly connected with the offence of which they are suspected and that they are unwilling for these matters to be visually recorded, the suspect should be given the opportunity to tell the interviewer about these matters after the conclusion of the formal interview.

2.10.17.3 **KEYNOTE**

For complaints made in interview, see para. 2.10.10.5.

2.10.17.4 ### (e) Changing the recording media

4.11 In instances where the recording medium is not of sufficient length to record all of the interview with the suspect, further certified recording medium will be used. When the recording equipment indicates that the recording medium has only a short time left to run, the interviewer shall advise the suspect and round off that part of the interview. If the interviewer wishes to continue the interview but does not already have further certified recording media with him, they shall obtain a set. The suspect should not be left unattended in the interview room. The interviewer will remove the recording media from the recording equipment and insert the new ones which have been unwrapped or otherwise opened in the suspect's presence. The recording equipment shall then be set to record. Care must be taken, particularly when a number of sets of recording media have been used, to ensure that there is no confusion between them. This could be achieved by marking the sets of recording media with consecutive identification numbers.

(f) Taking a break during the interview

4.12 When a break is taken, the fact that a break is to be taken, the reason for it and the time shall be recorded on the visual record.

4.12A When the break is taken and the interview room vacated by the suspect, the recording media shall be removed from the recorder and the procedures for the conclusion of an interview followed. (See *paragraph 4.18.*)

4.13 When a break is a short one and both the suspect and an interviewer remain in the interview room, the recording may be stopped. There is no need to remove the recording media and when the interview recommences the recording should continue on the same recording media. The time at which the interview recommences shall be recorded.

4.14　After any break in the interview the interviewer must, before resuming the interview, remind the person being questioned of their right to legal advice if they have not exercised it and that they remain under caution or, if there is any doubt, give the caution in full again.

2.10.17.5　**KEYNOTE**

For breaks in interview, see para. 2.10.10.7.

2.10.17.6

(g) Failure of recording equipment

4.15　If there is a failure of equipment which can be rectified quickly, the appropriate procedures set out in *paragraph 4.12* shall be followed. When the recording is resumed the interviewer shall explain what has happened and record the time the interview recommences. If, however, it is not possible to continue recording on that particular recorder and no alternative equipment is readily available, the interview may continue without being recorded visually. In such circumstances, the procedures set out in *paragraph 3.3* of this Code for seeking the authority of the custody officer or a sergeant will be followed.

2.10.17.7　**KEYNOTE**

For failure of recording equipment, see para. 2.10.10.9.

2.10.17.8

(h) Removing used recording media from recording equipment

4.16　Where used recording media are removed from the recording equipment during the course of an interview, they shall be retained and the procedures set out in *paragraph 4.18* below followed.

(i) Conclusion of interview

4.17　Before the conclusion of the interview, the suspect shall be offered the opportunity to clarify anything he or she has said and asked if there is anything that they wish to add.

4.18　At the conclusion of the interview, including the taking and reading back of any written statement, the time shall be recorded and the recording equipment switched off. The master recording shall be removed from the recording equipment, sealed with a master recording label and treated as an exhibit in accordance with the force standing orders. The interviewer shall sign the label and also ask the suspect and any third party present during the interview to sign it. If the suspect or third party refuses to sign the label, an officer of at least the rank of inspector, or if one is not available, the custody officer or, if the suspect has not been arrested, a sergeant, shall be called into the interview room and asked, subject to *paragraph 2.5*, to sign it.

4.19　The suspect shall be handed a notice which explains the use which will be made of the recording and the arrangements for access to it. The notice will also advise the suspect that a copy of the tape shall be supplied as soon as practicable if the person is charged or informed that he will be prosecuted.

2.10.17.9　**KEYNOTE**

For the conclusion of an interview, see para. 2.10.10.11.

2.10.18

5 After the Interview

5.1 The interviewer shall make a note in his or her pocket book of the fact that the interview has taken place and has been recorded, its time, duration and date and the identification number of the master copy of the recording media.

5.2 Where no proceedings follow in respect of the person whose interview was recorded, the recording media must nevertheless be kept securely in accordance with *paragraph 6.1*.

2.10.18.1

KEYNOTE

Any written record of a recorded interview shall be made in accordance with current national guidelines for police officers, police staff and CPS prosecutors concerned with the preparation, processing and submission of files.

2.10.19

6 Master Recording Security

(a) General

6.1 The officer in charge of the police station at which interviews with suspects are recorded or as the case may be, where recordings of interviews carried out elsewhere than at a police station are held, shall make arrangements for the master copies to be kept securely and their movements accounted for on the same basis as other material which may be used for evidential purposes, in accordance with force standing orders.

(b) Breaking master recording seal for criminal proceedings

6.2 A police officer has no authority to break the seal on a master copy which is required for criminal trial or appeal proceedings. If it is necessary to gain access to the master copy, the police officer shall arrange for its seal to be broken in the presence of a representative of the Crown Prosecution Service. The defendant or their legal adviser shall be informed and given a reasonable opportunity to be present. If the defendant or their legal representative is present they shall be invited to reseal and sign the master copy. If either refuses or neither is present, this shall be done by the representative of the Crown Prosecution Service.

(c) Breaking master recording seal: other cases

6.3 The chief officer of police is responsible for establishing arrangements for breaking the seal of the master copy where no criminal proceedings result, or the criminal proceedings to which the interview relates, have been concluded and it becomes necessary to break the seal. These arrangements should be those which the chief officer considers are reasonably necessary to demonstrate to the person interviewed and any other party who may wish to use or refer to the interview record that the master copy has not been tampered with and that the interview record remains accurate.

6.4 Subject to *paragraph 6.6*, a representative of each party must be given a reasonable opportunity to be present when the seal is broken and the master recording copied and re-sealed.

6.5 If one or more of the parties is not present when the master copy seal is broken because they cannot be contacted or refuse to attend or *paragraph 6.6* applies, arrangements should be made for an independent person such as a custody visitor, to be present. Alternatively, or as an additional safeguard, arrangement should be made for a film or photographs to be taken of the procedure.

6.6 *Paragraph 6.4* does not require a person to be given an opportunity to be present when:

(a) it is necessary to break the master copy seal for the proper and effective further investigation of the original offence or the investigation of some other offence; and

(b) the officer in charge of the investigation has reasonable grounds to suspect that allowing an opportunity might prejudice any such an investigation or criminal proceedings which may be brought as a result or endanger any person.

(d) Documentation

6.7 When the master copy seal is broken, copied and re-sealed, a record must be made of the procedure followed, including the date time and place and persons present.

2.10.19.1
KEYNOTE

For breaking master recording seals, see para. 2.10.12.1.

2.10.20   7 Visual Recording of Interviews by Secure Digital Network

7.1 This section applies if an officer wishes to make a visual recording with sound of an interview mentioned in section 3 of this Code using a secure digital network which does not use removable media (see *paragraph 1.6(c)*) above.

7.2 *Not used.*

7.3 The provisions of *sections 1* to *6* of this Code which relate or apply only to removable media will not apply to a secure digital network recording.

7.4 The statutory requirement and provisions for the audio recording of interviews using a secure digital network set out in *section 7* of Code E should be applied to the visual recording with sound of interviews mentioned in *section 3* of this Code as if references to audio recordings of interviews include visual recordings with sound.

2.10.21   Interviews on Behalf of Scottish Forces and *vice versa*

The CPS, in consultation with the Scottish Crown Office, has produced guidelines in relation to the potential admissibility of interview evidence when officers from England and Wales conduct interviews on behalf of Scottish forces and *vice versa*. These interviews relate to people subject to cross-border arrest as provided by ss. 136 to 140 of the Criminal Justice and Public Order Act 1994 (see **General Police Duties**, chapter 4.5).

2.10.21.1
KEYNOTE

Suspects in Scotland: Interview Evidence Required for Prosecutions in England and Wales

Under the legislation governing prosecutions in Scotland, the suspect is not entitled to legal representation during an interview. Suspects are not warned that a failure to answer questions may harm their defence. Failure to answer questions cannot harm their defence. Interviews under caution are, however, subject to guidelines which incorporate judicial precedent fairness to the accused.

In investigations of any great seriousness, English/Welsh constables should attend in Scotland, arrest the suspect and bring him/her back to their jurisdiction for interview. If such an arrest is made, the arrested person

---

must be taken either to the nearest designated police station in England or a designated police station in a police area in England and Wales in which the offence is being investigated (s. 137(1) and (7)(a) of the Criminal Justice and Public Order Act 1994).

Scottish officers do not have any statutory or common law powers to detain or arrest a suspect without warrant who is believed to have committed an offence in England and Wales. If there is insufficient evidence for the issue of a warrant, and the case is not sufficiently serious to justify officers travelling to Scotland, Scottish officers can be requested to invite the suspect to attend a police station on a voluntary basis for interview under caution.

When it has not been practicable for an English/Welsh constable to make an arrest, but a constable has gone to Scotland to interview a suspect following arrest or detention by a Scottish constable for Scottish offences, or a person has voluntarily agreed to be interviewed, the English/Welsh constable should comply, in so far as it is practical, with the PACE Codes of Practice, in particular:

- A suspect not under arrest or detention should be told that he/she is not under arrest or detention and that he/she is free to leave.
- A suspect should be told that he/she may seek legal advice and that arrangements are made for legal representation when required. An appropriate adult should also be present when interviewing a youth or a mentally disordered or mentally handicapped person.
- An English/Welsh law caution should be administered. When appropriate, officers should warn arrested suspects of the consequences of failure or refusal to account for objects, substances or marks (s. 36 of the 1994 Act) and the failure or refusal to account for their presence in a particular place (s. 37).
- The interview should be audio recorded if possible.
- If it is not possible to audio record the interview, a contemporaneous written record of the interview should be made. The suspect must be given the opportunity to read the record and to sign it.

Scottish constables interviewing suspects in Scotland when they are aware that the interview is required for a prosecution in England and Wales, should comply with Scottish law. In addition, in so far as it is practical:

- A suspect should be told that he/she may seek legal advice and that arrangements are made for legal representation when required. A solicitor may be present during any subsequent interview if the suspect requires. An appropriate adult should also be present when interviewing a youth or a mentally disordered or mentally vulnerable person.
- When it is certain that the interview evidence will only be used in English/Welsh courts, the appropriate English/Welsh caution should be used.
- The interview should be audio recorded if possible.
- If it is not possible to audio record the interview, a written contemporaneous record of the interview should be made. The suspect must be given the opportunity to read the record and to sign it.

English/Welsh officers should assist interviewing Scottish officers by providing a schedule of points to be covered in an interview. This could include a list of appropriate questions.

2.10.21.2   **KEYNOTE**

Suspects in England and Wales: Interview Evidence Required for Prosecutions in Scotland

- English officers do not have any statutory or common law powers to detain or arrest a suspect without warrant who is believed to have committed an offence in Scotland. If there is insufficient evidence for the issue of a warrant, and the case is not sufficiently serious to justify Scottish officers travelling to England or Wales to exercise their cross-border powers under the Act, English or Welsh officers can be requested to invite the suspect to attend an interview on a voluntary basis for interview under caution.
- Where a Scottish officer has attended to interview the suspect, the Scottish form of caution should be given.

- English and Welsh constables interviewing suspects in England/Wales when they are aware that the interview is required for a prosecution in Scotland, should comply with the PACE Codes of Practice, save that a Scottish caution should be used in the following terms:

You are not obliged to say anything but anything you do say will be noted and may be used in evidence.

The use of an English/Welsh caution may render the interview inadmissible in Scotland.

Scottish officers should assist the interviewing officers by providing a schedule of points to be covered in an interview and a possible list of appropriate questions.

In all circumstances, officers should ensure that suspects fully understand the significance of a caution or warning.

Appendix 2.1

Summary of PACE Code of Practice for the Detention, Treatment and Questioning of Persons under s. 41 of, and sch. 8 to, the Terrorism Act 2000 (Code H)

As stated at the start of chapter 2.10, Code H has been introduced and applies to people in police detention following their arrest under the Terrorism Act 2000, s. 41; the latest revision applies after midnight on 26 October 2013 notwithstanding that the person has been arrested before that time. The main changes to Code H mirror changes to Code C, these are in regards to safeguards for 17-year-old suspects and for suspects who do not speak and understand English as required by the EU Directive on the right to interpretation and translation in criminal proceedings (see EU Directive 2010/64/EU).

Code H is not reproduced within the Manual but should be available in custody suites and at police stations. Generally, the provisions to Code H are mirrored (with modifications as necessary) in the current version of PACE Code C and *vice versa* in order to ensure consistency; however, in relation to reviews and extensions of detention there are significant differences from the equivalent provisions in PACE Code C owing to the changes made to maximum detention times by the Terrorism Act 2006.

Code H has been expanded in scope to incorporate provisions relating to the post-charge questioning of terrorist suspects. Part 2 of the Counter-Terrorism Act 2008 provides that a judge may authorise the questioning of a person by a constable after that person has been charged with a terrorism offence or an offence with a terrorist connection. The post-charge questioning provisions of the 2008 Act also introduce a new mandatory code for the video recording with sound of such questioning.

Section 1—General

This section covers the scope and applicability of the Code (which are, by definition, different from the equivalent provisions of Code C); it also covers the availability of the Code, definitions, applicability to the deaf, blind and speech impaired, and the use of reasonable force, and in these respects follows Code C.

> *Note 1N The powers under Part IV of PACE to detain and release on bail (before or after charge) a person arrested under section 24 of PACE for any offence (see PACE Code G (Arrest)) do not apply to persons whilst they are detained under the terrorism powers following their arrest/detention under section 41 of, or Schedule 7 to, TACT. If when the grounds for detention under these powers cease the person is arrested under section 24 of PACE for a specific offence, the detention and bail provisions of PACE will apply and must be considered from the time of that arrest.*

Section 2—Custody Records

This section follows Code C. It covers general requirements for making custody records, including the exemption for counter-terrorism officers from disclosing their identities on custody records and provisions as to access to custody records by detainees' solicitors and disclosure of those records to them.

Section 3—Initial Action in respect of arrested individuals

Code H broadly follows Code C in respect of detainees' rights and arrangements for exercising them but differs in a number of respects:

- the record will indicate that the arrest was under s. 41 as opposed to indicating the offence in respect of which the arrest was made—Note 3G indicates that, where an arrest is made on grounds of sensitive information which cannot be disclosed, the recorded grounds 'may be given in terms of the interpretation of "terrorist"' set out in s. 40(1)(a) or (b);
- there is a specific provision to the effect that risk assessments do not form part of the custody record and should not be shown to the detainee or his/her legal representative;
- there are provisions relating to the initial steps that may be taken in connection with the identification of suspects;
- the custody officer is allowed to direct custody staff to carry out certain actions in relation to a detainee's rights and entitlements, need for medical treatment and the risk assessment process.

Section 4—Detainees' Property

This section of Code H includes a simplification of the circumstances in which a custody officer should search a detainee to ascertain what he/she has in his/her possession but there is no material change in comparison with Code C.

Section 5—Right not to be Held Incommunicado

This section allows a detainee to be visited by those in whose welfare the detainee has an interest. The detainee's right to have someone informed of his/her whereabouts closely follows the equivalent section of Code C but there is much more detailed guidance on visiting rights. A requirement is imposed for custody officers to liaise with the investigation team to ascertain the risks presented by visits. Where visits from relatives etc. present a risk, consideration of more frequent visits from independent visitor schemes is suggested. Visits from official visitors ('official visitors' may include accredited faith representatives and MPs) may be allowed subject to consultation with the officer in charge of the investigation. Note 5B indicates that custody officers should bear in mind the effects of prolonged detention under the Act and consider the health and welfare benefits that visits bring to the health and welfare of detainees who are held for extended periods. However, Note 5G reminds officers that the nature of terrorist investigations means that they need to have 'particular regard to the possibility of suspects attempting to pass information which may be detrimental to public safety, or to an investigation'.

Section 6—Right to Legal Advice

The principal difference from Code C is that there is provision for an authorisation to be given whereby a detainee may only consult a solicitor within sight and hearing of a qualified officer (a uniformed officer of at least the rank of inspector who has no connection with the investigation). This section also introduces additional safeguards for detainees who change their mind about wanting advice.

Section 7—Citizens of Independent Commonwealth Countries or Foreign Nationals

Section 7 shows no material change from the equivalent Code C provisions.

Section 8—Conditions of Detention

The main differences from Code C are that there is specific reference to allowing detainees to practise religious observance and to the provision of reading material, including religious texts. Police should consult with representatives of religious communities on provision of facilities for religious observance and handling of religious texts and other articles. The benefits of exercise for detainees, particularly in the cases of prolonged detention, are emphasised. If facilities exist, indoor exercise is to be offered if requested or if outdoor exercise is not practicable. Although the same restrictions on putting a juvenile in a cell apply as under Code C, there is no requirement to include occasions when a juvenile is so confined on the custody record.

Section 9—Care and Treatment of Detained Persons

Section 9 of Code H begins by requiring that, notwithstanding other requirements for medical attention, 'detainees who are held for more than 96 hours must be visited by a healthcare professional at least once every 24 hours'. In all other material respects, the provisions are the same as under Code C.

Section 10—Cautions

Insofar as relevant, the provisions on cautions closely follow those of Code C.

Section 11—Interviews (General)

There are no material differences from Code C under this section. The Code H equivalent is, however, much shorter, reflecting the fact that not all instances covered by the Code C equivalent are relevant to detention of terrorist suspects.

Section 12—Interviews in Police Stations

The only material difference here is set out at para. 12.9:

> 12.9 During extended periods where no interviews take place, because of the need to gather further evidence or analyse existing evidence, detainees and their legal representative shall be informed that the investigation into the relevant offence remains ongoing. If practicable, the detainee and legal representative should also be made aware in general terms of any reasons for long gaps between interviews. Consideration should be given to allowing visits, more frequent exercise, or for reading or writing materials to be offered. *See paragraph 5.4, section 8* and *Note 12C.*

Note 12C indicates that consideration should be given to the matters referred to in para. 12.9 after a period of over 24 hours without questioning.

Section 13—Interpreters

The requirements for accredited interpreters to be provided for deaf or non-English speakers, for both general custody procedures and interviews, are the same as under Code C.

Section 14—Reviews and Extensions of Detention

This section contains significant changes from the equivalent provisions in Code C, section 15, owing to the changes made to maximum detention times by the Terrorism Act 2006. It is set out in full below.

14 Reviews and Extensions of Detention under the Terrorism Act 2000

(a) General

14.1 The powers and duties of the review officer are in the Terrorism Act 2000, Schedule 8, Part II. See *Notes 14A and 14B*. A review officer should carry out their duties at the police station where the detainee is held and be allowed such access to the detainee as is necessary to exercise those duties.

14.2 For the purposes of reviewing a person's detention, no officer shall put specific questions to the detainee:
- regarding their involvement in any offence; or
- in respect of any comments they may make:
  - when given the opportunity to make representations; or
  - in response to a decision to keep them in detention or extend the maximum period of detention.

Such an exchange could constitute an interview as in *paragraph 11.1* and would be subject to the associated safeguards in *section 11*.

14.3 If detention is necessary for longer than 48 hours from the time of arrest (or if a person was being detained under TACT Schedule 7, from the time at which the examination under Schedule 7 began, a police officer of at least superintendent rank, or a Crown Prosecutor may apply for a warrant of further detention or for an extension or further extension of such a warrant under *paragraph 29* or (as the case may be) 36 of Part III of Schedule 8 to the Terrorism Act 2000. See *Note 14C*.

14.4 When an application is made for a warrant as described in *paragraph 14.3*, the detained person and their representative must be informed of their rights in respect of the application. These include:
(i)   the right to a written notice of the application; *See Note 14G*.
(ii) the right to make oral or written representations to the judicial authority / High Court judge about the application;
(iii) the right to be present and legally represented at the hearing of the application, unless specifically excluded by the judicial authority / High Court judge:
(iv) their right to free legal advice (see *section 6* of this Code).

(b) Transfer of persons detained for more than 14 days to prison

14.5 If the Detention of Terrorists Suspects (Temporary Extension) Bill is enacted and in force, a High Court judge may extend or further extend a warrant of further detention to authorise a person to be detained beyond a period of 14 days from the time of their arrest (or if they were being detained under TACT Schedule 7, from the time at which their examination under Schedule 7 began). The provisions of *Annex J* will apply when a warrant of further detention is so extended or further extended.

14.6 *Not used*
14.7 *Not used*
14.8 *Not used*
14.9 *Not used*
14.10 *Not used*

(c) Documentation

14.11 It is the responsibility of the officer who gives any reminders as at *paragraph 14.4*, to ensure that these are noted in the custody record, as well any comments made by the detained person upon being told of those rights.

14.12 The grounds for, and extent of, any delay in conducting a review shall be recorded.

14.13 Any written representations shall be retained.

14.14 A record shall be made as soon as practicable about the outcome of each review and, if applicable, the grounds on which the review officer authorises continued detention. A record shall also be made as soon as practicable about the outcome of an application for a warrant of further detention or its extension.

14.15   Not used

Notes for Guidance

14A   TACT Schedule 8 Part II sets out the procedures for review of detention up to 48 hours from the time of arrest under TACT section 41 (or if a person was being detained under TACT Schedule 7, from the time at which the examination under Schedule 7 began). These include provisions for the requirement to review detention, postponing a review, grounds for continued detention, designating a review officer, representations, rights of the detained person and keeping a record. The review officer's role ends after a warrant has been issued for extension of detention under Part III of Schedule 8.

14B   A review officer may authorise a person's continued detention if satisfied that detention is necessary:
(a)   to obtain relevant evidence whether by questioning the person or otherwise;
(b)   to preserve relevant evidence;
(c)   while awaiting the result of an examination or analysis of relevant evidence;
(d)   for the examination or analysis of anything with a view to obtaining relevant evidence;
(e)   pending a decision to apply to the Secretary of State for a deportation notice to be served on the detainee, the making of any such application, or the consideration of any such application by the Secretary of State;
(f)   pending a decision to charge the detainee with an offence.

14C   Applications for warrants to extend detention beyond 48 hours, may be made for periods of 7 days at a time (initially under TACT Schedule 8 paragraph 29, and extensions thereafter under TACT Schedule 8, paragraph 36), up to a maximum period of 14 days (or 28 days if the Detention of Terrorists Suspects (Temporary Extension) Bill) is enacted and in force) from the time of their arrest (or if they were being detained under TACT Schedule 7, from the time at which their examination under Schedule 7 began). Applications may be made for shorter periods than 7 days, which must be specified. The judicial authority or High Court judge may also substitute a shorter period if they feel a period of 7 days is inappropriate.

14D   Unless Note 14F applies, applications for warrants that would take the total period of detention up to 14 days or less should be made to a judicial authority, meaning a District Judge (Magistrates' Court) designated by the Lord Chief Justice to hear such applications.

14E   If by virtue of the relevant provisions described in Note 14C being enacted the maximum period of detention is extended to 28 days, any application for a warrant which would take the period of detention beyond 14 days from the time of arrest (or if a person was being detained under TACT Schedule 7, from the time at which the examination under Schedule 7 began), must be made to a High Court Judge.

14F   If, when the Detention of Terrorists Suspects (Temporary Extension) Bill is enacted and in force, an application is made to a High Court judge for a warrant which would take detention beyond 14 days and the High Court judge instead issues a warrant for a period of time which would not take detention beyond 14 days, further applications for extension of detention must also be made to a High Court judge, regardless of the period of time to which they refer.

14G   TACT Schedule 8 Paragraph 31 requires a notice to be given to the detained person if a warrant is sought for further detention. This must be provided before the judicial hearing of the application for that warrant and must include:
(a)   notification that the application for a warrant has been made;
(b)   the time at which the application was made;
(c)   the time at which the application is to be heard;
(d)   the grounds on which further detention is sought.
A notice must also be provided each time an application is made to extend or further extend an existing warrant.

14H   An officer applying for an order under TACT Schedule 8 Paragraph 34 to withhold specified information on which they intend to rely when applying for a warrant of further detention or the extension or further extension of such a warrant, may make the application for the order orally or in writing. The most appropriate method of application will depend on the circumstances of the case and the need to ensure fairness to the detainee.

14I   After hearing any representations by or on behalf of the detainee and the applicant, the judicial authority or High Court judge may direct that the hearing relating to the extension of detention under Part III of Schedule 8 is to take place using video conferencing facilities. However, if the judicial authority requires the detained person to be physically present at any hearing, this should be complied with as soon as practicable. Paragraph 33(4) to (9) of TACT Schedule 8 govern the hearing of applications via video-link or other means.

14J   Not used

14K   Not used

Section 15—Charging and post-charge questioning in terrorism cases

This section is included in full as it is not mirrored in Code C

15 Charging and post-charge questioning in terrorism cases

(a) Charging

15.1 Charging of detained persons is covered by PACE and guidance issued under PACE by the Director of Public Prosecutions. Decisions to charge persons to whom this Code (H) applies, the charging process and related matters are subject to section 16 of PACE Code C.

(b) Post-charge questioning

15.2 Under section 22 of the Counter-Terrorism Act 2008, a judge of the Crown Court may authorise the questioning of a person about an offence for which they have been charged, informed that they may be prosecuted or sent for trial, if the offence:
- is a terrorism offence as set out in section 27 of the Counter-Terrorism Act 2008; or
- is an offence which appears to the judge to have a terrorist connection. See *Note 15C.*

The decision on whether to apply for such questioning will be based on the needs of the investigation. There is no power to detain a person solely for the purposes of post-charge questioning. A person can only be detained whilst being so questioned (whether at a police station or in prison) if they are already there in lawful custody under some existing power. If at a police station the contents of *sections 8* and *9* of this Code must be considered the minimum standards of treatment for such detainees.

15.3 The Crown Court judge may authorise the questioning if they are satisfied that:
- further questioning is necessary in the interests of justice;
- the investigation for the purposes of which the further questioning is being proposed is being conducted diligently and expeditiously; and
- the questioning would not interfere unduly with the preparation of the person's defence to the charge or any other criminal charge that they may be facing.

See Note 15E

15.4 The judge authorising questioning may specify the location of the questioning.

15.5 The judge may only authorise a period up to a maximum of 48 hours before further authorisation must be sought. The 48 hour period would run continuously from the commencement of questioning. This period must include breaks in questioning in accordance with *paragraphs 8.6* and *12.2* of this Code (see *Note 15B*).

15.6 Nothing in this Code shall be taken to prevent a suspect seeking a voluntary interview with the police at any time.

15.7 For the purposes of this section, any reference in *sections 6, 10, 11, 12* and *13* of this Code to:
- 'suspect' means the person in respect of whom an authorisation has been given under section 22 of the Counter-Terrorism Act 2008 (post-charge questioning of terrorist suspects) to interview them;
- 'interview' means post-charge questioning authorised under section 22 of the Counter-Terrorism Act 2008;
- 'offence' means an offence for which the person has been charged, informed that they may be prosecuted or sent for trial and about which the person is being questioned; and
- 'place of detention' means the location of the questioning specified by the judge (see *paragraph 15.4*), and the provisions of those sections apply (as appropriate), to such questioning (whether at a police station or in prison) subject to the further modifications in the following paragraphs:

Right to legal advice

15.8 In *section 6* of this Code, for the purposes of post-charge questioning:
- access to a solicitor may not be delayed under *Annex B*; and
- *paragraph 6.5* (direction that a detainee may only consult a solicitor within the sight and hearing of a qualified officer) does not apply.

Cautions

15.9   In *section 10* of this Code, unless the restriction on drawing adverse inferences from silence applies (see *paragraph 15.10*), for the purposes of post-charge questioning, the caution must be given in the following terms before any such questions are asked:

'You do not have to say anything. But it may harm your defence if you do not mention when questioned something which you later rely on in Court. Anything you do say may be given in evidence.'

Where the use of the Welsh Language is appropriate, a constable may provide the caution directly in Welsh in the following terms:

'Does dim rhaid i chi ddweud dim byd. Ond gall niweidio eich amddiffyniad os na fyddwch chi'n sôn, wrth gael eich holi, am rywbeth y byddwch chi'n dibynnu arno nes ymlaen yn y Llys. Gall unrhyw beth yr ydych yn ei ddweud gael ei roi fel tystiolaeth.'

15.10   The only restriction on drawing adverse inferences from silence, see *Annex C*, applies in those situations where a person has asked for legal advice and is questioned before receiving such advice in accordance with *paragraph 6.7(b)*.

Interviews

15.11   In *section 11*, for the purposes of post-charge questioning, whenever a person is questioned, they must be informed of the offence for which they have been charged or informed that they may be prosecuted, or that they have been sent for trial and about which they are being questioned.

15.12   *Paragraph 11.2* (place where questioning may take place) does not apply to post-charge questioning.

Recording post-charge questioning

15.13   All interviews must be video recorded with sound in accordance with the separate Code of Practice issued under section 25 of the Counter-Terrorism Act 2008 for the video recording with sound of post-charge questioning authorised under section 22 of the Counter-Terrorism Act 2008 (see *paragraph 11.8*).

Notes for Guidance

15A   *If a person is detained at a police station for the purposes of post-charge questioning, a custody record must be opened in accordance with section 2 of this Code. The custody record must note the power under which the person is being detained, the time at which the person was transferred into police custody, their time of arrival at the police station and their time of being presented to the custody officer.*

15B   *The custody record must note the time at which the interview process commences. This shall be regarded as the relevant time for any period of questioning in accordance with paragraph 15.5 of this Code.*

15C   *Where reference is made to 'terrorist connection' in paragraph 15.2, this is determined in accordance with section 30 of the Counter-Terrorism Act 2008. Under section 30 of that Act a court must in certain circumstances determine whether an offence has a terrorist connection. These are offences under general criminal law which may be prosecuted in terrorism cases (for example explosives-related offences and conspiracy to murder). An offence has a terrorist connection if the offence is, or takes place in the course of, an act of terrorism or is committed for the purposes of terrorism (section 98 of the Act). Normally the court will make the determination during the sentencing process, however for the purposes of post-charge questioning, a Crown Court Judge must determine whether the offence could have a terrorist connection.*

15D   *The powers under section 22 of the Counter-Terrorism Act 2008 are separate from and additional to the normal questioning procedures within this code. Their overall purpose is to enable the further questioning of a terrorist suspect after charge. They should not therefore be used to replace or circumvent the normal powers for dealing with routine questioning.*

15E   *Post-charge questioning has been created because it is acknowledged that terrorist investigations can be large and complex and that a great deal of evidence can come to light following the charge of a terrorism suspect. This can occur, for instance, from the translation of material or as the result of additional investigation. When considering an application for post-charge questioning, the police must 'satisfy' the judge on all three points under paragraph 15.3. This means that the judge will either authorise or refuse an application on the balance of whether the conditions in paragraph 15.3 are all met. It is important there-fore, that when making the application, to consider the following questions:*

- *What further evidence is the questioning expected to provide?*
- *Why was it not possible to obtain this evidence before charge?*
- *How and why was the need to question after charge first recognised?*
- *How is the questioning expected to contribute further to the case?*
- *To what extent could the time and place for further questioning interfere with the preparation of the person's defence (for example if authorisation is sought close to the time of a trial)?*
- *What steps will be taken to minimise any risk that questioning might interfere with the preparation of the person's defence?*

This list is not exhaustive but outlines the type of questions that could be relevant to any asked by a judge in considering an application.

16 Testing persons for the presence of specified Class A drugs

The provisions for drug testing under section 63B of PACE (as amended by section 5 of the Criminal Justice Act 2003 and section 7 of the Drugs Act 2005), do not apply to persons to whom this Code applies. Guidance on these provisions can be found in section 17 of PACE Code C.

Index

disclosure of defence interviews and
    alibis 2.7.10.7
examination-in-chief
    general principles 2.4.15
    leading questions 2.4.15.1
further evidence 2.4.18
hostile witnesses 2.4.8.11
identification (Code D)
    confrontation by witnesses 2.9.11
    eye witness identification 2.9.4
    visual identification 2.9.4.1–2.9.4.10
live links 2.4.9
oaths and affirmations 2.4.14
oral statements through interpreters 2.4.12
overview 2.4.8
re-examination 2.4.17
refreshing memory 2.4.11

service of process 2.2.3
special measures
    directions 2.4.10.2
    eligible witnesses 2.4.10.1
    statutory provisions 2.4.10
victims' personal statements 2.4.13
Written charges 2.2.2
Written statements under caution 2.10.6

X

X-rays 2.8.25

Y

Youth Courts
    attendance of parents or guardians 2.1.9.2

constitution 2.1.9
restrictions on persons present
    and reporting restrictions
    2.1.9.1
Youth Justice System
cautions 2.5.4
child safety orders 2.5.5.6
parenting orders
    binding over of parent
    2.5.5.3
    breaches of order 2.5.5.2
    compensation orders 2.5.5.4
    importance 2.5.5
    statutory provisions 2.5.5.1
statutory basis 2.5.2
youth offending teams 2.5.3
Youth offending teams 2.5.3